THE
GOOD
FIGHT
THAT
DIDN'T
END

THE
GOOD
FIGHT
THAT
DIDN'T
END

Henry P. Goddard's ACCOUNTS OF
Civil War AND Peace

EDITED BY CALVIN GODDARD ZON

The University of South Carolina Press

© 2008 University of South Carolina

Published by the University of South Carolina Press
Columbia, South Carolina 29208

www.sc.edu/uscpress

Manufactured in the United States of America

17 16 15 14 13 12 11 10 09 08   10 9 8 7 6 5 4 3 2 1

Library of Congress Cataloging-in-Publication Data

Goddard, Henry Perkins, 1842–1916.
  The good fight that didn't end : Henry P. Goddard's accounts of Civil War and peace / edited
by Calvin Goddard Zon.
    p. cm.
  Includes index.
  ISBN 978-1-57003-772-6 (cloth : alk. paper)
  1. Goddard, Henry Perkins, 1842–1916. 2. United States. Army. Connecticut Infantry
Regiment, 14th (1862–1865) 3. Connecticut—History—Civil War, 1861–1865—Personal
narratives. 4. United States—History—Civil War, 1861–1865—Personal narratives.
5. Connecticut—History—Civil War, 1861–1865—Regimental histories. 6. United States—
History—Civil War, 1861–1865—Regimental histories. 7. Goddard, Henry Perkins,
1842–1916—Political and social views. 8. Soldiers—Connecticut—Norwich—Biography.
9. Norwich (Conn.)—Biography. 10. Baltimore (Md.)—Biography. I. Zon, Calvin Goddard.
II. Title.
  E499.514th .G25 2008
  973.7'8—dc22

                                                                                    2008030335

The editor would like to acknowledge the work of Nancy Emison on the index.

This book was printed on Glatfelter Natures, a recycled paper with 30 percent postconsumer
waste content.

This book is dedicated to my mother, Mary Goddard Zon,
    for lighting the torch,
to my wife, Laurel Ellen Blaydes,
    for fueling the torch,
and to my children, Cary Goddard Zon and Daniel Chapman Goddard Zon,
    to whom the torch is passed.

I have fought the good fight,
I have finished the race,
I have kept the faith.

2 Timothy 4:7

CONTENTS

List of Illustrations   ix

Introduction   xi

PART 1   From Journalist to Cavalryman

1   A Connecticut Yankee Is Commissioned   3

2   Goddard Goes to Washington   5

3   Goddard in Baptism of Fire with His "Connecticut Squadron"   17

4   Parading through Fredericksburg and Engaging Rebel Infantry   22

5   Goddard Resigns from the Harris Light Cavalry   27

PART 2   The "Fighting Fourteenth"

6   Organizing the Regiment   33

7   Sergeant-Major Goddard Takes to New Life in the Infantry   37

8   The Regiment Pursues Lee into Maryland   47

9   The Regiment's Baptism of Fire at Antietam   55

10   A Long, Hard Wait at Harpers Ferry   62

11   Back to Virginia, with a New Commanding General   87

12   Disaster and Heroism at Fredericksburg   98

13   A Demoralized Army Again Changes Commanders   112

14   Wounded at the Battle of Chancellorsville   149

15   Staff Duty with General Tyler as Gettysburg Turns the Tide   154

16   Staff Duty, Hospital Stay, Draftees, Substitutes, and Deserters   166

17   Another Change of Duty—Pleasant Living as an Artillery Officer   190

18   A Gauntlet of Bullets at Morton's Ford   201

19   Goddard Reluctantly Resigns from the Army   207

PART 3   Fighting for Principle before and after the War

20   Goddard Recalls Candidate and President Lincoln   221

21   Stories of Confederate and Union Friends and Reunions
      after the War   232

22   Maryland's Notable Confederate Sympathizers   259

23   Post–Civil War Politics and Race Relations in Maryland   266

24 Concerning Booth, Fritchie, Randall—Setting the Record Straight   280

25 Racism and Veterans' Poverty in Hartford   284

26 Impressions of a Changing South—Industry, Charm, and "Savage" Women   297

27 An Honest Republican Revolted by the 1876 Election   304

28 The Civil War Redux?   310

29 Goddard's Friend and Dinner Companion, Mark Twain   319

30 Preserving the Legacy, Welcoming Former Foes   325

31 Conclusion   328

PART 4   The Brother Who Did Not Return

32 Alfred Mitchell Goddard   331

Index   339

About the Editor   361

ILLUSTRATIONS

Following page 117

Goddard as journalist for the *Norwich Bulletin*

Goddard as a second lieutenant in the Harris Light Cavalry

Ike Bromley

Col. Hugh Judson Kilpatrick

Brig. Gen. E. W. Whitaker

Capt. Marcus Coon

Mary Woodbridge Goddard

Henry Perkins Goddard in the 14th Connecticut Volunteer Infantry

Connecticut governor William A. Buckingham

Maj. Gen. Abner Doubleday

Maj. Gen. John E. Wool

Maj. Gen. George B. McClellan and his wife

Lt.-Col. Sanford H. Perkins

Col. Theodore G. Ellis

President Abraham Lincoln

Maj. Gen. Ambrose Burnside

Maj. Gen. Edwin V. Sumner

Maj. Gen. William H. French

The armory at Harpers Ferry

Maj. Gen. Joseph Hooker

Maj. Gen. Winfield Scott Hancock

Gen. Robert E. Lee

The monument to the 14th Connecticut at Gettysburg

Goddard's older sister, Julia Goddard Piatt

Goddard's younger sister, Mary "May" Goddard

Maj. Gen. John Sedgwick

Following page 231

Recruitment poster for the 14th Connecticut

Goddard in the early 1870s

Harriet Beecher Stowe

Samuel L. Clemens

Maj. Gen. Daniel Sickles

Maj. Robert Anderson

Poster for a Union veterans' reunion at Fredericksburg, Virginia

Candidate Goddard

Alfred Mitchell Goddard

Brig. Gen. Edward Harland

A. M. Goddard's telegram to his mother

INTRODUCTION

The life of Henry Perkins Goddard, native of Norwich, Connecticut, is a colorful slice of American history from the 1850s to the early years of the twentieth century. A scrupulous journalist with a lifelong passion for principle, Goddard rose to a captaincy in the most battle-scarred Connecticut regiment in the Civil War, the 14th Connecticut Volunteer Infantry, which first fought at Antietam and last fought at Appomattox as part of the Second Corps of the Army of the Potomac. At the battle of Fredericksburg, his bravery under fire saved the life of his regiment's commander.

In a constant stream of letters to his family and reports to his hometown newspaper and *Harper's Weekly*, Goddard captured the drama and significance of the Army of the Potomac's major battles and vividly described his life as a soldier—first during a short stint in the cavalry, then in the infantry, later as a general staff officer, and finally as an artillery officer—and assessed the parade of generals he encountered. His opinions of George McClellan and Joseph Hooker wavered during the course of the war, but Winfield Scott Hancock, his 2nd Corps commander, remained "a knight in whom we all believe" (199).

After the Union's success at Antietam and what Goddard called Lincoln's "freedom-breathing" Emancipation Proclamation, the young man's original fight to save the Union became also a fight to end slavery. But as the war dragged on with no end in sight, he wrote that the issue of emancipation was even more controversial among Northerners and his fellow soldiers than the increasing amounts of blood being shed to preserve the Union. Such divided Northern opinion, combined with Union defeats on the battlefield, caused Goddard to fear the war's outcome and even question its goal of emancipation. In the end, however, he stood firm for duty and principle, as in his vehement rebuke of the "peace Democrats" who would abandon the cause of Union and freedom.

But his story does not end with the war. In the decades that followed, his newspaper writings from Connecticut, then Baltimore, and from his travels to the South addressed boldly and honestly the festering issues of race left unresolved by the war, emancipation, and Reconstruction. Although no radical regarding Reconstruction and yearning to heal the war's wounds, he used his pen to attack racism in Connecticut and his adopted state of Maryland and to defend the rights of African Americans.

Goddard developed an interest in politics beginning at age fifteen, when he campaigned for "Fremont and Freedom," the antislavery candidate John C. Fremont in the presidential campaign of 1856. As an eighteen-year-old, high school–educated reporter for the *Norwich Bulletin*, Goddard covered the 1860 campaign visit to Connecticut of Abraham Lincoln, for whom he had campaigned throughout eastern Connecticut as part of the Wide Awakes, a group of young partisans of the emerging Republican Party. Years later he described the charisma that emerged from the homely, rumpled "son of the soil" from the West as he "spoke the truth" about "the great problem confronting us" (223).

He relates amusing and little-known anecdotes about candidate and President Lincoln gleaned from his postwar acquaintance with some of the principals of the recently ended fight. The second of the four times he saw Lincoln was at Antietam, where, he reported, the president, reviewing the troops, "looks more care-worn than ever" (62). It was after Antietam that Lincoln announced his plan to issue the Emancipation Proclamation. Years later Goddard recalled "the marvelous sadness" of Lincoln's eyes as the president rode down the blue column with Major General McClellan, whom he would soon have replaced as army commander.

Goddard in War

Goddard served in the Union army from March 1862 until May 1864, first using his family connections to obtain a commission as a second lieutenant in the 2nd New York Volunteer Cavalry, then, in June 1862, enlisting as a sergeant major in the 14th Connecticut. Soon promoted to lieutenant, he later served on Maj. Gen. Dan Tyler's staff while recovering from wounds received at Chancellorsville and ended his military service as a brigade artillery officer. The son of a lawyer and grandson of a member of Congress, he was driven to leave his comfortable life as a journalist by a sense of duty to God, country, Connecticut, and family.

Traveling to Washington in 1862 to join his cavalry regiment, dubbed the "Harris Light," he turned down an offer to travel with the army as a correspondent for the *New York World*, preferring, he underlined in his letter, "to fight" (7). He found the temptations of camp life less than expected; and though he pledged not to gamble or to drink, the latter pledge was somewhat relaxed as the war, of which he had expected a quick end, dragged on. He feared death less than he had anticipated, content to leave his "fate in the hands of God" (52).

During his three months in the New York cavalry regiment's "Connecticut Squadron"—so called because two of its companies were composed mainly of Connecticut natives—under the command of dare-devil Col. Hugh Judson "Kill Cavalry" Kilpatrick, he participated in his first engagement and was stung by the loss of a brave friend, one of many such losses he would experience during the war. He complained that incompetents were being commissioned and promoted on the basis of "influence and wealth" (12) rather than military experience and merit. His initial experience of war ended when the death of his father, coupled with his captain's animosity, prompted him to resign and return to Norwich.

After taking care of family business, he again said goodbye to his mother and two sisters and joined the newly formed 14th Connecticut Volunteer Infantry as a sergeant major and was soon commissioned a second lieutenant. In less than a month the raw volunteers got their baptism of fire at Antietam, the bloodiest single day in U.S. history. For three hours on that bucolic September day, the regiment exchanged fire with Confederates entrenched in the Sunken Road (Bloody Lane) before advancing "towards the center of the fight, . . . in the face of a most terrible fire of artillery and infantry, . . . a merciful Father has spared me a little longer" (58).

Dispatched next to Harpers Ferry, where over twelve thousand Union troops on Bolivar Heights had recently surrendered to Stonewall Jackson, he spent several weeks without his baggage and fresh clothing. There, meditating in John Brown's engine house and yearning for an effective army commander, he reported that officers and men were "getting sick of the long war" (74).

Following the disastrous Union defeat in December 1862 at Fredericksburg, where he was saved by his bullet-scarred canteen and commended by the regiment's colonel he courageously rescued on Marye's Heights, he described an army increasingly demoralized and having no confidence in its new commander, Maj. Gen. Ambrose Burnside. While privately expressing pessimism in letters to his family about the war's outcome, he was more upbeat in his reports to the *Norwich Bulletin*, where he drew his sword against the "peace" Democrats who appeared in the spring of 1863: "The miserable Copperhead Democracy in Connecticut has disgusted us all so completely, that should Tom Seymour be elected governor, or the draft resisted, we will whip the traitors in front and then go to Connecticut to drive Tom Seymour and his crew into the Long Island Sound" (133).

The Union defeats brought yet another change of command of the Army of the Potomac, and Goddard described the army's improved morale and material conditions under Major General Hooker, who rides down the long blue line of review with President Lincoln. The optimism was short lived: in early May 1863 Gen. Robert E. Lee scored his greatest victory with the outnumbered Confederate forces at Chancellorsville. In the face of the surprise attack by Stonewall Jackson, Goddard rallied his men but was struck in the head and felled by a piece of cannon shell. Repeating a familiar pattern for the Army of the Potomac, Hooker retreated back across the Rappahannock.

While recuperating from his wounds, he visits Baltimore and networks with some influential relatives and acquaintances, including Major General Dan Tyler, who asks him to join his staff as aide-de-camp. Goddard accepts, but his staff duties in Wilmington, Delaware, keep him from participating with "the Fighting Fourteenth" in the victory at Gettysburg in early July 1863. He laments his absence from a long-sought Union victory. However, his moving description of his regiment's bravery in repulsing Pickett's charge on Cemetery Ridge was so telling that it was published in *Harper's Weekly*.

Although Goddard enjoyed the pleasant life and small luxuries of a staff officer, he was eager to return south to "the dear old boys" of the 14th (173). When he returns to what had been a regiment of volunteers, he finds its new draftees and substitutes to be an "<u>awful</u> hard set," including a "big ruffian" he is forced to confront (175, 176). Desertion was rampant among the conscripts, but when the regiment engages at Bristoe Station, the newcomers proved their mettle.

Still physically unable to resume the long marches and other rigors of the infantry in the late fall of 1863, Goddard—who had served in the cavalry, the infantry, and general staff—reinvented himself again, this time as an artillery officer in his brigade. Facing rebel forces across the Rapidan River in early 1864, Goddard came under fire for the fifth time during the war. In what he calls the "too little known" battle of Morton's Ford (206), where the 14th suffers heavy casualties, he dodged enemy bullets as he raced his horse to reposition the artillery.

Ulysses S. Grant, named general in chief of the Union armies in early March 1864, "has pleased the army by his first official step—in pitching his headquarters with the troops in the field," Goddard noted approvingly (213). With a victorious three-star general in command, reinforcements on the way, and a new determination among officers and men, he boldly opined in the *Norwich Bulletin* that Richmond could be taken by summer. He correctly predicted, however, that General Lee, having the confidence of "his army and of the so-called Confederacy as no other general on this continent. . . , his men will fight as they always have fought, desperately" (213).

As Grant prepared for the final drive toward Richmond, all brigade artillery officers on loan from the infantry were ordered back to their regiments. Shortly after being promoted to the rank of captain, Goddard—judged physically unfit by a panel of surgeons to resume infantry duty—was honorably discharged from the army. "It was <u>very hard</u>," he wrote his mother, "but I am heartily convinced that I have done my whole duty under all the circumstances" (216).

Having "seen the elephant," he observed that, contrary to press reports, "a regiment that has been under fire is <u>never</u> anxious for another fight." It is "the <u>sentiment of honor</u>" and sense of "pride" that "does the business" (132). He described the attitude of mortally wounded soldiers toward death, claiming he "never saw a soldier . . . fearing death after being mortally wounded. . . . They all seem to trust in forgiveness" (211).

He pleaded with his older brother, Alfred Mitchell Goddard, who was employed as an engineer in the Sandwich Islands (Hawaii), "as you love me <u>never go to war</u>"

(136), citing the possibility that neither of the family's sons will survive the war, leaving a mother and two sisters to fend for themselves. The book concludes with a brief section about Alf, who, ridden with guilt over his absence from the righteous war for union and emancipation, returns from Hawaii to enlist. Commissioned a first lieutenant in the 8th Connecticut Volunteer Infantry in the Army of the James on August 9, 1863, he was mortally wounded on May 7, 1864, at age twenty-seven, in the battle of Walthall Junction near Petersburg, Virginia, during Grant's Bermuda Hundred campaign to take Richmond.

Goddard after the War

Goddard moved from Norwich to Hartford, Connecticut, in 1867, and then to Baltimore in 1882, leaving journalism to become an insurance executive. However, he retained his passion for writing, whether it be theater reviews (he was president of Baltimore's Shakespeare Club) or articles on the social and political issues of the day.

Although a staunch defender of the political and legal rights of the formerly enslaved, Goddard's view of African Americans sometimes reflected an ambivalence common among nineteenth-century white Americans both during and after the Civil War. Although as a young lieutenant he eschewed the radical label of "abolitionist," he was inspired by Lincoln's "freedom breathing" (63) Emancipation Proclamation. And after the war when the issue was joined, he consistently stood up for fair and decent treatment of blacks, in the North and the South.

In the early 1900s, living in what he calls the "Southern city" of Baltimore, he expresses in newspaper articles his dismay about racist incidents and practices in largely segregated Maryland, a former slave state. He decries "negrophobia" and the politicians in the state who exploit it. Running as a Republican for the Maryland legislature in 1907 on the platform "An Honest Election Law," he attacked the Democrats who dominated state politics for their use of complex "trick" ballots to disenfranchise African Americans and recent immigrants. He lost the election but expressed gratitude for the support from "some very dear old Confederate soldiers, who proved as magnanimous in peace as they were brave in war" (277). Goddard, in turn, campaigned for his friend Henry Kyd Douglas, an ex-Confederate colonel and former staff officer to Stonewall Jackson.

Writing in a Baltimore newspaper in 1910, he defended Harriet Beecher Stowe, a friend and neighbor from Hartford, and her book *Uncle Tom's Cabin* against an attempt to remove the book from public libraries in Maryland. He calls the book "a great tract [that] served its end" of bringing on an "inevitable" civil war (273). On the other hand, he says that the book is not an accurate picture of the antebellum South, while he imagines Thomas Dixon's *The Clansman*—a novel and play written as a rebuttal of a 1901 theatrical production of *Uncle Tom's Cabin*—to be a realistic portrayal of the postwar South. *The Clansman,* which served as the basis for D. W. Griffith's film *Birth of a Nation,* ignores the positive aspects of Reconstruction and seems to justify the use of Ku Klux Klan violence to redeem the Reconstruction South from carpetbaggers, scalawags, and freedmen. Goddard's comments say much about the temper of the times in which "separate but equal" had become the law of the land and the Southern recollection of Reconstruction, and even slavery, had become widely accepted in both the North and the South. However, Goddard took strong issue with a Lost Cause apologist in New England, writing, "Condone or disguise it as we may, back of all questions of loyalty to state or nation was the question of African slavery, the bedrock which the southern confederacy was founded" (314). While today some Southerners and revisionist writers wax nostalgic about the Lost Cause, such was not the case with Goddard and his contemporaries. Reflecting on the war's outcome, Col. Charles Marshall, the staff officer who accompanied Lee to his meeting with Grant at Appomattox, tells a Baltimore audience in 1892 that "in view of all that has happened, . . . let us reverently thank God" (285).

Goddard's view of Reconstruction (1866–76) is somewhat ambivalent. Writing from Selma, Alabama, in 1870, he defended Reconstruction, observing that although some Northern transplants may rightfully be called "carpetbaggers" or "demagogues," others were "gallant gentlemen" holding offices "which they alone of the loyal men were intelligent enough to fill" (299). He also welcomed the advent of equal rights for the freedmen, now able to serve on juries in the South.

However, writing four years later in a New England journal following a visit to Montgomery, Alabama, to commemorate Decoration Day, he reflected a less positive view of Reconstruction among Northerners during its waning period, urging fellow Northerners "to do all in our power to bury past hates" although "this may seem to some an unpropitious time to urge gentle charity and friendship to old opponents when ill-advised men have thrown one of the loveliest of southern states into apparent opposition to federal authority. But let me tell you that we of the North are not blameless that they have done so. By sustaining a set of wanton adventurers who were no more true Unionists than camp-followers were true soldiers, we have helped to lay upon them a grievous burden" (298). Two years later, following the famously contested presidential election of 1876, the last federal troops were withdrawn from the South, ending a Reconstruction about which Northerners such as Goddard had become weary and conflicted.

In 1909 Goddard noted approvingly Maryland's "self-Reconstruction" (1864–67), during which its "radical constitution" of 1864 (266) was repudiated and the political privileges of ex-Confederate soldiers and sympathizers were restored.

Goddard's view of the South changed after the war. During the war years he frequently referred to "the cursed 'secesh soil' of Virginia" (49); after the war he took a liking to the South, which he claimed possessed "the most romantically interesting history of any portion of our country" (266). Visiting a rebuilt and revived Richmond, he paid a call on a hospitable Gov. Fitzhugh Lee, a nephew of the renowned Confederate general, who invited him to make his home in the city that took the Union army four long years to reach.

Married twice to Connecticut women after the war, his first wife dying early in the marriage, he never lost his eye for pretty ladies—Southern belles in particular. As a cavalryman he pranced through Fredericksburg, "trying to catch a glimpse of my fair Southern inamorata—a Miss Herndon [niece of naval commander William Herndon], whom I have seen but once, but it was 'love at first sight'" (29). In postwar Baltimore he becomes a friend and theater companion of the brave and beautiful blockade runner Hetty Cary, who had sewn clothing and flags for Maryland Confederates, which she spirited across the Potomac into Virginia.

Never abandoning his principles to political expediency, Goddard chastised his prominent Republican friends who winked at the ballot chicanery and deal making that allowed Rutherford B. Hayes to become president over Democrat Samuel Tilden after the 1876 election. And in the election of 1880, he reluctantly opposed his "well-beloved corps commander" (306), Gen. Winfield Scott Hancock, after Hancock refused to repudiate a forged letter smearing James A. Garfield.

His friendships and conversations after the war with high-ranking Union and Confederate officers, politicians, and Mark Twain, his Hartford neighbor and dinner companion, provide the reader with some amusing and little-known historical anecdotes. His stories involving President Lincoln, for example, include one of how Lincoln devised a joke that made a stiff Mrs. Lincoln burst into laughter. Another story relates Secretary of War Edwin Stanton's defiance of Lincoln's signed order. His anecdotes about Twain include hidden gems garnered from lectures and dinner conversations with the great humorist.

He writes moving obituaries of the veterans of the 14th Connecticut, including William B. Hincks (who enlisted as a private, won the Medal of Honor at Gettysburg, and left the army as a major) and Col. Sanford H. Perkins (commander of the 14th until his wounding at Fredericksburg, where Goddard, himself wounded, helped carry him off the field). He also reminisces about departed Union and Confederate field officer friends he met after the war, including Col. John R. Kenly of the 1st (Union) Maryland regiment and Colonel Douglas, who served as adjutant general of Maryland after the war and fought in the Spanish-American War.

Goddard delved into investigative journalism as he took it upon himself to set the historical record straight over such controversies as where John Wilkes Booth was buried; whether Barbara Fritchie flew the Stars and Stripes during Stonewall Jackson's occupation of Frederick, Maryland; the origins of "Maryland, My Maryland," the state's pro-Confederate anthem; and the devotion to the Union cause of Fort Sumter commander Maj. Robert Anderson, who was disavowed by his wife's Southern family. On one intriguing and largely unexamined historical question regarding Major General McClellan, Goddard seems unsure of the answer and perhaps unwilling to believe the proffered evidence. Correspondence to a Baltimore newspaper in 1904, from persons having first- and secondhand knowledge of events more than forty years earlier, claimed that after the battle of Antietam, McClellan proposed in a letter to General Lee "to end the Civil War by uniting their forces to march upon Washington and compel peace" (310).

In a reunion of the regiment in Madison, Connecticut, on September 17, 1872 —the tenth anniversary of Antietam—a Hartford newspaper reported that "Capt. Goddard made the closing speech. He begged the members of the regiment to remember the gratitude we owe to those at home who sustained us during the war. Whatever perils, griefs or woes time brings us in its flight, we must never forget our duty to that country that called us into this organization ten years ago, and for whose salvation we must pledge our lives, our fortunes and our sacred honor" (233).

Goddard died of pneumonia in his adopted home of Baltimore on April 5, 1916. He was seventy-three years old. His attending physician was his only child, twenty-four-year-old Calvin Hooker Goddard, whose middle name paid homage to General Hooker, a second cousin of his mother, Lida Acheson Goddard, who with her son Calvin attended her husband at his deathbed. They had been married for thirty-four years.

The brave soldier was buried at Arlington National Cemetery with military honors and the sound of a trumpet. Those in attendance included companions from the Military Order of the Loyal Legion of the United States.

Calvin Hooker Goddard became a U.S. Army colonel. He served in three branches of the service (medical, ordinance, and military police) and was also a military historian, but he is best known for having pioneered the science of forensic ballistics in the 1920s and '30s.

The younger of Calvin Hooker Goddard's two daughters, Mary Goddard Zon, was my mother, and she inherited several old trunks of ancestral keepsakes. The trunks contained H. P. Goddard's faded newspaper clippings spanning five decades and his Civil War letters, most of which had been copied out by typewriter and placed into scrapbooks shortly after the war by his older sister.

For Christmas 1997 my mother presented me with a wonderful gift: a genealogical history, elegantly written and illustrated. My mother's history briefly mentions Henry Perkins Goddard and other New England ancestors, including the Reverend Thomas Hooker, founder of colonial Connecticut, but its focus is the Virginia ancestors, whom she traced back to Jamestown and who included Confederate field officers. My mother wrote in her unpublished book that her next family history would be devoted to the "verbose" Goddards, "who seem to have had pens surgically attached to their hands at birth." As she began to gather up H. P. Goddard's writings from the trunks in 1991, a long illness overtook her and prevented her from proceeding with the project. She died in 1997.

As my mother's only child, I inherited the precious literary contents of the trunks and also my great-grandfather's cavalry and infantry swords, belt buckles, insignia, field diaries, Bible, photo albums of the Civil War figures he depicts in his writings, and the bullet-ridden canteen that saved his life at Fredericksburg. I feel deeply thankful to have carried the torch she handed to me.

Part 1

FROM JOURNALIST TO CAVALRYMAN

1

A Connecticut Yankee
Is Commissioned

D riven by a sense of patriotic duty, Goddard used his family's political connections to obtain a commission as second lieutenant in the 2nd New York Volunteer Cavalry. On March 3, 1862, leaving his father, mother, and two sisters in Norwich, he heads to Washington with a pair of engraved pistols, the gift of a family friend, and a New Testament from his mother. He was studious and quick to learn the ropes of military service. During his cavalry service from early March to May 1862, his regiment engaged in several skirmishes on its way to Fredericksburg, Virginia, and Goddard lost a courageous friend in action.

Organized in July 1861 at Scarsdale, New York, by Col. J. Mansfield Davies, the regiment was nicknamed the Harris Light Cavalry in honor of the Senator Ira Harris, who assisted Colonel Davies in raising its six companies of men from New York, Connecticut, New Jersey, and Indiana. Senator Harris presented the regiment with a flag bearing his likeness and the inscription "Harris Light Cavalry," which the regiment proudly carried and gallantly defended during its engagements. The Harris Light captured three Confederate generals and their men at Sailor's Creek near Appomattox as well as three railroad trains filled with crucial munitions and food days before General Lee's surrender. In early 1864 the Harris Light was part of a cavalry expedition that made a daring but failed attempt to free Union prisoners held in Richmond's Belle Island prison, when Brig. Gen. Hugh Judson Kilpatrick (who followed Colonel Davies as the regiment's commander; both men were promoted to major general during the war) led some 3,000 cavalrymen in a daring raid through the outer line of Confederate defenses surrounding Richmond—the only Union unit to pass through these defenses during this period. During its four years of service in the Army of the Potomac, the Harris Light lost 9 officers and 112 enlisted men in battle and 1 officer and 235 enlisted men of disease—106 of them while prisoners.

The regiment's so-called Connecticut Squadron, mostly comprising men from that state, formed Company C and Company D, to which Goddard belonged. The two companies were organized by Capt. W. H. Mallory, a native of Watertown,

Connecticut, who had moved to New York City and had seen three months of service in Duryée's Zouaves, 5th Regiment New York Infantry. In early August 1861 Mallory opened recruiting offices in Hartford and Litchfield counties, to which men came from all parts of Connecticut, and by the end of the month Mallory took two full companies to a training camp near New York City.

The regiment was first assigned to the defense of Washington, as part of Maj. Gen. Irwin McDowell's Department of Northeastern Virginia, until March 1862, when Goddard joined it at Camp Palmer in Arlington, Virginia, one of sixty-eight major forts that ringed the city during the war. (After the rout of the Union army at the battle of Bull Run in July 1861, McDowell was replaced by Maj. Gen. George McClellan as commander of the new Division of the Potomac, which McClellan designated as the Army of the Potomac on August 20, 1861). McDowell began leading some 10,000 federal troops (part of the new Department of the Rappahannock), including the Harris Light Cavalry, to Falmouth, Virginia, across the Rappahannock River from Fredericksburg in March. The original plan was for McDowell to continue south to Richmond, by way of Fredericksburg, to join forces with McClellan, whose army on the peninsula would come up the James River to Richmond. McDowell's troops were to board trains and travel the Richmond, Fredericksburg, and Potomac Railroad line. However, most of the rail lines and bridges south of Alexandria, Virginia, had been destroyed. To rebuild the railroad and construct new bridges, McDowell established his headquarters near Falmouth at an elegant mansion known as the Lacy House.

～

Norwich Bulletin, March 24, 1862

[author unknown]

Henry P. Goddard, who, for the past three years, has been connected with the local department of the *Bulletin,* has received and accepted the appointment of Second Lieutenant in Co. D of the Harris Light Cavalry. He joined his regiment near Arlington Heights on Sunday, and expected to march Southward with them on Monday. He carries with him into his new vocation the best wishes of all who have been associated with him in this office, to whom his many good qualities of head and heart have endeared him. We shall miss his cheerful disposition and genial manners, as well as his faithful services and devotion to the interests of his employers. We know that in whatever position he may be placed, he will be faithful, true and honest, and that his work will be well and promptly performed.

2

Goddard Goes to Washington

March 4, 1862, Ebbitt House, Washington, D.C.[1]

Dear Father,

[Taking a sleeper car to New York and then Philadelphia, he writes,] Arrived here at 7 A.M. today. Came on with Wm. Bond as far as Philadelphia, and a Mr. Gallaudet, of Deaf and Dumb notoriety[2] and a fine fellow.

Strange to say, I slept through to near Washington, only waking three times for about five minutes at Havre De Grace and Baltimore. At the former place, the sleeping car is run on to the top of the ferry boat. An "horrid man" in the cars was relating anecdotes when we left Philadelphia about the cars being blown into the water on numerous occasions and the great danger, etc. I had no idea I should sleep until we had passed that place, but I did not know we had reached it until we had crossed the ferry and were starting on the further side. Rising at some ten miles from Washington, I found that we had reached the seat of war as the entire length of road was guarded by sleepy sentinels.

1. The Ebbitt House, established in 1856, was Washington's most historic boarding-house and saloon, frequented by Presidents Grant and Johnson and other luminaries.

2. Thomas Hopkins Gallaudet, a founder of the first school of higher education for the deaf, later named Gallaudet University, in Washington, D.C.

March 5, 1862, Ebbitt House, Washington, D.C.

Dear Mother,

[After taking a stagecoach from the Ebbitt House to Georgetown, walking across Aqueduct Bridge (replaced after the war by the Francis Scott Key Bridge) and trudging for an hour-and-a-half through deep mud to Arlington House,[1] he was ushered into Col. Davies tent.] The only party in the tent was a young man with private's pants and a torn shirt, smoking a cigar and shaving himself by a piece of looking glass. I bowed to him and said, with no idea but that of complimenting some subordinate, "Is this Col. Davies?" "Yes," he replied. "Have I the pleasure of addressing Mr. Goddard?" I apologized for being covered with mud, when he apologized for his own appearance but said I would get used to that.

Soon the Regimental Adjutant, Lovell, came in, then Lieut. Col. Kilpatrick and Adjt. Armstrong. I was introduced to all and watched them have a wrestling bout.

Pretty soon dinner was ordered and the Colonel, Adjt. Lovell and I dined on boiled fish, roast beef, prairie chicken, tapioca pudding and coffee and porter as drinkables. After dinner the Colonel dressed to go into town to a reception given by Miss Kitty Chase[2] at her residence. Finding that I had no horse he insisted that I should ride in on one of his; he wanted me to try it without stirrups but that did not go down.

First the Colonel and I rode out to the parade ground where the Lieutenant Colonel was drilling the regiment. It was a splendid sight—1,200 horses maneuvering in every manner guided entirely by the sound of the bugle.

My horse was very restive and I had hard work to hold him, till the colonel showed me how to guide him by a gesture of the hand, and what military orders to give him. Such a ride as we had into town. The mud two feet deep, the Colonel firing his pistol every few minutes to train his own steed which was the most restive of all; the Adjutant spurring his horse over ditches and into the canal on the tow path. Had I any but a cavalry saddle I should have broken my neck.

Col. D. lent me the "Cavalry Tactics" and I am to stay here studying several hours per day, until he (Davies) gets an answer to his letter to Governor Morgan asking my appointment as second lieutenant.

1. Arlington House, today known as the Custis-Lee Mansion, was the home of Robert E. Lee and his wife, Mary Custis Lee, until April 1861, when Virginia seceded from the Union and Lee, choosing loyalty to his state, was commissioned a major general in Virginia military forces. Federal troops under Brig. Gen. Irvin McDowell took up positions around Arlington House, and military installations were erected at several locations around the 1,100-acre estate. On June 15, 1864, Brig. Gen. Montgomery Meigs, who commanded the garrison at Arlington House, appropriated the grounds as a military cemetery—Arlington National Cemetery.

2. Kitty, or Kate, Chase was the daughter of Ohio politician Salmon P. Chase, President Lincoln's treasury secretary and later chief justice of the United States. She is best known as a society hostess during the Civil War and a strong supporter of her widowed father's presidential ambitions, which would have made her First Lady. Beautiful and intelligent, she was twenty-one at the time of Goddard's entry.

March 6, 1862, Washington, D.C.

My Dear Sister,

I visited the Capitol today and was shown all over it by Geo. Pratt[1] from cellar to dome. Visited both houses. The House is just like a boy's school when the teacher is out. It would be better if composed of women.

Senate—I like this body. Vice President [Hannibal] Hamlin is a jolly appearing old farmer who clears out when anybody makes a long speech. [Charles] Sumner, Mass., and [Ira] Harris, N.Y., are the only good looking Senators. [Charles] Fessenden, Maine, is the smartest man—I heard him squelch [president pro tempore of the Senate Solomon] Foot of Vt. But oh, how disappointed I was in his looks. Instead of the splendid head and noble presence I expected, I saw only a wiry, sharp faced and voiced, pettifogging lawyer.

Preston King [of New York] is an old lump of fat. [Lazarus] Powell [of Kentucky] a brandy bottle. [Edgar] Cowan of Pa. has no heart for this cause. His speech on the confiscation bill showed it. [Lot] Morrill from Maine replied ably today. [John] Foster [of Indiana] looks 'seedy' and [James] Dixon [of Connecticut, a family friend] 'anxious.'

Our national advocates. Bah! Let me make one exception. I had a full view of Hon., now Brig. Gen., Andrew Johnson, and he looks like he is one of nature's noblemen. It was his last day in the Senate.

1. George Pratt (1832–1875), a poet and writer of history, was a member of the Connecticut General Assembly from the Norwich area during the war.

March 6, 1862, Washington, D.C.

Dear May,

I saw Ned Stedman [a lawyer/writer friend from Norwich] at the Attorney General's office today. He was very kind and wants me to air his horse two or three hours per day, which I shall probably do. Ned is still chief Washington correspondent of the *World* and says that the Army of the Potomac will move within a week under the command of Maj. Gen. McDowell. He has obtained a leave of absence from Judge [Attorney General Edward] Bates and goes with the main column. All the papers are hiring correspondents by the dozens and Ned has orders from the *World* to spare no expense and to engage four subordinates. He offered John J. Piatt the position of going with Gen. Banks' division and, he refusing, wants me to go: to start immediately for Harpers Ferry and go with Gen. [Maj. Gen. Nathaniel] Banks everywhere—expenses paid and a fair salary, the amount of which would be the usual rate of $1 to $2 per day above expenses. I shall peremptorily decline the offer as I won't go with the army without going to fight. Don't let mother write me to take the place as I shall not do it anyhow.

March 9, 1862,
Washington, D.C.

Dear Julia,

Today has been one of the loveliest Sundays I ever enjoyed—beautiful weather, good spirits. This morning I unfortunately was half an hour too late to cross the Potomac with A.H. Almy and the *Tribune* correspondent; so I went to the nearest church—the Church of the Epiphany, Episcopal; Rev. Dr. Hale had a fine sermon and splendid music.

Tonight all Washington is in excitement at a report that the rebel steamer Merrimac has come down to Hampton Roads and sunk and burned the federal vessels stationed there. People are afraid that she will come up the Potomac and shell this city, but somehow I don't feel alarmed about it. This is an easy place to dodge shell in, even if the water is deep enough for her to come up and if she can get past Fort Washington.

March 22, 1862, Washington

Dear Mother,

Tomorrow AM I report to Col. Davis and unless he orders me home shall start with the regiment Monday and may not be back here for months.

Why I did not report today—and with shame I own it as it brings on all my old fears—is that I actually could not ride my horse, hired, over the Long Bridge [later named the Fourteenth Street Bridge], he compelling me to return and more than that—after getting off to try and lead him over, I could not get on him again and had to sneak back to town $4 out of pocket and so downhearted!

All packed and ready to start. Have packed my valise nearly full, stored what I want at the Ebbitt House and ordered my trunk sent on by express. Had no time to get any photographs taken. Will do so first chance. I think the regiment is going to Fortress Monroe [Union fort located at Hampton Roads, near Yorktown, Virginia], thence to Richmond. Hope so.

March 23, 1862, Camp Palmer,
Arlington, Virginia

Dear Julia,

I have bought a horse of the late Adjutant Lovell for $150.00 and shall get a saddle etc. of the Quartermaster to complete my equipment when, if my baggage gets out from Washington, I shall be ready to go with the regiment tomorrow afternoon or Tuesday morning.

We are going down the Potomac in steamboats to Yorktown where we shall have a great fight probably—thence 'On to Richmond' on the James River.

My horse was recommended to me by the Colonel and every officer in the regiment as gentle and perfectly drilled. I am attached as 2nd Lieut. to Company D, Col. Davies making the appointment on Governor Morgan's [Edwin D. Morgan, New York governor, 1861–62] promise to confirm all his appointments.

I am in trouble about a servant. Neither the Capt. or Lieut. have one. I have hired a man to take care of my horse and shall detail one to black my boots etc.

March 25, 1862, Camp Palmer, Arlington, Virginia

Dear Father,

Here I am alive and well and not on the road to Richmond yet though at this moment we can see the transports coming up to Alexandria which are to take McDowell's Corps down the Potomac to Fortress Monroe.

I rode into town yesterday and finished purchasing my equipments and brought out my baggage. You would have laughed to see me riding down Pennsylvania Avenue with an Orderly, ten paces behind, carrying my baggage—myself in full uniform, strap, buttons, sash, belt and sabre.

We are very comfortably situated here and I know that the officers and men who know me do not dislike me. I am very fortunate in not being a party to any of the thousand quarrels in the regiment and shall ever seek to keep clear of them.

If it was an infantry regiment, I would go to battle today if I could. But I feel when riding about that a Captaincy in infantry could not induce me to get off and walk.

My dear Father, I assure you that I am satisfied, and indeed I am fortunate that I keep so quiet that nobody seeks to tempt me. I shall <u>not</u> drink with anybody and am glad that I have already taken a stand where temptation does not come to me as strongly as I expected.

March 26, 1862, Camp Palmer, Arlington, Virginia

Dearest Julia,

Now then for my 'blue' feelings as per your letter. In the first place the Colonel— I suppose I am looked upon as one of his 'pets,' but still I don't much like him. He has acted in an un-officer-like way in trying to make me trade my horse for his wind-broken chestnut. Last night the Chaplain came round to advise me to trade—great business for <u>him</u>, of whom more anon.

Then the Lieut. Col. is always running down the horse. Lieut. [J. Nelson] Decker says that they are in league to get him for the Colonel. It is undignified to say the least but can't move me. I like my horse and shall keep him.

Chaplain Stone is the meanest, most selfish man in the regiment and though he has a pleasant way with him, has no religious principle of any stamina. For example, he has preached but four or five times since he joined the regiment in August last. (<u>Don't make this public</u> as a private is to be punished for writing home that fact to a newspaper in Hudson, N.Y.). Last night, when he came into the tent, I asked him if he would have a glass of water. He said, 'No, but if you have anything better, I shall not object.' A pretty answer to give to a young officer in camp; a pretty man he is. The rest of the field and staff I like much.

March 26, 1862

Dear Mother,

Yours and Julia's letters were handed to me yesterday as I was on the eve of starting to witness a review of Maj. Gen. McDowell's entire corps d'armee at Bailey's Cross Roads. The whole regiment went as part of the corps. It was a glorious sight—35,000 men marching and counter-marching on an immense plain with music, flags, salutes etc.

McDowell is a splendid officer in appearance at least. Mounted on a magnificent white charger, he galloped up and down the lines of thousands of cheering soldiers, followed by a staff large enough to form a company of cavalry.

Oh such a glorious ride as I had back! My horse is a beauty. He can out trot any horse in the regiment and can gallop like the wind. The road was smooth and the night beautiful.

March 27, 1862, Camp Palmer
Arlington, Virginia

Dear Mother,

Here I sit this lovely day in the Headquarters of the Officer of the Guard as a supernumerary, learning the duties as my turn to fill the post approaches.

Looking out of the entrance to the tent the smooth waters of the Potomac glistening in the sunshine are seen stretching for miles for miles away in either direction, with the great city of Washington in its magnificent incompleteness directly opposite.

March 29, 1862
Arlington, Virginia

Dear Julia,

Yesterday I went on drill for the first time and got along very well. I now know my place in the company, how to act as an officer of the guard, and how to do at dress parade.

The officers have nightly recitations in the Tactics at the Colonel's tent. I was very much astonished last night to see what a set of ignoramuses they were. I did as well as any of them and know myself that I can beat any of them in a month.

A singular thing in this regiment is that nearly every officer in it has been under arrest for some triviality save Lieut. Decker, who hates the Colonel more than any of them.

I am changing my own opinion with regard to the Colonel as I find that he thinks well of me. I like him for that, and again in that some of the best officers in the regiment swear by him. I think he is a gentleman, rather indolent and rather a martinet. He has done some very singular things though, as nearly every officer in the regiment had to buy his commission of him for solid cash.

We take our meals, and excellent food we get too, at an old Negress a short distance from camp for 75 cents per diem.

As for seeing service soon, it's the sooner the better, for if I can do well on the battlefield, I am all right and it will excuse any little mistakes. Besides, it's easier to lead a company into action than to a company drill. All you have to do is to take your place, draw sabre and charge. I look upon as much a part of my business as wearing shoulder straps. Then if wounded or killed I shall know that it was in a good cause and feel assured that though unworthy of Our Father's mercy in the hereafter, I am no more so than I was in Norwich.

Indeed I think I fear Death less than ever before and feel more dependence on Him. My temptations here are actually, to my great astonishment, infinitely less than in Norwich. My Captain and Lieut. drink very rarely, if at all. Gambling is the curse of the regiment and you may rest assured that I shall keep from it.

National Republican, March 30, 1862
"Justice in the Army"

Camp of Cavalry, Near Arlington, Va.

Editors *National Republican*:

In your issue of the 29th instant, you struck at a vice the growth of which is exercising a depressing influence upon the spirits and honest aspirations of our soldiers; and in reading that article, the true and tried soldier feels that in you he has an advocate and friend, ready and willing to bring to bear upon the military abuses of the day the power and influence of the press.

Not alone, however, in the appointment of "outsiders" as brigadiers over officers whose skill and courage has been tested on the battle field, is injustice and want of appreciation seen and surely felt; but by extending, as it does, to the appointment of subalterns, the evil, with all its blighting effects, is brought directly home to the great body of the army.

For instance: a second lieutenancy is vacant; next in rank stands an orderly sergeant, a man of sound discretion, fair education, correct habits, and, from eight months' instruction in camp duties, military discipline and drill, well qualified to fill the place to which he is by law entitled, and to wear upon his shoulders the mark of an officer. But no; both his qualifications and just claims are ignored; merited promotion is refused him, and by the aid of the lever that moves the world, a pampered pet of wealth and fashion, in the shape of a pale-faced, beardless boy, or a drawing room fop, is raised from the lap of unmanly and enervating luxury, and presented to a company of camp-worn or battle-scarred soldiers as an officer to be by them "respected and obeyed as such." Ignorant of camp duty, military discipline and drill, he is not capable of imparting instruction to the men; and even if this disability were removed, his feeble arm cannot swing a sabre, or guide a war horse. A few weeks of camp life uses him up—a sick furlough is obtained, and Government pays him an ample salary for parading the Avenue or lounging in graceful ease around the fashionable hotels, while the *soldier*, whose qualifications are in every respect superior to his own, and over whose head he was promoted, remains in camp, and does double duty, at fourteen dollars per month.

What wonder, then, that dissatisfaction exists in regiments where such injustice, such open transgressions of military law, are practiced and allowed; and what conclusion is left for the soldier to form, but that, because he cannot command influence and wealth, the country for which he fights cares not for him, and will not protect him in his rights.

Patriotism and honest ambition are the two great incentives to the soldier— override him in the gratification of the latter, and the former will eventually die out, and when it is gone, he is fit for nothing; and no surer method of destroying the one and quenching the other can be adopted, than this unjust, this ungrateful system of appointments and promotions.

"Give us competent officers" has been, and still is, the cry. If our country would have them, let her take the proper measures to get them, and stop this hotbed culture of brigadiers, colonels, captains and lieutenants. Let the laurels a soldier has won rest upon his own brow, not to be torn away to decorate the head of a military ignoramus.

SOLDIER

April 4, 1862,
Arlington, Virginia

Dear Mother,

Last night I read two chapters of *McClellan's Tactics* to our non-commissioned officers, explaining what I could, relating incidents and answering questions. When I came back I found both Captains asleep and my bed blocked up with logs to the ceiling, a trick of that abominable Decker. As Decker sleeps with the Orderly I could not punish him then; so I made up my mind that Captains [William H.] Mallory and [Marcus] Coon were accessories, so I built a barricade of logs, water pails and trunks at the door, covered their bed, in which they were sleeping, with saddles and went back to Lieut. Compton's tent and slept with him, Lieut. Hasty being absent. This morning Captain Mallory swears he'll put me under arrest if I ever do it again.

Everything gets stolen here and the less one has the better. My beautiful little looking glass was stolen the third day after I got here, and Lieut. Decker's second horse was taken last night.

April 7, 1862,
Arlington, Virginia

Dearest Parents,

We have just received marching orders for Manassas and the South, the destination of McDowell's Corps having been entirely changed. We leave in about two hours.

The scene in the Colonel's tent was very affecting. The Colonel was thunderstruck. Lieut. Colonel Kilpatrick cried for joy, and Major Davies looked like the little despot he is.

Good bye, God bless you all. Send me nothing for the present. On to Richmond —this time without question.

April 7, 1862,
Bristoe Station, Virginia

Dear Mother,

The papers of Sunday announced the formation of a Department of the Rappahannock under General McDowell.

The story here is that McClellan left on Friday last for Fortress Monroe, supposing that McDowell would follow with his whole corps, but that McDowell, who is jealous of McClellan, had the orders countermanded, the new department created, and his corps ordered here, intending to go this way to Richmond and reach it in advance of McClellan, [Maj. Gen. John E.] Wool, or [Maj. Gen. Ambrose] Burnside, and be hailed as the true hero.

My man shot a sheep yesterday in the sight of the camp in broad daylight, and he with eight others was caught and sent to the guard house while the Q.M. took the sheep. The boys have just been released and fined $5.00 apiece to pay the owner.

The Colonel and Quartermaster will have our nice mutton for dinner.

Yankees have already opened eating houses in Fairfax and Centreville. The latter is the strongest position I have ever seen, infinitely more so than Manassas.

The country the other side of Bull Run is perfectly beautiful, stretching away for miles in a smooth prairie with range after range of hills in the distance, while in the dim blue ether, miles to the westward, can be descried the lofty summits of the Alleghenies. Yet not an acre of land was cultivated and not a soul visible save the teamsters and guard. The only bar to perfect delight was my lame leg and the number of dead horses with which the country is strewn.

We reached Manassas about 4 PM and while waiting for forage, got an excellent dinner at the New York Saloon for 62 cents.

While waiting here I rode up to the only house where there was a light and found a very intelligent Negro, his wife and daughter. He said he had been a slave (thank God he is not now) of William Warl, whose house was General [Maj. Gen. P. G. T.] Beauregard's headquarters at the Battle of Bull Run.[1] His master fled early in March with all his children and grandchildren. He said the Rebels talked big till the battle of Dranesville [Union victory, December 20, 1861, in Fairfax County, Virginia, near Washington, during McClellan's operations in northern Virginia], since when they had been very apprehensive. He was rejoiced to see federal troops, but a regiment which passed two days before ours used him shamefully.

You see the Negroes are allowed to select from their master's grain enough for themselves and then give the rest up to the Government. He had taken ten bushels of corn and a quantity of wheat and stored them in the mill just opposite his house. The wheat he had just ground into flour when this regiment came up and, regardless of his expostulations, declared it was all secesh property, seized the corn and emptied the flour in the run. The poor fellow went to Q.M. General at Manassas who told him to go somewhere to a rebel stack and take a certain quantity of unthreshed wheat, but refused to give him a letter to protect him from its being seized after he had threshed and ground it. I gave him ten cents and told him to hook all the rebel property he could find and hide it in his cellar or somewhere where nobody could find it.

1. The first battle of Bull Run on July 21, 1861, also known as the battle of Manassas, was the first major battle of the war.

April 9, 1862,
Bristoe Station, Virginia

Dear May,

Such horrible weather as we have had for 48 hours and as still prevails you never saw in Norwich. At 11 AM Monday a storm of snow, rain and sleet commenced which now continues without any prospect of its clearing up. The suffering of the men in their miserable shelter tents (the officers fare no better) with the rain and snow pouring down and the camp a mass of deep, red mud are beyond description. Most of them have found quarters all about the country for miles in homes, barns, haystacks, etc.

Roll call is a farce, dispensed with in most companies, and the men do little but growl, eat and sleep. The horses are worse off than the men. My poor Kilpatrick like the rest wallows in the mire with his head and tail a mass of ice and is ugly and spiteful.

Every man here abouts swears he is a union man but daily proof arises that such and such a one is Secesh. We have a bag filed with peanuts in common with every company in the regiment, confiscated by Captain Mallory, and luxuriate in them.

We have seized enough smokes and chewing tobacco of the best quality to supply the regiment for a month. We have just found a barrel of salt pork and dried beef and another of corn and oats. We shall live like princes.

April 10, 1862,
Bristoe, Virginia

Dear Father,

We received two mails today with letters to me from Governor Buckingham [Connecticut governor, 1858–66] and Mrs. Abbott and two from Mother dated Sunday and Monday. The same train brought the owner of this house who rushed down here and examined his stock. He swears by all that's holy that he is a union man and we finally settled with him by the occupants of the whole house paying him $6, which made my share only 75 cents, which is moderate as I had to pay that sum every day for meals at Camp Palmer.

Have just got news that McClellan has taken Yorktown and moved to within 30 miles of Richmond. We expect to leave tomorrow. Hope my next will be from Richmond.

April 12, 1862
Bristoe, Virginia

Dear Mother,

Still here but expecting to leave daily. [Brig. Gen. William] Franklin's[1] whole division are returning from the South of us back to Alexandria to reinforce General McClellan.

Lieut. Compton and 20 men of our squadron went out foraging yesterday with Colonel Kilpatrick, and such a headlong chase as he led them. He rode at a gallop all the way, never minding fences, ditches, rivers or anything else. That man is the greatest dare devil alive. The party captured seven secesh horses, but late last night the owners appeared to claim them. As Kilpatrick is Provost Marshall, the complaints had to be made to him and so they will probably get their horses back.

The weather is superb, and the mud is rapidly drying up. Our only hindrance in an advance movement will be the swollen condition of the brooks which are difficult to cross, but now rapidly falling. That is a feature in Virginia. Before a storm you see a little attempt at a brook, say a foot wide by six inches deep. After a storm the brook will be a little river, four feet deep and ten wide.

1. Franklin was then commanding the 6th Corps.

In Camp, Callett's Station,
Seven miles from Bristoe
April 14, 1862

Dear Mother,

Further South than ever, slowly but surely the rebellion is being wound in the anaconda coils of the great army of freedom. Slowly, but surely, we near Richmond. Ah, how we hope to revel in the homes of that accursed city.

Sunday morning the regiment formed on the parade ground and in accordance with Secretary Stanton's proclamation religious services were held and thanks given to the God of battles for our recent victories. Dr. Stone prayed impressively and Colonel Davies made an excellent address. We gave three cheers for the cause and dispersed to form in line, mounted, at 12 AM to proceed further. The march was without incident save that we passed McDowell's headquarters and I had an excellent full-faced view of that lord of our destiny.

April 16, 1862,
In Camp, Weaversville,
Near Catlett's Station

Dear Father,

Monday night I had my first experience in one of the most interesting, exciting and dangerous phases of a soldier's life—picket duty.

We rode all over creation, searched a dozen houses, fed our horses with corn at the residence of the richest secessionist in the county, who was at home and not very happy to see us. One of my men split a turkey with his sabre while I shut my eyes—today I had a nice piece of roast turkey for dinner. Then we took a station and for an hour half my men kept dismounted at their horses sides while the other half slept. I watched with them.

While watching we saw the rebels exchange signal lights somewhere miles off. Our guide was a Negro servant of Lieut. Smith's who escaped from the county (Fauquier) a month since and knows every road from here to the Rappahannock.

At dawn we darted away into the enemy's county, some four miles, but saw nothing and retraced our steps, bringing back all the pickets and arriving at camp about 9 AM.

We shall have a chance soon to show that Connecticut blood is as good in the Army of the Potomac as anywhere else.

3

Goddard in Baptism of Fire
with His "Connecticut Squadron"

Norwich Bulletin, **April 20, 1862**

"Army Correspondence: From McDowell's Advance"

Falmouth, Va., opposite Fredericksburg

Dear Bulletin,

At last the sons of Connecticut stand upon the banks of the beautiful Rappahannock. The Connecticut Squadron in the Harris Light Cavalry have, in the words of the Lieutenant Colonel, "passed through the baptism of fire," and, as I predicted in my last letter, have nobly maintained the honor of their State, though they mourn the loss of one of the finest officers in the regiment.

On Monday, April 17th, the regiment left Catlett's station and marched 22 miles to Stafford, Va., where the rebel pickets were discovered and the regiment halted, while the 1st battalion was ordered forward for a charge through the village.

The two Connecticut companies were placed at the head of the battalion, and Lieut. Decker of company D, at the head of the first platoon as advanced guard. As Major Davies gave the order to "Charge," the battalion started and dashed down the road like the wind. After riding two miles we heard picket shots, and Lieut. Decker's voice came ringing back to us to urge us still faster onward, and then pressing the spurs to his horse he disappeared in advance with his platoon. Two minutes later, as we turned a corner in the road, we saw his bleeding corpse and a wounded rebel begging for "Quarter." Decker was shot through the heart by the rebel upon whose head his sabre was just descending. Then I saw what a soldier's grief can be. Old men cried and, raising their hands, vowed to God that Decker's death should be avenged.

A few minutes later we captured five prisoners and a rebel camp with all its stores, but their main body had fled. We bivouacked in their camp till midnight, when we advanced against their main body a mile further on, where, through the treachery of our Virginia guide (a villain named Hewett, who said he came to Virginia from Norwich, Conn., twenty years since), the regiment was led into an ambuscade, where it was exposed to a galling fire of rebel infantry. The night being pitch dark and the horses wallowing in the mire, an advance was impossible till daylight, when the troops (a whole brigade having arrived) chased the rebels across the Rappahannock, and though too late to save the bridge, shelled the fugitives till Fredericksburg was deserted by all save citizens.

So after eight months of patient waiting, the Connecticut boys enjoyed three fights within eighteen hours, and distinguished themselves throughout.

Lieut. J. Nelson Decker was a resident of Newburgh, N.Y., and before the commencement of hostilities had been in the dry goods business in New York City. . . . No man was more loved and respected in the regiment, and none understood his duties as well. His remains lie in a pleasant churchyard at Falmouth, where he was buried with military honors. Yet he has not died in vain.

> *For how can a man die better than facing fearful odds,*
> *For the ashes of his fathers,*
> *The temple of his God.*

Falmouth, Virginia
April 20, 1862

Dear Mother,

Here we are encamped in a beautiful little town opposite Fredericksburg. I have but five minutes to write and will simply state that I was with my platoon in an action on the 18th at Stafford, Va., five miles hence, in which poor Lieutenant Decker was shot through the heart and instantly killed. The rebels got his horse and traveling valise in which he carried all his own and my valuable toilet articles.

We captured the man who shot him, and I was left at Stafford Court House overnight with a guard and four prisoners while the regiment marched on. I rejoined the regiment with my guard and five prisoners in the afternoon, having during the day been engaged in the care of the dead, wounded and prisoners, preparing the body of Decker for a coffin, holding a wounded man of Co. E while the doctor was at work, and sitting all night with a cocked revolver in charge of five prisoners, desperate villains, large enough to eat me easily.

Our force is 5,000 strong, under command of General [Christopher, then a brigadier general under McDowell] Auger.

Falmouth, Virginia
April 20, 1862 (Sunday)

Dear Mother,

Here we lie on an open hill, the highest in the vicinity, with Falmouth at our feet on this side, the Rappahannock and Fredericksburg on the other. I have already bathed my head in the Rappahannock just below the burning bridge while a rebel horseman was directly opposite me on the other bank, not an eighth of a mile. Had I a carbine, I should have shot at him, but I did not fear that he could hit me, as it was foggy and he was too high up the bank to get a good aim at me; so Fred Compton and I bathed right on in his presence without saying "by your leave."

Lieut. Col. Kilpatrick issued a capital order to the regiment last night—congratulating us on our conduct Thursday and Friday—and indeed we won praise from all, as two companies of the Pennsylvania ran away when our boys came up and took their places. At any rate, Kilpatrick will immortalize us though it may cost us our lives. His only order to us through the charge through Stafford was, as he dashed down the lines, "Now, boys, they say that up North we don't know how to ride. Perhaps we don't. Let's show them whether we do or not."

Oh, what a ride that was. For three miles we charged like a whirl wind. At any rate, whatever mistakes I may make, I know my place in the company in battle and what orders to give and have a horse that never will let those behind him run him down.

Stealing is the great fault here. I have had stolen in this camp two blankets, a cup, a bag of oats, my last pair of spurs and a handkerchief which I placed on the horse which followed Decker's body to the grave. Everybody tells me the only way is to "find" things in return.

Contrabands come into the camp by the dozens, and I intend to secure one soon. The Adjutant got a splendid one yesterday who had just come from the service of a confederate officer in Fredericksburg. I could have had him had I a tent, but through Coon's [captain of Goddard's Company D] and Mallory's carelessness at Bristoe, the Captain and I have had to sleep with three of our men.

We expect to stay hereabouts for a few days, then to occupy Fredericksburg, and then, then "on Richmond"—only 60 miles.

Camp Auger, Falmouth, Va.
April 22, 1862

Dear Sister May,

Yesterday was one of those vile, rainy days so common in Virginia, but which I never experienced North. Mud everywhere and as I have no tent of my own, I had to sleep in a mud puddle in Coon's servant's tent with nothing but wet blankets for covering. It was the worst phase of a soldier's life that I have yet experienced. I think I should prefer to go into action once a week than endure such weather as often.

At 3 A.M. I could stand it no longer and got up and went to a camp fire where I rested till 5 A.M. when I got my clothes dry and then went to Lt. Compton's tent where I found a cover (as I always can in his quarters) and slept there till 6 A.M. (roll call) as sound as a "bug in a rug."

I have hired a contraband from Fredericksburg who knows all about horses but is otherwise green as a servant.

Monday I was out all day with a foraging party. We were very short of rations and fodder at this time and on this trip I bought a dozen eggs of a colored "aunty." I carried them in my handkerchief. A little later when we were galloping across a muddy field, I essayed to jump a brook. The horse slipped on the farther bank and fell upon my right leg. I shouted to Compton who galloped down to me and called out, "Hope you have not broken the eggs." I had them in my hand but was pretty mad and replied, "Get this horse up and off my leg or I will throw every one of them at you." He laughed and pulled the horse up. The mud was soft and I was not hurt.

The Negroes everywhere give us "hoe cake," and it tastes good I assure you, though at home you would not eat it without butter and molasses. I got a good supper at the home of a woman whose property I protected from the soldiers the day I got here by sending a note to the Provost Marshall for her, for which she is amazingly grateful.

The people of Falmouth express much astonishment at the discipline of our soldiers. General Auger is very particular and I do not believe five dollars worth of property has been dislocated, while our officers have spent more specie in town than the people have seen for months. They say that if the truth had been known in the South, we should have received a warm welcome, but that they expected we would rob and pillage every house in the place. This, it is claimed, is why there are no unionists here. There were none who dared own themselves such, but were forced to talk "secesh" though they now pray (so a woman with a brother in the rebel army tells me) that our army may never return North except in triumph.

I have had two compliments since our fight:

1) Major Davies has appointed me acting Battalion Adjutant while he is absent, and

2) Corporal Buck of our company, an old militia captain, in course of conversation tells me that in common with the whole company he was at first indignant at my appointment and "forgot" himself so much as to denounce me soundly (I quote his exact words), "But now the boys had seen that I roughed it just as they did, bore what they bore and was in my place in our first action and unavoidably absent from the second, they hold me in much higher respect."

At present I like my place and hope yet to master thoroughly my duties. I dislike Captain Coon's never telling me any of his intentions. He is a brave, fearless soldier, but is not and never was a gentleman in manners or feeling. Personally I like Colonel Davies, but I hear that even his cousin, the Major, says he must resign.

We shall cross to Fredericksburg as soon as we can get a pontoon bridge across. The rebs will probably shell us as we cross, and then run away—though we may have the big fight there. So my darling I may never return. Just remember,

"Whether on the scaffold plank
Or in the battle's eye
The noblest place for man to die
Is where he dies for man."

I enclose some beautiful azaleas which grow here about in the greatest luxuriance—far prettier than any I saw North.

Falmouth, Virginia
April 23, 1862

Dear Mother,

We removed our camp yesterday some three quarters of a mile back into the woods, leaving the hill which was in full view of Fredericksburg, and would have been dangerous if the rebels had commenced shelling us.

We have splendid quarters as we built a large frame and put four shelter tents over it. It's the most pleasant situation I have yet enjoyed in my camp experience.

In my account of our fight which I sent the *Norwich Bulletin* I said we were deceived and led into an ambuscade by a man from Norwich named Hewett. It has since been proven that he is the most thoroughgoing Unionist hereabout and had been persecuted by the rebels as such. It was through his ignorance of their plans that he got us into the "fix." Please have the *Bulletin* correct my error.

I never was so entirely happy in the army as now. It is one of April's most beautiful smiles. I sent May flowers from the Rappahannock's banks.

Colonel Davies, it is said, tried to rejoin us but General Auger sent him back as "sick" at General McDowell's injunction. He is now ill in Washington. I may never see him again.

God bless you all, Harry

4

Parading through Fredericksburg and Engaging Rebel Infantry

Falmouth

May 6, 1862

Last evening our whole regiment under Col. Davies crossed the Rappahannock on a pontoon bridge and escorted Generals McDowell, [Brig. Gen. Rufus] King and [Brig. Gen. Marsena] Patrick over to Fredericksburg. We then reconnoitered all the roads for about five miles in each direction. As senior 2nd lieutenant of the squadron, I now command the 2nd platoon. Lt. Hasty leads the 1st platoon and as advance guard captured a rebel lieutenant on picket duty, seizing also his horse and all his arms which he delivered over to Gen. King, who presented them to Hasty, though about a dozen men claimed the horse of the captive. I did not witness the capture as at the time I was carrying orders from Col. Davies to Maj. [Alfred N.] Duffie, who was reconnoitering another road, and also reports to Gen. Patrick.

When I rejoined the squadron, I galloped down the lines at their head, with Union pickets acting as skirmishers. We heard the rebel pickets falling back and Lt. Hasty begged to be allowed to charge them. But Gen. Patrick refused. We were then under Maj. Duffie. Just then Col. Davies sent for us to come up and act as his guard as the rebels were in view on the other end. We wheeled and were starting when Gen. McDowell came up and ordered us to remain where we were, and sent orders to Gen. Patrick and Col. Davies to retire immediately as it was growing dark and he did not wish the reconnoiting pushed any further. Lt. Hasty and his pickets were called in and we made a right-about wheel and pushed to the front of the column escorting Duffie's battalion and the General's back to town where Col. Davies joined us with the balance of the command. When we resumed our places at the head of the column, mine being now the advance platoon, I had to repeat the Colonel's orders at the top of my voice.

We marched all through the city of Fredericksburg, which is quite a large and pleasant city, with some fine horses, large workshops, a good depot and gaol.

The colored people threw us bunches of lilacs and laughed in their joy to see the "fine gentlemen's." We saw but few whites, the men appearing as they do in any city, except not all well-clothed. The women—the old ones—looked as sour and bitter as persimmon, such an "I would like to cut your head off" expression as I never saw before and don't wish to see again. The young ladies, and we saw some elegantly dressed ones, looked half mad, half pleased to see such a lot of good-looking fellows in handsome uniforms, in short, looked much as coquettes do anywhere. One of the prettiest frowned as I saluted her in passing, but, as soon as her mother's back was turned, honored me with such a very sweet smile that seemed to me _inviting_ as it surely was _enticing._

We passed the town until dark when we re-crossed on a new and much sturdier bridge, canal boats being used for pontoons instead of the inflated bags. It would amuse you to see a cavalry regiment crossing one of these wobbly pontoon bridges. The men all dismount and lead their horses, and such a swaying and jiggling to and fro on an uneven surface you never saw. One would think that men and horses were all drunk, making a foolish effort to "walk the plank." Matters run more smoothly in our squadron now. Whitaker is a sincere Christian though not of gentle birth. I can but be sorry for him. Mallory is the only officer in the squadron who seems to be well born, but his moral principles do not seem lofty.

Wood ticks are little insects that get on and even into one's body, and it is very difficult to pull them out. The violets were charming. They brought the door step right before my eyes.

Falmouth, May 9, 1862

I begin to wish I was in any other than the Connecticut squadron of the regiment as I find its officers are the most opposed to Col. Davies, who is behaving splendidly these days. All the _field_ officers treat me very well, if my Captain was only disposed to help me, I should have no trouble, but he does all he can to torment me.

Marching orders have come. Thank God.

Falmouth, May 13, 1862

Dear Julia,

Last Friday, Company D crossed the river to Fredericksburg and went into camp on the river road with Company L on the "Telegraph Road," the one the regiment had previously reconnoitered. That night I went on picket with 12 men, the present Orderly Sgt. and a corporal. We expected an attack and were watchful, as we saw the rebel pickets the day before. Saturday AM I was relieved and rode over to C's offices at Falmouth, where I found letters announcing Father's serious illness, and receiving Gov. Buckingham's message as to the troubles in the regiment.

Applied for a week's leave of absence to go to Connecticut. On my return, I found our camp moved closer to the city on a splendid shady lawn, bordered by a running brook with a high hill shadowing our camp. An infantry company are camped close by.

While I was asleep, Capt. Hasty took 40 men and went down to the telegraph lines for two miles where they arrested two women and an old man and made them harness up an old carriage and drive up to the city and take the oath of allegiance of Gen. Patrick. While there, two companies of rebel infantry tried to flank Hasty's men but he retreated in haste though a carbine shot came within three feet of him. Gen. Patrick was pleased about his conduct.

At 10 PM that day, Maj. Duffie came up with two companies of his battalion and ordered Capt. Coon to move up in support of Capt. Walters, who had been driving in rebel pickets on the "Telegraph Road" every night. We moved over and encamped alongside Walters.

At 2 AM Sunday, Hasty and I got orders from Gen. Patrick to go on a reconnaissance with Capt. Walters and Lt. Plumb. We got about a mile beyond the scene of Hasty's late adventure when the rebel pickets opened on us, carbine balls flying all about us. They then galloped off and we captured their hats and blankets and, having accomplished our orders in locating them, returned to camp. Sunday morning I visited Falmouth and in the afternoon returned to camp.

Soon after, I heard firing on the river end and at once called out the company and awaited orders. The three regiments of infantry in camp very soon went past on the double quick.

We did not move and in an hour the infantry returned and we heard the whole story. It seems that Maj. Duffie went out with his whole battalion on a reconnaissance. Lt. Hasty was over there, and finding an advancing platoon of Company L under a Sgt., volunteered and obtained leave to command it. He dashed ahead, and, in turning a corner in the road, encountered eleven rebel infantry, with guns at a "ready" but not aimed—at 300 yards, Hasty ordered a charge. When within 30 paces, one of the rebels raised his gun and took aim. Hasty shouted, "Lay down your arms or I will blow out your brains." Our men had their carbines ready to fire, but the rebels all dropped their guns instantly and Hasty received the surrender of the whole party with their Lieut., who formally delivered up his sword and also surrendered two cavalrymen's and their horses. Here a large rebel force appeared and drove the whole battalion back, killing Maj. Duffie's horse and nearly hitting Gen. Patrick. Soon after, our infantry support reached Duffie, whereat he drove the rebels back beyond their original starting point. Hasty dined with a Tribune reporter and gave him the surrendered sword, delivering up his other captives to the General, except a shot gun. See if he doesn't get a great "puff" in the N.Y. Tribune. He is quite the hero here.

About 7 PM our pickets commenced firing on the Telegraph road. Capts. Coon and Walters were each down in the city, awaiting orders. Hasty told me to have the men saddle up while he went to see what the noise was about. I did so and heard Lt. Plumb doing the same. We remained in our saddles an hour. While waiting we heard great cheering in all the camps across the river and heard three more shots from the pickets. Our pickets, who had come down to supper, rushed back to their post and a force of infantry stood in readiness. Just then Capt. Coon came up and told us that Norfolk and Portsmouth were taken and the "Merrimac" was blown up, and that Duffie's battalion was ordered back to Falmouth, and that we were to return to our picturesque camp and picket the river road.[1] We gave three rousing cheers, when the Capt. said to me, "What the d——l have you the men in line for?" I told him that the enemy had opened on the Telegraph road, which astonished him and he rode up to see about it.

Then we heard the cheering pass up and down our side of the road till it seemed there must be two divisions instead of one brigade this side. Gen. Patrick's orderlies were sent up the road but ere long returned with Coon and Hasty who said the rebels had attempted to drive in on the pickets but that the cheering had led them to make a hasty retreat. Hasty was sent with 24 men on picket while Duffie returned to his camp. We lay down and slept quietly for the first time since we crossed.

Yesterday I came to Falmouth and went to see Gen. King about my leave of absence. He was very pleasant. He was formerly editor of the Milwaukee Herald and lately of the Bulletin as well. He says there will be no advance for 10 days and I can do as well as not.

The appointments were made as announced except that Whitaker is made Sgt. Major. He is _mad_, though everyone but Coon tells him to take it. If the governor will put me in a Connecticut regiment, "Goodbye Harris Light." General Patrick has forbidden further reconnaissance lest we bring on a general engagement.

I notice in today's mail a letter from Norwich for Lt. Hasty. What does it mean? It frightens me a little.

While on the other side, four deserters came in who had been impressed into the rebel service. They are from Maine, New York and Michigan and say (which is corroborated by the contrabands who come in) that on Saturday the Confederates had 500 men within five miles of Fredericksburg, under Brig. Gen. [John R.] Anderson [A. P. Hill's division] of Porto Rico Island fame, with six pieces of artillery. They were fine fellows and the story of the year's impressment (they were taken from the Norfolk Navy Yard) was very interesting.

The contrabands coming in so frightened a secesh officer that he ran away from his dinner and left his secesh cap—a pretty one which I shall try to bring home.

Hasty and I get on splendidly and Coon likes me much better. He has offered me use of the secesh horses for $50.

I have received a letter from Mrs. Decker which I shall read to the company and then send to you. She is a Cornelia[2] in patriotism though an uneducated woman, as her letter shows.

If Father is dangerously ill, send for me at once as the only son at home must come to him, regardless of the consequence.

1. The Confederate ironclad *Merrimac,* or *Virginia,* was blown up on May 11, 1862, near Norfolk, Virginia, to avoid its being captured.

2. Cornelia of ancient Rome has been regarded as a perfect example of a virtuous woman who was devoted to her two sons, her "jewels," who died violently.

5

Goddard Resigns from the Harris Light Cavalry

Falmouth, May 15, 1862

My Dearest Mother,

Tuesday night on my return to camp, Hasty found Mrs. Abbott's letter and informed me that my worst anticipations were realized and that my dearest Father had left this world for one better and holier. I was stunned and immediately walked away and prayed to God to sanctify the loss to the Fatherless. Yet it did not overwhelm me as it would at home, as I live in daily anticipation of losing my friends or my own life.

That night we had to muster out again as cannonading was heard way down the river road, but it resulted in nothing.

Hasty acted like a brother and in that lonely field in Fredericksburg, far away from home, with a vigilant foe in our front, administered consolation in a manner I never can forget. I forgive him all his faults now (which arise from his youth) for his kind words to me that lovely moonlight night. If he survives this war and I do not, remember him as the comforter of your boy in his hour of affliction. I have made every effort now to get a leave of absence and filed them with Gov. Buckingham's letter requesting the same. God bless and preserve you all, my darlings. I know I am needed at home and must get there, and if I resign it will only be to join another regiment later.

May 17, 1862, Washington, D.C.

My Dearest Mother,

Gen. McDowell refused my application for leave, tho it had been approved and strongly recommended in all preceding headquarters. Hence I decided to take a 48-hour pass to Washington, which Gen. King gave me, and I came up here to communicate more directly with you and consider what to do. I rode from Falmouth to Aquia and took my horse to the steamboat, which left at 7 AM. Gen.

McDowell and his staff were on board and I got well acquainted with all the latter. Stopped at the Willard hotel[1] that night. Have called on E. C. Stedman and John J. Piatt.

Your dispatch came safe, and I shall rejoin the regiment tomorrow—resigning only if it becomes absolutely necessary. I feel it is still my duty to fight my country's battles in some capacity and somewhere. Don't despair, dear Mother. Many and many a Cornelia have given and must give their children's blood to save our dear country. If I am true to myself, death in this course can be but sweet.

1. As a guest of the historic Willard Hotel, Julia Ward Howe wrote the words to "The Battle Hymn of the Republic," and the Lincolns stayed there before moving into the White House, two blocks distant.

May 20, 1862
Fredericksburg, Va.

Darling Mother,

Rejoined the company here today. Regret to say that the old company troubles are as bad as ever. Whitaker refused to become Sgt. Major and is very "cranky." I went out yesterday to see the rebel pickets with Lt. Col. Kilpatrick, Maj. Duffie and Mr. Chas. H. Webb of the New York Times. They are in plain view of our pickets all day—some 300 yards apart—and exchange some shots every night. My commission from Gov. Morgan of New York came today. Had there been any disposition on the part of Capt. Coon, I should ere this be entirely satisfied here. But I am almost weary of this incessant struggle against his sullen dislike and Whitaker's ingratitude. Fortunately, none can charge me with showing fear in any of our skirmishes.

My horse is also no longer any good. My whole course has been heavy since I joined. In fear of being thought an arrogant fool, I have tried to please all and to learn from all and hence have not now the respect that I should have demanded. I have studied hard in all the manuals and have been laughed at for that and told that <u>practice</u> was what I needed—yet wherever possible I have been deprived of opportunities for drilling and parading the men.

May 21, 1862
Fredericksburg, Va.

My Dear Sister,

As Coon is in Falmouth and Hasty in Washington, I am in command of my company here. While reclining in my tent (thank God I have one to myself now), one of the pickets came in to report that a flag of truce had come to the lines, and he had come to see me for orders. The flag of truce was on a C. S. marked wagon drawn by two horses, with a Confederate soldier for driver, with a gentleman and his daughter (a beautiful miss of 20 years) as passengers.

I made the driver get out and wait while I examined the papers, which showed the gentleman to be a consul from Bremen, Germany, at Savannah, Georgia, with passes from authorities at both Richmond and Washington. I wanted to send to Gen. Patrick for instructions but Whitaker urged me to take the men there. So I put one of our men in the wagon as driver and rode alongside with Whitaker to the General's headquarters. The consul was a very pleasant gentleman but both he and the lady were much exhausted by their long trip.

Arriving at headquarters I went directly into Gen. P's room and related all the circumstances. He said I should have sent word to him before admitting the flag, but that as it was my first experience and the passes were all right, it was very excusable. Instead of the awful tyrant that I expected, I found him a very pleasant gentleman whom I am happy to serve. I got acquainted with his staff officers and found them splendid fellows.

To return, Gen. Patrick wrote a letter to Gen. McDowell for instructions and sent us to McDowell's chief of staff at Falmouth. We then rode over there with the letter, but found Gen. McDowell himself in the headquarters. He read the note and ordered a pass issued to Washington for the travelers.

Gen. McDowell then asked me a few questions about our officers. I humbly disagreed with his opinion that Coon and Greer are good officers.

The "Great Mogul" of our destiny had his hat off and I had a full view of him—though predisposed against him, I must say that he is a splendid looking man, apparently of much intellect. He had a map of the country south of the Rappahannock before him upon which all his thoughts seemed centered. What he said to me did not seem to distract his attention from his map. He has a large forehead and to a strong intellectual development combines strong animal development. He looked to me as a lion prancing before his prey.

Returning to Gen. Patrick, I found his staff devoted to the young lady. I had the baggage sent to a hotel and the wagon back to the picket line, with a letter from Gen. Patrick to Gen. J. R. Anderson, the Confederate commander on our front, who was his class mate at West Point.

I wish you could see me some afternoon, when I am galloping out to the front to watch secesh pickets or prancing my horse through Fredericksburg, trying to catch a glimpse of my fair Southern inamorata—a Miss Herndon,[1] whom I have seen but once, but it was "love at first sight." Fredericksburg is one of the loveliest of cities.

1. Belle Herndon.

Washington, May 27, 1862

My Dear Julia,

I have resigned my commission in the Harris Light Cavalry and came up here to settle my accounts with the Paymaster. I took this step after a long conference with Col. Davies, who advised it, and have the warmest recommendation to Gov. Buckingham from all the field officers of the regiment and my squadron officers.

After a brief visit home to render what help I can, I shall certainly re-enter the service.

I have a secesh sabre to bring home, captured when Decker was killed.

Shall be home Friday.

Yours ever, Harry

Goddard's Notes, 1882

Among the most beautiful of Fredericksburg young ladies was Miss Herndon, who subsequently became the wife of President Arthur. I saw her often but did not know her formally, though I knew who she was as her father[1] had always been one of my heroes.

I left the "Harris Light" because I found it intolerable to endure the Captain's dislike and lack of help: while I was slowly and gradually winning friends and learning my duty, I found I could do better to start in a new regiment with some experience than to stay in an old where all had a year's start of me.

It was a wise step and one I never regretted. Later in the war, Generals Kilpatrick, Davies and other officers of the Harris Light all became good friends of mine and many of the same are such to this day.

On my way home, I called in New York on Mrs. Col. Davies, Mrs. Kilpatrick and Mrs. H. E. Davies Jr.—all very kind.

1. Navy commander William Lewis Herndon, a renowned explorer and seaman, died in 1857 while in command of the steamer *Central America*, which sank in a gale off Cape Hatteras, North Carolina. Herndon went down with the ship after supervising the loading of women and children into lifeboats. His daughter Ellen Lewis Herndon married Chester A. Arthur and died in 1880 before Arthur became president. His niece Belle Herndon is Goddard's "fair Southern inamorata."

Letter of Commendation Written on Behalf of H. P. Goddard

Headquarters of the Harris Light Cavalry
Camp Auger near Fredericksburg, Va.
May 24th, 1862

We take pleasure in certifying to the bravery and good conduct of Lieut. H. P. Goddard in the actions of the 17th and 18th of April, and in subsequent skirmishes of this regiment. He also regrets that his sad bereavement should compel so gentlemanly an officer to reign his commission in this regiment.

J. Kilpatrick, Lt. Col.
J. M. Davies Jr., Major Commdy 1st Batt.

Part 2

THE "FIGHTING FOURTEENTH"

6

Organizing the Regiment

The 14th Regiment, Connecticut Volunteer Infantry, was in the greatest number of battles, sustained the highest number of combat casualties, and captured the most enemy flags of any Connecticut regiment in the Civil War. Organized in May 1862, the regiment of 1,015 officers and men was officially mustered into service on August 23, 1862. The new volunteers received their baptism of fire at the battle of Antietam, September 17, the bloodiest day of the Civil War. As part of the 2nd Corps, Army of the Potomac, the "Fighting Fourteenth" participated in thirty-three other engagements, including Fredericksburg, Chancellorsville, Gettysburg, Bristoe Station, Morton's Ford, the Wilderness, Spotsylvania, Cold Harbor, the siege of Petersburg, Reams Station, and the surrender of Robert E. Lee's army at Appomattox Court House. The regiment took more than a thousand prisoners during the course of the war.

At Gettysburg it was the 14th Connecticut that captured the Bliss barn and farmhouse from Confederate sharpshooters in what has been called a "small epic" that proved important to the Union repulse of Pickett's charge, where the regiment's thin line formed a key link defending Cemetery Ridge. For heroism in capturing rebel flags at that high watermark of the Confederacy, two members of the regiment were awarded the Medal of Honor.

After it was first organized, 697 substitute and volunteer recruits were added to the regiment—making a total of 1,712 men who served in its ranks. When it was mustered out on May 31, 1865, it numbered 234 officers and men. Its casualties during its nearly three years of service were as follows: killed in action, 132; died of wounds, 65; died of disease, 169; discharged for disability prior to the regiment's muster-out, 416; missing at the regiment's muster-out, 6.

The regimental band was commonly regarded as the best in the Army of the Potomac (Maj. Gen. Joseph Hooker was among those who called it so), and it was likely the most heroic, for during the battle of Chancellorsville, as the 11th Corps fled pell-mell from Gen. Thomas "Stonewall" Jackson's surprise attack and fell into the startled ranks of the 2nd Corps, the band quickly grabbed their instruments and played "The Star-Spangled Banner" and other patriotic anthems—inspiring the regiment and other units in the corps to form a line against the advancing Confederates.

Soon after joining the regiment in June 1862, Goddard wrote his mother, "Please keep my interesting letters from the 14th, as they will serve to form a connected history of my small part in the great drama of the 19th century" (42).

~

Excerpts from *History of the Fourteenth Regiment, Connecticut Vol. Infantry,* by Charles D. Page (Meriden, Conn.: Horton Printing Co., 1906)

The call of the President in 1861 for five hundred thousand men had been fulfilled, and the last of Connecticut's quota (13,037), the Thirteenth Regiment had left New Haven March 17th., and were doing duty at Ship Island.

These were the conditions when May 21st the War Department signified its willingness to accept from Connecticut one regiment as its part to form a contingent of fifty thousand men for a "Camp of Instruction" at Annapolis, Md.

The next day, May 22, the governor directed that "volunteers be received sufficient to form one regiment to be known as the Fourteenth Regiment of Infantry, to serve three years or during the war unless sooner discharged." . . .

The regiment was ordered to rendezvous at Hartford. The camp was located on the New Haven turnpike about two miles from Hartford and was called Camp Foote in honor of Commodore Foote, who had merited popularity and esteem in his native state for his gallant conduct at Forts Henry and Donelson.

May 22nd Dwight Morris was appointed as Colonel. Colonel Morris of Bridgeport was well known throughout the state. He . . . had graduated from Union College in 1832, and was a member of the General Assembly of Connecticut for six years from 1845, and again in 1880. . . .

No one at that time would have ventured the prophecy that this very regiment, conceived for the dull duties of a "Camp of Instruction," was destined to play an important part in some of the most sanguinary battles of modern times, and do valiant service in some of the pivotal actions of the great conflict.

Assistant Surgeon Dr. Levi Jewett in his diary estimates there were about two hundred and fifty men enlisted when he joined the regiment, July 14th. This was nearly two months after the call had been made for volunteers.

Suddenly all these conditions changed. Reverse followed reverse with the Union army, and the tide of rebellion swept westward and northward until the loyal people of the North were depressed and alarmed.

Governor Buckingham joined with the governors of all the loyal states requesting the President to "call out a sufficient number of men to garrison the cities and military posts that have been captured by our armies and to speedily put down the rebellion that now exists in several Southern states."

President Lincoln therefore issued an order for the enlisting of three hundred thousand more men. Connecticut's quota in this call was 7,145.

July 1st Governor Buckingham issued a call for this number of men to form six more regiments. Immediately following the call the Governor issued an impassioned address and appeal for volunteers: . . . "Close your manufactories and workshops, turn aside from your farms and your business, leave for awhile your families and your homes, meet face to face the enemies of your liberties!"

Meetings to promote enlistments were held in nearly all of the cities and larger towns of the state. These meetings were addressed by some of the best known men, and were characterized by the most intense patriotic enthusiasm and fervor. The effect of the Governor's appeal and the influence of these meetings were electrical. Young men flocked to the recruiting offices eager and earnest to enlist in the service of their country. The "lonely squads" of the Fourteenth Regiment, that had passed up and down the dusty field of "Camp Foote" for weeks, felt the impulse of the new enthusiasm and every day brought new members to its ranks. . . .

The regiment numbered 1,015 men and were to be armed with Springfield rifles, with the exception of Companies A and B, which were to be equipped with Sharp's rifles (14–16).

No Connecticut regiment ever took to the front a more noble representation of the best elements of the state than did the Fourteenth. Many of the men had already become moving forces in the social, religious, commercial, and industrial activities of the state. . . . It was indeed a regiment from the state at large, a regiment of the people. No less than eighty-six towns were represented upon the roster (17).

August 25th, the day for the regiment to break camp and start for Washington arrived. We will let Dr. Jewett, a participant, tell the story of the departure. He says, . . . "We left camp with bands playing and flags flying, marching to the dock in a column of fours. As we moved the crowd increased and when we reached the corner of Main and State Streets, it became so dense that we could hardly make progress. Reaching the dock, six companies boarded the steamer 'City of Hartford' and four companies upon the transport 'Dudley Buck.'

When we reached Middletown, it seemed as if the whole city had turned out to meet us. . . . Many came to the boats with baskets of fruit and food, which were greatly appreciated by the 'boys.' At Cobalt a great gun on the hill gave us a roaring 'God-speed' and there were hearty greetings from a crowd of friends at Middle Haddam." . . .

Slowly the steamer and transport steamed out of the Connecticut River into the broader waters of the Sound. At the right lay the old state dear to the hearts of those on board, their birthplace, the scenes of their ambitions and hopes, and the homes of those they loved who were left behind. Slowly they passed the familiar hilltops, the rugged cliffs, the undulating shore and the broad fields that floated back to the western sky. So the twilight drifted into the shadow and the shadow into darkness, and the fair scene was hidden from view. Alas, how many were never permitted to look upon it again! (19).

7

Sergeant-Major Goddard Takes to New Life in the Infantry

After a short visit home, Goddard—with letters of recommendation from Connecticut governor William A. Buckingham and field officers of the Harris Light Cavalry—is appointed sergeant major of the newly recruited 14th Connecticut Volunteer Infantry. At Camp Foote, two miles from the State House in Hartford, volunteers from across the state swell the ranks of the new regiment during the summer of 1862. Goddard spends his days "drilling and being drilled" (41) as his regiment awaits orders to move south and join the Union forces in Virginia, which are being driven from the gates of Richmond back toward Washington. Although he is generally happy with his new life in the infantry (a reason he had cited for joining the cavalry was to avoid long marches on foot), he expresses disdain for most of the candidates vying for election as company officers. (During the Civil War, line officers were often elected by their men.) He is eager to become an officer again and also eager for one big fight that will end the war, a common theme during that stage of the four-year conflict.

In early May 1862 the overly cautious Maj. Gen. George B. McClellan finally began to move the massive Union army he had assembled on the Virginia Peninsula toward the Confederate capital of Richmond. At the battle of McDowell, Virginia, on May 8, the Confederate general Stonewall Jackson won the first victory of his Shenandoah Valley campaign. The campaign, which was intended to relieve pressure on Richmond by threatening Washington, ended with Confederate victories at Cross Keys and Port Republic. On May 31 Gen. Joseph E. Johnston was wounded at the battle of Fair Oaks (Seven Pines) on the Virginia Peninsula, and General Robert E. Lee assumed command of what he soon names the Army of Northern Virginia. After the costly Seven Days' campaign that ended July 1 near Richmond, McClellan continued his withdrawal back toward Washington. President Lincoln called for three hundred thousand new volunteers on July 2 and told his cabinet on July 22 that he planned to emancipate the Southern slaves when conditions are more favorable.

~

Goddard's Account of Joining the 14th Connecticut Volunteers

[From a preface written shortly after the war]

Having resigned a commission as 2nd Lieutenant in the Harris Light Cavalry May 26, 1862, for reasons stated in my "War Letter Book No. 2," I returned to my home at Norwich, Conn.

After a brief visit there to my recently widowed Mother and two sisters, I determined to re-enter the Union service in a Connecticut Infantry regiment.

To this end I first visited at Hartford, Conn., Col. Henry C. Deming of the 12th Conn. Vols., which Regiment was then at Ship Island, Miss., in the "Dept. of the Gulf." He was very cordial and at once offered to make me a Lieut. in his Regiment, but advised me to enter the newly called 14th Conn. My fears of the climate of the Gulf Dept. decided me not to enter Col. Deming's Regiment.

June 3rd, 1862. I called on Col. Dwight Morris, the Colonel of the new 14th, at Bridgeport, Conn. With letters of recommendation from Gov. Wm. A. Buckingham and from the field officers of the Harris Light Cavalry, I offered to Col. Morris then and there to be appointed Sgt. Major of the new Regiment. Col. Morris seemed much pleased with my credentials, said he had 15 applications for the post. He said he would consult Gov. Buckingham and then advise me. I told him the story of the course of my leaving the Cavalry, with which he seemed perfectly satisfied. Col. Morris told me that he should make his entire staff "chiefs up to the nines."

After a brief visit to Donald G. Mitchell, my uncle, whose lovely Southern wife was naturally most unhappy about our Civil War, and to New York City where Judge Henry E. Davies [New York Court of Appeals, 1859–67] and family were most kind, and where Mrs. Col. [Judson] Kilpatrick, an East Hadden, Conn., lady, I found most charming, I returned to Norwich.

June 9th, 1862. I was summoned by Col. Morris to Camp Foote at Hartford, Conn., where the 14th Conn. was to be recruited. The only officers then commissioned were Col. Dwight Morris of Bridgeport, Conn., and Lt. Charles F. Dibble of New Haven, Conn.

Camp Foote, Hartford, Conn., June 12, 1862

Dear Mother,

Have been appointed Sgt. Major of the Regiment, the 14th Conn. Vols. and am in command of the camp, which consists of seventy-five recruits, with no commissioned officers present. It is the old camp of the 8th Conn., pleasantly situated in a meadow about two miles from the State House. The Colonel is very kind and lets me go and come much as I please. The Adjutant will come Monday. He is unknown to me.

Camp Foote, June 22, 1862

Dear Mother,

Lt. Charley Weld of the regular army has just called on me, accompanied by the Adjutant, [Theodore G.] Ellis, who appeared in full uniform for the first time. Charley is a fine fellow, but has now put on a little "style" as a regular. He was very cordial.

Capt. [William] Tubbs is here, but I have charge of the camp when the Adjutant is not here. The Adjutant is a gentleman and a scholar and we get on very well.

It's very dull here and will be till the Regiment fills up and is ready to start for the front.

Camp Foote, June 28, 1862

I am sorry to hear of Gen. Fremont's resignation of command[1] and of noble Hunter [Maj. Gen. David Hunter] demoted for employing negroes,[2] so as to save some of his soldiers.

I enjoy myself here hugely. Have little to do in the heat of the day and am not suffering the heat of Virginia. I have the friendship of all the field staff and the respect of every man in the regiment and appreciate their good wishes. You would be surprised to see the presents brought me—cherries, strawberries, flowers, cigars, etc. Our rations are brought to our tent at all meals, and dishes washed for us. Yet I am very strict with the men, so much so as to surprise myself as it is not natural, but I think it well for me to acquire the habit.

Sgts. [James R.] Nichols and [Edwin] Wilcox—each of whom has been in service—give us lessons in the Manual of Arms, and I watch the company drills.

I never was more content in my life and am ready to wait for a commission until I earn it. I won my spurs at Falmouth and if necessary will wait till I can win my spurs in battle.

P.S. Adjt. Theodore Ellis is a <u>Bostonian</u> in manner as well as in birth, thinks he knows better than anyone else, and snarls and scolds severely at times, and dislikes to show that he has any milk of human kindness. Yet he is admirably well read, always says what he thinks and is a gentleman. He treats me better when we are alone and is more confidential with me than with anyone here. He sees that I have the best of social connections and friends, and he is doing me good daily, for he makes me <u>particular</u> instead of negligent, which naturally I am. I like him better than anyone else here and should hate to lose him.

1. Maj. Gen. John C. Fremont, then head of the army's Mountain Division in West Virginia, sustained several severe defeats against Stonewall Jackson's successful Shenandoah Valley campaign. Placed under the command of former subordinate Maj. Gen. John Pope in an army reorganization, he angrily resigned his post, ending his military career.

2. In May 1862 Hunter declared slavery abolished in the Department of the South—South Carolina, Georgia and Florida—but his declaration was quickly revoked by President Lincoln. However, he was not demoted.

Camp Foote, June 29, 1862

Maj. Sanford H. Perkins arrived today. He is a short but energetic looking man and is said to be an excellent officer. He has just come from the front, having been a Captain in Col. R. G. Tyler's 10th Conn. Heavy Artillery. It is said that Col. Tyler is indisposed at Gov. Buckingham, who has promoted many of his Captains, for making his regiment a "yeast pot" for raising officers for other commanders.

We have been mustered into U.S. service. I supped with Adjt. Ellis. He tells me he was at Norwich at our Bi-Centennial in 1859.

Camp Foote, July 4th, 1862

Dearest Mother,

On this anniversary of the birth of our nation, I send a line to the dearest friend I have on earth. One year ago who could have foreseen where the country would now stand? With 75,000 three-months volunteers we calculated to restore the supremacy of the Union and that by the Fourth of July 1862 we should celebrate the restoration of the Union, stronger and more enduring than ever.

Where do we stand today? We have raised 600,000 three-year volunteers and fought nearly one hundred battles, yet we are called upon for 800,000 more men to wind the thing up, and we will raise them too, and they will be volunteers, not drafted men. Where will the Fourth of July 1863 find the country? One year ago we were a united family! Since then, our boys have been under fire and imperiled by land and sea, by day, by night, and yet all are safe—two have returned in safety to your arms, while our father, whom we should have least thought was near his end, has gone from us and is beyond the reach of mortal suffering. Does this does show us that truly God holds us in the hollow of his hand! Is it not the duty of every man of honor to offer his musket, or sword, aye his life even, to his country in her hour of need?

Ah Mother, you know not how much I am pleased here. I write a good deal every day and yet never miss the Sergeant's drill under Maj. Perkins, or the general Superintendence of the company drills. I get along splendidly with the courteous old gentlemanly Colonel, the prompt military Major, and exacting Adjutant. I admire and like them all exceedingly, and cannot but know that I am liked by all. So now I am beginning at the beginning, and learning every step of a pursuit I like, while I am so much ahead of the men in general military knowledge, that I am respected by all. Now I know this sounds like conceited balderdash, but I write this once, only to prove to you that a man must know the principles of his business to do well and not to be pushed or jump into it. I shall not write anything or say anything about my field officers, as I have resolved to follow your advice, but assure you that I like them exceedingly.

—Your affectionate son ever, Harry Goddard

Camp Foote, July 5th, 1862

Dear Mother,

Just as I had directed my letter to Julia I am called on to enroll the names of some men from Waterbury who had just come into camp. Entering into conversation with one of them, the most intelligent, who was in charge of the squad, I took occasion to ask about Capt. Marcus Coon of Co. D, Harris Light Cavalry, "an old friend of mine." He expressed much surprise when I said that Coon was a good soldier. He said Coon obtained his Captaincy in the 1st Conn. Vol. by cheating, and did not come home with a good reputation, and took scance any of his men into the Harris Cavalry with him, (which I knew to be a fact) and moreover that he was noted in Waterbury as a hard case and a low drunkard. I listened attentively but did not express any unfavorable opinion of Coon, though I did say that Coon was an old rascal. The man was surprised to hear me speak so well of Coon as an officer and said he could hardly believe it.

Well the past is dead and I am glad I am out of it. The only men I shall keep up an interest in that regiment are the Col., Lieut., Major P., Adjt., and Compton. Did I tell you that Whitaker[1] wrote me that he had received no appointment since I left, and in an un-Christian spirit, I must say that I am glad of it. I shan't cry if he never gets one.

I went down to Hartford to see the friends last night, and enjoyed them much. I have to work pretty much all the time now, at writing, drilling and being drilled.

With the exception of the loss of my father, and losing a large salary when I should have been helping you, I never was happier in my life, and feel that I have a right to be proud of coming in with a set of perfect strangers, and so soon have won the good opinion of all.

How then to win a commission and then to be in one big fight to wind up the war and then return home, where we shall, I hope, be united for good or evil, for better or worse, is the sum of my ambition.

Yours lovingly, Harry P. Goddard

1. Edward Whitaker earned the Medal of Honor while a captain in the Harris Light Cavalry for bravery at Reams Station, Virginia, June 29, 1864; later he served as chief of staff to Gen. George Custer and bore the flag of truce at Appomattox.

Camp Foote, July 8th, 1862

Dear Mother,

Did you get my long letter of Sunday? Please keep my interesting letters from the 14th, as they will serve to form a connected history of my small part in the great drama of the 19th century.

Mort Hale has been elected 1st Lieutenant of the Norwich company [Company E] and Charley Baldwin 2nd Lieutenant of the Middletown [Company B].

Camp Foote, July 23rd, 1862

My Dearest Mother,

Lt. Col. [Dexter R.] Wright has been made Colonel of the 15th C.V. This gives Major Perkins a chance to be Lt. Col. and Adjt. Ellis to be Major.

Bromley [Ike Bromley, publisher of the *Norwich Bulletin*] made me a very pleasant visit today. He will do anything for me, and make all his political friends, from Senator [James] Dixon down, help me to anything I wish here or elsewhere. I prefer for the present to depend on the Governor and Col. Morris. Bromley said he stole a picture of May [Goddard's younger sister][1] at Thompsons. It was so pretty he could not help taking it for his wife.

I have had a splendid letter from beautiful May. She is receiving lots of attention and I am happy to hear it. Lou Reynolds must look to her laurels or May will have a Brigadier before Lou gets a Lieutenancy.

                                        Yours ever, Harry Goddard

1. Mary Goddard was nicknamed May; she later became the wife of Louis Comfort Tiffany.

Camp Foote, July 28th, 1862

Thank God you are my Mother whom I love beyond all earthly things, if I do sometimes seem to be a selfish indifferent boy.

The letters you sent by Lt. [Morton] Hale came safely to hand and were enjoyed. Poor Alf, how his heart must turn to his home, but he cannot but be happy in knowing that he is doing his duty to his God and his Mother to whom he is indebted for his noble soul.

I have before me your two notes of the 25th and Julia's [his older sister] letter of the 27th. Julia is enjoying herself and I am glad of it. So is darling May, whom I am now feign to confess is fast winning the name of being the prettiest girl in Norwich. Ah, if my dearest, gentlest Father was alive, how he would rejoice in the sweetness of his favorite child.

Mother, I never realized Decker's death[1] nor could I realize Father's until now. Thank heaven he has escaped the present turmoil and terrible times, and looks on us with loving eyes without sharing in our afflictions. In pace.

Very happy to hear of Uncle Louis' return. Give him my best regards, and tell him it cost me more struggling to resign my commission in the Harris Cavalry than he can probably ever imagine. I did it from a sense of duty, but it cut my pride to the quick, and yet since then I have thought it for the best—until the recent gallant exploits of that regiment under Col. Davies and Lt. Col. Kilpatrick at Beaver Dam [the battle of Beaver Dam Creek, June 26, 1862, first of the Seven Days' battles of the Peninsula campaign]

Do you know, Mother, that reading of those splendid dashes kept me awake half one night with mortification and pain. I would have given all on earth to have been there. I wrote Col. Davies a congratulatory letter, and am so glad that under Gen. Pope he is receiving his just dues after McDowell kept him under so long.

Bromley is doing nobly and I am glad of it. Capt. [James B.] Coit is making himself very obnoxious to the officers of the 14th (at least they say so) by the liberties he takes in overriding the Adjt., etc.—it won't do.

Forty-two men came in from Rockville today and sixty-two are expected from Danbury tomorrow, which will make us about 475 strong. September will not find us in Connecticut. Col. Morris was never in the army, but has studied military science at home and abroad. I find he makes me wear a silk sash, officer's sword, etc.

Yours ever, Henry P. Goddard

Serg't Major, 14th C.V.

1. Goddard's friend J. Nelson Decker was a lieutenant killed during Goddard's first engagement in the Harris Light Cavalry in Stafford, Virginia.

Camp Foote, Aug. 10th, 1862

My own dear Sister,

I have been blue all this week that I would not write—camp sickness all day and feverish nights. I am disgusted with running hither and thither, saluting and being deferential to some incompetent Lieutenants, who don't know enough to give the order "About-face."

Why some are such fools that they salute me first, take off their hats in my tent—and yet I have got to respect them. We have dress parades nightly and acting Adjt. Hale (and a splendid looking officer he is too) and I have to work like beavers. He is sick too, and hates to move about as much as I do, yet I won't leave till Ellis gets here. I have tried hard to get a commission as there are lots of chances, or would be if I had brass enough, and anybody to back one, yet it seems so mean to run out a man who has worked hard to receive it, for mind you, I respect a gentleman if he knows nothing of military matters, but let me show you an example of our style.

Company G is composed of three united squads under Capt. [James B.] Coit and they have not enough men to elect more than two officers, and all are too much afraid of the others to hold an election, and the consolidation has not been approved by its Colonel.

There are five candidates; Coit is one. He is very fair spoken and has promised some six lieutenants, and curses them all behind their backs. He makes outrageous mistakes whenever on duty and usurps authority everywhere.

2nd. Hill of New Haven is a little fool who doesn't know beans about the military, and his lieutenant says was in jail once for passing counterfeit money.

3rd. Stone of Putnam is a country bumpkin discharged as a private from the 5th C.V. as much for worthlessness as anything else having a cross-eye. He plays leap-frog with the privates, and offers fifty-cents a piece for a vote; these men recruited about twenty apiece and then united. They have about sixty-two mustered in and it is the most insubordinate street in the camp.

Then there is Hotchkiss, whom Hill promised to make 1st Lieut., a black leg and gambler of New Haven, who swears Hill shall never have an election.

Fifth, there is Len Robinson of Norwich whom Coit is working to make 1st Lieut. If I were a civilian and they should come into my office, I would not make one of them a printer's devil. I am disgusted with such men and feel as if I wish I could be shot in the first action rather than endure it much longer. It is unbearable.

Now for a bright side. I am allowed more privileges than most Sergt. Majors, have plenty of money, and the men think I hold a "big office." I love my Col. and respect my Lt. Col. I have hosts of friends among the officers, but the men think I am pretty severe. I have a warm friend in Lt. Hale, who is now the best line officer in the regiment. I never want to be adjutant of a regiment—I have seen too much of it.

Tell Mother this letter is private, and that I am very pleasantly situated, send lots of love, etc. Will try and be down this week. Thank Heaven I have three real friends, and I don't believe in the proffered friendship of any others—Mother, Juli and May. Yours ever, H.P.G.

Camp Foote, Aug. 18th, 1862

Dear Mother,

I had made all my preparations to go home on Saturday and was getting ready when Gen. [Brig. Gen. Dan] Tyler came here with Frank Bond. He greeted me pleasantly and so did Frank. Just after, he sent the Lt. Col., who said he must revoke my leave, and so I am very much afraid that I cannot get home again at all. Friday night I saw the General in his room. Saturday night I called on Maj. Weld with Adj't. Ellis, and then took him (or Alice Weld did) into the Aikens where we had a very pleasant party.

We are very busy indeed here as we have orders to make out all the company muster rolls by noon tomorrow, and that every company must be organized and full by that time. Col. Morris got one company (Davis's of New London), which makes eight organized today—promising me a 1st Lieutenancy and wanting me to do this and then that and then nothing at all, so that I could do nothing. The election today where he had promised [Thomas F.] Burpee a Captaincy resulted exactly according to the Lt. Col.'s and Adj't.'s ideas in throwing matters into confusion worse confounded. The men elected Coit captain and Crosby 2nd Lieut. The brave Capt. Burpee whose "resignation after scandalous treatment from his colonel," repeated his former experience on the same ground a year since by crying. I had all the work I could do in my own dep't. How I don't blame Col. Morris a bit, but I shan't bother him any more. He promised me a Lieutenancy yesterday, but he is so good-natured that he cannot refuse anybody, and so I shall be agreeably disappointed if he gets me a place, and not at all angry with him if he doesn't; tomorrow must decide; it can't be put off any longer as the regiment must be mustered in tomorrow night. Tonight, I feel as if I did not care a cent whether I get one or not.

Yours affectionately, Harry

Excerpts from *14th C. V.: Regimental Reminiscences of the War of the Rebellion*, by Henry P. Goddard (Middletown, Conn.: C. W. Church, 1877)

Every Fourteenth man will recall with pleasure the merry days at Camp Foote, Hartford, where we were first enlightened and rather surprised to discover that butter and milk were not government rations, that each man was not allowed a wall tent to himself, that the only horses provided infantry-men were of wood, with pretty acute edges at that. In those days the raw recruits would present arms to a sergeant major they had never met before and say "Halloa Sam" to captains they had always known.

Ah! Those two months at Camp Foote; how slowly our ranks filled up at first, and how rapidly toward the last, under the impetus of Lincoln's call for "Three Hundred Thousand More," until at our last dress parade we turned out a full thousand strong. What crowds of visitors we had from Hartford, and what tender words they bestowed upon us; among those who came oftenest was the great war governor, the courtly head of the house of Buckingham, the stern, but soldierly, Gen. Dan Tyler, who except Gen. [Maj. Gen. John A.] Dix, was the oldest West Pointer who served in the Union Army, and who still carries his years, and honors, with erect head and unbent frame; the beautiful, and accomplished, Mrs. Senator Dixon [wife of James Dixon, U.S. senator from Connecticut, 1857–69] and her daughters, both of whom later gave most of their time while in Washington to hospital service.

What a friendly rivalry we had with the 16th Connecticut, who were encamped next to us, as to which should first be filled up, and off for the war, and how we cheered them when we met them thereafter once, and only once, during the war, on the morning of Antietam battle.

At last came the day of our departure, when we marched down the streets of the Charter Oak city [Hartford], which was all alive with flags and the waving of handkerchiefs in the hands of her fair daughters, whose eyes filled with tears as our magnificent band—afterwards pronounced by Gen. Hooker second to none in the Army of the Potomac—played "The girl I left behind me," leading us to sob—some for the girls we had left, others because we hadn't any girls to leave behind.

Then came the sail down the ever beautiful Connecticut, when all Middletown, throbbing with loyalty, turned out to cheer us as we passed. The people of the Forest city [Middletown], loyal then, loyal now, and loyal evermore, demonstrated it by sending their own best blood to that gallant regiment, with the injunction of the Spartan women of old to return with their shields or on their shields: to this people I appeal today to know if your braves did not obey that high behest. When you recall how we sent back to you on their shields the bodies of Gibbons, of Crosby, of Canfield, of Huxham, Brooks and many others, I know how your tearful eyes will testify to their patriotism, integrity and valor.

Right here may I be pardoned for paying personal tribute to one of Middletown's private citizens, Hon. Benjamin Douglas [mayor], for the general support that he gave to the soldiers and their families all through the war. Here in his own home the facts are so well known that it is not necessary to rehearse them, but those of us who saw his tears when he visited us after Antietam and saw our depleted ranks, want to thank him now for the comfort he gave us then, and for the courage with which he labored in the dark days of the war.

As we passed out of the Connecticut that night, I remember standing with Johnny Broatch on the after-deck of the boat, for a last look at the dear old state, whose good health we drank, emptying a half-pint flask that a worthy relative had filled, telling me that unless I was badly wounded, it ought to last me through the war (5–6).

8

The Regiment Pursues
Lee into Maryland

The regiment travels by ship and rail from Hartford, Connecticut, to Arlington, Virginia, where they make camp at Fort Ethan Allen, one of more than eighty forts that now ring Washington. "Once again my feet touch the cursed 'secesh soil' of Virginia," Goddard writes (49). Along the route, the regiment parades, without incident, through the "semi-secesh city" of Baltimore, now under martial law following the bloody riot of April 19 against the 6th Massachusetts regiment on its way to defend Washington. Impressed by the regiment, the commanding general in Baltimore sends the 14th straight to Washington to prepare for action. From high ground at Fort Ethan Allen, commanded by then colonel Abner Doubleday, Goddard can hear the distant thunder of cannons August 29–30. Learning that the cannonading occurred at a second Union defeat at Bull Run in August 1862, Goddard notes the army has no confidence in commanding Maj. Gen. John Pope (commander at the Second Bull Run in August 1862) nor in Maj. Gen. Irvin McDowell (Union commander at the First Bull Run), and yearns for the return of McClellan, "the only General that the soldiers love" (50). Emboldened by his victory, Lee invades Maryland, with the 14th Connecticut—"with banners flying and bands playing" (57)—in hot pursuit. Certain that a big battle looms, Goddard takes comfort from Bible verses but looks to avenge the death of his friend Lt. Decker of the Harris Light Cavalry, his former regiment.

After the defeat of Maj. Gen. John Pope's army at the second battle of Bull Run (Second Manassas), only twenty-five miles southwest of Washington, President Lincoln replaced Pope with the popular Maj. Gen. George B. McClellan as commander of the what McClellan named the Army of the Potomac. Lincoln valued McClellan's administrative ability while recognizing his chronic affliction with "the slows." While moving most of his Army of Northern Virginia north through Maryland, on September 9 Gen. Robert E. Lee sent Maj. Gen. Stonewall Jackson's corps on a successful mission to capture Harpers Ferry and its garrison of some twelve thousand Union troops. With the town in Confederate hands on September 15,

Lee's supply line coming out of the Shenandoah could be extended west of the Blue Ridge Mountains without fear of interruption. By winning a big victory in a Union state, Lee also hoped to win recognition for the Confederacy from Great Britain and other European nations. The stage was set for a decisive engagement.

∼

In Camp near Fort Ethan Allen
Opposite Chain Bridge, Va.
Aug. 31, 1862

My Dearest Mother,

The 14th Reg't C.V., which left camp last Monday at Hartford, has lived fast since they left, having been pushed right into the field, and having been for those days in daily prospect of a fight.

As I have little time to write, and don't know how soon this will be allowed to go, I will just extract from my diary.

Aug. 25th. The 14th C.V. broke camp and left Hartford at 3 P.M. on the steamer City of Hartford and propeller George C. Collins. I was on the latter vessel, with four companies of the left-wing under Major [Cyrus C.] Clark. We had a most gratifying fare well from the people all along the river, and we had a delightful trip.

Aug. 26th. The left-wing arrived in New York at 10 A.M., saw Col. Almy. The entire reg't embarked on the Hill Von Hull at 11 A.M. and sailed to Elizabethport, N.J. There we embarked on the cars, the field and staff having a car to ourselves, and rode without change of cars all night.

Aug. 27th. Reached Harrisburg, Pa., at 6 AM and got breakfast. Our train was shifted onto the Northern Central road by which we went to Baltimore. I have been much interested in the lime kilns and coal mines of this state, and find Adj't Ellis a very agreeable companion—he giving me the whole history and describing the machinery of the mines. We reached Baltimore after a gratifying reception in Northern Maryland, and disembarked from the cars at 8 P.M. We marched through the streets of this semi-secesh city, passing by Maj. Gen. [John] Wool at the Eutaw House, giving him three rousing cheers, then proceeded to the Washington depot and halted. Supper was furnished to all the companies at the Union Relief Rooms, and we rested in the street, awaiting orders, as the Colonel had only orders to report to Maj. Gen. Wool at 5:30 PM. Maj. Gen. Wool (and a splendid looking man he is—just as pictured in the Rebellion Record) and Col. Morris rode down to us. We go direct to Washington, as Gen. Wool on seeing our regiment changed his purpose and said to Col. Morris, who stood beside him, "A very fine regiment, Sir, not a drunken man in it—that's altogether too fine a regiment to stay around Baltimore." He then wrote an order as follows: "Chief Q. M., furnish transportation to Washington for Col. Morris with his fine regiment." The Q. M. was astonished at such a message from Gen. Wool, and said it was unexampled for him to praise a new regiment. We left at 6 P.M. and did not reach Washington till 3:30 A.M.

Aug. 28th. Arrived in Washington. The men went into barracks. I breakfasted with Lieut. [Theodore] Stanley at Clay's Hotel. At noon we crossed the Long Bridge, and once again my feet touch the cursed "secesh soil" of Virginia. We marched to Camp Seward near Hunters Chapel Va., where we go into a Camp of instruction under Gen. Silas Casey. The 18th C. V. is guarding Fort McHenry Baltimore and drinking all the N. Y. 7th has left in the city. We find two companies of the 1st Conn. Artillery garrisoning Fort Richardson. Close by our Camp, having returned today from the Peninsula, the rest of the regiment is in other forts.

Aug. 30th. Received marching orders at 2 A.M. when our men had not a musket. We dealt out muskets and cartridges and rations, and leaving knapsacks and everything behind, (I did not bring here my rubber blanket) started at 7 A.M. We marched up past Arlington and the old camp of that glorious regiment—the Harris Light Cavalry. Ah me, why will that regiment persist in winning glorious laurels in every action? By the way, it is commonly reported in the Waterbury Company [Company C] in this regiment that Capt. [Marcus] Coon [his disagreeable company commander in the Harris Light] has been shot by one of own men. If so, I am sorry.

Crossed Aqueduct Bridge to Georgetown. Marched up on the Maryland side to Chain Bridge and then crossed the Potomac, and encamped close by Fort Ethan Allen, occupying the rifle pits outside of the Fort, as an attack is hourly expected. We have a strong position, but our men never handled muskets till today. Col. Abner Doubleday, the Fort Sumter hero,[1] in command of the fort, threw us into these pits. We are very proud of our reputation. Heavy cannonading can be heard in the direction of Centreville.

Aug 30th. No fight yet. Gen. [Maj. Gen. John] Sedgwick's division of McDowell's army arrived in the morning, but left at noon to go down and guard the camps near Hunters Chapel, leaving only three of the new regiments here, who are all greener than we, and the garrison. The cannonading is louder and nearer, and very constant. It is reported that one must march. God help us to do our duty. Later our forces are said to have won a glorious victory! All honor to Gen. Pope. McDowell has redeemed the disgrace of July 21st on the same field of Bull Run. As the cannonading was so very heavy that it must have been a bloody action.

Aug. 31st. Sunday in camp. Rainy and wet. Not a blanket have I here, and my old boots are full of holes. We are all very anxious to get back to our camp and tents. I have never come into a field better provided, nor ever had less on hand than here. Am perfectly well and happy.

Yours ever, Harry Goddard

1. Doubleday was a captain of the federal garrison when the Fort Sumter fell in April 1861; later he was a major general commanding 1st Corps at Gettysburg.

Camp near Fort Ethan Allen
Sept. 1, 1862

As I understand the New York Herald reports the 14th C. V. as annihilated, I take pains to inform you that we are all well, having held possession of our rifle pits in face of the foe (anywhere from 3 to 5 miles distant) under the guns of Fort Ethan Allen. Col. Doubleday gets scared once or twice a day, and turns us out in quick time, but it amounts to nothing as yet, although our advanced posts are not more than five miles from us. Troops are flying about in all directions. The Conn. 5th (now reduced to only 250 men) is near us, and the 1st Conn. close by. Heavy cannonading is going on again today north and south of us, not west as hitherto. I don't know anything about the war, having given up trying to, and I don't believe anybody knows anything about it. After Bull Run No. 2, the Army has no confidence in Pope, swear they will shoot McDowell, and say that McClellan and [Maj. Gen. Franz] Sigel are the only decent commanders. The Peninsula army will follow nobody but McClellan, and the army of Virginia nobody but Sigel. As for me, I am as happy and contented as a King, never took things more philosophically in my life.

As to Ellis, I really begin to pity him. Every Captain in the regiment hates him, and the field officers begin to evince dislike, while Lieutenants and privates d—n him. I really believe I am the only man in the regiment that shows him any friendship. He told me today that he didn't like this regiment and should apply for a transfer.

All we do is to lie here and be detailed to do dirty work in the vicinity. No drill, no nothing, and the men half scared to death in fear of Stonewall Jackson. Pshaw, this is a civil war with a vengeance, like a handle to a jug.

Gen. Pope wrote his "victory" dispatch while fleeing from Bull Run. He says, "The enemy sent a flag of truce to bury their dead." From the best information that is an awful lie. We sent a flag of truce and were refused, and sent another flag and begged for poor Phil Kearney's body.[1] "Oh God, for a man with a head, heart and hand."

The 15th Conn. is near Hunters Chapel, the 16th some miles ahead of them near Falls Church, the 18th in Baltimore, and we at Chain Bridge, four miles above Washington on the Virginia side. The 62nd N.Y. has just encamped along side. Have received no letters yet in the regiment—not a man.

Yours while life lasts and evermore, Harry

1. Philip Kearney, a longtime professional and popular soldier, distinguished himself in the Peninsula campaign, rising to major general commanding the 1st Division of the 2nd Corps. Following the second battle of Bull Run (Second Manassas), he was killed while mistakenly riding into enemy lines.

In the woods, "Camp Defiance," two miles above Rockville, Md.
Sept. 9th, 1862

My darling Mother,

Here we are "in the woods" fourteen miles from where I last wrote, and on the Maryland side of the Potomac. We are brigaded, divisioned and corps'ed as follows. Maj. Gen. [Edwin] Sumner, Corps, Maj. Gen. [William] French, Division, Col. [Dwight] Morris, Brigade. We are to march today or tomorrow to Harpers Ferry. There are within three quarters of an hour's call of us, 120,000 troops— Sumner's, [Maj. Gen. Nathaniel] Banks', Sigel's, [Maj. Gen. Jesse] Reno's (late McDowell's) Corps! We expect to demolish Jackson "entirely" before he can get back to Virginia. So McClellan leads us again? I saw him Sunday night. Do you know he is the only General that the soldiers love? The Peninsula soldiers will die for him any moment. Your charges of his delay at Bull Run No. 2 we never heard till we saw them yesterday in Soslie's Illustrated Paper. Pope is denounced for trusting McDowell and they do seem very intimate. Sigel is the hero of the hour. Poor Fred Compton has yielded up his life to his country's cause. He was a gentleman by nature if not by birth. I loved that man more than I am given to love men ordinarily. He was a friend in every sense of the word. May God receive him to an eternal home of Happiness. True it is that each night finds us "days much nearer Home." Write me whenever anything good or bad happens to my friends as I rarely see the papers.

What am I to make of Kemp's queer conduct? I am so sorry for the Abbotts, but will not judge Kemp till I know all the facts. May I let the Norwich boys here know that he has resigned, or is it private yet?

I received yours and Julie's letters Sunday, the day we left Fort Ethan Allen. They were very gratefully received, but I have nil them by me to answer. We march at 1 today, seven miles and a half in some direction and I hasten to close. "Glad tidings" is with me always and I like it, as it is a link that binds me to you. Today the 9th, the passage from Philippians 1: 2–3 [Grace be unto you, and peace, from God our Father, and from the Lord Jesus Christ. I thank my God upon every remembrance of you.] is one of my favorite wishes when I feel good.

Tell Alf not to enlist—beg him not to, as he is not needed.

Yours ever, Harry Goddard, Sgt. Major, 14th C. V.

Camp near Clarksburg, Md., Sept. 11th, 1862

Dear Mother,

No mail from home since Sept. 2nd. I resume my journal.

<u>Sept. 9th.</u> After camping near Rockville, Md., for the night, we marched seven miles from our camp in the woods, and encamped in a large field with the whole

Corps d'armie around us. Michael McVay, an old man in Lieut. Coit's company, died on the march from exhaustion.

Sept. 10th. Lieut. Coit's company buried McVay on a hillside in his blankets, as no coffin could be obtained. Lieut. Coit managed to the best of his ability and showed a tender admirable spirit. McVay has two sons in the same company, who were mourners. A Catholic priest conducted the ceremonies. We marched three miles further and encamped in the woods in line of battle, the second line of the army on the left. Jackson and his rebel hordes are supposed to be near and we expect a battle momentarily. God defend the right and help me to do my duty to my Mother, my Country and my God.

Lieut. Hale has been detached as ordinance officer to Gen. French. I had the pleasure of recommending his name to Col. Morris for the appointment. He has not yet entered upon his duties. We have grown to be very intimate, but I like nearly all the officers.

Chaplain [Henry S.] Stevens and I are getting to be great friends. I only wish I was always good, but somehow my wicked heart does get the control too often. "Glad tidings" is a great comfort morning and night.

Saw Gens. Sumner and French today. The former is a very old man, and the latter looks like [Maj. Gen.] Ben Butler and has a comical habit of winking all the time.

Sept. 11: We marched at dawn some three miles, passing through the town of Clarksburg, Md., with music playing (we have a splendid band) and colors flying. We encamped just outside the town on the tip of a large verdant hill commanding a beautiful view. We have 90,000 troops are here and the rebels are within a few miles in force. Sure this time Sedgwick [commanding 2nd division of Sumner's 2nd Corps] attacks the enemy today or tomorrow. When he draws them out, we are all to go in and do our best to crush Jackson forever. It will be a great fight and a hard one. The blood of the noble Decker and Compton cries for vengeance. God give me the strength to do my part.

The texts for today are beautiful. "The Lord thy God walketh in the midst of the camp to deliver thee, and to give up thine enemies before thee." "Him that cometh to me I will in no wise cast out."

Now Mother I don't want you to think me so very good, for I tell you truly, that since my profession of Christianity, I have not lived as I should have done, and have often, often sinned heinously, and doubtless many believe me a hypocrite. Yet I do say that I am better in the field than at home, dread death less, and on this march have felt a strong Christian hope oftener than ever before, often doubting myself, and the sincerity of my feelings. I never doubted in my whole life the truth of every word in the Bible, and am content to leave my fate in the hands of God. I enclose some flowers, plucked on the march. I have learned to love all natural beauty, for it reminds me of your love.

Forever yours, Harry Goddard

Excerpts from *14th C. V.: Regimental Reminiscences of the War of the Rebellion*, by Henry P. Goddard (Middletown, Conn.: C. W. Church, 1877)

How pleased was Col. Morris as he stood by old Gen. Wool's side as we marched through Baltimore, to hear that old veterans of four wars exclaim, "A splendid Regiment, not one drunken man in the ranks; too good a regiment to be sent anywhere but to the front!"

Do you remember how pleased we were to go into that "permanent camp of instruction" at Washington, where we were to spend the winter, but how before we had stayed twelve hours we received marching orders, ere muskets had ever been in the hands of the men, and we had to spend our only night in the camp engaged in unpacking the arms-chests, and issuing the muskets and ammunition for the march to Fort Ethan Allen. We spent a week at that fort, while the reverberations of the cannon of the second battle of Bull Run, and the red face of Col. Doubleday, who appeared every few moments to tell Col. Morris that a fight was imminent, kept us on the *qui vive*.

Here it was that the torn and tattered veterans of the Army of the Potomac, fresh from the swamps and battles of the Peninsula campaign, excited our wondering interest as they marched by on their way to the front. But how they repaid our deprecatory looks at the condition of their clothes and accoutrements with their jeering "Hulleo children! Poor boys, dark blue pants, soft bread three times a week, three hundred miles from home and ain't got but one mother apiece."

It was here that the officers of Company K had occasion to find fault with their company cook for being so tardy in getting breakfast for the boys. The cook, an ex-Methodist elder from Norwich, pleaded in extenuation that it was his invariable habit to give an hour to his devotion after reveille. "By George," said Capt. (now Gen.) Coit, "if you can't get time to cook, you had better stop praying." "Or pray that you may learn to cook," added Sergt. (now Lieut.) Charles Austin. It was here too that the Madison boys (Co. G) concluded that steel-plated "bullet proof" vests were too heavy a load to carry, and dumped the lot with which they had been provided by friends at home into the Potomac.

The Maryland campaign followed in which the Sergeant Major [Goddard] established his reputation as a vocalist by his one song, which ran somewhat after this fashion: "Reveille at three a.m. and march at early dawn." How the company commanders used to "cuss dreffull" when they heard that song resounding through the company streets at the close of a long day's march in that sweltering weather.

In this campaign the 14th was for the first time brigaded—with the 108th New York and 130th Pennsylvania. Col. Dwight Morris of the 14th was assigned to the command of the brigade of 3,000 green troops, and, with a single aide, Adj. Ellis of the 14th, who acted as assistant Adj. Gen'l, and but two orderlies, so handled the command all through that campaign as to win for it the commendation of that battle-scarred veteran, Gen. E. N. Sumner, who then commanded the 2nd army corps, in which we served throughout the war.

It was in this campaign that two privates of the 108th New York of his Brigade were one day brought up before Col. Morris for sheep stealing. The corpses of their victims were on their backs when captured. They were ordered to throw them down, and evidence of guilt being conclusive, the men were sent off to the corps provost marshal. Johnny, the Col.'s cook, at once seized the mutton, saying, "Will you have this for breakfast, Colonel?" Col. Morris quickly turned his back, while Lieut. Col. Perkins, turning sharply to the offender, said, "Don't you know better than to ask such a question? Take that carcass away," and then *soto voce* to the sergeant major, "Goddard, keep your eye on that mutton and see that the cook has it well done for an early breakfast for the field and staff mess."

Perhaps there wasn't much foraging in those days. Why the right and left general guides, (Ned Smith of Co B and Fred Taylor of Co A) did nothing but "confiscate" things, and "Pony" Prior of Co. B was not much better. Col. Broatch will recall that intensely hot day when Ned Smith brought to us as a result of his day's labors only a can of condensed "Tom and Jerry" (6–8).

9

The Regiment's Baptism
of Fire at Antietam

Goddard describes the march through Maryland on the way to the new and untried regiment's baptism of fire at Antietam. Along the way the troops march through Frederick, where they are warmly greeted by Union sympathizers. The engagement on South Mountain, the prelude to Antietam, is heard as distant rumble. The next day, September 15, he hears "heavy firing towards Harpers Ferry" where General Jackson captures the war-wasted town and its huge federal garrison. On the sixteenth, "we lay in reserve during an artillery fight in the morning, shells whistling over our heads, keeping us on our bellies." On the seventeenth the regiment falls in at 3 A.M. and crosses Antietam creek. (Company B quickly captures Confederate sharpshooters inside a spring house on the Roulette Farm.) Moving into the cornfield, the regiment exchanges fire for three hours with Confederates entrenched in the Sunken Road (Bloody Lane) and then advances "towards the center of the fight" under "a most terrible fire of artillery and infantry." The 14th was in the extreme advance line when the battle ended that evening. "Throughout the whole action, I felt completely in God's hands." He reports 21 of the regiment killed, 74 wounded, and 32 missing.

The battle of Antietam was the bloodiest day in American history, with 12, 400 Union and 10,700 Confederate losses. Although the battle itself was basically a stalemate, General Lee's heavy losses forced him to retreat into Virginia, and the failure of his foray into the North meant no immediate help from Europe. This "victory" gave President Lincoln the opportunity he was waiting for to announce the Emancipation Proclamation, effective January 1, 1863. Lincoln also decided to relieve McClellan of the command of the Army of the Potomac because of the general's failure to use opportunities to crush Lee's army and end the war. Outnumbering Lee's army—eight-seven thousand to forty thousand men—McClellan had failed to engage a quarter of his army, including a fresh corps that was ready to exploit the breaking of the Confederate center at Bloody Lane, and had also failed to pursue Lee's retreating army vigorously. Three days before Antietam, McClellan had delayed sending troops to South Mountain when Lee's battle plan, enclosed in a cigar wrapping, fell into his hands. Knowing McClellan's hesitant disposition, Lee had gambled successfully by dividing his army, sending Jackson's corps to Harpers Ferry, where it captured some twelve thousand federal troops two days before the big battle.

~

Excerpts from *History of the Fourteenth Regiment, Connecticut Vol. Infantry,* by Charles D. Page (Meriden, Conn.: Horton Printing Co., 1906)

When the Fourteenth had passed through the cornfield and stood on a little ridge on the side next the enemy, there burst upon them a perfect tempest of musketry. The line of troops in front had passed well into the open field. It seemed to melt under the enemy's fire and breaking[,] many of the men ran through the ranks of the Fourteenth toward the rear. No enemy could be seen, only a thin cloud of smoke rose from what was afterwards found to be their rifle-pits. As by one impulse the line halted on the edge of the cornfield and opened fire. Probably they did then but little damage as the enemy were well protected, but upon our side the bullets whistled past, cutting off the cornstalks, and every moment some one of the men would fall.

This rifle-pit was the Sunken Road which at this time was plentifully filled with a quota of Confederate men while the line of troops skirted the crest of the hill above them, thus able to fire over their heads (37–38).

This fence at the farthest side of the cornfield was the farthest advance in that direction and a monument has been erected to mark the line by the State of Connecticut. They remained in this field about three hours according to Colonel Perkins's report. The regiment fell back to and over the fence separating the cornfield from the meadow where it was reformed, an order being given to support General Kimball of Richardson's division. The men were then marched back by the left flank to the Roulette house, . . . round the barn to the lane known as the Roulette lane, coming from Bloody Lane to the Roulette buildings, extending in the same general direction through the Roulette fields; to a position by a wall of the Roulette lane, which Colonel Morris [brigade commander] was ordered to take and hold which he did "with the Fourteenth Connecticut alone" (39–40).

Camp near Sharpsburg, Md. Sept. 20, 1862

My dear sister Jule,

I started to give you my Adventure in search of Seceshdom and will continue from my last, though it seems tame since the battle.

Sept. 12th. Marched at 8 AM, passing through Hyattstown, Md., just vacated by the rebels, who were shelled out by our troops yesterday. We encamped a quarter of a mile from Clarksburg near Urbana. Indices of a hasty rebel retreat are numerous.

Sept. 13th. Marched at dawn. Advanced five miles, crossed the Monocacy, having a most beautiful panorama of the city of Frederick and the river valley. Cannonading is going on in the mountains, beyond the city. Gen. McClellan has just ridden down the lines and has been greeted with rapture and applause. He is a handsome little fellow and attracts his troops wonderfully, but somehow he does not impress me much. Later we marched through Frederick at 10 AM with banners flying and bands playing. Nearly every house displayed a Union flag, and we had a glorious warm reception from the Union people, who are in the majority. Encamped a mile from town. Gen. Burnside rode by us tonight amid great cheers. He is a man.

Sept. 14th. We left camp at 7:30 AM and crossed a section of the Blue Ridge near Middletown, Md., where we rested. A heavy engagement took place on South Mountain while we lay in reserve. Several hundred were killed, among them Maj. Gen. Reno. We pushed on and encamped on the battlefield at midnight.

Sept. 15: The rebels were defeated yesterday and fell back. I am awfully exhausted. We marched at 11 A.M., following up the retreating rebel army. Passed through the pretty town of Boonesboro, Md., where are hosts of wounded and captured rebels. McClellan and Burnside passed us again today. Encamped at Keedysville in range of the enemy guns. Hear heavy firing towards Harpers Ferry.

Sept. 16: We lay in reserve during an artillery fight in the morning, shells whistling over our heads, keeping us on our bellies. The 8th, 11th and 16th Conn. Vols. are close by with Gen. Burnside. Major [Alfred N.] Duffié's battalion of the Harris Light Cavalry and the Brooklyn 14th are near. Had a long talk with Charley Tiffany of Norwich of Co. D, H.L.C., Gen. [Brig. Gen. Marsena] Patrick's orderly.[1] He says that Whitaker is 2nd Lieut. of Co. G and that the balance of the regiment is at Bailey's Crossroads drilling new recruits. Six companies were nearly annihilated at Bull Run No. 2, where poor Compton was taken prisoner. As soon as they found what regiment he belonged to, the rebels killed him, slowly putting seven revolver balls in him before he died. My God is not that horrible. Fred would not have harmed the hair of a prisoner. May God in Heaven punish them for this. Lieut. [Walter M.] Lucas Co. D is acting Adj't, as Ellis is acting asst. Adj't to Col. Morris.

Sept. 17: We fell in at 3 A.M. and had 80 rounds of cartridges passed out to each man. We advanced three miles from our bivouac, crossing Antietam creek. We advanced in line of battle with the rest of the brigade through the woods, while we were shelled like fury and marched into a cornfield while the musketry commenced. For three hours we fought here, wavering two or three times, but holding our ground till the whole Corps fell back a little. The rest of our brigade scattered at the first fire, but rallied and fought on their own hook. We then marched towards the center of the fight, fell back once, then advanced, crossed a hill in the face of a most terrible fire of artillery and infantry, and at 3:30 PM rested under a hill where we were shelled till night ended the story, having lost a large number of officers and men—killed, wounded and missing. We numbered 800 this AM. At six PM we number 315. It has been the biggest fight yet, but a merciful Father has spared me a little longer. It may be my turn next.

Sept. 18th. Our total killed is 21, wounded about 74, missing 32. Capt. [Jarvis] Blinn (Co. F) and [Samuel] Willard (Co. G) were killed in the fight, and Lieuts. Coit, [George] Crosby and [William] Sherman, and Sgt. [Thomas] Mills (Co. H) wounded. No artillery fight today, but as we held the foremost position in the center, their sharpshooters are peppering bullets at us, so we have to keep flat on our backs all the time. Col. Morris, Lieut. Col. Perkins, Major Clark and Adj't Ellis behaved splendidly yesterday. The Lieut. Col. and Adj't both had their horses shot. Capt. [Robert] Gillette, appointed from Hartford, Conn., arrived and took command of Co. H.

Sept. 19th. The enemy have skedaddled from our front, and we rejoined the rest of our brigade. At 2 PM we moved a short distance into the woods and encamped in column of divisions, with our whole Corps.

Sept. 20th. Commissary Sergt. [Julius W.] Knowlton has been made acting Brigade Commissary. By order from Gen. Halleck [Maj. Gen. Henry, general in chief], can carry no non-commissioned officers baggage, and I have to send my valise to Boonesboro, Md., to be stored. I have got to pack my things hereafter, carrying only a rubber blanket and blouse. We lay back of the battle field, where the dead and wounded lie in tiers.

Now I am content where I am, but it will look as if I had not done my duty if I am passed over in promotion, when I have been highly complimented by officers and men. I cannot have any baggage and it comes rather rough, no clean shirts or stockings or anything but dirt. Any how there is some fun in misery. Let the wild world sway as it will, I'll be gay and happy still.

Yours jubilantly, Harry Goddard

1. Patrick commanded the 3rd Brigade, 1st Division, 1st Corps.

Camp in woods near Keedysville, Md.
Sept. 21st, 1862

Dear May,

Today I have a chance to write by a Mr. Doten of Bridgeport, who was so anxious about this fight that he has come here to see if his son was safe, and finds him entirely well.

Ah, May, the battle was a terrible one, from 9 AM to 6 PM we were under a tremendous fire—shot, shell, grape, cannister, bullets and buck shot. Men fell in heaps all over the field. Poor Capt. Willard [Samuel F. Willard, Goddard's Company G commander] was shot in the face. I had been borrowing his spy glass, a half an hour before, and chatting merrily with him. Lieut. Coit, who was fairly chosen to a Captaincy, but made a Lieutenant, received two rounds and was taken to a hospital. Next morning a Captain arrived from Connecticut to take command of his company, appointed by Gov. Buckingham and the Adjutant General. "Sie Tempora Sie Hominas." Lieut. Sherman, formerly conductor on the Shore Line, is slightly, and Lieut. Crosby of Co. K, seriously wounded. Our colors are riddled with bullets. Do you know that throughout the whole action I felt completely in God's hands, and had a presentiment that I should come out safe, and that Mother knew that I was in danger, but that she also felt that I should be saved.

Yesterday I had to send my valise back to Boonesboro and with it my Bible. I cannot carry it or any shirts, but those on my back. I am not strong enough to carry a knapsack, and there are none to be had if I could. My reduced baggage is as follows: 1st what I have on; 2nd a skeleton knapsack holding two blankets, my blouse, two pair stockings, five handkerchiefs, a roll of linen, and one or two little knickknacks from my valise; 3rd a sword, belt, pistol, cartridge box, cap pouch, haversack, and canteen complete my equipments. What a change from the exquisite dandy Local Editor with his collars, ties, coats, caps, flirtations and worldliness every way, or from the dashing harum-scarum Lieutenant of the best Cavalry Regiment in the Army, flirting with Senators' daughters on the steps of the Capitol, or charging twenty-five miles in ten hours. A singular world, is it not? Yet I have no reason to repine. I am respected, loved, almost always happy, and have such a dear, dear Mother, and sisters, and two Fathers in Heaven, to guide and watch over me. Oh if I was really good, but sin rolls up against me in the past and present. Rev. Mr. Stevens preached today. Text, "Blessed are those that seek Righteousness for they shall be filled." He had an immense audience and preached well. Poor me was under orders all the time, detailing and writing. It was too bad. My text tonight (sunset) is Isaiah 14, and a comforting one too.

Col. [Henry W.] Kingsbury of the 11th [Connecticut Infantry] is killed, also Capt. John Griswold of the 11th. Poor Cousin John, who came thousands of miles to serve his country, has fallen in her defense. "The blood of the martyrs is the seed of the Church." Don't expect my promotion. I don't, and I didn't care for it in the blood of those who fell, I would not give half as much for a commission in that way, nay had rather be where I am than have an officer lose his life. We are encamped in a beautiful field—waiting orders, expect to be sent to Harpers Ferry soon. It is a beautiful sunset, and a serene Sabbath eve, but on yonder green hill lie thousands of dead, Union and rebel soldiers in their last sleep.

Yours forever, Harry Goddard

Excerpt from *14th C. V.: Regimental Reminiscences of the War of the Rebellion,*
by Henry P. Goddard (Middletown, Conn.: C. W. Church, 1877)

Some of us recall that scene on the night of the battle of South Mountain when Lt.
Lee smelt whiskey in the air, and Capts. Davis, Carpenter and Hart fell out of the
ranks and followed up the smell till they found a distillery a mile away. Those of
us who had answered to their names at the roll call made after dark that night were
rewarded when these officers returned, bringing full canteens with them. There
were so many dead bodies on the field that night that the whiskey was in demand
as a *preventive*.

On the night of the 15th of September we bivouacked at Keedysville in a field
of pigs. No sooner were arms stacked than the whole command went pig-hunting.
Lt. Col. Perkins at once sent word to company commanders that the animals must
not be harmed as they belonged to a good Unionist. When I delivered this order to
Capt. Gibbons, he repeated it to the non-commissioned officers, who in turn
repeated it to the men. Corp. Harry Lloyd, ex-telegraph operator, had already captured a fat little porker, but buttoning his blouse over him shouted, "Boys do
you hear, the captain says 'Let those pigs alone.'" "Wee, wee" went the little pig
under the blouse. Punching him in the head Harry muttered "keep quiet a minute,
can't you?" then aloud, "Boys, let those pigs alone." "Wee, wee" repeated the porker.
Harry looked at me in despair and then muttered, "Come down to B Company
mess to supper in an hour."

I went back to headquarters, reported the order delivered, and an hour later
was enjoying a good supper with Capt. Gibbons and Lts. Broatch, Lucas and Hale,
and if Harry Lloyd and Jim Cairnes (that thief of the world) did get it up, no questions were asked concerning the roast pork and the roast chickens that were furnished us. Poor Lloyd was mortally wounded at Fredericksburg and died soon
after. I saw him after the battle and offered any assistance. His reply was that all he
wanted was for me to fill his pipe, as his right arm was useless. "I shall have to be
a left handed operator," he added with a smile.

My reminiscences have come down to that beautiful day when

> "Up from the meadows rich with corn,
> Clear in the cool September morn,"

the sun arose upon Antietam creek and the thousands of foemen encamped on
either bank of it, destined ere nightfall to be engaged in one of the great battles of
the war of the rebellion, a battle of which we may say at least, that Connecticut has
no reason to blush for the conduct of her regiments engaged therein, raw recruits
though many of them were. Our list of losses in that battle tells its own story, as
does the fact that throughout the whole contest the fourteenth never retreated,
either with or without orders, and was in the extreme advance line when the
battle was ended. It is on the anniversary of this battle that we have now gathered

for twelve years, and hope to gather annually as long as there are any of us left who can walk, talk, or shake hands.

The heroic and many of the pathetic incidents of the Antietam fight are so well known to you all that I will pass them by for the nonce and today dwell mainly on its humorous incidents, for scarce ever yet was a fight in which any Yankee was engaged but what he could find some food for mirth even in the shadow of impending death. There was instance was Lt. Galpin, then Orderly Sergeant of Co. B, complaining that the confederates sent their bullets so close to his head while he lay in that famous plowed field, that he couldn't make out his morning report with any comfort or precision. Ah those morning reports, how they bothered poor Walt Lucas, then acting adjutant, who wasn't much used to that sort of work, and who said to me, when Adjutant Ellis, then assistant adjutant general, sent back his consolidated report a third time for correction, "Sergeant Major, I will give you a box of cigars if you will tell me how to account for these fifteen men that my report omits." "Let's put them down as 'Missing in action,'" said I. "Done," said Walt, and the report went back all right at last. But that night was Walt's last night as adjutant, for which at dress parade he interpreted Gen. [Maj. Gen. Darius N.] Couch's[1] "Circular," to Brigade Commanders, to read "Circular Brigade Commanders," that finished him, for the excuse that with Gen. [Brig. Gen. William] French's[2] round belly in mind he supposed generals might be spoken of as "circular" didn't avail.

It was in the Antietam battle that I was talking with Corporal Fred Beebe of "B" company, when a bullet struck him in the leg. Some of us picked him up at once, when I felt a strange curiosity inspired by an article on gun shot wounds, that I had read the day before, and inquired "Fred, how does it feel?" In his pain, Beebe turned to me and growled out, "That's a d—— pretty question to ask a man at such a time as this." He was borne off the field, and soon after discharged for disability, and from that day to this I can get him to give no other answer to any question I ask him. It was in this fight that Capt. [William H.] Tubb's colored boy, Tyler, "skeedaddled," appearing three days after to excuse himself, on the plea that when shot and shell began to fall about him, he thought every hair on his head a bugle, and every bugle playing "Home, Sweet Home."

How grittily Lieut. [James E.] Comestock held up the regimental colors that day after poor Tom Mills was killed, how neatly Gibbons flanked a lot of rebels in the Roulette house, and how coolly some of B's boys climbed Roulette's apple trees and shook down the fruit while under infantry fire, and how conspicuous was Col. Morris on his calico-colored horse, how active Lt. Col. Perkins, and how cool Major Clark and Adjt. Ellis (8–10).

1. Maj. Gen. Darius N. Couch, commanding 1st Division of 4th Corps at Antietam.

2. Brig. Gen. William French, commanding 3rd Division, 2nd Corps at Antietam, promoted major general in November 1862.

10

A Long, Hard Wait
at Harpers Ferry

After Lee's retreat to Virginia after Antietam, the 14th Connecticut was among the units dispatched to the strategic location of Harpers Ferry, Virginia, where Jackson had captured a Union garrison of some twelve thousand on Bolivar Heights before rejoining Lee at Sharpsburg. Harpers Ferry, the site of John Brown's raid in 1859, changed hands eight times during the war. The Confederates having destroyed the bridges, the regiment wades across the Potomac—its band playing "John Brown's Body" and "Dixie." Goddard meditates in John Brown's engine house. Lincoln issues his "freedom breathing proclamation" (63), and a week later the President "rode through our camp . . . accompanied by Gens. McClellan, Sumner, French, Williams, etc. . . . He looks more care-worn than ever" (67–68). Feeling discouraged, Goddard yearns for a winning general and doesn't believe generals McClellan, McDowell, Halleck, or Pope fit the bill. "Hooker the dauntless, Sigel the unconquerable, or Burnside the chiseler . . . all these have only been successful with small armies," he writes prophetically (19). Goddard arrests some stragglers and converses with a captured rebel sergeant who "talked fight to the bitter end" (64). He enjoys two "splendid" meals from a Unionist who was "the first man arrested by old John Brown" (63–64). He is promoted from sergeant-major to second lieutenant of Company G. He pleads—there are many such pleas in his letters home—that his older brother Alfred, an engineer building canals in the Sandwich Islands (Hawaii), stay out of military service. He expects a big battle in the vicinity that never comes. The regiment's baggage and knapsacks still haven't arrived from Fort Ethan Allen, and he begs his mother to mail him $20 "or I shall be shoeless soon," and with "nothing to eat" (73). When the tattered and demoralized regiment finally gets marching orders, its "17 line officers . . . signed a paper peremptorily refusing to move until they got their own and men's baggage" (84).

McClellan's failure after the battle of Antietam to pursue Lee vigorously as the Confederate commander retreated back to Virginia prompted Lincoln to pay a visit to the general two weeks later. Still the Army of the Potomac doesn't move south for another month, and the approaching winter will make movement more difficult.

∼

Bolivar Heights, Harpers Ferry, Va.
Sept. 25th, 1962

Dear Mother,

No mail from home since we left Fort Ethan Allen. Has Alf come home? If so, beg him not to enlist for your and for my sake. You need him at home, and thousands more must fall ere this rebellion is ended.

My valise was not sent back to Boonesboro, but is here, and I hope will be still carried, as the Lieut. has got over his little "tiff" with me, which arose from my refusing to detail men for him unless ordered by the Colonel's authority.

I nearly fainted on the march here from carrying my blankets, till asst. Surgeon Dudley [Frederick A. Dudley], took them awhile on his horse, then private Jerry Corbett of Co. B put them on top of his knapsack and "toted" them across the river. (I shall not forget this kind act). Here is my journal.

Sept. 22nd. Broke camp at 3 AM and marched through Sharpsburg, crossing Antietam creek, till we neared the Potomac, then down the Maryland bank till we passed wooded Maryland Heights.

As we approached the Potomac our fine band struck up "Away Down South in Dixie" as we waded the river about waist deep, and wobbled about on the iron of the bridge there, played "Jordan am a Hard Road to Travel," and as we entered Harpers Ferry, about 5 PM on a lovely evening, "John Brown's Soul Is Marching On." I hope the old hero is where he could hear that and watch the scene. Harpers Ferry presents a scene of desolation, it having changed hands about a dozen times. Encamped on Bolivar Heights where Col. Miles[1] surrendered one week ago. A strong position but commanded by Maryland Heights and Loudoun Heights of the Shenandoah. We have a most magnificent view some 20 miles in our front, with the Potomac on our right and the Shenandoah on our left.

Once more my feet press the thrice accursed soil of Virginia. Shall I ever leave it? God only knows.

Sept. 23rd. Regiment went out on picket duty. Adj't [Walter M.] Lucas and I acted as aides de camp to Col. Perkins and arrested some twenty stragglers.

President Lincoln issued his freedom breathing proclamation. Sanis Deo.

Sept. 24th. Got a splendid breakfast and dinner from a Union planter at our picket station. It seemed like home, the family were so pleasant. His name is Alstadt[2] and he was the first man arrested by old John Brown. Our forces have taken all his forage, and the rebels all his edibles. A hard case for him. Regiment was relieved and returned at camp at 6 PM.

Sept. 25th. Nothing of importance so far today. The rebel pickets are about a mile and a half right in view of our pickets. I had a long talk with several paroled rebels yesterday. The Sergeant commanding was very intelligent and talked fight to the bitter end. Will this war ever end?

Our forced marches from Fort Ethan Allen to this point were most exhausting, and nearly half the regiment is sick. About nine line officers of the 28 are reported fit for duty, the rest are all along the road from Ethan Allen. I am pretty well.

Do write often, and if ever we get mail, I shall enjoy it. We expect to remain here some time, but of course don't know how long. Ask May if she attended to my wish about that hair. If not, do so immediately.

Cheerfully yours, Harry Goddard

1. Col. Dixon Stansbury Miles, the Union commander at Harpers Ferry, surrendered his twelve thousand men on nearby Bolivar Heights to Stonewall Jackson following an intense artillery barrage. Two days before the battle of Antietam, it was the largest surrender of Union forces during the war.

2. John Alstadt, along with some of his slaves, was among those detained on October 17, 1859, by John Brown's raiding party at Harpers Ferry, but he was not the first.

Camp at Bolivar Heights
Harpers Ferry, Va., Sept. 26, 1862

Dear Mother,

I have just been appointed Acting 2nd Lieutenant of Co. G of this regiment, with the understanding that my name will be nominated to Gov. Buckingham for the position. The company is from Madison. Capt. Willard, its commander, was killed at Sharpsburg, 1st Lieut. [Edward W.] Hart is in command, 2nd Lieut. Sherman (formerly conductor on the Shore Line Road) was wounded at Sharpsburg, and is now in hospital somewhere in Maryland. Hart and Sherman are to be promoted. They are splendid fellows.

S'gt [John C.] Pelton of Co. B has been appointed S'gt Major. I report to Lieut. Hart at 8 AM. Today Acting Adj't [Lt. Walter M.] Lucas was sick and I (still S'gt Major) acted as Adj't at Guard. Mounting and Dress Parades. It is almost unparalleled for a noncommissioned officer to act, but there is actually no Lieut. now on duty in the regiment who could do so, and I made the battalion hear me too, to my great surprise. Major [Cyrus C.] Clark conducted the parade. He and I are getting to be great friends. No more trouble about my valise or blankets. Lt. Marion Wait of the 8th Conn. fell at Antietam Creek, pierced with five bullets—a kind-hearted soldier and a true patriot, he sleeps his last sleep. I am writing in the shade of a candle and cannot keep on the lines very well.

You would have laughed to see me washing my clothes in the Shenandoah River yesterday. I washed a flannel shirt, 2 pairs flannel drawers, 5 pairs stockings, 2 collars, 18 handkerchiefs, and 1 pair gloves with hard soap, scrubbing them on a flat rock, and bringing them to the camp to dry. It took me three hours, and I think that Bridget would think them just fit for the wash tub now. I had a splendid bath at the same time.

Send me one pair of Infantry 2nd Lieut. straps.

Truly God is good to your boy

Lovingly yours Harry P. Goddard
For the last time S'gt Major 14th C.V.

Camp at Bolivar Heights
Sept. 28th, 1862

Dear Julia,

No letters from home since we left Fort Ethan Allen. Is it not shameful? The Chaplain may say what he pleases, but he could have attended to it. The guard left at that post numbering 125. Arrived yesterday, having been some ten days on the road. Lt. [James F.] Simpson, who was with them, says that they told him in Washington some days before he left, that there were then over four bushels of letters for the regiment.

I tent now with Lieut. [William W.] Hart of G Company, but do very little company duty, as Lucas being sick I have to do all the military duties of the Adjutant, such as conduct the Guard mounting, Dress Parade, etc. and though not detailed as Acting Adj't, the Lieut. Col. saying he must have some company officers on duty in the regiment (most being sick), yet Lucas sends for me to help him out, whenever he is called on to do any that Sergeant Major [John C.] Pelton can't do, so that I am virtually detailed from my company.

Don't have my promotion announced in the newspapers as the Lieut. Col. took pains to say Acting 2nd Lieut., and that I might have to go back to the Sg't Majority.

The 130th Penn. Col. [Henry I.] Zinn is in our brigade. Its Adj't and Sg't Major are both nullities and skedaddled at Sharpsburg. Three days after the battle, while we were on the march, I being on my post at the left—and in rear of the regiment with Col. Zinn's regiment just behind—the colonel rode up to me with a pleasant "Good morning Sg't Major. If I had just a Sg't Major I would make him Adj't double quick." I laughed and we turned the conversation.

Heard a fine sermon today by Mr. Stevens from Romans I.16.

Major Clark and I are getting to be great friends. He has conducted all parades while I am Acting Adj't, and so I see a great deal of him, and go to him for information on all points.

The line officers have got up a very foolish petition, which most of them have signed, to have this regiment detached from the brigade and sent some where to rest and drill. It will have no effect, save to make Cols. Morris and Perkins down on the signers. I couldn't see signing it.

Oh I do want to hear from home so much. Keep on writing regularly; your letters will always interest me, if I don't get them till the war is over.

These heights afford the most magnificent view I ever beheld. I have a notion we shall march tomorrow, as that will make a week here, and we have stayed at no place longer than that since we left Connecticut.

Yours,

Harry Goddard, Act'g 2nd Lieutenant Co. G

Camp on Bolivar Heights
Sept. 30th, 1862

Dearest May,

Yesterday we had a battalion drill, and I commanded Co. F and was agreeably disappointed by doing admirably well.

Acted as Adj't at Guard Mounting. Lieut. Sherman of Co. G, wounded at Sharpsburg, resumed command of the company yesterday, but is not fit for duty. 1st Lieut. Hart is very sick, and last night I commanded the company at dress parade.

General orders No's 8 and 9 were read appointing Lieut. George A. Morehouse of Co. A Acting Adj't, Ellis Acting Ass't Adj't General, and promoting Sg't Major Henry P. Goddard to be 2nd Lieut. of Co. G. 14th C.V., and Sg't J. G. Pelton of Co. B to be Sg't Major per order Lt. Col. S. H. Perkins, commanding. The nominations go north today and will of course be confirmed and my commission forwarded. I inclosed today an envelop addressed to Mother my Sg't Major's warrant, and some flowers from the battlefield of Sharpsburg. The regiments are all being inspected today and I think we shall start for Richmond in a day or two. Hard times and hard fighting in a distant country are ahead. This time we must take Richmond, or give it up forever.

Lieut. Hart will have to be sent to Harpers Ferry if we march soon, and Sherman's wound will keep him off duty, so I shall probably be in command for some days. The Lieutenants are good fellows, and tonight an order will be read making Hart Capt. and Sherman 1st Lieut. People come here from Connecticut daily. Some say no letters from us have reached home. Now I have written eight letters, including the two today, since I left Fort Ethan Allen. They have been mailed at various points and must reach you at some time. Many of our officers are rather sorry they came; it is rather amusing.

I am officer of the Guard today. It is stupid.

Yours ever,

Lieut. Harry Goddard

Co. G, 14th C.V.

Camp on Bolivar Heights
Sept. 30th, 1862

Dear Mother,

I have written May today and enclosed a brief note to you in an envelope with my warrant, and some flowers with it.

We got our mail today. Hurrah, Hurrah, Hurrah! I had seven letters from home. So Alf has been home and gone away. Poor noble brave brother mine, he has endured what I never would have had perseverance or endurance to do.

Thank God I am once more a commissioned officer, and if providence spares my life, fifty dollars a month of my one hundred and three shall be devoted to household expenses. The only trouble in the army is that pay days are few and far between. Don't fear that I shall ever resign again as I had almost rather die.

Poor Alf, how hard for you not to have him longer at home. His nature was always nobler than mine. Thank Heaven he did not enlist as a private. Don't ever urge any friend of mine to do so.

Later. . . . Being officer of the Guard, I was called away to attend to turning out the Guard at Dress Parade. Orders were read promoting the 1st and 2nd Lieut's of Co. F and Co. G (and making me 2nd Lieut. of Co. G) and Q. M. S'gt [William A.] Comes 2nd Lieut. of Co. F. This fills all vacancies, and we for the first time have 30 line officers. God pity Mrs. Abbot. You are not the most afflicted mother in Norwich.

It is growing dark and I must close. We shall march soon in all probability, and my letters will be fewer, briefer, farther between and longer in reaching you, but remember I am with you in my prayers. Within a month I shall probably be dead, or in Richmond. It is Col. Dwight Morris who commands our brigade. Major Clark is well, sends regards and says "secesh have not molded" his death bullet yet. It <u>was</u> a hard old fight. Glad that John is on Sigel's staff. Pope blusters much.

Yours, Lieut. H. P. Goddard

Camp on Boliver Heights
Oct. 4th, 1862

Dear Mother,

Two more letters from home today. It is so jolly to get letters from home. It always puts me in good spirits.

Speaking of the feeling we had at Antietam, I believe it is sympathetic, and that when I do fall—killed or wounded—you will feel it.

I don't like Pope too much—too much gasconade, just like little Mack.

Journal Continued

Oct. 1st. President Lincoln rode through our camp today, accompanied by Gens. McClellan, Sumner, French, Williams [Maj. Gen. Alpheus Williams, commanding 12th Corps at Antietam], etc. We gave him a fine reception. He looks more care-worn than ever. Drilled the company in loading and firing, and was in command of them at dress parade.

Oct. 2nd. Drilled the company in loading and firing. Lieut. Col. Perkins (after drill) sent for me, and said I had made several mistakes in the morning drill, and as he had promoted his noncommissioned staff without regard to anyone's opinions, he wanted me to study and do well. I told him I did not understand company drill yet, but would study and do better.

Regiment went out on picket. Co. B and our company remained at the reserve post—Mr. Alstadt's. This gentleman was made prisoner by John Brown in Harpers Ferry in 1859. He has a fine old Virginia home.

Oct. 4th. Drilled the company in loading and firing and did well. Am getting very much interested in the manual of arms. Have studied and now understand it. Battalion drill in the afternoon. Officers take part according to rank. Eight commissioned officers present. I was in command of Co. C. Very hard drill but my part was easy, and got through it well, through some of the line officers got "blessings" the "wrong side of heaven" from the field officers.

Have been in command of the Company ever since I ceased to act as Adjutant, save on two occasions. Lieut. Sherman commanding at the President's reception, and when out on picket. Capt. Hart is quite sick, and Lieut. Sherman's wound troubles him so he can do very little duty. I am more serene with the Company than either of them, and expect to be disliked by the men for a while, but liked in the end. The material of the company is excellent: stout, strong, New Haven country farmers, and Long Island Sound fishermen; very many religious men, and with drill and discipline it will be one of the finest in the regiment.

Capt. Hart and Lieut. Sherman are gentlemen and we agree admirably. I am very very happy here, my only sorrow being in the thought of my poor dear lonely Mother and sick sister, and brother turning his face from all he loves and hiring away o'er distant seas. But, he is right. His duty calls him there, mine calls me here. The 20th and 21st Connecticut regiments are encamped at Sandy Hook, two miles the other side of the Potomac this AM. Some of them came over here and I sent a note to Kit Brand of the 21st, but I hear they moved up the Potomac to join Burnside tonight, and I shall not see them at present.

Regarding the 26th Conn. Vols., what sort of colonel is Tom Kingsley? Joe Selden Lieut. Col!! Ed Ells 1st Lieut., that's rich too. I mean to ask Gen. Burnside to make me a Brigadier next. Do you know that I am almost the only line officer in the regiment that has been constantly on duty. I was off duty one night and half a day at Fort Ethan Allen, and that is all since leaving Connecticut, while nearly every officer and man from Col. Morris down has been or is on the sick list. Diarrhea is the great complaint, but my health is excellent. I got acclimated last April and it doesn't affect me now. There are not over twelve line officers on duty at this time. Did Lieut. Coit go home? If so, call him and give him my best wishes. "This is a faithful saying, and worthy of all acceptation, that Christ Jesus came into the world to save sinners." I marked that text one month ago, and have since realized its truth. My candle is going out, so good night. Love to all friends.

Your loving son, Harry P. Goddard

Camp on Bolivar Heights, Va.
Oct. 8th, 1862

Dear Mother,

The regiment has orders to strike tents and move today. We are still of Provost Duty (that is, myself and 40 men) but expect to be called in every moment.

I went out this morning and met Lieut-Col. [William B.] Wooster of the 20th C.V.; the regiment is coming over to encamp on Loudoun Heights. All of Sumner's corps is moving, apparently to the other side of the Shenandoah.

You know my first straps were spoiled. Well, this morning a bought a pair for $2.50, and had just got them sewed on, when Sherman sent down my things from camp, and some mail matter that I did not get last night, including the shoulder straps forwarded by mail. I was so mad. I should not have bought the new ones, but on this duty one must wear some emblem of rank.

The different corps are merely changing positions, as some corps on Loudoun Heights, and some of the troops in Pleasant Valley are going into camp on Bolivar Heights. Our regiment's baggage has not arrived yet, so officers and men will have to move without their clean clothes. It is tough.

The 20th Conn. Vols is resting in the street in front of us. I have just been talking to Col. [Samuel] Ross, and one of the captains is up here. Mr. Norton has just been here and bid me Good Bye, making me a present of $5.00. He is too kind. The regiment is going up the Shenandoah Valley, and I expect to join them before I can write again.

Later. The whole army is moving and troops are passing constantly. The Provost Marshall says we shall be relieved tomorrow, and promises transportation for our things.

I quarter with the 1st Lt. of the 1st Minnesota, which regiment has just passed, and I hear the 14th Conn. has also gone. The 20th is in a Brigade commanded by Brig. Gen. Thomas L. Kane. I had a full view of him. He looks the hero, and proved it, at Cross Keys [the battle of Cross Keys, June 8, 1862, a victory for Stonewall Jackson during his 1862 Shenandoah Valley campaign] where he was wounded and a prisoner.

Yours ever, Harry

Journal continued

Oct. 6th. Two battalion drills, nothing important. Our cavalry driven in on a skirmish today. Our army is fortifying Maryland and Loudoun Heights. This place will soon be impregnable. The finest sunset tonight I ever witnessed. It reminds me of Church's "Twilight in the Wilderness."[1]

Oct 7th. Battalion drill in the morning. Have nightly lessons at Lieut. Col.'s tent now. Moved our quarters into a splendid Sibley tent[2] with Co. B officers.

Oct. 8th. Inspection by one of Gen. Sumner's officers in the morning. He gave all the officers "fits" for not wearing shoulder straps. They all took them off the day before the fight, except Lieut. Crosby, who would not, and he was the most seriously wounded of the lot. I told him I had been recently promoted and had none. "Button up your coat then, sir." There he had me. Capt. Hart is very sick; he can keep nothing on his stomach, and seems to be growing worse.

Was detailed as Judge Advocate and Recorder of a court of Inquiry, Major G. C. Clark presiding. I have to report all the proceedings. It comes natural, but you must not even say I am in the Court Martial as such things are kept as quiet as the doings of a jury at home. Lieut. Sherman is in command today but insisted on my drilling. He lacks confidence in himself, but is a splendid fellow though not at all posted on military.

Love to all, Lieut. Harry Goddard

1. Frederick Edwin Church (1826–1900) painted the landscape "Twilight in the Wilderness" in 1860.

2. The Sibley tent, modeled after the teepee of the Plains Indians, was eighteen feet in diameter, twelve feet high, and held about a dozen men.

Near Harper's Ferry
Out on Picket, Oct. 10th, 1862

Dear May,

Marion Hart was not so bad a boy. If God considers true geniality and kindness of heart and deed, and whose earnest patriotism and expressed willingness to die for his country, Marion Wait will not suffer in his sight.

Oct. 9th. The Court of Inquiry assembled in the morning and came to a decision and adjourned. I wrote up the record, which was signed by Maj. Clark as President and myself as Recorder and forwarded to Gen. French. Regiment went out on picket in the afternoon.

Oct. 10th. Out on picket. Had battalion drill in the morning; in afternoon drilled the company in wheeling and marching.

In camp, evening. We have come in from picket. I have moved up to Capt. [William H.] Tubb's quarters as Capt. Hart is very sick and fretful, and has to be alone. Adj't Ellis has gone home on twenty days sick furlough. Gen. Sumner is off on 30 days furlough.

Good night, Harry

Harpers Ferry, Va.
Oct. 11th, 1862

Dear May,

A damp, wet, rainy morning, my darling, and the men who have no blankets or overcoats, having thrown them away on the field of battle as most of them did, by Col. Perkins' advice, will suffer in these miserable old tents today. Personally, I will not be very comfortable. You know we have five Sibley tents—one for the officers of each two companies; G and B tent together, but Lieut. Hart is sick and wants an attendant all the time, so I left and moved up to Capt. Lulls' Sibley, he being the only officer on duty in Co.'s E and K.

1st Lieut. Hale of Co. E, being detached, stays at Gen. French's headquarters. 2nd Lieut. Baldwin [Charles O. Baldwin, resigned December 19, 1862] of Co. E is sick downtown. Capt. Gillette of Co. K [resigned December 20, 1862] is sick out towards the picket lines and the two Lieut.'s at home wounded.

Bolivar Heights today affords a far different view from that from that which you would have seen in 1860. Instead of being crowned with thick woods, its surface presents only here and there a noble elm, which the destroyers could not but spare in fortifying the Heights. Turning your head to the South, you behold across the Shenandoah the lofty crests of Loudoun Heights on which day and night immense fires are blazing to clear them of trees, so that the fort being erected there cannot be approached.

Across the Potomac on Maryland Heights, the loftiest summit of all, whole regiments are at work with axes and spades, and a fort is rapidly making itself visible on the Heights. Looking north you see the Potomac, ordinarily calm and peaceful, but today lashing itself in madness with the storm, winding its most crooked path between the mountains.

Northeast of us, between Maryland Heights and Loudoun Heights, lies the village of Harpers Ferry, beautiful cottages, and the magnificent ruins of the Arsenal and Armory burnt by Lieut. Jones[1] to save them from rebel hands. Then there is the Gap between Maryland and Loudoun Heights where the Potomac glides through 500 or 600 feet below the level of the mountains, unites with the Shenandoah, then expands, and starts for Washington. But looking west, the view is the most beautiful. Standing on these heights where we are encamped and which descend peacefully some 300 feet below with just such a grade that you can walk down. We have a sweep of twenty miles of beautiful undulating valley, interspersed here and there with wooded patches, where lurk the pickets of the army of Jackson, who is any-where that McClellan can't catch him. Today the whole scenery has a wild weird look, prophesizing battles and victories, defeats and death, and when I think of the wrangles and discussions of our Generals and of the people of the North, all hav-ing and expressing their separate views, and doing nothing, I feel discouraged and feel fearful that our best blood flows in vain.

> "But the little birds sang east,
> And the little birds sang west,
> And I smiled to think God's greatness
> Flows around our incompleteness,
> Around our restlessness His Rest."

Your loving brother, Lieut. Harry P. Goddard

1. On April 18, 1861, Lt. Roger Jones of the U.S. Army set torches to the armory and arsenal buildings to prevent their capture by an approaching Virginia militia.

Camp on Bolivar Heights
Oct. 13th, 1862
Dear Mother,

I am dead broke, and really have nothing to eat. I must also have a pair of boots so I want nearly thirty dollars. Send me that amount any way. There is much talk about Sumner's Corps going into winter quarters here, but I cannot believe it though things look so. It is preeminently a fighting corps and cannot be left behind.

Journal continued

Oct. 11th. Rainy, damp, dirty day. In Capt. Tubbs' tent all day with Charley Hale, who brings Norwich news up to Tuesday. He comes out to get some position under his brother. I am very sorry to hear of Kemp's exceedingly ill health. I begin to believe that it must have influenced his resignation, and to feel that we must look with charity upon the other cause. Remember his temptations, rank, money and situation being placed in the "Modern Sodom" as New Orleans is well termed. Who knows but that I should have been in the same position under the same cir-cumstances. "Judge not that ye be not judged."

Oct. 12th. Officer of the guard today. Capt. Hart was removed to the hospital.

Oct. 13th. We are going out on picket this afternoon. It is so wet and nasty and my boots are so thin that I hate to go. It makes me so mad to see other officers eat-ing fresh bread and butter, and apples and sweet potatoes, etc. when Sherman and I are broke and have to live on crackers and pork.

Do send me money. Lieut. [Walter M.] Lucas has joined Co. B. Visitors come here every day from Connecticut, bringing things for other companies, but not a soul from Norwich. A man from Preston visited Tubbs, and he has had two boxes from home—one directed to Washington was four weeks coming, and another directed to Harpers Ferry, two days. It's provoking—no money, no letters, nothing to eat, raining, and have got to go out on picket—way out to the Shenandoah this time. I declare I won't write any more till I feel better. Rejoicing in rank and hope, but nothing to eat and nothing to buy it with.

Yours ever, Lieut. H. P. Goddard

Harpers Ferry
Oct. 14th, 1862
Dear Mother,

Last evening, I got your letter just mailing one. We went out on picket. I had command of my company, which was pushed out to the Shenandoah River, and placing nine tents encamped with my reserve on the bank of the most beautiful of rivers, watching the river and railroad track. This is the end of Oct. 13th.

Oct. 14th. We remained at our post all day. I had a very interesting conversation with a Union Scout who passes everywhere by order of Gen. Banks. Just when coming in I captured an old darkey who has been ferrying people across to "Secessia." I laid several traps to catch him, but he made three trips before I nabbed him, which I did just as we were starting home. The old fellow is honest himself, but has been carrying across female informants of whom he was glad to tell. I marched him back to camp and reported him to the Major. (Col. Perkins is sick at Harpers Ferry.)

Got Uncle's letter today dated the 9th. I tell you again that _that_ money letter has not come, and will not if expressed to Washington, as some packages have been received here which lay there five weeks. Some come straight through when directed to Harpers Ferry, but let me assure you that it is not good to send by express, as one third of the matters don't come. Send me directly by mail twenty dollars. I need it or I shall be shoeless soon. The fifteen dollars is lost, and I never expect to see it. I have written so a dozen times, and repeat, the letter never came. And if expressed, never will, and I want twenty dollars mailed. Again, some regiments here have not been paid for six months and don't expect any sooner than that. Once more, I will take any staff place or any thing above my present rank up to a Colonelcy and jump at the chance. Military is played out with me. It cost me one commission, but won't stop my taking anything I can get.

Don't be too hard on Kemp; remember that he has been more tempted than any of us, and again don't tell ever why he resigned, and I don't believe anybody else will. Kit Brand has been made 1st Lieut. Of Co. K, 21st Regiment C.V. Joseph Stanley the 2nd Lieut. was Lloyd Green's coachman. Commissary S'gt. Joe Plunkett has also been promoted. Col. [John] Spiedel was right when he said to Col. [William B.] Ely, "I would like to live in that Norwich where every man is born a commissioned officer." Tell May to write me who Annie Berkeley is engaged to. I am resigned to it. Love to all, and all the Abbotts. <u>Do send me the money.</u>

Yours very hard up, Lt. H. P. Goddard

Camp on Bolivar Heights
Oct. 16th, 1862

Dear Mother,

Last night a large force went out from here, and this morning we can hear cannonading and see the smoke of battle some five or six miles out towards Charlestown. We had orders for a division drill at 9 AM, but as soon as we got into regimental line had orders to stack arms and be ready to fall in at a moment's notice. Just after we broke ranks I found J. W. Newcomb Jr., formerly of the New Haven Palladium, now of the New York Tribune. He called in and being an old friend of mine and of Lieut. Sherman's we had a pleasant chat. He says the whole disposition of the campaign will depend on today's doings, and thinks that we shall have a great battle today. If so, we shall be in it. One month tomorrow since Antietam was fought and we have it all to do over again.

Well, officers and men in the Union and rebel armies are getting sick of the long war, with no definite results, and ask, "When will it all end?" But we must obey orders and do our duty. That's what we came for, and if we can only realize that "He doeth all things well," we can be contented.

<u>Oct. 16.</u> Have stated what has happened up to 10 AM., save that we all have the "Virginia Quick Step." Uncle Sam knows what that is He had it at Ship Island.[1] Cannonading has just commenced again. Later we are ordered to Harpers Ferry to guard Commissary stores. This shows no battle impending.

Harry

1. Union troops under Maj. Gen. Benjamin Butler occupied Ship Island, a barrier island off the coast of Mississippi, early in the war—in November 1861. The island was used as a prison and as a launching post for the capture of New Orleans by fifteen thousand Union troops in April 1862.

[October 17]

Dearest May,

After closing my letter to Mother yesterday we fell in, and marched down to the Ferry where the regiment was divided into four parts, one guarding Commissary stores on the Shenandoah, another crossing the Potomac and going to Sandy Hook, Md., two miles over, and another to Knoxville, Md., about six miles. The fourth division was again divided, Co. B guarding King street, and our company being held in reserve in an old parsonage of a Catholic church. We sent out half the company at a time to guard the pontoon bridges, the whole regiment being in what is called Quartermaster business. Had we not been thus detailed, we should have left Harpers Ferry and gone to the front yesterday, as Gen. Hancock, after taking Charlestown last night, sent for more troops immediately, and many of those regiments about our camp went out. The regiment that are relieved here had only been in 24 hours, so I suppose we shall be relieved this afternoon, and go back to camp. If so we shall have to push on very soon, as it looks as if a great battle is impending near Charlestown. It will be greater than Antietam in the number of troops engaged. My straps came yesterday by Express, but my money letter has never arrived.

I suppose it is useless to urge any one to send me by mail, as I have begged in my letter for a fortnight, and it will do little good as I have yet to wear my hole-y-torn boots in the advance into Virginia, not having received any money with which to get a new pair, or have these repaired. Then I have nothing to eat, save what the company force upon me out of their rations. Well, I won't grumble.

Right behind this house is "Jefferson's Rock" where Thomas Jefferson was wont to sit and meditate on the beautiful scenery and write his stirring thoughts. He said it afforded the finest view he ever gazed upon. The rock is of limestone, and is now supported by four freestone pillars, and is covered with names. I sat on the rock and chipped off a piece to send home at the first opportunity.

In front of this Parsonage is a neat Catholic church with its gilded cross pointing heavenward, inspiring thoughts of Him who died to save his enemies, while we fear to die for our friends. The church is about the only building in the place that does not show the effects of war.

One of our men died today; he has been sick ever since he came here. We shall have to bury him here as the Express agents will take none but embalmed bodies. I see troops crossing the Potomac and surmise that is the regiment that is to relieve our men at Sandy Hook and Knoxville, so I suppose we shall be relieved in a few minutes. If so we shall be pushed to the front and you may expect a big battle about Sunday or Monday. It will be impossible for me to telegraph so you must wait official advices, and remember that in the words of the heroic Elsworth,[1] "He who noteth the fall of a sparrow will have some purpose in the fate of men like me."

Write me to whom Annie B. is engaged. I can bear it without pain now. Annie has many good qualities, and with a good husband will make an excellent wife. Kit Brand is now Lieut., esteemed highly by his Colonel, and a promising young officer of Abraham Lincoln's forces. Well, the war is making brethren of us all, as the poem reads that I sent Mother yesterday.

Write often, darling. Will it be too much for you to write twice a week? You may not have to do it but for a little while, and I do so love to get letters. Keep Mother in good spirits. She is too sad. You are the only child at home now well enough to take good care of her.

There is more religion in my company than in the whole Harris Light Cavalry. Now don't think I am very good, because I am very wicked, and do many things I ought not, but I hope God will make me good yet. The army is a hard place, but He is everywhere.

In the piazza of a house in front of me, two little girls have been singing. It affects me to remember my younger days, with a pleasant sadness, a mood that often comes over me lately.

With warmest love,
Your very aff[ectionate] Brother Harry

1. Elmer Ellsworth, a colonel of the New York Fire Zouaves whom he recruited from the city's firefighters, is remembered as the first casualty of the Civil War. In the summer of 1860, Ellsworth went to Springfield, Ill., to study law in Abraham Lincoln's office and to help Lincoln in his campaign for president. On May 24, 1861, the day after Virginia seceded from the Union, Ellsworth led his men across the Potomac River from Washington to Alexandria, Virginia, to secure the railroad station and telegraph office. On his way he noticed a Confederate flag atop the Marshall House Inn. With four of his men, Ellsworth quickly ascended the stairs and cut down the flag. On Ellsworth's way down the innkeeper killed the twenty-four-year-old colonel with a shotgun blast to the chest. Cpl. Francis Brownell immediately shot the innkeeper to death. Lincoln had an honor guard bring Ellsworth's body to the White House where it lay in state May 25. The body was then moved to New York's City Hall where thousands paid their respects to the first man to fall for the Union. Volunteers flocked to join the Union's ranks in response to Ellsworth's death, "Remember Ellsworth" became a patriotic slogan, and a New York regiment called itself the "Ellsworth Avengers."

Camp on Bolivar Heights
Oct. 18, 1862

Dear Mother,

I tell you this army must go into winter quarters somewhere. This weather is very cold and soon the roads will be impassable. Our army is not anxious to advance, but begins to have a feeling that fighting won't end the war. It is too bad, but they do talk so. Well, we will hope for the best. The Post-master here says the Government delays all matter for soldiers over its roads. Some of our men have just got boxes expressed five weeks since. We had a very impressive funeral over [Private Cornette M.] Crampton, who died in the hospital yesterday. We buried him in the village church yard. I am officer of the guard today.

Yours very truly your son,
Harry Goddard

Camp on Bolivar Heights
Oct. 21st, 1862

My own Darling Sister Jule,

I was detailed as officer of the guard yesterday, and as the regiment went out on picket last night, I shall be on forty-eight hours. I am glad it happened so, as last night we got another mail, and I got your letter of Oct. 15th enclosing the long-lost $20. In addition my commission came yesterday bearing date Sept. 14th, and I have received the straps sent me by uncle Lou. Capt. [Elijah W.] Gibbons was officer of the day and instead of being out on that cold stupid picket duty, I am pleasantly sitting in our warm room, writing and smoking a good cigar. Have had a good breakfast of toasted bread and butter, as now I have money enough to buy something to eat. Indeed I am very happy; besides I have just put on a clean lot of underclothes, a luxury not another line officer can experience, as no baggage was brought from Fort Ethan Allen, save Field and Staff (commissioned and non-com). Then I have found an old darkey to do all my washing, and can now pay to have it done. How long we shall remain here I cannot say. Lieut. Col. Perkins and Major Clark are having their tents floored, and act as if we are going into winter quarters, but I cannot believe it possible. I suppose Gen. Schenck [Maj. Gen. Robert C. Schenck, commanding Middle Department at Baltimore] will resign now he is elected to Congress [from Ohio]. I would like to be with him. Some time ago I sent home my warrant as Sg't Major, and some flowers from Antietam. Did they ever reach home?

Your loving Brother,
Harry

Camp on Bolivar Heights
Oct. 21st, 1862

Dear Mother,

Quarter past nine P.M. sitting in cold tent writing, while it is raining hard outside. Sunday nothing happened of interest, save religious service in the morning. The regiment came in from picket duty at 4 P.M.

Monday I was on the sick list—all day feverish. Cured myself with a good supper of sweet potatoes and toast. Today we have a target-shoot in the morning. As Sherman is officer of the day, I had command of the company. We made some excellent shots, as good as any in the regiment. This afternoon I drilled the company in double-quick marching and wheeling. Now then for our camp life. At 5:30 A.M. Reveille when commanding officers report to Adj't and Orderlies to S'gt Major.

> At 6 A.M. Breakfast. At 7 A.M. Sick call when about 650 sick report
> to the Surgeons. At 8 A.M. Guard Mounting.
> 10 to 12 M. Company Drill.
> 12 M. Dinner
> 2:30 P.M. to 4:30 P.M. Battalion Drill.
> 5 P.M. Dress Parade.
> 6 P.M. Supper.

7 P.M. Tattoo

9:30 P.M. Taps.

Every third or fourth day we go out on picket. The posts are now some three miles towards Charlestown and on the railroad instead of a half a mile out as before Hancock's [Maj. Gen. Winfield Scott Hancock, commanding 1st Division, 2nd Corps] reconnaissance. I shall try and get to Harpers Ferry tomorrow, and get a pair of shoes. I shall order a new suit of clothes and boots from Norwich as my government pants are giving out, and my old dress coat is pretty well worn out by Sg't Major Pelton, and I told him to keep it and give me a dollar. It was worn out when I got here.

We have a Sibley tent for the officers of Co. B and Co. G. At this moment Capt. Hart is very sick in the hospital, and has applied for leave to go home. He is very homesick and if he can't get a leave, I fear he will be very apt to resign. The officers are thus engaged—Lieut. Sherman is Officer of the Day and playing High Low Jack on a box with 1st Lieut. [John C.] Broatch and 2nd Lieut. [Walter M.] Lucas. Captain Gibbons of B Company is lying on his back on the straw, bothering all hands with asking questions about tactics which we cannot answer. I am writing on a box table, with a candle in a bottle. "Officers, too much noise in this tent." Good night till tomorrow.

Yours lovingly,

Harry

"On Picket" in the Shenandoah
Oct. 24/62

Am again in the same duty on the same spot as before, but Lt. Sherman is with me now. It is very dull and am sitting here in an old building. I resolve first to write home, second to go bathing in the river which flows at my very feet.

Journal

Oct. 22nd. Very high wind. Drilled the company.

Oct. 23rd. Division inspection by Gen. French in AM followed by Brigade drill under Gen. F. and Col. Wallis. I begin to like "Old Blinky" as the boys term Gen. French from his habit of incessant winking. Some have termed him "the Gin Barrel."

On our return to camp, I had a call from Lt. C. A. Brand of the 21st Conn. with two of his friends. Was very glad to see him. "Kit" never looked or appeared as well in his life. Capt. Tubbs and I got the party up a dinner. As this was extra good for these parts, I enclose bill of fare:

Ham, fried

Potatoes, Irish and sweet, boiled

Salt, pepper, butter

Bread, fresh and soft
Pies
Sweet cider

Is not that a good dinner?

Went out on picket as a regiment on the Charlestown road where we lay in reserve. At 7 PM our company was ordered to the Shenandoah to relieve a company that had been forgotten. We had a hard tramp up the road, getting here at 8 P.M.

Oct. 24th. On picket. My boots are played out. I only hope that we shall not advance till I can get to Harpers Ferry and get a pair. There are many indications of an advance. Some talk of "winter quarters" but I don't believe the North will stand that. My cry is

> "Oh for a General—
> One with a head, heart and hand,

Like one of the simple great ones gone by." Where is he? Has America the Man? Is it McClellan? Fourteen months trial answers "No." Is it Halleck? Answers "No." Is it McDowell? The dead from three battle fields answer "No." Is it Pope? Bull Run No. 2 from its bloody field answers "No." Whence shall we look? Maybe to Hooker the dauntless, Sigel the unconquerable, or Burnside the chiseler. Yet all these have only been successful with small armies, as had McClellan, Fremont and Pope. Was not Napolean right when he said, "It takes a very great man to command 100,000 men." If so, have we the man to command a million men?

In camp 9 PM Capt. Hart was today removed to the division hospital, and after just having had a visit from his father-in-law, consulted with Capt. Gibbons and then sent in his resignation on the grounds of continued ill health with no prospect of recovery here. The poor fellow cannot get a "leave" and would likely die here. Lt. [Charles O.] Baldwin of Co. E resigned for the same reason. Capt. R. H. Gillette of Co. D, who has been ill, goes home in citizens clothes, never having been mustered in. Capt. H. Polk Hammock of Co. D did the same thing a few weeks since. He will not retire, but Gillette will re-enter service if possible.

Your loving Harry

Bolivar Heights
Oct. 28, 1862

Dear Mother,

Just in from picket. We now go to that duty at morning instead of eve.

Journal

Oct. 25. Officer of the guard today. Capt. [Samuel H., Company H, dishonorably discharged September 17, 1863] Davis of New London, detailed as Officer of the Day, was placed under arrest for noise after "Taps." Charges were filed by Maj. Clark.

The father of Lt. Baldwin arrived from Middletown to take his sick son home where he will resign on account of ill health. Mr. Baldwin brings news of the death of 2nd Lt. [George H. D.] Crosby of Co. K at Middletown from his Antietam wounds. It seems as if I was fated to lose the commander I most esteem. Crosby was one of our best young officers.

Oct. 26. Rainy. I spent the day in Capt. Tubb's tent entertaining Lt. Hale of the staff and Capt. Harris of the 18th Conn. We succeeded in making a fire in the tent and were very comfortable.

Oct. 27. Went on picket at 8 AM. Very cold. Whiskey rations served to the men and helped them.

Oct. 28. Back in from picket. Lt. Sherman had some New Haven visitors. Henry B. Norton of Norwich called while we were all on picket. Many troops are moving out of their camps. Please send me some mittens as cold weather approaches. Last night our regiment turned out but six officers for Dress Parade—the cold and the bad water having made many ill of diarrhea.

Gen. Couch is in command of the Corps in Gen. Sumner's absence.

Yours affectionately,
Harry

Harper's Ferry
Oct. 29, 1862

Dear Julia,

Here I sit in a comfortable room in the third story of a building opposite the Railroad bridge, writing on a table with every needed accommodation and this grand letter from home.

This morning I had to testify in the court martial of Capt. Davis. The President of the court martial was Lt. Col. Marshall, 10th N.Y.

By the way, our Brigade Quartermaster whom we all laugh at is Capt. Augustus More of Lecminster, Mass., formerly Col. of the 21st Mass., which he had to resign after shamefully staying behind his regiment when it went from Annapolis.

Again, do you remember my fair inamorata of Fredericksburg, Va., Miss Belle Herndon?[1] Well, in reading an old paper today an account of the noble Capt. Herndon, U.S.N., lost on the Central American after he had saved all the women and children. I find that Miss Herndon must be a relative of his as his home was in Fredericksburg. She was <u>beautiful</u>, at any rate.

Tell Mother that I brought Corporal [Frederick S.] Ward in to see Mr. Norton tonight, and will look out for him as he is the best corporal in my company. To tell you the truth, the 14th C.V. <u>has</u> suffered fearfully since we left Fort Ethan Allen, where all officers baggage and knapsacks were left and have never been brought up, though all the officers of other regiments have got theirs. Then again the Lt. Col. told the men to throw away all overcoats and blankets at Antietam, and men are <u>dying daily</u> on Belair Heights for want of clothing. As soon as Gov. Buckingham found out about it, he sent Mr. H. B. Norton on to investigate. There is great blame some where and Mr. Norton is bound to find out where. Officers have now the same shirts for seven weeks and our regiment is now in truth what the Hartford folk called us in jest, "The Lousy 14th." Half the officers have lice, men have had to draw new clothing to be deducted from their pay, and the regiment is terribly demoralized. The Col., Lt. Col. and Major will tell you this, "Somebody is terribly to blame" and before God and man will have to answer for at least <u>ten</u> deaths. I have never written of this as I have suffered less than anyone, and had resolved never to write a blue letter again as long as I lived.

We now expect the baggage tomorrow as it has been started and seen in the cold. Tonight I have been detailed on this duty Private Guard, and the regiment have orders to march tomorrow with three days' rations and 60 rounds of cartridges. I think it a grand reconnaissance in force as they leave every thing behind, but many think it a grand advance.

Make Mr. Norton tell you about the troubles in the 14th as I shan't allude to them again.

<u>Thursday, Oct. 30th.</u> The Quartermaster has just been down here. He says at the time the regiment was to start. They received orders to stack arms in line of battle and await orders.

We have just heard of Gen. [Maj. Gen. Ormsby] Mitchell's death[2] on the Charleston and Savannah Road and the woundings of Cols. [John L.] Chatfield and [John] Speidel,[3] that the 6th Conn. Regiment has been very fortunate heretofore but now suffers with the rest.

This is very pleasant duty and I shall probably remain on it until the Army leaves Harpers Ferry. You need not send the $20. I wrote you last as I have received the last $7 as well as the $20 first forwarded. The baggage is expected here today and I guess it will all be right. Tell Mother that what she says about Kemp in her last letter rather staggers me, but she must remember that I don't know what he is charged with.

Lt. [Theodore H.] Stanley is under arrest and will be tried by court martial for leaving camp for 24 hours without permission to visit a sick man. He may be cashiered and yet his private character is irreproachable.

There was only half a Norwich company in the 21st regiment under Stanley. Kit is 1st Lt. and Stanley 2nd Lt.

The reason Norwich men all get commissions is because they win them. It is a fact and Cols. Ely and (may I hope) Morris will tell you so.

Ever your loving brother,
Harry Goddard

1. Belle Herndon was the niece of the U.S. Navy captain William Lewis Herndon, who became a hero after he went down with his mail ship in a storm off Cape Hatteras, North Carolina, in 1857. During his service in the Harris Light Cavalry in the spring of 1862, Goddard rode through Fredericksburg in the hope of catching a glimpse of the young lady.

2. Maj. Gen. Ormsby Mitchell, commanding Dept. of the South, died of yellow fever.

3. Col. John L. Chatfield and Lt. Col. John Speidel were wounded at the battle of Pocotaligo near Beaufort, S.C., a Union defeat on October 24, 1862.

Harpers Ferry, Oct. 30, 1862

Dear Mother,

The regiment has orders to strike tents and move today. We are still of Provost Duty (that is, myself and 40 men) but expect to be called in every moment.

I went out this morning and met Adj't Arms and Lieut-Col. Wooster of the 20th C.V.; the regiment is coming over to camp on Loudoun Heights. All Sumner's corps is moving, apparently to the other side of the Shenandoah.

You know my first straps were spoiled. Well, this morning I bought a pair for $2.50, and had just got them sewed on, when Sherman sent down my things from camp, and some mail matter I did not get last night, including the shoulder straps forwarded by mail. I was so mad. I should not have bought the new ones, but on this duty one must wear some emblem of rank.

The different corps are merely changing positions, as some corps on Loudoun Heights, and some of the troops in Pleasant Valley are going into camp on Bolivar Heights. Our regiment's baggage has not arrived yet, so officers and men will have to move without clean clothes. It is tough.

The 20th Conn. Vols. is resting in the street in front of us. I have just been talking to Col. [Samuel] Ross, and one of the captains is up here. Mr. Norton has just been here and bid me Good Bye, making me a present of $5.00. He is too kind. The regiment is going up the Shenandoah Valley, and I expect to join them before I can write again.

Later. The whole army is moving and troops are passing constantly. The Provost Marshall says we shall be relieved tomorrow, and promises transportation for our things.

I quarter with the 1st Lt. of the 1st Minnesota, which regiment has just passed, and I hear that the 14th has also gone. The 20th is in a Brigade commanded by Brig. Gen. Thomas L. Kane, brother of Dr. Kane. I had a full view of him. He looks the hero, and proved it, at Cross Keys, where he was wounded and a prisoner.

Yours ever, Harry

Harpers Ferry, Oct. 30th, 1862

Dear May,

Capt. Church Howe, under whom I have been serving here on provost duty came out as Adj't of Col. Gerard, 15th Mass. He was under Gen. Charles P. Stone in the disastrous fight at Balls Bluff, where Col. E. L. Baker of Oregon (U.S. Senator) died so gallantly. He (Howe) thinks that Col. Stone has been most unjustly treated by the government for that affair in having been imprisoned for alleged treachery.[1] He tells many stories that, if substantiated, and I believe them, had me to agree thereto.

I must tell you a funny story of our worthy 14th Colonel. One day while drilling his brigade on Belair Heights, he wished the 14th to form in "close column by division," that is, close up en masse. Not knowing the proper order to give, he called Lt. Col. Perkins and said, "Colonel, you know what I want. Get the men up together—Bunch 'em. Bunch 'em." The story got out and from thenceforth "Gen. Bunch 'em" is a nick-name applied to him.

Yours, Harry

1. The battle of Ball's Bluff, also known as the battle of Harrison's Landing or the battle of Leesburg, took place on October 21, 1861, in Loudoun County, Virginia, at a Potomac River crossing. In the second largest battle in the east, after First Bull Run/Manassas, some two thousand Union troops under the command of Col. Charles P. Stone were routed, many driven over the steep river bluff, by a Confederate force of some sixteen hundred men. Col. Edward D. Baker, a sitting U.S. senator from Oregon and a close friend of President Lincoln's, was killed. Stone became a scapegoat for the defeat but was later exonerated.

Harpers Ferry, Oct. 31st

Dear Mother,

Still here. The regiment is eight miles from here, across the Shenandoah. Fitz John Porter's corps are passing today. We shall be relieved when the present Provost Marshall is relieved.

Paymaster General Fitch [William Fitch, paymaster-general of Connecticut, rank of colonel] and his wife were here today. She is a connection of the Nortons, and a very pleasant lady. I sent home by Col. Fitch an ambrotype that I had taken here today. It is horrid, and Lt. [Chris] Heffelfinger of the 1st Minnesota on Provost duty with me, who had his taken at the same time, swears they are both "awful," and he won't send his home. But to tell the truth, I do look pretty "seedy," as do all the other officers of the 14th.

Our baggage did arrive today, and if the regiment only lays still for a day or two, I will get it, otherwise not. Now for a secret. When the regiment got marching orders, the 17 line officers—which were all who were present—signed a paper peremptorily refusing to move until they got their own and men's baggage. Fortunately I knew nothing about it, being down here on Provost duty. Col. Morris sent word to the officers that it was downright mutiny, and they were liable to the severest penalties. They requested him to return the paper. He replied, "Not until the regiment moves." They all left with the regiment.

I have every thing safe here sent me by Lt. Sherman, who ought to have put them in the Quartermaster's wagon. I shall either hire a donkey to take my baggage with me to the regiment, or else leave it with the regimental baggage, which has just arrived here. I wrote a long letter to the Bulletin last night; it is signed "Omega." I had a long letter from my friend Lieut. Whitaker. Mallory has been promoted to Major.

I have a good pair of shoes and have thrown away my boots as there was no use to mend them.

I have not completely lost faith in McClellan yet, but as to Pope, Bah. He is a blustering, begging liar in my opinion. This army can never serve contentedly under him again.

We join the regiment tomorrow ten miles out. My baggage will be transported.

Yours lovingly, Harry

Norwich Bulletin, **November 5, 1862**

Harper's Ferry, Va., Oct. 30, 1862

Dear Bulletin,

The grand Army of the Potomac is again moving. Division after division are today appearing and disappearing in the narrow streets of this once so beautiful village. Sumner's corps has gone, and with it our regiment, the 14th Connecticut. Being detached from my regiment in charge of a Provost Guard detailed from it, I remain till tomorrow to follow with the Provost Marshall and pick up stragglers. So I have had an opportunity to see the whole movement today.

Among the regiments which passed was the 20th Connecticut, with its full ranks, beautiful banners (the $500 State flag presented by the Governor being much admired) and handsome field and staff officers. Col. [Samuel] Ross is as jolly a man and as strict a soldier as ever. Lieut. Col. Walter and Maj. [Philo B.] Buckingham maintain their urbanity and good looks; and Adjt. Charley Arms (whom I met for the first time since leaving Conn.) giving me a hearty shake of the hand carried me back to Old Norwich. I gave him a Bulletin, which he said was just what he wanted.

Right behind the 20th came Brig. Gen. Thomas L. Kane to whose brigade they are attached. He is a brother of the distinguished Dr. Kane; was Lieut. Col. of the Pennsylvania Bucktails, wounded and taken prisoner at Cross Keys, afterwards paroled, exchanged and made a Brigadier. He has a look a "terrible earnestness," He will hear more from this man.

Then Gen. Couch, now commanding Sumner's corps, rode by, laughing and joking, but mind you, he knows what he is about.

Soon after came our own Fourteenth, with their splendid brass band. Not with the swelled ranks and full knapsacks and happy faces with which they marched through Hartford one day last August. But with thinned ranks, scanty clothing and shot-riddled colors, and stern, sad, but determined faces, and a strong, steady step. Antietam Creek can explain the difference, as can the graves of Blinn [Capt. Jarvis E. Blinn, Company F, killed at Antietam], Willard [Capt. Samuel F. Willard, Company G, killed at Antietam], Crosby [2nd Lt. George H. D. Crosby, Company K, mortally wounded at Antietam], and many more in the quiet sod of your State. The 14th do not murmur at that, but have had some ground to complain of the fact that all their baggage was left at Washington, and that though they have lain idle here five weeks, they have not received it. A portion of it has just arrived here and the rest is expected tomorrow, so if the regiment does not push ahead too fast, it can be got to it.

I have just been enjoying Harper's Ferry by moonlight, have gazed at the view which Thomas Jefferson pronounced "Worth a trip across the Atlantic," (Jefferson's Rock is famous here to this day); have meditated in "John Brown's Engine House," where a Union provost guards rebel prisoners. Oh John Brown, John Brown truly our Norwich poet expressed it when he said that in hanging, you were sowing Dragon's teeth soon to spring up and hiss like vengeful serpents over the fiery South. You are avenged!

Over the ruins of the once magnificent arsenal sad thoughts came over me that treason should have caused all this, but gratitude to the United States officers who by fire prevented so important a possession from falling into the traitors' hands.

The Potomac and Shenandoah glisten in the sheen of the moon ard their gradually rising waters are hailed as a better preventive against Stuart's raids than—must I say it—all our grand army.

Over the rivers of lower Maryland and Loudoun Heights, and again we mourn that treason—at home this time—should have caused the surrender of these almost impregnable heights.

Returning to my headquarters, I hear that some of our secesh prisoners in the room above are anxious to take the oath of allegiance, while all are well satisfied with their treatment as prisoners.

The guard quietly patrol the halls and a comfortable fire burns in our fireplace. We have very nice headquarters here, but the army is moving and tomorrow we shall rejoin our regiment.

Several officers of the 14th are very sick and have or are about to resign on account of their health, as it is almost impossible to get a furlough. We have just heard of the death of 2nd Lieut. Crosby of Lieut. Coit's company from wounds received at Antietam. He was a Christian soldier and brave to rashness. Farewell, comrade. Your memory will be enshrined in our hearts while the memory of this accursed rebellion lasts.

We must prepare to move tomorrow. "On to Richmond this time." Dare we hope it.

Excerpt from *14th C. V.: Regimental Reminiscences of the War of the Rebellion*, by Henry P. Goddard (Middletown, Conn.: C. W. Church, 1877)

Then came the crossing of the Potomac and entrance into Harper's Ferry. How appropriately our band played that day "Away Down South in Dixie" as we entered the river, "Jordan am a hard road to Travel" as we plunged about on the stones and railroad iron with which the bottom of the river was strewn, and "John Brown's Soul is Marching On" as we climbed up the further bank into the historic village. Who will ever forget the miseries of that camp on Bolivar Heights, with the enemies encountered in the deserted tents of D'Utassey's Germans[1] that we dug up and used, and how long a struggle we had with those greybacks, almost as persistent, and hard to get rid of as the Confederates in our front. Here it was that the officers and men of the 14th, destitute of baggage, from red tape negligence that it vexes us to recall even now, used each one to wash his only shirt in the Potomac or Shenandoah, and sit on the bank au naturel, waiting for them to dry (10–11).

1. Col. Frederick d'Utassy commanded a brigade of New York and Illinois troops, many of German descent, on Bolivar Heights above Harpers Ferry. The brigade surrendered to Confederate forces under the command of Gen. Stonewall Jackson on September 15, 1862.

11

Back to Virginia, with a
New Commanding General

The regiment finally gets its marching orders and heads south through Virginia's Loudoun Valley, with the Blue Ridge and the enemy close by to the west, and it gets a new commanding general. "Maj. Gen. McClellan, having been relieved of the command of the Army of the Potomac, we had a grand review from 8 A.M. to 10 A.M., the general riding past us and bowing to the cheering, he was accompanied by his successor, Maj. Gen. Burnside. . . . Curse the politicians who drove him from his place just as his plans were developing," Goddard writes home (89). Increasingly confident of his own military proficiency, he feels "a proud satisfaction that there is now no lieutenant in the regiment I am afraid to drill against." He enjoys a sumptuous Thanksgiving dinner celebration, but contends with a lice infestation and a blinding snowstorm. As the army approaches Fredericksburg, midway between Washington and Richmond, he anticipates "one of the greatest fights of the age. . . . If we win, Richmond is ours. If we lose, we are whipped indeed" (92).

President Lincoln replaced McClellan as commander of the Army of the Potomac with Maj. Gen. Ambrose E. Burnside, who had displayed dogged persistence in the costly taking of "Burnside Bridge" at the battle of Antietam. Impatient with McClellan's slowness to follow up on the success at Antietam and to seize the opportunity to trap and destroy Lee's army before it could recross the Potomac, Lincoln had reputedly told him, "If you don't want to use the army, I should like to borrow it for a while." Burnside told Lincoln that he considered himself unfit to command the army, but Lincoln ignored him. So the general, notable for giving his name to the "sideburns" facial hair style, reorganized the army and secured Lincoln's approval for a new campaign against Richmond.

Near Upperville, Va.

Nov. 5, 1862

Dear Mother,

We left Harpers Ferry Nov. 1, crossed the Shenandoah river, marched a few miles and bivouacked.

Nov. 2nd. Came to the old camp of the 14th where we found Capt. Tubbs with regiment guard, which my detachment of provost guard joined. We then made a long march in the fields all day, and at night came up with the regiment at Snicker's Gap.

It was on this march that I had my simple conversation with [Brig.] Gen. Dan Butterfield [commanding 1st Division of Maj. Gen. Dan Sickles's 5th Corps] of Sickles' corps. I was at the head of our little command of 100 men, Capt. Tubbs in the rear, and we wished to get into the main road, where it was easier marching. But the troops that had the road would give us no chance to get in till I noticed a gap just ahead of Butterfield's division. I called out to Tubbs, "Captain, we will put our men in just ahead of this division," whereat Gen. Butterfield in full uniform, gold sash and all, glanced at me from his stately steed and ejaculated, "Not by a d——d sight, young man." That settled the question and ended our dialog.

Nov. 4th. In bivouack. Lt. Douglas of Middletown, Conn., who with several civilians from Connecticut, has accompanied us from Harpers Ferry, left for home. He was very kind to me. Said the name of "Goddard" was known and respected throughout the state.

Nov. 5th. Heavy picket firing this morning. Burnside is in advance of our regiment. [Brig. Gen. Ludwig] Blenker and his Dutchmen [the mostly German-speaking 11th Corps] on our left. Our army is on the south side of the Blue Ridge; Lee's on the north. We are securing gap after gap to prevent their getting on our flank. Our plan of campaign appears excellent and the "Johnies" will have to fight or fall back on Richmond.

Gen. Couch now commands our corps. You can find Upperville on any map of Virginia. If they won't fight us here it would look as if we must catch and fight them at Port Royal on the Manassas RR., but it looks as if there must be a fight for this gap variously known as Paris, Upperville or Ashby's Gap.

Your loving son, Harry

Near Rectortown, Va.

Nov. 7, 1862

Dear Julia,

We broke camp at 10 A.M. The regiment was detailed as guard to the baggage train and our company deployed as skirmishers. Encamped at night at Rectortown on a pleasant slope. None of my baggage came up and I rolled about the camp fire all night.

Nov. 7. Walked back three miles for my baggage and blankets. Letters from home. Heavy fall of snow (we are in the vicinity of the Blue Ridge Mountains) all day, and the privates suffer in their little shelter tents, but we have a fire in our Sibley and are very comfortable. I bought two pounds of fresh beef of the Brigade Commissary—a really nice Sirloin steak, and with some flour from a neighboring mill had my cook gel me up a fine dinner of steak and hot griddle cakes.

Newspapers follow us everywhere. I have one here published yesterday in Philadelphia. We are pushing towards the Manassas Gap RR only three-fifths of a mile away.

Gladstone M.P tells the truth of us I fear. The New York election is very bad, but it's useless to deny that in the army itself there are many who would accept any kind of peace.[1]

Yours always, Harry

1. William Gladstone, a leading member of the British Parliament, made a speech at Newcastle, England, in October 1862 in which he predicted success for the Confederate States of America as a new nation—a speech for which he later expressed regret. "Peace" Democrats made significant headway in the November 1862 congressional and gubernatorial elections.

Warrenton Junction, Va., Nov. 10, 1862

Having had no chance to mail my letters since the 7th, I will continue.

Journal. Nov. 8th. Broke camp at 8 A.M. and marched through Rectortown, Va., crossing the Manassas Gap R.R. and through Salem, Va., (looks much like Salem, Conn.) And bivouacked two miles beyond the latter town. Had left my blankets in the train, which did not come up and had to sleep on bare ground.

Nov. 9th. Left camp at 8 A.M. and marched 10 miles to Warrenton Junction, the most of a town I have seen in Virginia, and a place of great strategic importance as it is the junction of the roads from Washington and Richmond. Encamped near the town.

Nov. 10th. Maj. Gen. G. B. McClellan, having been relieved of the command of the Army of the Potomac, we had a grand review from 8 A.M. to 10 A.M., the general riding past us and bowing to the cheering, he was accompanied by his successor, Maj. Gen. Burnside.

It was a splendid sight, but a sad day for the Army. Curse the politicians who drove the general from his place just as his plans were developing. I never was a McClennanite till this last campaign, which has been managed splendidly. We have seized and held every gap in the Blue Ridge before him us and got in the rebels rear here at Warrenton, and now he to whom we owe all this is removed.

It is worse than Fremont has ever received. Poor Little Mac, nobly hast thou done and thy name and fame are dear to every American soldier. I tell you that you at home have no idea how his soldiers love that man and how down-hearted they are today. You know I never worshiped the man but I say of him as of Gen. Fremont—it is a shame to remove a general on the eve of battle.

General Sumner is here again in command of his corps. I expect we shall move directly to Richmond without waiting for the rebels to attack us. God grant that we may get there.

Yours ever, H.P. Goddard

P.S. My box has just come from Harpers Ferry. Everything O.K. save the spoiled edibles, and the huckleberry spilled over everything.

Warrenton Junction, Va., Nov. 13th, 1862

Dear Mother,

That smoking tobacco is splendid. Hard at work on our company's books. Hart and Willard left our books in an awful state. (There are four of them.) and as the necessary documents are in the officers' baggage and missing company chests, it is almost impossible to straighten them, but field and staff are poking us up. Lt. Sherman [William J. Sherman, resigned January 23, 1863] lacks confidence and does not take hold as he ought to; he is too considerate of the feelings and position of his men at home and doesn't like to have me "pitch into" them, so that Co. G from being one of the best is getting to be one of the worst in the regiment.

I do wish we had a Captain. Thereon hangs a tale. Last night at dress parade a list of promotions was read. All good appointments save that Lt. [John C.] Broatch[1] Co. B, second ranking 1st Lt., is overslaughed when he is acknowledged to be one of the best officers in the regiment because he is going home on sick furlough, in face of the fact that all the new Captains are on the sick list. 2nd Lt. [James F.] Simpson of Co. C is overslaughed by Lt. [Wilbur D.] Fisk of Co. I.

Broatch is my most intimate friend and I pray heartily that he may yet be our Captain. Simpson is my next friend and he talks of resigning. I hate to form a friendship as all my friends are unfortunate. Lt. Crosby of Co. K was one; he is dead. Lt. Baldwin of Co. E [Charles O. Baldwin, resigned December 19, 1862] was another and he is home on leave very ill. A grand inspection is ordered and I remain here as Officer of the Guard. (I went on last night and am on till 5 P.M.) Gen. [Maj. Gen. Henry] Halleck [general in chief] is said to be here and I presume will review the troops.

As for my military knowledge, I assure you that I feel a proud satisfaction (perhaps it may be conceited) in knowing that there is now no Lieutenant in the regiment I am afraid to drill against. Infantry drill and discipline suit me, so does (soon I won't say that) infantry fighting—for a march, a dash, or picket duty, give me cavalry. I would rather be 1st Lt. of cavalry than Capt. of infantry—above all give me an adjutantcy. Still I am very, very happy—from being ninth in the list of 2nd Lt. I am now fifth.

It's splendid weather—good for a campaign—and I expect marching orders soon, but the fatal Southern winter is upon us and that horrid weather will stop operations.

Hoping and praying that I may be ever ready. I wish love to all, Harry.

P.S. Col. Morris is sick. Col. [Oliver H.] Palmer of the 108th New Jersey commands the brigade. Col. Perkins, Maj. Clark, Capt. Gibbons, and Lts. Sherman, Broatch and Lucas unite in a most unqualified approval of Mother's cookies and return their thanks. Tell Lillie that Lt. Broatch, who is sick and going home on furlough, admires her and her caramels exceedingly. He is handsome, single, and from Middletown.
H.P.G.

1. John C. Broatch was promoted to captain, Company A, January 1, 1863.

Camp at Dellaplain, Va., Nov. 24th, 1862

Dear Mother,

Positively nothing to write since Nov. 21st. We are here doing nothing. Expect to stay a week or so until our forces occupy Fredericksburg. We shall either move into winter quarters at Aquia Creek, or else rejoin our division and on to Richmond—most probably the latter.

If I should be killed it would be almost impossible for you to get my pay as I have never been mustered as a Lieutenant. This red tape is a nuisance. Still I am as happy as any officer here and more so I am now second ranking 2nd Lt.

Harry

Dellaplain, Va., Nov. 25th, 1862

Dear Julia,

There is literally nothing to write about here. Our brigade is in detached service guarding this depot of the army.

As soon as the Aquia Creek R.R. is rebuilt, the depot will be removed to that point and this brigade either sent there for winter quarters or rejoin French's Division and march on to Richmond. The latter I think the most probable, provided our forces take Fredericksburg. That city is 12 miles from here and I expect to hear the cannonading to commence hourly.

The probability is that we won't be engaged in that fight unless the day is against us.

We expect to have a good time Thanksgiving day. Religious exercises in the morning, with music and speeches by Col. Morris and Capt. Davis. In the afternoon we shall have a greased pig, etc. Our dinner, alas, will probably be coffee, fried hard bread and beef. All this provided we are here.

The 8th, 11th, 16th and 21st Connecticut Regiments are all at Falmouth.

Did you get my letter from here of Nov. 21st? If not, let it pass for dead. We were laying in a mud hole in a drenching rain and I was blue.

It seems as if a battle at Fredericksburg has just commenced. 11 A.M. The cannonading is heavy. It will be one of the greatest fights of the age. I am satisfied that if we win, Richmond is ours. If we lose, we are whipped indeed.

Later—the firing has stopped again. What does it mean?

Thank God—Alf is not in the Army. Who would have thought that I could ever have got so used to war as to sit here cooly writing home while a great battle was going on 10 miles away.

Never fear to send provisions. I should have starved but for the last. Next time send bread, crackers, butter, cheese, ham, tea, pickles, cookies. That is, choose from that list.

Lt. [Samuel] Fiske of Co. K ("Owen Brown" is his literary nom de plume) is an excellent man and a good preacher.

The straps came by mail all right. I am ashamed of the McClellanism of my Rectortown. And am glad the Bulletin did not publish it.

And now my darling Sister, I write you the farewell lines. We know not but we may be called into the impending action at any moment and I may not write again for many days. May God give us the victory and guide a poor humble sinner to do his duty and accept his fate, whatever that may be.

Harry

Dellaplain, Nov. 29th, 1862

Dear Mother,

I will continue my journal.

<u>Nov. 26th.</u> Damp, dark, miserable day.

<u>Nov. 27th.</u> Thanksgiving day. Had made preparations for a big supper, but the committee who went for beef, etc. got aground in the Potomac Run and did not arrive till Nov. 28th. I am chairman of committee on preparations for tent tables and decorations, which has been done in style. At 5 P.M. had undress parade. Speeches by Lt. Fiske and Chaplain Stevens. A fine time.

<u>Nov. 28th.</u> Heard of death of Hospital Steward A. Y. Mullen, one of the best Christians I ever knew. When I was on the non-commissioned staff, we were very intimate. He died at Harpers Ferry.

Our company was detailed as permanent guard at the wharf, a half-mile from camp. Moved our tents there. I still eat and sleep in camp, but spend rest of time with Company. Lt. Sherman being on the sick list, I was alone, but Lt. Galpin [Charles W. Galpin, dishonorably discharged December 20, 1863] of Co. A, recently promoted from 1st Sgt Co. B, was detailed as my acting 2nd Lt. He as usual got drunk, made an ass of himself, and was returned to the regiment and placed under arrest. I hope he will be cashiered as he is an habitual drunkard and should never have been promoted.

In the evening we had a grand postponed Thanksgiving supper. Our supper room was two Sibley tents connected by a "fly." The poles were decorated with evergreen, hemlock, laurel, and holly. The Bill of Fare was—

1st course. Salt Beef Soup and hard crackers
2nd course. Roast Turkey, Fresh beef, Chicken, Tea.
3rd course. Cakes, Cheese, Cookies, Apples, Hot Whiskey.

We had a very pleasant time. Col. Perkins was present and everything passed very pleasantly and soberly. Col. Perkins made a speech while Capt. Davis (the life of the 14th) kept us laughing two hours by a humorous narrative of the adventures of the committee of the food. You know every line officer is "dead broke" and many items procured by banter with contrabands; coffee, tea, etc. obtained "by Tick" of the Brigade Commissary, by stealing, by shooting, and by credit at the sutlers.

Nov. 29th. Today is lovely and I sit on the beach of Potomac Run, writing on a barrel head. Gen. Burnside went to Washington yesterday; he is not to blame for the present delay. It is unavoidable that the attacks on Fredericksburg are delayed.

If my health lasts I shall stay in the army till the war ends. My health is not tip-top though don't worry about me. All I mean is that I dread this out of door life in this damp spot if we winter about here.

The box was the best gift I ever had. Our division were sorry to lose Mac. Thought they are willing to try Burnside. Your arguments against Mac are good, but Pope I believe is a gigantic humbug and braggart. Fitz John Porter [major general dismissed from the army following his court-martial relating to Second Bull Run] I always distrusted.

What you say about whiskey is very true. Once in a while I drink it, but not often or immoderately, nor "on the sly." Am glad to hear that Kit has enlisted, also that Charlie Bierne of Springfield, Mass., has gone to war; it will make a man of him.

The tobacco was most acceptable. I smoke much but never chain smoke. Enclosed find a rose picked on the banks of the Potomac Nov. 27th, 1862.

Harry

Dellaplain, Va. Dec. 2nd, 1862

My dear Mother,

As indications are that we shall join our division and the Grand army within 48 hours, I will write you from here where we have facilities that we may not have soon again.

Journal.

<u>Nov. 30th.</u> Bright, clear lovely weather. Boiled and washed all my underclothes and found to my astonishment and horror, that at last following the example of our Surgeon and nearly every line officer, I really am one of the Lousy 14th. It nearly drove me mad with rage. I found after boiling no less than 20 dead "animals" on one shirt. Sic transit.

<u>Dec. 1st.</u> Our company was ordered from guard at the wharf and rejoined the regiment. Got letter from home with a splendid pair of mittens.

<u>Dec. 2nd.</u> Officer of Guard. Now for business a moment. If I am killed, it will be very hard for you to get my pay as Lieutenant as no muster role has been made out since my commission, which you will find in my valise.

Again, me. Sherman and I were together buying articles on credit from the Brigade Commissary. I sign all the orders and have only Sherman's verbal promise (good if we both live) to pay half the amount on pay day when we settle up. If I fall see to this as Uncle Sam will be sure to deduct the amount from my pay.

If I am wounded, send some one to take me home, that is, if it is serious. All I own on earth of pecuniary value, after paying my debts to Mother, my books—to be divided between May and Jule, my sabre, sword, pistols, etc. to be preserved in the family, and my letters burned.

Personally I am well except a slight trouble in my throat and a few visitors, which are daily growing fewer.

Adj't Ellis returned today, as sarcastic, sardonic and Bostonian as ever, he greets me more warmly than he does any line officer. He would die like a Spartan, with a sardonic grin—there's grit in this man. Dr. [Levi] Jewett, 1st Asst. Surgeon, also rejoined us today. So we have two of our Surgeons here now.

Tonight is beautiful with a glorious moon, and in our Sibley with an open fire and chimney, we have just got fairly comfortable. It will be just our luck and I feel sure that we shall move tomorrow for Falmouth.

My text tonight (2nd Corinth.) is consoling and though I do not claim to feel assured of a heavenly hereafter, I feel tonight that I would rather accept a grave than in peace at home break a Mother's heart in evil doing. Mother's arguments have much affected me and I hope I can truly say with her, "Death Before Dishonor."

With much love to all, Harry

Falmouth, Va., Dec. 9th, 1862
Journal

<u>Dec. 4th.</u> Wrote the Norwich Bulletin.

<u>Dec. 5th.</u> Rainy, snowy, dreary. Charles Smith, a private, died in a fit. This is the seventh man we have lost therein. Sent all their bodies home, except that of one killed at Antietam that we never found.

<u>Dec. 6th.</u> Our Brigade was relieved at Dellaplain and started in the mud to rejoin the division at Falmouth. We had a hard march and reached Falmouth at 4 P.M. Encamping in the snow some two miles back of my old camp of the Harris Light last spring, but far different are the surroundings of this winter day to that of the lovely spring we had here then. The rest of the division have been here long enough to build good huts and have got all the dry wood long since—so we have today to burn green wood.

<u>Dec. 7th.</u> Very, very cold and the smoke from the wet pine was so terrible all over the camp that its effect added to that of the blinding glare from the snow was such that I never suffered such agony in all my life. My eyes felt as if full of needles, and in sheer despair I would at times dig up the snow till I reached the earth on which I would fasten my eyes till I could get a brief respite from pain. The whole regiment is suffering in the same manner as myself. Letters from home were the only cheer I had today.

<u>Dec. 8th.</u> A little better weather. Began laying out a new camp and building log huts for the night.

<u>Dec. 9th.</u> Pleasant. Our "contraband," a hair-lipped darkey, was so badgered and frightened by some of the new tales of how the Johnies would treat him if captured that he ran away last night and I had to do our own cooking today while Sherman superintended the projects of the new camp.

I did some work on the company books. Notwithstanding we have had orders from Headquarters to prepare log huts, etc., everything indicates a speedy advance on Fredericksburg. Col. Bob Tyler, who is now here with two batteries of the 1st Conn. Heavy artillery, says we shall have a fight in 48 hours. If so it will be a second Bridge of Lodi[1] for whatever army tries to cross the Rappahannock, with the opposing batteries as now posted, has got to do it in the face of the most terrific stream of shot and shell. God grant that we may all say "ever ready."

<u>Dec. 10th.</u> I was sent out with a wood chopping detachment as Col. Perkins has decided to keep on erecting huts until ordered to move. Maj. John Ward of Norwich of the 8th C. V. called to see his brother Fred [First Lieutenant Frederick B. Hawley] of my Co. The 15th and 27th C. V. have just joined this army and we have near us the 8th, 11th, 15th, 16th, 21st, and 27th. Our new Capt. of Co. G (Seymour) joined us today, but has not yet decided whether to accept the promotion or return to his 1st Lieutenancy of Co. C. [Frederick J. Seymour promoted to captain November 12, 1862, but not mustered. Discharged December 24, 1862.] F. M. Hale of Norwich is here to see his son Lt. [Morton F., Company E] Hale.

Yours, Harry

1. The bridge stormed by Napoleon Bonaparte's victorious French army in 1796 in the face of intense Austrian artillery during the First Italian campaign.

Norwich Bulletin, December 11, 1862

"From the Fourteenth Regiment"

Dellaplain, Va., Dec. 3, 1862

Dear Bulletin,

It is said that a calm always precedes a storm. It is probably this deceptive calm now prevailing about here that gives me hardly an item of importance from the Fourteenth, and the Army of the Potomac, or of the Rappahannock, if more proper.

The grand army lies at Falmouth gazing across the narrow Rappahannock at the rebel grand army in Fredericksburg. McDowell's old headquarters, the splendid Lacy mansion, is now the headquarters of the Eighth Connecticut. The pickets of both armies daily converse across the narrow river, and every morning the smoke of over one hundred thousand camp fires rises to Heaven from both sides of the river. Today an immense army of men eat, drink, and are merry on each side. Tomorrow may find thousands engaged in deadly combat, and ere night the blood of hundreds may be crying to God.

The Eighth, Eleventh, Sixteenth and Twenty-first Connecticut Regiments lie at Falmouth. The Fourteenth, with the rest of Col. Morris' brigade, is on guard duty at this depot of army supplies, but expect to join the main army very soon.

All things indicate the near approach of the third great attempt to "On to Richmond." Our wagon trains are being cut down, and we are notified that we shall receive no mail for three weeks. The feeling in the army is, "Let's have the thing done with. Better fight it out now even if we get whipped, than prolong this infernal war any longer." But we don't mean to be whipped, though.

The Fourteenth had a very pleasant time on Thanksgiving day, and on the Friday evening following (our arrangements for Thanksgiving being broken up by unavoidable circumstances), our line officers had a grand Thanksgiving supper. The tent and table were decorated with evergreen and holly. The bill of fare embraced chicken, turkey, roast beef, cakes, apples, and all the delicacies of the season. Altogether we had a very nice time.

Among the recent promotions in the Fourteenth is that of First Sergeant James E. Nichols of Norwich, of Company E, to be second lieutenant of Company I. The promotion will no doubt be as gratifying to his friends at home as it was to his friends here.

Capt. Tubbs has been quite ill, but is getting better. Lieut. Hale is still on Gen. [Maj. Gen. William H.] French's staff and is as hearty and happy as ever. We are hoping soon to see Capt. James B. Coit, recently promoted, back with his company [Company K].

Excerpt from *14th C. V.: Regimental Reminiscences of the War of the Rebellion*, by Henry P. Goddard (Middletown, Conn.: C. W. Church, 1877)

In our next change of base what a view that was from Snicker's Gap, with the campfires of both armies in view as they raced down each side of the Blue Ridge, in route to the Rappahannock.

Who was there will ever forget that Thanksgiving dinner at Belleplain, held the day after Thanksgiving, owing to the fact that the foraging committee—Capts. [Samuel H.] Davis, [Isaac R.] Bronson and [Samuel W.] Carpenter—got the little boat, in which they had gone out, stuck in the mud and had to go ashore across the creek, and wait twelve hours, till Capt. Bronson could lighten her by eating half her cargo of mutton and persimmons. The bill of fare of that dinner was mutton broth, roast mutton, roast duck, and hard tack, with Sprenkle's jumbles, persimmons and hot whiskey punch for dessert. Sergt. [Samuel] Webster was caterer as usual, drank more punch and told more unmatchable stories than anyone else.

What a day it was when we marched back to Falmouth in a blinding snowstorm, and pitched our camp in a lot where the wood was so green and wet that it was almost impossible to get any fires started (11).

12

Disaster and Heroism at Fredericksburg

Goddard describes the brave crossing of the Rappahannock by the 7th Michigan, and the devastating pillaging and bombardment of Fredericksburg before the battle. He describes the hopeless charge up the strongly fortified Marye's Heights, where he was wounded in the leg, saved by his canteen, and where his heroism saved the life of Lt. Col. Sanford H. Perkins, his regimental commander. Of the 300 members of the regiment before the battle, he said 125 reported for duty, and "men who will come in will probably swell the number to 200. . . . So much for the brave 14th C.V., which not more than 15 weeks ago left the state 980 strong. Two field and 15 line officers went into the fight and only four came out unhurt" (105, 104). He writes that "this useless massacre of men has disgusted me with Burnside. He is a dead lion. . . . The army is pretty badly demoralized now and all of us say a good many hard things of our commanders, of the prospect of the endless war, of disgust with fighting to free the Negro, etc." (104–5). However, Goddard's short report of the battle to the *Norwich Bulletin* is matter of fact and does not reveal the pessimism of his letters to his family.

Instead of continuing to move south toward Richmond from the Warrenton area toward Culpeper as Lee expected, Burnside shifted his army to Falmouth, across the Rappahannock River from Fredericksburg, where it could be more easily supplied. Burnside's plan was to cross the river and take Fredericksburg before Lee caught on, but a bureaucratic snafu delayed the arrival of pontoon bridges. By the time the army had crossed the river, under heavy fire, Lee's army was firmly dug in on Marye's Heights overlooking Fredericksburg. Burnside nevertheless decided to proceed with his attack. The result was a massacre, as Union infantry charged up the long slope into a firestorm of musketry and artillery fire. When the first assault failed, Burnside ordered five more, reminiscent of his strategy at "Burnside Bridge" at Antietam. However, the assault on heavily-fortified Marye's Heights was a futile disaster, and by the end of the day twelve thousand Union soldiers had fallen. Lee lost fewer than five thousand troops. Two days later Burnside retreated with his battered army back across the Rappahannock.

~

Excerpts from *History of the Fourteenth Regiment, Connecticut Vol. Infantry,* by Charles D. Page (Meriden, Conn.: Horton Printing Co., 1906)

The morning of the 13th was foggy and the position of the enemy could not be seen nor our own guns on the opposite side of the river. It was generally rumored in the regiment that it would be the Second Brigade that would attack the stronghold of the Confederates. This was no mistake. About nine o'clock the regiment was suddenly ordered to fall in and obeyed, leaving their half cooked salt beef on the fire. They marched to Princess Anne Street and halted between the church and court house, the former of which was used as a hospital and the latter as a signal station. . . .

The regiment was here ordered to prime and fix bayonets. Shells came crashing down into the city, tearing down brick walls and scattering death and destruction around. One would fall amid a group of men, burst with noise, and in a few moments pale and mangled forms with bloody garments would be carried by in silence. The regimental officers here dismounted and sent their horses back over the river. At noon "Forward Fourteenth" was again the word and they moved down the street, some times on the double quick, to the depot, turning square to the right on to one of the only two bridges by which they could cross the canal and gain the plain in front of the enemy's position. The firing of a dozen rebel guns came to a focus on each of these two points. Lieutenant-Colonel Perkins ran on foot at the head of the regiment cheering the men by his voice and example. The path was narrow and uneven and the ranks a little disordered. Across the causeway they filed and to the right near a stone wall, behind which a number of wounded lay. Some of the faces were already white with the strange pallor of death though it was but so lately that the fight had commenced. Still on and on, out into the open field under the full fire of the enemy's guns. Here the regimental line was reformed and the men ordered to lie down. While lying here several shells burst directly over the left wing of the regiment, causing much suffering in their ranks. . . . Soon the order came to rise and move forward again on the double-quick. This brought the regiment to the very front just under the heights occupied by the enemy's artillery and very close to the sunken road in which were posted the rebel infantry.

Chaplain H. S. Stevens in his "Souvenir of the Fourteenth Regiment" [1893], says concerning this moment:—"Into a 'slaughter pen' indeed, were the men going, but with brave hearts they pushed forward, the officers cheering them on. Soon they filed to the right by a half wheel, for this road was far to the left of the point to be charged, until the line came under the partial shelter of a slight mound, and formed to the left of Andrews. . . . The guns on Taylor's Hill fairly enfiladed the position doing deadly work, particularly at the left of the regiment, as they did in the 10th New York near. It was a moment when men's hearts are stricken with a dreadful expectancy, for the outlook was horrible. [Brig. Gen. Nathan] Kimball's veterans were ordered on, and bracing for the fray, they made their straight, fierce rush at the stone wall, only to be hurled back by the leaden storm flung out at them by tiers of musketry as barks are beaten back by raging gales. Then [Brig. Gen. George] Andrews' brave fellows were ordered up to the charge to meet a similar fate. There was a rush, a cheer, a crash of musketry with a tempest of bullets driven straight at their breasts, and the lines dissolved, stragglers or clusters firing here and there, but chiefly dropping upon the ground to be exposed as little as possible. Then the Second Brigade ["Irish Brigade," 2nd Brigade, 1st Division, 2nd Corps, commanded by Brig. Gen. Thomas F. Meagher] was ordered 'up and at 'em.' Ah, that charge! A few rods brought the line to the flat ground directly in front of the old 'Fair Grounds,' indicated at that time by some remaining tall posts and some high boards clinging here and there to the rails. Here Colonel Perkins shouted his last command to the Fourteenth. He dashed ahead and his brave boys followed. A few rods over ground every foot of which was lashed by artillery, and the leveled guns on the direful wall[,] coolly waiting[,] spoke out in unison terrific" (81–85).

The loss to the regiment was killed, 1 commissioned officer, 9 enlisted men; wounded, 10 commissioned officers, 82 enlisted men; missing, 20 enlisted men; total loss, 122 (95).

Captain Elijah W. Gibbons, of Company B . . . when the new call for troops was made, . . . speedily enlisted a full company of the young men of Middletown. Henry P. Goddard, afterwards captain of Company B, says of him:—"A personal pride in dear old 'B' Company doubtless affects my judgment, but I think no survivor of the regiment but will agree with me that no company in the regiment, all things considered, ever looked or did much better. And this was owing to one man more than any other, and that man was Elijah W. Gibbons. From the time the regiment left Hartford until his mortal wound, he was never absent from his company a day. He led them gallantly at Antietam where, by a quick flank movement of his company, he enabled the regiment to capture a large posse of rebels in the famous Roulette house. At Fredericksburg he was advancing courageously with the regiment when a rebel ball shattered his thigh, and he fell. He was picked up by the men who loved him so dearly, and conveyed to the Falmouth side of the river, where he lingered in great suffering, but sweet resignation, for six days, until the 19th of December, when he died" (98; citing Goddard's *Memorial of Deceased Officers of the Fourteenth Regiment, Connecticut Volunteers,* 1872).

Fredericksburg, Va., Sunday, Dec. 14, 1862

My Dear Mother,

I am here in hospital, in the once elegant residence of a Mr. Gardiner, slightly wounded in the upper part of the left leg. It is a mere scratch. I can walk about and offer assistance to the other wounded here, but shall not be able to march again for five or six days as my leg is too stiff. I have the bullet that hit me in my pocket; it only cut to the flesh about one-half inch deep and then fell out. My canteen has two bullet holes through it, my overcoat one hole made by a piece of shell, one by a buck shot and one by the bullet that hit me with a compounding hole in my blouse, pants and drawers. Don't be anxious on my account as I shall be well in a week.

Now then for my journal with full account to date:

Dec. 10th, Regiment inspected by Lt. Col. Perkins in afternoon. Went out this same PM on picket to a glorious spot. Read letters from Mother of Dec. 5th and two papers.

Dec. 11th, At 4 AM we were ordered in from picket and at 6 AM started to take part in the siege of Fredericksburg. We left our camp tents standing. My valise, maps, chest and blankets are all there with one of the wagoners. Just note this. You may have to remember it if we do not return to that camp.

We marched down to the railroad near the Lacy Mansion[1] and there rested all day while our artillery shelled the city so that we could lay the pontoon bridge. The rebels did not reply with artillery, but had a brigade of infantry in the cellars of the city who kept picking off our men trying to lay the pontoon. After numerous ineffectual attempts, at 6 PM the 7th Michigan, disgusted at the delay, jumped into the pontoon boats and, pushing them across the river under terrible fire, gained the other shore, formed, charged up the hill and drove the rebels out of the lower streets. The 17th Massachusetts followed, then laid the bridges and, taking their colors, charged through the city. Howard's Division then crossed, when the rebs threw one shell over near our Division, when we bivouacked for the night about one-half mile from the river. The troops on the other side drove the rebs out of their cellars, some regiments bayoneting every cursed sharpshooter they found. At 10 PM we held the whole city when there was an order to pillage the city, which was done so thoroughly that $500,000 will not cover the damage. The 27th Connecticut lay near us all day. They are in Hancock's Division of our Corps.

Dec. 12th: At 6 AM our Division crossed and at 8 AM we formed a line in Caroline Street, rested all day, while the remainder of the Right Grand Division[2] crossed the river. The enemy threw shells at the bridge all day, two of which burst among us, wounding three of our regiment. The city was thoroughly pillaged that day in a manner beyond description. Every house and store in the city bears the marks of our terrific bombardment, and is riddled so thoroughly it will cost millions to restore the city to its former beauty. Dead and wounded rebs lay everywhere and every house and store has been ransacked. The boys are all eating pickles, preserves, hams, flour cakes, etc., out of silver, glass and china, smoking 10 cent cigars and $2 per pound tobacco, stuffing their pockets with chewing tobacco valued at $1.50 per plug and reclining on sofas, reading from private libraries.

I cannot begin to describe the scene. Imagine Norwich shelled, full of dead and wounded and everything you hold most dear scattered in the streets, and you will have some idea of Fredericksburg as it is today.

Friday night the enemy rested in houses along the line of battle formed at morning. We have gone into the riddled homes for quarters for the night. We are reading the Bible together.

Earlier I went over the river with 100 men to draw rations for the regiment, returning to sleep on a feather bed.

Dec. 13th: The proudest day in Harry Goddard's life.

What I write of today, you will excuse because I am so situated that I must be egotistical. I don't mean to blow but to tell the plain truth about the battle of Fredericksburg so far as the 14th C. V. is concerned. At 8 AM we marched up and rested in line near the church. The battle had already begun just in rear of the town and several shells struck near us. Lt. Simpson of Co. C was stunned by one of them. We then marched down the street and halted in front of Gen. [Maj. Gen. Darius N.] Couch, who gave Gen. French his orders. French did not like the orders. I heard him expostulate with Couch but to no avail. Then we filed down through the depot and here the shells began to fall lively and the men began to skedaddle. Some of my own men ran away here, but not many. (I recall seeing one of our light batteries trying to get into position behind the depot, but the horses were almost instantly killed and guns dismounted so as to be of no service.) Then across the railroad to the right, under a fence where lots more hid in a ditch. Then a turn to the left and up a hill where the brigade formed and lay under a fence protected by a rough old brick-work of some sort. Here we were under a cross fire from two batteries and the shells did fall lively enough.

Their artillery had it all their own way and ours could get no position and in short we had no artillery on our side all day, save what few shots were fired by our batteries on the other side of the river. Col. [Oliver H.] Palmer of the 108th N. Y. V. was in command of our brigade, (Col. Morris being sick at Falmouth!)

Here we lay some time when we were ordered to "About Face" and marched back and lay down on another hill to let the Irish Brigade charge over us—which they did in style. Men were now pouring on to the field by thousands, and I found a skedaddler from a Madison Company of the 27th C. V.—forced him into our company where he did good service. Then we rose up, ran back to our former position, when our gallant Lieutenant Colonel Perkins drew his sword and gave the order "Forward."

We started up and away—over the hill, over fences, over ditches, up to the extreme front where rebel bullets falling like hail were sounding the death rattle of many (ah! so many) noble Union soldiers. Here we halted and poured forth volley after volley at the infernal cowards hidden in their breastworks. The grape and cannister were mowing our men down in swaths. Shells actually crushed the bones of men like glass. After ten minutes or a little more, I observed that my company had melted away, not a man of them to be found. Capt. Gibbons was no where near and I looked round to see our color bearers running back and all the troops just starting to leave. I hesitated a moment, but saw Col. Perkins wave his sword and cry "Fall in," "Form in order," "Don't go back!" I swung my sword up and shouted "Form," "Form here," "Don't run!" But could see none of our regiment save three or four of Co. B. The whole army had commenced to run like blazes. I turned again to the Colonel to see him struck in the neck and to catch him as he fell.

I grasped and waved my sword, shouted and screamed "For God's sake, come back 14th, come and save your Colonel." Three of Co. B came and that was all the regiment left there. The Colonel begged us to carry him off the field, when we pledged our lives to him to save him, or die, or be taken with him. We bore him a few yards when a bullet struck me in the leg and I looked for somebody to relieve me in carrying him, when I found one of Co. E.

Thus relieved I ran at a skedaddler in a ditch (from a New Jersey regiment I believe) and told him he must help carry our Colonel or I would run him through. He did so and we bore him safely to a house near the depot, where I found plenty of the 14th to make reliefs to carry him. I was now quite faint, and resting on Lt. Nichols of Co. I and private [Alson A.] Kelsey of Co. G, we accompanied the bearers of the Colonel off the field down to the hospital near the river. Here we laid him down in the parlor of the house where I now write and Dr. [Philo G.] Rockwell dressed his wounds. I went out on the back stoop and examined my own, to find it a mere scratch, requiring nothing but bandages and application of water, which Lt. Nichols applied.

In a few moments Dr. Rockwell came out to dress my wounds, having been ordered by the Colonel to do so. I showed him it was nothing but a scratch, and he told me to keep quiet, and he re-dressed and re-bandaged it. In a few moments Corp. Hart of my company came in and told me that he feared Corp. Fred Ward was dead as he saw him lying on the field and asked if he was wounded. Ward said, "Yes." "Badly?" inquired Hart. Poor Ward grit his teeth and said, "Tell them I was not afraid." Since then I have heard nothing of the dear boy, whom I had learned to love, but have strong hopes that he may be in some of the hospitals. Don't tell his people that he may be dead, but when they find out, tell them that he was a noble Christian patriot. I loved him as a brother.

In a few moments Hart came out and said the Colonel was speaking very highly of me to the night surgeons and men there. By the by I went in to see him. Lying there bleeding at the neck, with the Sgt. Major joining him, he grasped my hand and said, "Goddard, you are the man. You stuck by me. You were clear to the front rallying our brave boys. God bless you, Goddard. Oh my poor boys. I saw them wounded and dying on the field. Oh my poor boys, how they butchered them. My brave boys, how they fought. Oh, my God, my God. Where is the Major and Capt. Gibbons? (Alas both are wounded and Gibbons left on the field.) Goddard, were you hurt bringing off your Colonel, poor boy? Oh, all my poor boys!"

For the first time since I left home I cried like a child to see my dear brave Colonel, he there fearing he must die. Oh my God, what a horrible thing war is. All the afternoon shot and shell fell around the hospital and the cries of "Doctor, doctor" and "Water, water" are too pitiable. I am ashamed of my scratch when I see some such horrible ghastly wounds. At night the firing ceased and I made a comfortable bed of two bundles of blankets I picked up coming off the field. Half I gave poor Lt. [William A.] Comes who is wounded much worse than I am. (Died soon after)

We held our ground in front today. Capt. Davis of Co. H is in command of what is left of our regiment and has gathered all told 104 men. If we could lay still a week, the number may be brought up to 225, not more. So much for the brave 14th C.V., which not more than 15 weeks ago left the state 980 strong. Two field and 15 line officers went into the fight and only four came out unhurt.

Dec. 14th, I am still here rendering all the assistance I can but I am pretty stiff. Hope to be sent across the river soon so that I can get my things at our old camp. There has been no firing today but the battle has got to be fought and won.

Thank God for my preservation, praying Him for victory.

I am

Your loving son Harry Goddard

Dec. 15th I am safe in our old camp at Falmouth. All our wounded are brought over, or have evacuated.

1. The Lacy Mansion was a brick plantation house located on high ground in Fredericksburg near the battle. During the battle it was used as a hospital to treat wounded 2nd Corps soldiers. Clara Barton was among those who tended to the needs of the wounded there. It is now part of Fredericksburg National Military Park.

2. Maj. Gen. Ambrose Burnside, assuming command of the Army of the Potomac on November 7, 1862, streamlined the army's organization by partitioning it into thirds that he named "grand divisions." Burnside's orders called for Maj. Gen. William B. Franklin's Left Grand Division to roll up Gen. Stonewall Jackson's corps, after which Maj. Gen. Edwin V. Sumner's Right Grand Division, including the 2nd Corps, would advance against Marye's Heights to the north. An initially successful advance by Franklin's troops was reversed by

Jackson's counterattack that routed the Union troops, but Sumner nevertheless was directed to press his attack against the heavily fortified heights.

Letter from Julia Goddard to her brother Alfred Mitchell Goddard

Dec. 15th

Dear Alf,

In great haste I have copied Harry's letter which reached us yesterday. It will relieve your anxiety concerning him. Capt. Tubbs of the 14th arrived in town yesterday; he was slightly wounded and came home, but Harry would not quit his post. The dear boy behaved splendidly they all say—the last to leave the field, he brought his Colonel with him. Harry, though only 2nd Lieut., has been in command of his company for some time.

French [Maj. Gen. William French, commanding 3rd Division, 2nd Corps] took 7,000 men into the fight in his Division and brought out 2,000.

God bless you,

Your loving sister, Julia G. Piatt

<u>Dec. 15th</u>: Sunday our corps lay idle, and Monday morning the wounded were carried over to the hospitals in Falmouth—those lightly wounded back to the old camp here, and Monday night the whole division was ordered back to its old headquarters at Falmouth, as it is almost totally demoralized, and it will take some time to reorganize it.

Norwich Bulletin, December 26, 1862
"From the Fourteenth Regiment"

Falmouth, Dec. 16, 1862

Dear Bulletin: Again the Fourteenth Regiment has been through a fiery ordeal; again it has done its duty well and nobly; again are its recently patched colors riddled with shot and shell; again it has lost brave men by scores, and today it gathers together at this spot where it started eager for the fray, numbering about one hundred and twenty-five men all told. Men who will come in will probably swell the number to two hundred, which is the maximum that we hope to report for duty for some months to come. The regiment numbered some 300 before the battle.

The regiment left camp here at 6 o'clock A.M., the 11th. All that day we lay near the Lacy mansion, watching the terrific bombardment of the city of Fredericksburg by our artillery. About sunset all efforts to lay the pontoon bridge having failed, the Seventh Michigan Regiment (may it be forever honored) jumped into the pontoon boats and pushed across the river under a terrific fire from the enemy's sharpshooters concealed in the city. They formed on the other bank, and charging up the hill, cleared the path. Other regiments followed, and soon a whole division had crossed, and after a running street fight cleared the city of rebels. The rest of the army bivouacked for the night on the Falmouth side.

Friday we crossed at dawn, and forming a line in Caroline Street, rested during the whole day, while the remainder of the Right Grand Division crossed. The enemy threw shells at the bridge all day, two of which burst among us, wounding three of our regiment. The city was thoroughly pillaged that day in a manner beyond description. Every house and store in the city bears marks of shells, and is riddled so thoroughly that it will cost millions to restore the city to its former beauty. Friday night the army rested in houses along the line of battle formed at morning.

Saturday, Dec. 13th, we fell in at an early hour and marched down Main Street, filed through the depot where shot and shell began to fall, and the skedaddlers to be taken suddenly sick. Then we marched up to an old earthwork where we began to catch the humming bullets. Here we lay while the Irish brigade charged over us. Then our gallant Lieutenant Colonel drew his sword and gave the order "Forward." Then on, on, over the hill, over fences, over ditches, up to the extreme front where rebel bullets falling like hail where sounding the death knell of many (ah! so many!) noble Union soldiers. Here we halted and poured forth volley after volley at the infernal cowards hidden in their breastworks.

Alas it was useless; we had no artillery support to silence their batteries for us to charge up the hill, and the grape and cannister were mowing down our men in swaths. To advance was hopeless and the order to retreat was given. The whole corps commenced to fall back. Colonel Perkins shouted: "Form in, don't go back." There was a pause. We looked at the Colonel. The boys fired one more volley in the direction that his extended sword pointed, but it was too late. Just then two shots struck the colonel and he fell. He was born off the field by some of those on the left to a hospital, and then we began to count up the dead and wounded. Our division was relieved and the scattered regiments formed near the river.

Sunday our corps lay idle, and Monday morning the wounded were carried over to the hospitals in Falmouth—those lightly wounded back to the old camp here, and Monday night the whole division was ordered back to its old headquarters at Falmouth, as it is almost totally demoralized, and it will take some time to reorganize it.

We went into the fight with two field and sixteen line officers. The following are the casualties among them as far as ascertained:

Lieut. Colonel Perkins, two bullet wounds in the neck, serious; Major Clark, severe contusion of a shell in side; Capt. Gibbons, Company B, in hip, dangerously; Second Lieut. Canfield, Company B, killed; Capt. Carpenter, bullet in left heel, severe; Second Lieut. Simpson, Company C, slightly bruised by explosion of a shell; Capt. Tubbs, Company E, struck by piece of shell in neck and shoulder, slightly; First Lieut. Stanley, Company F, ball through left lung, dangerous; Second Lieut. Comes, Company F, two bullet wounds in hip and thigh, dangerous; Second Lieut. Goddard, Company G, bullet wound in left leg, slight; First Lieut. Lee, Company H, bruised in shoulder by piece of shell; Capt. Bronson, Company I, several severe bruises; Second Lieut. Hawley, Company K, in right heel by bullet, slight.

Capt. Tubb's Company has nine wounded; none from Norwich. Capt. Coit's Company has some half-dozen wounded and missing. Private Nelson J. Beaumont of Norwich, of this Company, is slightly wounded in the leg. Capt. Fred Ward, of Company G., brother of Major Ward, of the Eighth, and a noble little patriot, was seen wounded on the field, and has not since been heard from. We hope, however, he is in one of the numerous hospitals in Falmouth.

What is to be the next move we know not, but only know that this regiment cannot be got together and be properly armed, equipped and officered for some time to come. Capt. Davis, of New London, is in command of the battalion.

Yours ever, Omega

Falmouth, Va., Dec. 17th, 1862

My Darling Mother,

Safe back in our old camp, I resume my Journal.

The night of Dec. 14th, I spent in a hospital pretty lame. I had an opportunity yesterday to save some things from being stolen from the old home of Capt. Herndon, the U.S. Officer who died so grandly at his post (years before the war) while in command of the Steamer "Central America" or "George Law." You remember how I always admired the story.

I ran off the would-be pillagers and had the family property protected by a guard. I think the sword was saved. I certainly hope so. I remember that when here with McDowell's army in May last, the prettiest woman in Fredericksburg was his niece, Miss Belle Herndon. I hope she is safe. I suppose she must have left the city before the bombardment, as did most of the inhabitants.

<u>Dec. 15th.</u> Early in the morning, was ordered across the river with other wounded. Crossed the pontoon bridge and finding no other accommodations, Capt. Tubbs and I, after a toilsome march, found our way to our old camp, which we reached about 5 P.M. and rested. About 11 P.M. the regiment came in under Capt. Davies, the city having been evacuated. The Siege of Fredericksburg and this useless massacre of men has disgusted me with Burnside. He is a dead lion. Gen. Sumner we think "the bull in a china shop" that Phil Kearny[1] is said to have termed him.

It is said that Gen. French refused to order our division to go on the field and is under arrest.[2] Certainly we had no orders on the field from any general officer, and Howard [Maj. Gen. Oliver O. Howard, commanding 2nd Division, 2nd Corps] was the only one I saw after we passed the depot. He was fearlessly exposing himself.

The army is pretty badly demoralized now and all of us say a good many hard things of our commanders, of the prospect of an endless war, of disgust with fighting to free the Negroes, etc.

Dec. 16th. A good mail from home.

Dec. 17th. Capt. J. H. Piatt visited me in camp. He is now on Sigel's staff. Lt. Sherman is quite sickly with fever. This leaves the orderly Sgt. in command of the Co. as Capt. [Frederick] Seymour resigned without ever having assumed command and Capt. Tubbs has got a leave of absence and gone home. Poor Fred Ward I fear is dead as I can get no report of him in any hospital.

So even Jon abandons Gen. Pope. I even prefer Fitz John Porter. "Not much fighting this winter" as Jon predicted on Dec. 8th. Lo! I should say <u>not</u> with this little bullet in my pocket and a game leg received since Jon wrote Burnside had gone to Richmond, with a vengeance this time.

Thank Jon, dear Mother. Even as you prayed Dec. 13th and then wrote, God saved your Son.

Harry

1. Maj. Gen. Phil Kearney was killed at Chantilly, Virginia, September 1, 1862, during the second Bull Run / Manassas campaign.

2. Evidently a false rumor.

Excerpt from *14th C. V.: Regimental Reminiscences of the War of the Rebellion*, by Henry P. Goddard (Middletown, Conn.: C. W. Church, 1877)

What a day it was when we marched back to Falmouth in a blinding storm, and pitched our camp in a lot where the wood was so green and wet that it was almost impossible to get any fires started.

Then came that great day at Fredericksburg, of which a London Times' correspondent, who sat by Gen. Lee's side and watched the charges of the 2nd Corps, wrote that "no men on earth could be braver than those who thrice essayed to carry Marye's Heights." The vacancies in our ranks that night, alas, never to be filled, attest to the truth of his assertion.

It was while waiting to charge these heights that Capt. Townsend was first to descry a balloon ascending from our army headquarters at Falmouth, across the Rappahannock, and, noting that a rebel gun was turned upon it, shouted "they are firing at the balloon." "Good God," said Davis. "Townsend is afraid they were firing at the balloon. I should think *somebody* was firing at *us*." As we were at the time under a terrific fire, the point of the joke was clearly seen, and in the face of impending death a shout of laughter went down the ranks.

A moment later the order came to charge, and there was no laughter then, but grave, earnest faces, as we attempted to scale those heights, under a cross fire of grape and cannister that actually crushed the bones of men, like glass. Here young [1st Lt. Theodore A.] Stanley and [2nd Lt. David E.] Canfield were killed, and Capt. Gibbons—who the night before read to us out of a Bible found in the city— and poor [2nd Lt. William A.] Comes were mortally wounded. What a picture was that when our gallant Lt. Col. Perkins fell at the head of his command, where with drawn sword he was crying, "Forward 14th." He wound was a bad one, but not fatal, and it was a singular coincidence that two of those who bore him off the field (Capt. [William] Murdock and the writer) were bearers at his funeral in New Britain just twelve years later.

Reminiscences of this battle alone would take more time than I have for the story of the whole of our term of service. But the fact that fifteen out of eighteen officers and fully fifty percent of the men engaged were killed or wounded, tells the story of that day, of which Gen. French remarked as we came off the field that it was a "—— hot day for the 13th of December."

How strange it was to note that all through the battle, the tomb of Mary, mother of Washington, was uninjured by shot or shell, and was even the resort of a few snow birds, who seemed to mind the great strife about them as little as the dead woman there buried (11–12).

Letter from Julia Goddard to her brother Henry P. Goddard

Sunday, Dec. 21st, 62

Harry My Dear Boy,

How is that stiff leg tonight and how the brave soldier boy standing on it? We always valued your letters, my boy, but never was one of them so thankfully received, so proudly read and so thoroughly enjoyed as that one you wrote in Fredericksburg on the 14th and which reached us Friday. I was down town when the mail came in, hoping for yours. The mail brought yours of the 14th and I jumped into a Hack and rode up to bring yours to Mother, for walking was too slow. You may believe that Mother, May, and we all were glad to get it. You may know too sir that we are all immensely proud of it. Uncle Lou says "the Boy is a brick." Mother says, "God help him." May's eyes fill with tears as she says "He is splendid!" To it all I say Amen—God help him—as I told you the other day, you are the Hero of the hour, everybody inquires after you, half the town has been here to give you the kindest messages. The wounded Lieut. who would not quit his post reflects honor upon his mother and sisters at home.

Mrs. H. B. Norton came in to hear your letter—everybody wants to hear it. I copied it yesterday for Alf G. and sent it by the California mail of yesterday.

I went down to see Capt. Tubbs yesterday. Tubbs said his wound is not much and it does not seem to be, but he is sick otherwise. He has a shocking cough. He gives a grand account of you, my boy, and I enjoyed talking with some one who had just come from you.

One thing dear Harry, I am sure you have earned promotion and I think your sticking to your post when others slightly wounded have left for home will ensure it to you. Oh my boy, when I think of your marvelous escape in that fatal field, I bow down in thankfulness to God for his mercy to us—you came literally "back from the jaws of death."

Mother and May are both writing you. You must send me word if you want anything sent to you and how. There's a suit of clothes already for you and a pair of boots, which I will send anytime that you are sure of receiving them.

Your loving sister, Julia

Letter from Lt. Col. Sanford H. Perkins to Lieut. Henry P. Goddard

Wolcottville, January 21st, 1863

My dear Goddard,

I have been contemplating writing you for some time and should have done so before this, had I not been called upon to answer numerous letters received from my friends in the State—but as the saying is—better late than never. I am improving so far as wounds are concerned; my shoulder is very lame yet. I would like to see you all. We are having today a severe and cold windy snow storm. I hope it does not extend to the Army of the Potomac.

I desire Lieut. to thank you in more than usual manner and also to express to you my admiration of your conduct amid the thundering of artillery and under the terrible storm of iron hail on the 13th of Dec. I have said I desire to thank you for your assistance in bearing me off the field and kindness in attending to my wants. Words, Lieut., can not express my feelings, but when I say I owe my best wishes and thanks that come from my heart, believe me and accept them. And I wish to know the names of those three men who assisted you. I remember the countenances but I did not get the names. The true soldier I admire and I thank God that my lot has been cast among so many as compose the rank and file of the 14th Regt.

We read the news journals here from day to day anxiously, but up to this time nothing has been said in regard to the Army of the Potomac that leads us to believe that you are to be moved soon. I do not design to express a wish that the Army may remain idle and Rebeldom remain unpunished. But I sincerely hope that the 14th may not be called into battle again soon. There is no news of importance in the land of steady habits, except among political circles, and in this channel so many doubts are entertained as regard the future and final results that I propose not to mix in just now. McClellan's stock continues to rise and I say to it, God Speed. Mrs.

Perkins joins with me in best wishes for your safety, and her best regards. Please remember me to <u>all</u> rank and file, <u>friends</u> and <u>enemies</u> in the 14th regiment. Give each one of the latter one dollar for me and believe me

Sincerely your friend

And obedient servant

Sanford Perkins, Lieut. Col., 14th C.V.

13

A Demoralized Army Again
Changes Commanders

Demoralization and defeatism in the ranks and doubts about pursuing the war dogged the army following the disastrous defeat and heavy losses at Fredericksburg. Goddard writes his younger sister, May, "You must not think me sorry that I volunteered. I shall stick to the last so long as there is a man left in the Regiment . . . but it is without hope of victory that we shall move next . . . against an earnest, united South, you can see how demoralized is our own army" (117, 120). Yet the twenty-one-year-old second lieutenant takes pride in his regiment and his company, which he temporarily commands while its captain is away on sick leave. Company G, he writes, "is fast getting considered the best." The regiment gets a new commander following the severe wounding of Lt. Col. Perkins at Fredericksburg. While "ready and willing . . . to give my life to save the Union" (126), he says the issue of abolition should be subordinate to that end. As an election nears for governor of Connecticut, he attacks the Democratic "peace" candidate and his supporters as traitors and vows that if the candidate is elected, "the soldiers will whip the rebels in front quicker, to go home and knock down the men that talk treason in our rear" (130–31). After Lincoln names General Hooker to replace Burnside, and the new commander gets busy revamping the demoralized army, Goddard reports, "'Fighting Joe' is rising daily in higher esteem in his army" (130). Goddard is promoted to first lieutenant and takes part in a long review of his 2nd Corps and three other corps by Hooker and President Lincoln. He recommends for promotion as noncommissioned officers those men who have best performed their duty, not those with influential friends back home. He continues to plead with his older brother, Alfred, not to join the army.

Heavy rains following the battle of Fredericksburg kept the army bogged down across the Rappahannock in what was called Burnside's "Mud March" by a dispirited army licking its wounds at Falmouth. Unlike the hapless Burnside, the Army of the Potomac's new commander, the self-confident Maj. Gen. "Fighting Joe" Hooker, was more than eager to take command. Hooker was quick to relieve the troops' severe material needs and restore esprit de corps to the ranks. Assembling the largest army ever in North America, Hooker devises a battle plan he calls perfect. "May God have mercy on General Lee, for I shall have none," he boasts. Hearing this, Lincoln noted, "The hen is the wisest of animals because she never cackles until after the egg is laid."

~

Excerpts from *History of the Fourteenth Regiment, Connecticut Vol. Infantry,* by Charles D. Page (Meriden, Conn.: Horton Printing Co., 1906)

January 31st the band of the regiment, always a favorite, being the best band in the corps, went down to army headquarters by invitation and serenaded General Hooker, who had meantime replaced General Burnside in command of the Army of the Potomac. The regiment soon saw a great change in rations and clothing, with fresh bread every other day and plenty of fresh meat, potatoes, beans, peas and other vegetables. . . . This had a marked influence on the spirit and good feeling of the boys of the regiment (110).

Sergeant [Benjamin] Hirst speaks of the exchange of coffee and tobacco between the boys of the Union and Confederate armies. He says,—"On a fine day in the sunshine it is rather pleasant picketing the banks of the river and cracking jokes with the Johnnies on the other side. Some times we rig up a shingle for a boat, load it with coffee, set it adrift in the stream and watch it drift across to the opposite bank. How the Johnnies will watch it slowly drifting over and receive it like a long lost friend. They in turn will rig up a tobacco boat, and we take the same pleasure in receiving it. You can hardly realize that these are the same men who were shooting us down a few weeks ago, and may be, will be doing the same a few weeks hence" (111).

On Sunday, April 5th, President Lincoln reviewed the Army of the Potomac on a broad plain about four miles from the camp. Although the occasion was one of great interest, moment and pride to the members of the regiment some of them were not able to put on dress suits for the occasion. We cannot forbear quoting from Sergeant Hirst upon this subject. He says:—"The other day I was detailed with a squad to go on picket near the Lacy house, and arrived there at seven o'clock A.M. We were not relieved until ten o'clock the next day when we were marched about four miles out of our way to take part in a big review in honor of President Lincoln. . . . There was some swearing at the long march before us after being on duty twenty-seven hours, part of the time in the cold and part over a smoky fire, but there was no help for it, to the review we must go at once. The whole Army of the Potomac was there, dressed in its best bib and tucker, with their arms shining like burnished silver, while we were dirty, sleepy and ragged. Just look at us with our overcoats and knapsacks on, our blankets in a coil around our shoulders, a canteen filled with water, a haversack containing bits of beef, crackers and pork, three or four cooking utensils, such as frying pans, tin cups, old tomato cans, etc., hitched to various parts of our body. Of course, we were all well armed and some of us had axes besides. We were made into a division by ourselves, and I, with a gun on one shoulder and an ax, a five pounder, on the other, was placed as right guide to the division. After nearly the whole army had marched past and we came into sight, it was no surprise for me to see the President step a little nearer and wonder what damnation kind of men would come along next. However, if he, or his wife, or daughter asked any questions, I think they would have been surprised to learn that we were a fair sample of the army in light marching order. Just after we passed the President, we were moved at double-quick time for a quarter of a mile, just to show what stamina there was in Old Hooker's soft tack. We got back to camp just before sunset, thoroughly tired out with our two days exertions" (114–15).

Falmouth, Dec. 25th, 1862

Dear Julia,

My Journal for the past few days.

Dec. 19th. I applied for a 12-day leave of absence. Dr. Jewett signed a certificate that I would be unfit for duty in that time. Col. Palmer, commanding our brigade, approved it. We got Gen. French to sign it. Since then I have heard nothing from it, as I have got well and went on duty. Today I don't care much about it, but if it is granted I shall go home with the body of poor Capt. Gibbons, who has died of his wounds. It is an unpleasant duty, but it was Col. Perkins' last request before going to Washington that Gibbons' body should be sent home.

Lt. Sherman was taken with fever and is now in hospital quite sick. He too has applied for leave. I wish mine would come as I must be here January 1st if he is not, as it is the day we must make out our payrolls, and such a job as it will be. Nov. 1st we were on march and our copies of the September rolls in the company chest, which with the rest of the officers' baggage has not been seen by us since Sept. 6th. Every man on that roll has got to be accounted for on this.

Then another trouble is that we don't know the date of the acceptance of [Capt. William H.] Hart's resignation,[1] nor whether Seymour has ever been confirmed as Captain by the Governor, nor if he has the date of his appointment, nor where he is, as he never reported for duty, but left here the day of the battle and we have not seen him since.

Adj't Ellis says, "Nobody but the Lord can straighten out the papers of the 14th C.V. and He would not."

Dec. 22nd. Sent my canteen that saved my life home by Capt. Piatt, who made me another call. Be sure to preserve it, as the ball that hit me went through it, and Dr. Jewett says that my leg and perhaps life were saved by it.

The 14th turned out 6 officers and 120 men for Dress Parade tonight, Capt. Davis in command. The bodies of Capt. Gibbons and Lt. Comes have just been brought into camp. Red tape prevents anyone taking them to Connecticut.

1. William H. Hart, Company G, resigned October 29, 1862.

2. Frederick J. Seymour of Company C was promoted to captain of Company G on November 12, 1862, but not mustered. He was discharged December 24, 1862.

Falmouth, Va., Dec. 28th, 1862

Dear Mother,

Merry Christmas and Happy New Year. My journal reads—

Dec. 24th. Our Brigade was reviewed by Gen. Sumner. It is commanded by Col. [Robert C.] Johnson of the 12th New Jersey (a new regiment 1,000 strong with a fine band, just attached to our brigade.) The other regiments are the 14th C.V., 200 men; 108th New York, 200; 13th Penn, 130 men—its brave Col. [George W.] Zinn was killed at Fredericksburg while trying to make his men fight. Gen. [Brig. Gen. Alfred] Sully now commands the Division as French is on leave. An improvement.

We buried Capt. Gibbons and Lt. Comes in the little churchyard at Falmouth. It exhausted the entire list of officers to furnish bearers. The coffins were of plank torn from floors of ruined buildings and hence very heavy. Service solemn and impressive.

Dec. 25. Christmas day. Capt. [Isaac R.] Bronson of Co. I assigned to command our regiment received. Capt. Davis relieved. Commenced work on muster rolls and overcame the apparently insuperable obstacles so that my first copy in lead pencil was ready by 9 P.M. and is the best of the 10 companies.

Dec. 26th. Buried another private in my company and returning from funeral got letter with notice of the death of another. We have lost in Co. G as follows—

killed and died of wounds at Antietam, 3
died of disease, 7
killed and missing at Fredericksburg, 3
wounded at Fredericksburg, 4

A large proportion for one company in four months.

I am rather amused at the extravagant laudation of yours truly, but thank you all the same.

It's fun to see Capt. Bronson on dress parade in the Col's part. I do want and need my boots and coat very much, and if red tape will only delay my furlough (from which I hear nothing, but Hale says it will be given) till January 2nd. I shall come home to get them and to cure an abominable sore throat, but if it is granted before that, I shall not avail myself of it, as I must get out these muster rolls and see my men mustered as I am the only officer with them and they need me. Co. G and I are learning to get attached to each other.

I wish I could send home by somebody the bullet that hit me. I have it in my pocket.

Maj. [Henry] Ward of the 8th Conn. came here to see me yesterday about Fred [Corp. Frederick S. Ward, killed December 13, Fredericksburg]. He has strong hopes. I have none. But I report on my muster rolls "missing in action."

I enclose a 50 cent confed note for uncle Lou. I know it to be genuine as it was rifled from a store in Fredericksburg.

To all inquiring friends say I send love and that I don't feel my wound at all except at night when it's cold, then it aches a little.

Your devoted Son, Harry

Falmouth, Va., Dec. 30th, 1862

Dear Julia,

The dying days of the old year find us still in camp, expecting to move out at a moment's notice. A sad and mournful march will be our next one. Col. Morris away, Lt. Col. Perkins and Major Clark also both at home. [James D.] Merrill, Capt. of Co. A, resigned [December 20, 1862] and gone. Poor dear Capt. Gibbons of Co. G, dead. (Dec. 12 he read the Bible to us for hours in Fredericksburg). Lt. [David E.] Canfield of Co. B, dead, Capt. [Samuel W.] Carpenter of Co. C wounded.

Dec. 27th. Hard at work on the muster rolls. Went out on picket with Col. Morris and 100 men. Bought some tough "sweet potato pies" of an old darkey.

Dec. 28th. On return from picket duty we found in camp a number of gentlemen from Madison, Conn., on a visit to Company G. With quantities of "goodies."

Dec. 29th. At work on muster rolls.

Dec. 30th. At 4 A.M. received orders to be ready to move at a moment's notice. We were ready all day but tonight are as confused as ever in our Sibleys and log huts.

Finished our muster and pay rolls today. All done by myself. It was an awful job but it has been done right and Co. G. is ready to be mustered tomorrow.

I am very sorry to say that I have lost the bullet that hit me at Fredericksburg, but the canteen that it penetrated I sent you by Capt. Piatt. Our assistant surgeon, Dr. Jewett, says that the canteen saved my leg, and likely my life. Mother says that "my children will appreciate that bullet." I fear that she will never see either bullet or children.

I am well but very tired tonight.

Yours affectionately, Harry

Falmouth, Va., Jan. 3, 1863

Dear May,

On the last day of 1862, the Regiment was mustered by Capt. Bronson commanding—all our field officers absent—ill or wounded.

The Corps Surgeon-in-Chief called to see me as to my application for a leave. Made no examination but questioned me. I told him at I had reported for duty and that my leg had ceased to trouble me. He said, "Lieutenant, I am sorry you could not have kept it worse a few days." It was hard to have to remain here in such a filthy suit of old clothes as mine are now, knowing that my new suit awaits me at home. Yet I could not claim a leave now, with the other Lieutenant ill while Capt. Seymour has just resigned. So we have lost three Captains one way or another in the company in five months.

On Jan. 1st, all our back express matter came—brought through by Mr. Hart of Madison, Conn., after great trouble. There was a big bundle of clothing, etc. for poor Fred Ward, which I sent over to his brother, Major Ward. Also, a lot of edibles for him. Such of its contents that had not spoiled, I divided among his old comrades. I wrote his father today.

The remains of Privates Leffingwell and Redfield of our company were disinterred and sent home today.[1]

We expected a cavalry raid all night but it did not come.

Jan. 2nd. Got letters from Mother and Julia. Mr. Hart lost $6.00 worth of dress coats belonging to this Regiment while bringing our express matter. These coats have been following us ever since we left Ft. Ethan Allen. I am really ashamed to go on Dress Parade in this dirty old blouse and trousers now that so many of the officers have had friends in Washington go to their trunks and send articles therefrom.

Jan. 3rd. Officer of Guard. So Col. Morris "speaks highly of me." Well, I have not always done the same of him.

Yet you must not think me sorry that I volunteered. I shall stick to the last so long as there is a man left in the Regiment unless illness from lack of clothing or the rainy season comes, but it is without hope of victory that we shall move next. For one I am now firmly convinced that we cannot conquer the South, and the whole Army of the Potomac is of this opinion. That is why I hate to see it stated that the Army is <u>clamorous</u> for fighting, because it is not <u>now</u> true.

Yours affectionately, Harry

1. Ozias C. Leffingwell, died December 25, 1862; John D. Redfield, died December 14, 1862.

Postscript

(Note, 1887) This letter and those of the next 90 days were written in the darkest hours of the Civil War when the Union troops were more despondent than they ever were before or after.

Henry Perkins Goddard as a journalist for the *Norwich Bulletin*, 1860. From the collection of Eliza Wingate

Second Lieutenant Goddard in his cavalry uniform after joining the Harris Light Cavalry. From the collection of the editor

Ike Bromley, Goddard's editor at the *Norwich Bulletin*, who helped recruit a Connecticut infantry regiment. From the collection of the editor

Hugh Judson Kilpatrick, colonel of the Harris Light Cavalry, following his promotion to brigadier general. From the collection of the editor

Brig. Gen. E. W. Whitaker, a sergeant-major in the Harris Light Cavalry during Goddard's service in that New York regiment. From the collection of the editor

Capt. Marcus Coon, Goddard's company commander and nemesis in the Harris Light Cavalry, who was dishonorably discharged after Goddard resigned. From the collection of the editor

Mary Woodbridge
Goddard, Goddard's
mother. From the col-
lection of the editor

Henry Perkins Goddard
after joining the
14th Connecticut
Volunteer Infantry.
From the collection
of the editor

Connecticut governor William A. Buckingham, who issued a stirring call for volunteers to meet the state's quota requested by President Lincoln. From the collection of the editor

Maj. Gen. Abner Doubleday, a colonel at Fort Ethan Allen outside Washington, D.C., where Goddard and tens of thousands of other soldiers were stationed before moving south. From the collection of the editor

Maj. Gen. John E. Wool, age seventy-seven and the oldest general when the war began, commanded the Department of the East when he complimented the 14th Connecticut as they marched through Baltimore. From the collection of the editor

Maj. Gen. George B. McClellan and his wife. From the collection of the editor

Lt.-Col. Sanford H. Perkins, who commanded the 14th Connecticut until wounded at the battle of Fredericksburg. From Charles D. Page, *History of the Fourteenth Regiment, Connecticut Vol. Infantry* (Meriden, Conn.: Horton Printing Co., 1906)

Col. Theodore G. Ellis, adjutant of the 14th Connecticut, who assumed command of the regiment following Perkins's wounding. From Charles D. Page, *History of the Fourteenth Regiment, Connecticut Vol. Infantry* (Meriden, Conn.: Horton Printing Co., 1906)

President Abraham Lincoln, whom Goddard saw on four occasions before and during the war. From the collection of the editor

Maj. Gen. Ambrose Burnside, who commanded the Army of the Potomac after Lincoln's dismissal of McClellan, and who in turn was replaced after the disastrous Union defeat at Fredericksburg. From the collection of the editor

Maj. Gen. Edwin V. Sumner, who commanded the Right Grand Division at the battle of Fredericksburg. From the collection of the editor

Maj. Gen. William H. French, who commanded a division at the battles of Fredericksburg and Chancellorsville. From the collection of the editor

The armory at Harpers Ferry, the site of John's Brown's raid in 1859, in a photograph taken shortly after the war. From Charles D. Page, *History of the Fourteenth Regiment, Connecticut Vol. Infantry* (Meriden, Conn.: Horton Printing Co., 1906)

Maj. Gen. Joseph Hooker, commander of the Army of the Potomac after Burnside's dismissal, who in turn was relieved two months after the Union debacle at Chancellorsville. From the collection of the editor

(*left*) Maj. Gen. Winfield Scott Hancock, who commanded the 2nd Corps at the battle of Gettysburg. From the collection of the editor. (*right*) Gen. Robert E. Lee, commander of the Army of Northern Virginia. From the collection of the editor

The monument at Gettysburg to the 14th Connecticut on Cemetery Ridge. From Charles D. Page, *History of the Fourteenth Regiment, Connecticut Vol. Infantry* (Meriden, Conn.: Horton Printing Co., 1906)

(*left*) Goddard's older sister, Julia Goddard Piatt. From the collection of the editor.

(*above, right*) Goddard's younger sister Mary "May" Goddard, later the wife of Louis Comfort Tiffany. From the collection of the editor

Maj. Gen. John Sedgwick, a division commander at Antietam and Fredericksburg, who later commanded the 6th Corps. From the collection of the editor

Falmouth, Jan. 8, 1863

Dear Mother,

<u>Jan. 4th.</u> Came off guard duty. Had some difficulty with Capt. Bronson, commanding the regiment, but finally settled it amicably.

<u>Jan. 6th.</u> Was mustered out as Sergeant Major, dating back to Sept, 28, 1862, and in as 2nd Lieut. After being mustered, Lieuts. Nichols, [Charles W.] Galpin and I visited the Connecticut Brigade of the 9th Army Corps—some five miles further down the Rappahannock We called on Col. [Edward B.] Harland of the 8th Conn., Col. G.A. Stedman of the 11th Conn., and Col. [Arthur A.] Dutton of the 21st.

We had a delightful time. Col. Harland was very pleasant. He has received no box and was much amused, as I was, at your sending my boots to him as a "neighbor." He says, however, that if we are within "striking distance" and the box ever does come, he will send them to me.

Kit Boone would resign if he could get it accepted. I am happy to see that Joe Rockwell was promoted. I am afraid from what I hear that Baltimore is as bad for the 18th as is New Orleans for the 12th.

When I returned I came very near getting under arrest for going and had a very stormy time with Capt. Bronson. Somehow Capt. Bronson and I don't hitch, and yet he means to do right, and says "after all Goddard is a good fellow."

<u>Jan. 7th.</u> Officer of the Guard again today. Mrs. Hart of Madison brought our Deers coats which have been following us from Hartford since August 25th. Of the 1,000 sent from the state, only 425 were needed. Where are those 575 men who were to have worn the others? Ask of Antietam, Bolivar Heights and Fredericksburg. Poor Gibbons, Canfield,[1] Comes,[2] Stanley, Blinn, Willard, and Crosby[3] have fallen, and now we hear that Major Clark is paralyzed in the left arm and leg and may also die.[4]

I received one of the Deers coats and sowed on my left shoulder straps—also dress in a pair of government shoes so that I am a little more decent, as I had gotten so that I had almost decided not to appear in Dress Parade in my old shoes and torn blouse. So now if I was rid of vermin I should be happy, but (and all the officers are alike in this) it seems impossible to exterminate them. I have used the powder you sent me, but every few days I find that "The scent of the rose hangs around me still." When we next dress underclothing, I shall take a supply and wear all those splendid ones I brought from home. If <u>that</u> doesn't work, I shall either go crazy and shoot myself or resign and quit the country.

I was up all night on guard duty and am so sleepy I can hardly write. Please send me a Darning needle and some yarn for mending stockings.

As Sherman is away on sick leave I now am nominally as I long have been actually in command of my company. Since Capt. Gibbons died, my company turns out more men for duty than any, and was pronounced by the Inspector to be the cleanest in the regiment. It is fast getting to be considered the best.

Mr. Hart has presented me with a nice lot of very acceptable apples and potatoes.

1. Theodore A. Canfield, died December 31, of wounds at Fredericksburg.

2. Capt. Jarvis A. Comes, Company F, was killed at Antietam.

3. George H. D. Crosby, a second lieutenat in Company K, died October 23, 1862, from wounds suffered at Antietam.

4. Clark survived and was discharged on account of disability February 28, 1863.

Falmouth, Va., Jan. 11, 1863

<u>Jan. 9th.</u> Drilled company morning and afternoon. By the way I have taken hold. I now turn out the largest company in the regiment and shall soon have the best, as the two flank companies are fast being demoralized for lack of commissioned officers on duty.

<u>Jan. 10th.</u> Very rainy. Had to go on picket in the storm. "Tuff."

<u>Jan. 11th.</u> Cleared off about 2 A.M. Got one hour's sleep in the whole night. Got some edibles (hot pies and hot "biscuit") at an old Negro's who posted me as to the history of all my old acquaintances when I was on duty here with McDowell. I was much interested in his conversation. He fully vindicates from treachery Hewitt, our guide in that fight of April 19, 1862.

Found letters from home on return to camp. Thank God.

—Treat Capt. Tubbs well. He showed cool clear grit at Antietam and Fredericksburg.

—Glad to hear of Joe Rockwell's promotion in the 18th C.V. and that Mr. Stanley Trott has secured a good government position.

—Did I ever send you the funny lines a private extemporized about Col. Morris when he lost his road in marching us to Delaplain, and spent two days marching 17 miles to go but 8 miles they were!

"I looked to the east and I looked to the west,
And I saw old 'Bunch'em a'coming,'
Three bully regiment and he at the head,
And he didn't know where the deeble he was going."

Falmouth, Va., Jan. 14, 1863

Dear Julia,

Today my dear sister I hold the "responsible position of officer of the day." Ahem. I used to think that it was an awful big thing to strut around camp with one's sash tied across one shoulder, and long to be a captain and have that pleasure. Now we have so few officers on duty that all the officers alternate in the position while sergeants act as officers of the guard.

My head aches badly today, in consequence of eating too many griddle cakes with molasses. So you see I am still human.

A new order from Gen. Halleck is to the effect that hereafter commissioned officers shall be allotted only one shelter tent each. When we leave here our Sibley tents must be turned in. This is "Tuff." How do they expect a man to make out muster rolls and keep four sets of company books in a shelter tent? Still, "let her rip." We have lived so nearly like hogs for some time that I expect soon we will have to pen up the men to keep them from running away.

Yesterday two of my men discovered the orderly of the brigade commander in the act of robbing the mail. He is said to have been at this for some time, which accounts for your and I losing letters. Now it is hoped this will be put a stop to.

I have sent in my recommendations for non-commissioned officers in Co. G, and in doing so very likely have not suited the Madison people exactly. I have made it a principle to promote those who are always on duty and who did their duty on the battle fields without reference to their home friends.

I realize now all the care one assumes in commanding a company. You must see that clothing, rations, etc. are fairly distributed, must look well to the comfort of the men, and yet be firm and dignified, yet impartial and courteous. It's a hard job, especially in a volunteer regiment.

One rumor gladdens and inspirits the men more than any Northern Abolitionist would believe—that is that "Little Mac" [McClellan] is again to take the Army of the Potomac.[1] It's useless to deny that he is the idol of this army and men who swear by all that is great and holy never to cross the Rappahannock under Burnside, say they will follow Mac to the death or anywhere. I begin to wish him back myself for the life and spirit it would put into this corps.

We are ready for whatever fate has in store for us, but I say again that the army has no confidence in its commander and hence I sometimes fear none in itself. I dare not picture what I fear will be the conduct of such an army in the next great battle. Why, when the Johnies nail our men across the Rappahannock with "What are you fighting for?" men have even replied, "I don't know." Against an earnest united South, you can see how demoralized is our own army. When the rebels are similarly questioned, they reply, "To defend our country."

Let us hope for better days, here and hereafter.

Yours as ever, H. P. Goddard

1. The rumor was false.

Falmouth, Va., Jan. 16, 1863

Dear Mother,

We move at 5 A.M. tomorrow—we go up the river (we suppose) with three days rations and 60 rounds of cartridges. Nobody here knows what's up as we leave our camp standing while the whole army moves.

My commission is in my valise and Lt. Fiske of Co. K has the certificate of my muster as 2nd Lt. If anything befalls me don't be in too much worry till you know just what has happened. If you have to write, Sgt.-Major [John C.] Pelton is the nearest friend now here.

Gen. Burnside reviewed the corps yesterday—meeting the coldest of receptions from all save one or two new regiments.

Trusting in God who is over all.

Your loving son, Harry

Falmouth, Jan. 17, 1863

Dear May,

At 2 P.M. the 16th we got orders to be ready to march with 3 days rations at 5 A.M. today. At first all hands had a story that Gen. [Maj. Gen. Samuel P., commanding the Military District of Washington] Heintzelman had relieved us and that we were going to Washington, but when we got out for inspection it appeared that the whole army is under the same orders—that the pontoons have been sent up the river banks and that we are to leave our tents standing, so it's "On to Richmond" instead of "Back to Washington."

Well, it's not pleasant to move in this freezing cold weather, with nothing but shelter tents and no ambition in the regiment, but if I live, the name of any man who shirks, in this company, shall be published in the Connecticut papers. This "skedaddling" is played out.

At night the orders were modified and we are told to be ready to move Thursday at 5 A.M. with 3 days rations and 60 days rounds cartridges. I have an ordnance report to make out to Gen. [Brig. Gen. James W., head of Ordnance Department] Ripley before the 20th. Also a report of all changes in Co. G since Aug. 25th 1862 for the Adjutant General of Connecticut.

However we grumble, the old 14th will do its duty until, like the old guard of Napoleon, none is left to tell the tale. Let Connecticut treasure its history and fate, but let the credit be given where it belongs—to the gallant Lt. Col. Perkins.

God bless and keep the grand old Army of the Potomac, and if it fails in this fourth grand on to Richmond move, let the discredit be where it belongs.

Yours Lovingly, Harry

Falmouth, Va., Jan. 20th, 1863

Dear Mother,

My little text book of 20th—your gift reads, "The name of the Lord is a strong tower, the righteous runneth unto it and is safe."

Officer of the day today. At noon we received an order from Gen. Burnside that the Army of the Potomac is again to go into action with an enemy weakened by sending troops south and west and appealing to it to do its duty nobly. The order sounds like the last appeal of a sad but great heart that knows it is risking all on a single throw, but that the die must be cast.

Burnside I thank thee. Thou knowest that thou hast not the confidence of thy army, but issuing no vainglorious order. Tell us where we are going and what we have to do to win each other's confidence. God in Heaven grant that the army and the old 14th may do its duty. My company has been nearly spoiled by too much sympathy from home. Heaven grant its young commander aid to do his duty and to keep his men up to theirs. For the first time since Fredericksburg, I have a strange feeling that the tide is turned and that God will prosper us.

Don't be anxious when you don't receive letters. The government often stops the mail for a few days. Besides, we have ascertained that there has been considerable mail robbing in our division.

Capt. Bronson still commands the regiment. He has not distinguished himself although he is a sincere Christian and does the best he can, but he is not a <u>military</u> man.

The divisions of Hooker and Franklin have been moving past us all day. Franklin's troops from the extreme left are now going into bivouac near our camp.

One of my "missing" at Fredericksburg has just turned up a paroled prisoner. He was left under circumstances like those of poor Ward, and his father had written me.

<u>Jan. 21, 1863.</u> A dreadful storm last night. The center and left grand division bivouacked near us after their day's march. We expect to move today but last night's storm will delay the army fearfully as pontoon trains and wagons are broken down and stuck in the mud. Our Sibley blew down last night, but we were very comfortable compared to the poor boys on the move. It still rains and a cold nor'easter prevails. Has God forsaken us? Since the Battle of Fredericksburg, we have had splendid weather until last night.

Yours, Henry

Falmouth, Va., Jan. 22, 1863.

Dear May,

We have not yet moved though we expect to daily as the divisions of Hooker and Franklin have both "moved" and are both stuck in the mud. It has rained fearfully for three days and the roads are awful. Wagons, cannon, pontoons, etc., etc., are scattered all over the roads from here to Belleplain. A thick cloud of smoke was discernible this morning, and three guns heard on our extreme left. None know "what's up?" but the rain and mud will, I fear, spoil the new advance of the Army of the Potomac.

I do wish we could get paid. The Irish brigade of our corps stacked arms the other day and refused to move until their six months arrears are paid. Artillery was brought up and ordered to open fire upon them, but refused to do so. (Note, 1887.

I find this in the original but, at this date, cannot say whether it was a fact or rumor I wrote in 1863.)

Annie B. and Annie T. are both nice girls, but my own sister May Goddard is worth all the other girls in Christendom put together.

Your loving brother, Harry

[January 22, 1863]

Dear Mother,

Gen. Dan Tyler used to say, "Patriotism is a good thing to talk of at home, but it don't give a poor soldier his breakfast." "No, general, nor will it keep his body clean and clothe him when uncle Sam will neither pay him nor allow clothes sent him." Yet I will fight as long as our regiment is kept at the front, but the men are discouraged as I never saw them in my army life.

The Negroes about the camp are a bad lot and make it hard for one to keep up abolition sentiment.

Personally I admire Burnside as a gentleman, but he has entirely lost the confidence of his troops. Still I will not write to you such discouraging letters, but wait events. Love to all.

Your affectionate son, Harry

On Picket, Sunday Jan. 25, 1863

Dear Mother,

I hope you received the Confederate scrip I sent you from Fredericksburg. Please send me Owen Meredith's poems.

Lt. [John C.] Broatch of Co. B, whom we left ill at Warrenton Nov. 15, and who has been home, returned. This gives me another officer in our Sibley. He's a splendid fellow and we were always good friends. He spent two days at Norwich with Capt. Tubbs, was at the Hubbard Rhetorical Society Exhibition, and was to call on you next day when a telegram ordered him to Washington.

Send me anything you like by express, not forgetting butter. I need no coffee, sugar, or tea as we are supplied. A small box will do if you put in a mince pie and some butter. I wrote Kemp to send me some cigars and I would pay him.

Jan. 24. The grand advance has played out on account of the mud and fact that the rebs were fully prepared and actually called over the river offering to lay our pontoons for us if we would only cross. In Fredericksburg they put up a board in our sight painted, "Grand Advance—Burnside Stuck in the Mud." Poor Burnside—the whole army is laughing at his second "On to Richmond" and cursing his and its luck. Horses, wagons, pontoons, and artillery are stuck fast in the mud all around us while the infantry has all gone back into its old camps. The right grand division for once had the best luck as it did not leave its camps.

Went out on picket. Col. Morris and Adjutant Ellis have returned.

Jan. 25. Got my breakfast at the hut of the same darkey as two weeks ago. Bill of fare—salt junk, hot biscuit, coffee and sweet potato pies. The latter are excellent. Wish you could try one.

We live very well at Falmouth now as Burnside has issued an order compelling the brigade commissaries to trust officers, and the sutlers have just got in good stocks of goods. It's when moving that we suffer, but the weather is so horrible that I doubt if we move for some time now.

We get a daily mail and I love to get letters.

Give me the old 14th before any Connecticut regiment unless it's the 1st Artillery. If any of us ever get home our regimental colors—state and national—(they) will tell our story for us. We are very, very proud of these two colors. They are so tattered that we have had to sew them up, but will take out the stitches when we go home. Several color bearers have already lost their lives in their defense. God grant that they never fall into rebel hands while one 14th man survives.

I got a letter from Lt. Col. Perkins yesterday concerning my conduct at Fredericksburg that I send you to preserve with my commission.

Jan. 26th. It is said that Hooker is to relieve Burnside. What next? Dare we hope for Little Mac again? This corps hopes so.

Have built a bedstead today and shall no longer sleep on the ground.

Yours, Harry

Norwich Bulletin, February 4, 1863
"From the Fourteenth Regiment"

Falmouth, Va., Jan. 30, 1863

Dear Bulletin,

You remember the story of the thief who, while under charge of a constable, escaped from the wagon in which he was being conveyed to jail, and ran into the woods. The constable followed him for some distance, but the swamp crossed a deep brook, and pulling the bridge over after him, mounted a stump in the center of the morass and defied the constable to catch him. As there was no means of reaching him, the constable returned the warrant for his arrest with the following endorsement: "In swamp-'um, up stump-'um, can't get at-um."

Last week Gen. Burnside started the Army of the Potomac to cross the Rappahannock. The same day the army started, the elements started to prevent it, and at the end of three days, the center and left of the army were floundering in mud, and Gen. Burnside was compelled to make the same admission of "in swamp-'um, up stump-'um, can't get at-um."

On Monday of this week the army was startled by the news that Gen. Burnside was relieved and that Gen. Hooker succeeded him; also that Sumner and Franklin were. Tuesday night Gen. Sumner's farewell was read to us at dress parade. After all, we feel rather sorry to part with "Old Bull," who has so long been identified with us, and who never showed a white feather in all his long military career.

We are much amused by the discussion in the Northern papers as to whether the army shall go into winter quarters. Why, my dear friends, we have been in winter quarters ever since our first arrival at Falmouth, about the 20th of November, and what's more, expect to be until about the end of March. True, four plans have been made to fight the rebels, and once we have crossed the Rappahannock, but most of the regiments in the Right Grand Division still occupy the same log huts that we built on our first arrival here.

As to another "onward" move, I really wish some of our most clamorous would start with me after wood for our fire. We have to go about a mile, and I think the state of their toilets on their return would convince them that there is still some mud in Virginia, and that mud is something of an obstacle.

The Fourteenth regiment is in better condition and spirits than it has been for a long time. What we lack is officers. The junior captain, when we left Hartford, now commands the regiment, and we have present only eleven line officers. We miss Capt. Tubbs much, as he is an excellent officer, and if present would command the regiment, as we greatly fear that Lt. Col. Perkins and Major Clark are both too severely wounded to be with us for a long time yet.

Trusting that we may soon have pleasant weather, or an honorable settlement of this war in some manner, and assuring you that the Fourteenth regiment is still true and loyal to the old flag, I remain,

Yours fraternally, Omega

Falmouth, Va., Feb. 1, 1863

Dear Julia,

Another quiet Sunday in camp.

Tell Mother she is too hard on "Little Mac." No one ever questioned his patriotism and no one but he can reorganize and put spirit and infuse life into this army. The army and the people of the North do not seem to agree very well of late on many points.

Send Alf my fondest love and tell him I am so glad that he kept out of the army. He's nobly toiling where he is and is a better fellow than I am any day.

I was much pleased to hear that Lt. Col. Perkins had visited you. I wrote him he must do so.

I hear that I am to be promoted to 1st lieutenant. If so, I hope it will be in my own Co. G. as it is the largest and best in the line. Then we tent with the officers of Co. B and Lieut. Broatch of the company is the only officer on duty there and we are very intimate friends. He, Sg't Major Pelton and I mess together and have an excellent mess.

Tell Mother we are glad and yet sorry to lose "Old Bull" Sumner. He is ugly and works the troops hard, but is as brave as a lion. Gen. Couch succeeds him. Gen. Meade succeeds Hooker, and W.F. Smith succeeds Franklin. Gen. Howard of Maine now commands our corps. He is a good man and sincere Christian.

There is little news here. The ground is in an awful condition and I anticipate no general movement for a month at least. The pay master has not reached us yet, though some of the regiments of the corps have been paid.

We have built raised bedsteads in our Sibley and have sent to Washington for a little stove. As our sutler is now here, and the brigade commissary "trust" officers, we now live very well.

Falmouth, Va., Feb. 11, 1863

Dear Mother,

On Feb. 6th I sent home $250 to be appropriated as I wrote.

On the 10th I came in quite sick. Had been poorly and took a dose of castor oil, which pulled me down. Am better today.

The army and Northern people certainly are antagonistic as to Gen. McClellan. I regret it but it is true. I will say for Gen. Hooker that he is doing all in his power to reorganize a refractory and ill-disciplined body of men. Then too he gives furloughs to enlisted men. But after all, one glimpse of Little Mac at our head would do more than all Hooker strives to accomplish. Personally I don't care a copper as between Mac, Burnside and Hooker. I only record the feelings of the soldiers. Still, matters are certainly not as bad as they were quite recently.

Don't judge Franklin till you know. I have authority that he was not pleased with McClellan at Antietam. Burnside too has repeatedly said that McClellan was the only man to command this army.

I am ready and willing, I hope, to give my life to save the Union. If it's necessary to save slavery to save the Union, save it. If it's necessary to destroy slavery to save the Union, destroy it. But don't force us to fight for abolition regardless of the Union.

If we cannot save the Union, then let us stop fighting, and if the Negro wants freedom, let him fight for it himself. No race ever gained freedom without doing something for itself.

I am now 1st Lieutenant Co. B. Broatch promoted to Capt. Co. A.

Falmouth, Va., Feb. 14, 1863

Dear May,

Corporal [Frederick B.] Doten is now adjutant Doten. He is, I think in all respects, a perfect gentleman. But we had a little difficulty last night in which he was over-persuaded by others to play a practical joke on me. I was sick and irritable, saw through the "load," got mad, and demanded an apology from Doten. Capt. Bronson heard the fracas, demanded the facts, and told me the trouble was that Doten was the only one he could reach, while the others were the real instigators, but that Doten should make an apology at Dress Parade.

Then I begged him to let me take the matter in my own hands, which he finally consented to do. So I wrote Doten a sharp note and pitched into the other parties for using him. This A.M. Doten sent me a handsome apology and I wrote a pleasant note in return.

Tell the girls that they all behave scandalously in never writing me. I won't send my love to one of 'em. Seems to me they are horribly afraid of writing to a poor lieutenant out in the wilderness while they all flirt with Frank Norton or any other poor "Laggard in love and dastard in war." Pshaw, I'll cut all of them if they don't write me.

"Oh God for a <u>woman</u>, with a head, heart and soul

Like some of the simple, great ones gone by."

Give my love to everyone that hates me and to all that like me. Remind them of William Allen Butler's[1] lines:

> "Fool"! Says my muse to me,
> Look in thy heart and write."

Your loving brother, Henry

1. William Allen Butler (1825–1902), New York lawyer, satirical poet, and novelist.

Falmouth, Va., Feb. 19, 1863

Dear Mother,

Capt. Tubbs resigned the 15th. His papers have come up to corps headquarters. The same day Capt. Broatch's resignation was returned disapproved as medical certificate did not state that it was necessary to save life. Broatch has now resolved not to resign. Captain Davis has been put under arrest and will be tried by court martial for drunkenness.

On the 17th we had a very severe snowstorm and the whole regiment had to go out on picket way down to the Lacy House on the river some five miles from camp. It was awful. No fires, 16 hours on foot and my own pickets reached from the old pontoon bridge where we crossed Dec. 12th to Falmouth (two miles). The rebs were right opposite and some of their conversation with our men—which though prohibited is still kept up on the sly—was very amusing. To some of our men, a rebel called out, "You d—d fool. Why don't you build a fire?" "Against orders." "Then come over and warm yourself by ours." "No thank you. I have been in Fredericksburg once. Don't want to go again."

We returned in the rain yesterday, wet and miserable, but a good fire (I have a stove at last. I got it by luck for $3.00) and a good dinner and warm shoes made me very comfortable. But some of the men suffered much. Today is another nasty day. Capt. Fiske of Co. G and I have just backed a load of ash a mile and a half and have wood enough on hand for 24 hours.

My brother Alf writes a noble letter. I will write him as soon as I can. I would rather hear of almost anything than that Alf had gone to war. I never want to hear that.

Numerous 10-day furloughs are being granted. Our regiment is allowed to have 8 men—2 line and 1 field officer away at a time. By and by I may get a chance, but it will hardly be my luck. I expect to serve here three years unless I am killed. My health is not as good as usual—this damp weather. I had always good health until I got into Co. B. Now I have the diarrhea eight days and can't stop it, and a kind of "jumping" tooth-ache that nothing helps but cold water. Yet I am grateful for generally feeling cheerful and comfortable in a vile climate, in an unpleasant camp.

My cask has not arrived. Tubbs called for it in Washington and it had not arrived. To tell the truth, I never expect to see it as the Provost Marshall at Aquia Creek says he cannot transport express matter to Falmouth and will not. Yet I do not feel bad about it, save on your account, as I have plenty to eat now. Soft bread thrice and potatoes twice a week now. Why, I live as well in our mess as I did at home and am free to confess it.

You are too severe in your abuse of McClellan. Prayed all through western Virginia, and your "Fighting Joe" is a man that, though a splendid officer, does drink like a fish. This I know as there is a man in Co. G once master of the "stepping stones," which used to take Hooker from Mathias Point to Washington. He says General Sickles can out drink any officer but Hooker, who can get Sickles a little tight. But "Joe" never gets drunk himself. Hooker "blows" too much, reminding us of Pope's flaming proclamation and inglorious defeats.

The New York Tribune and Herald and Washington Chronicle are the only papers sold in this corps. Reading matter is scarce. Please send me Adelaide Anne Proctor's[1] poems.

Yours lovingly, Harry

1. Proctor (1825–1864) was an English poet of religious, social reformist, and feminist themes.

Falmouth, Feb. 21, 1863

Dear Julia,

Gen. [Brig. Gen. William] Hays assumes command of this brigade today. This sends Col. Morris back to command the regiment—though he is at present quite ill.

Hooker's stock is rising in the army. Even Gen. French is down on "Little Mac" now, so his son tells me.

We now report 28 men for duty in the company.

Yours affectionately, Harry

Falmouth, Va., Feb. 26, 1863

Feb. 22nd. Tremendous snow storm prevailed from 1 A.M. to 12 midnight. Snow deep. Suffered a little from cold.

A salute was fired from all the batteries in honor of Washington's birth-day.

Feb. 23rd. Capt. Fiske of Co. G relieved Capt. Bronson in command of the regiment, the latter being placed under arrest by Gen. French for not sending out a full picket detail as ordered. We line officers rejoice at the change.

I was temporary assigned to command Co. G and made out their muster rolls—all five in two days.

Feb. 25th. The rebel cavalry attacked our cavalry pickets in our rear and drove them to within half a mile of our camp. They took several, and we a few prisoners. A brigade of our division has gone in pursuit.

An order was read at dress parade from Col. Morris ordering Major Theo. G. Ellis to take command of the 14th C.V. After parade we all wished to know how it was and were informed that Major Clark's resignation was received last night and that he has been or would be discharged by Gen. Couch. We don't know whether Morris took upon himself to make Ellis major or whether the governor ordered it. Now I suppose Ellis will do as well as any one (anyone) as there are but three of the old captains left. One—Carpenter of Co. C—is absent wounded and the other two—Davis of H and Bronson of G—are under arrest and to be court-martialed.

I see by the papers that Daniel Whitaker[1] is now 1st lieut. of Co. D Harris Light Cavalry and acting adjutant, and his brother S'gt. Major [Edward] Whitaker[2] 2nd Lieut. of Co. D. Col. Davies must love Whitaker to keep him his adjutant. Why, the man can't write or spell correctly. We have just settled our mess bill from Feb. 5th to 26th inclusive. What do you suppose it is? For three it is $38.70. My share is $12.90. I am worried and nervous that you have not yet received the money I sent you. I wish I had half your coolness, but I had set my heart on clearing up all old debts with that money and doing something for the family, and paymasters visits are like angels—"few and far between."

My darling mother, liquor cannot be bought in this division. A general can have it brought him by a sutler, but no sutler can bring it to sell save by Gen. Hooker's order and he won't give it. The only liquor I have seen out here in Falmouth since Nov. 28th was commissary whiskey and that article has not been on hand for but five times this winter. Then it was issued to regiments going on picket in bad weather, 1–2 gill to a man. On such occasions I am glad to get it with the rest, though it's a very poor article. No other way can you get it save on doctor's order. Still, officers have been drunk in this regiment. They bought whiskey of the commissary of some brigade where the orders are not so strict as in ours. Col.

Morris was always down on it and officers could not get it. That's the whole matter. I would not get whiskey, save on such occasions as I have mentioned, if I could and couldn't if I would.

Well, this year will end this war for good or evil, and I am willing to try another campaign if it is done in earnest. Let's have iron men in an iron cause, and conquer or be conquered once for all.

Yours ever, Harry

1. First Lieutenant Daniel Whitaker was killed in action at Aldie, Virginia, on June 17, 1863.

2. Edward Whitaker was awarded the Congressional Medal of Honor for his actions at Reams Station, Virginia, on June 29, 1864. He was promoted to brigadier general at age twenty-three, becoming the youngest general in the Union army.

Falmouth, Va., March 1, 1863

Dear Mother,

The regiment has gone on picket duty but for once I was not detailed, but am lucky enough to have a day in camp.

Major Ellis makes a good regimental commander. We were mustered yesterday by our new brigadier, William Hays. He's a tough-looking customer.

I am in command of Co. I as Capt. Bronson is under arrest and both lieutenants of the company absent wounded. Capt. Sherman has resigned and been discharged. Ex-Capt. Hart is here visiting. He wishes he had not resigned.

I am alone today in our Sibley and very comfortable. Our stove is a treasure and we have two large elegant bedsteads of fine sticks. We have small branches of cedar for "feathers" and six woolen and one rubber blanket on our bed.—the Capt. and I. The tent is swept daily and kept clean and comfortable. I had some nice beans with Connecticut catsup for dinner with bread and butter. All the officers but myself have their good clothes here now.

I had a good bath today and then read chapter XXI of St. Matthew and feel lazy and comfortable. It's not so every day, with two drills, camp guard, "backing" wood two miles and three recitations in tactics each week.

We live, however, pretty comfortably and it's nonsense to say that the army is suffering this winter. "Fighting Joe" is rising daily in higher esteem in his army.

That McClellan "Baby Show" at Hartford was too much. You know they held the baby out of the Allen House window, wrapped in an American flag. Col. Morris says he wishes the baby had the chronic diarrhea as bad as he has got it. "Then the gaping loafer might not have found it so pleasant to stand below and stare."

I am far from being an abolitionist, but if Connecticut swallows Tom Seymour [a former governor of Connecticut who opposed the war effort and was openly sympathetic to the South] for governor on his platform, I vow that the soldiers will whip the rebels in front quicker, to go home and knock down the men that talk treason in our rear.

This command will, I think, be a final one. If fairly "licked," the Army of the Potomac can hardly be rallied again. If it fairly conquers, it will dictate none but the harshest terms to "Secessia." It's everything or nothing this time.

Uncle Don had best leave politics alone and devote his time to writing his long-promised history of Venice. Else his name and fame will perish with him.

I am very glad Alf has not joined the army. One of us is enough.

Lieut. [John A.] Tibbits was wounded at Antietam. He has been very ill of fever since his promotion, but is recovering. He is a very smart fellow.

Yours, Harry

Falmouth, Va., March 4, 1863

Dear Mother,

On Monday I received my First Lieutenant's commission dated back to Dec. 20, making me the ranking officer of the new lieutenants.

The express for this regiment has been partially received. I hear that my parcel is still at Couch's headquarters, where every thing is opened and examined, often resulting in thefts by the guard.

The weather has changed and a cold nor'wester is blowing. Wild geese going north. Hooker has postponed his review of this corps. As the almanac has it, "Expect a move about this time." which way nobody knows. Some say south under Sumner. Some say to the peninsular under Sumner. Some say to the peninsular under Hooker. But I think "On via Fredericksburg."

Yours as ever, H.P.G.

Falmouth, Va., March 5, 1863

Dear Mother,

I have the odds on Capt. Bronson now. He is awaiting the sentence of the court martial (I think it will be very light) and of course still under arrest. Capt. [Samuel A.] Moore of Co. F commands the regiment. The regiment has gone to be reviewed with the 2nd Corps by Hooker.

I am officer of the day commanding camp. Bronson wanted to go to the review as a spectator and had to get permission. I don't dislike him, but never want to see him in command again as he is not competent.

Capt. Davis is being tried by court martial. Major Clark has been appointed paymaster in the army. Good.

We shall like Ellis better than we thought, but he is too aristocratic for the volunteer service. He will yet be our colonel, as neither Morris nor Perkins will ever be fit for duty again.

Some of the "Harris Lighters" were here yesterday. Lt. Col. Kilpatrick was acquitted by general court martial and ordered "on duty." Col. Davies would not serve in the same regiment and has been transferred to the 12th New York Cavalry. Lt. Col. Kilpatrick was then made a brigadier general.

Most all my old friends have left that regiment. I am sorry for Col. Davies though he and Kilpatrick have always been scheming against each other and Kilpatrick beat him.

The weather is beautiful and we expect to move daily.

Yours as ever, H.P.G.

Falmouth, Va., March 7, 1863

No news except that Hooker reviewed our corps the 5th. I was unfortunately detained in camp as officer of the guard.

Lt. Col. Perkins returned the 5th to avoid being mustered out. He has applied for 15 days leave in order to have the bullet removed from his shoulder. Then he can tell whether he will ever be fit for duty. We are of course delighted to have him here again.

As to my opinion of women in general, I assure you I think them as a class infinitely superior to men—I have seen it in this war both North and South. I despise the Southern men, but think the women of the South must command respect in their heroic sacrifices in a bad cause. If it were not for the opinions of the women of the North, many a soldier of our army would not be here. Carlyle was right in saying "the worst woman is better than the best man." Mrs. Thomas Hart Benton said to Jessie when she married Col. Fremont, "Go to his church. All the religion a man has he owes to his mother. You must not try to supplant that."

You must remember that we are in winter quarters doing nothing. There is no excitement to call forth exertion, and soldiering of itself is not over pleasant to me. It's only the <u>cause</u> that keeps me in the field. Once I loved the business. Now I have tired of its monotony. But knowing that my life, fortune, and sacred honor are pledged to my country, I shall stay here as long as life and health permit.

Soldiering is mis-represented in the press. You read that the "army is anxious for a fight." The truth is that a regiment that has been under fire is <u>never</u> anxious for another fight. Ask Gen. Tyler or Col. Harland if this is not true. But that is no proof that it will not do its duty, as Charley Coit said to me recently, "Every new fight is dreaded more than the last, yet the regiment does better each one." The secret lies not alone in patriotism, or in religion, but it is the <u>sentiment of honor</u> more than aught else that does the business. You may ask the best Christian and ask the worst infidel fighting side by side what nerves them, and each will reply "pride." When the fight is over, then you can see who was sustained by a trust in God, who by patriotism, who by pride. Yet you rarely see a soldier fall doing his duty who dreads the future; it's singular but it's true.

Now I have been growling all winter in common with the regiment, vowing allegiance to McClellan, etc. But that miserable Copperhead Democracy in Connecticut has disgusted us all so completely, that should Tom Seymour be elected governor, or the draft resisted, we will whip the traitors in front and then go to Connecticut to drive Tom Seymour and his crew into Long Island Sound.

This regiment is proud of its 200 fighting men that are left, and we pity the Connecticut regiments not yet under fire.

My diarrhea is gone but I have a bad cough, yet think our doctor can break it up.

Your Loving Harry

Norwich Bulletin, **March 24, 1863**
"A Letter from the Fourteenth Regiment"

Camp of the Fourteenth Regiment
Falmouth, Va., March 18, 1863

Dear Bulletin,

I saw in the Hartford Times what purports to be an extract from a letter from a member of this regiment, in relation to Thomas H. Seymour and the ensuing State election. The writer days, "There isn't a man in the Fourteenth Regiment, now, so far as I can learn, that would not vote for the Democratic ticket." This statement I pronounce as an unqualified falsehood, or else the writer has closed his ears whenever politics were discussed in this regiment, and as they form a constant topic of conversation, this is decidedly improbable.

The true state of the case is that the Fourteenth Regiment has suffered much since it left the State, and that immediately after the battle of Fredericksburg there was too much croaking and complaining, but now the case is different. Under Gen. Hooker the regiment has fared well, in common with the whole army, and has been brought up into good condition. They know [Gov.] William A. Buckingham has shed tears of sympathy for their misfortunes and has done his best to alleviate them. They know Thomas H. Seymour thinks they are doing a wicked work in carrying on a crusade against Southern institutions, and that the men who nominated him think we had "better be in h—l than murdering our Southern Brethren."

The Fourteenth Regiment is composed mainly of men who can read and think for themselves, and, though there is some difference of political opinion (and *our* Democrats say they can hardly swallow Seymour), two thirds of our two hundred and twenty-five men for duty would, if they had the power, cast their votes for William A. Buckingham. And let me warn the Copperheads of Connecticut that a day of reckoning will yet come to hand. We do not propose, after fighting treason in Virginia through long and weary months, to allow treason to reign triumphant in Connecticut; and when we return home victorious, as we shall yet, I would remind them that the Fourteenth Regiment has been taught that traitors blood must be spilled to restore peace and happiness to our country, and may not be particular whether said traitors hail from Virginia or Connecticut.

Again I pronounce the statements in the correspondence published in the Times false. It was probably written by some one who was tired of the service, or of whom the service was tired.

You will hear from the Fourteenth again some day not far distant, but it won't be by their voting for Tom Seymour.

Yours ever, Omega

Falmouth, Va., March 10, 1863

My dear May,

It's cold and snows and sitting close to stove I write.

So Kit Brand has resigned from the 21st [Connecticut] and come home. What reason does he assign? I <u>did</u> think him patriotic, but if he says "all the boys want to and will come home," I reply, "So they will, but it will be as did the Spartans of old, 'with their shields or on their shields,' in either case undimmed by treachery or cowardice."

About January 1st when our corps was demoralized by defeat and dissatisfaction, we talked as we ought not, and I did say to Kit that "I was a Democrat and sick of it," never that "I would go home if I could." If he uses that phrase, contradict it to him and read just what I have written to everyone. Since then I have got into better shape and changed my mind. Am <u>not</u> a Democrat. Nay, I despise traitors at home more than those who stand in arms against us across this narrow stream—which will be memorable in American history.

I begin to look upon Falmouth as almost my second home. Half my time when in the Harris Light Cavalry was spent here and now we have been here since Nov. 18th, 1862.

You remember Jim Nichols, who used to be clerk in R.M. Haven's store. He is now 1st lieutenant of Co. K and as the only other Norwich officer, we are quite intimate. Tell his aunt Miss Nichols from me that he has grown very handsome in service and is an excellent officer.

It's pretty dull in camp now. In pleasant weather we have some good drilling, as I like the study and science of arms, but in the ordinary weather one tires of reading, writing, and smoking, and that's about all we do.

Tell Mother I should be very glad to heed her old advice and "spend my evenings at home."

Your affectionate brother, Harry

Falmouth, Va., March 14, 1863

My dear Mother,

I wrote you hurriedly on the 12th, when we were under arms expecting an attack. The cause of the alarm was that the rebs were seen to be moving up the other side of the river and the scouts reported them 15,000-strong at U.S. Ford, with much cavalry this side. But the alarm is over and as we are not under orders, I guess they did not cross.

Yesterday Capt. Fiske arrived with my coat. It is a beauty—a little tight under the shoulders, but a tailor is fixing it for me now. I want the bullion straps for that coat. The bullion straps <u>wear</u> best and I much prefer them. I have only one old pair of (my old cavalry) metallic straps for my blouse.

My dear Mother, I have little or no idea of a furlough. There are too many ahead of me. Lt. Nichols of Norwich will probably go next. He is going to Washington and will try to find that barrel, when he has orders to smash it and, taking out my pants, let everything else go. It's so provoking to think that but for that stupid Tubbs, I should have had it long since as express matter is received by the regiment in five or six days from Connecticut.

Our chaplain occasionally preaches to us. Maj. Gen. Couch still commands the corps. The grand division have been abolished. Sumner left this army on Hooker's appointment. Couch is a gentleman. Sumner a bull-dog.

Bronson and I are all right now. You know I temporarily command his company, and if there is a fight before he's released, he's going in as a private under me. But Davis and he will be acquitted soon.

Your loving son, Henry

Falmouth, Va., March 14, 1863

My dear brother Alf,

Forgive me my long silence now good brother. I have no good excuse for so long delaying an answer to your letter of last September, which reached me at Harper's Ferry in October.

Since then we have been through one campaign in Virginia—fought the bloody Battle of Fredericksburg, got whipped and changed our generals several times. Spent the winter in this little town opposite to the city of Fredericksburg, and are now preparing for a new campaign under "Fighting Joe" Hooker.

Our regiment has been out of the state six months and seventeen days with a full complement of field, staff, and line officers and 980 enlisted men. We now have no field officers present and death, disease, and resignations have brought us to that point that an officer who came out first lieutenant is now captain commanding the regiment. We report present for duty about 220 all told. Aggregate present and absent officers and men—700. Is not that a sad tale for six months service?

Sad but glorious; we have lost some of our best officers and men, but today the 14th Conn. regiment has a name and reputation in the field and at home that few regiments have earned in so short a time. Our torn and tattered colors, though twice repaired, tell our story.

But I am so glad you are not in this army—for several reasons, and as I told Mother, if you join the army I'll have naught to do with you. Why?

First, because one from a family is enough. If I get killed, you can help the family. But if you were here and both of us were killed, what would Mother do?

Second, it's no place for you. You are a sailor, not a soldier, and the army brings men up in the way they should not go, and the influence of army life would be very bad on you.

Third, because (I won't tell Mother this) I have little idea that the South will ever be conquered. The reason is that they are united—men, woman and children—and are fighting on their own soil, enduring and suffering the most hardships for their native soil. We are divided: half the army hates "niggers," the other half believe in abolition. Too many North are wearying of the war, and we in the field are not much inspirited to see state after state there go over to the Democracy.

As for myself I shall stay in the army just as long as my health lasts, and it has been very good so far. Not that I like army life. I hate it, but because I tendered my services to my country, I shall carry out the contract unless the rebels end it and me at the same time.

I have been well treated in this regiment. Came in S'gt. Major and am now fifth-ranking 1st lieutenant.

We have good quarters this winter and a pleasant time. Our table has been very good since "Fighting Joe" took command. He feeds well.

We have a Sibley tent for the officers of every two companies, and as we have no 2nd Lt. in our company, the captain and I sleep together in a bed of poles supported on crossed sticks, with evergreens for feathers. Two blankets under and three over us. A good stove in our tent adds to the cheerfulness and we are very grateful for such good quarters.

When in the field we "catch it" though. Very little transportation is furnished and it's hard work to get anything to eat. But then there is no use of grumbling and I am rarely guilty of that.

We are in a good cause and hoping and praying, almost against hope, for success. I am in to the bitter end.

But as you love me never go to war.

If I survive this war I will show you some relics when you come home.

Believe me, my dear brother.

Yours fraternally, Henry [addressed to Honolulu, Sandwich Islands.]

Falmouth, Va., March 18, 1863

My dear Mother,

St. Patrick's Day, the 17th, in the Army of the Potomac was devoted by the chief corps and division officers to comedy, nearly resulting in tragedy before the day was over.

Gen. Meager had a great celebration at the camp of the Irish Brigade, consisting of hurdle races, etc. Nearly all the generals in the army hereabout were present, including Hooker, Couch, Howard, Hancock, French, Hays, and brigadiers unlimited. Very many ladies—Mrs. Meager, Mrs. Gen. [Brig. Gen. Charles] Griffin and others being present. There was a great deal of fun and a great deal of liquor— several of our division officers as usual getting "slightly tight."

Just as the sack race commenced, heavy cannonading was heard up the river. Meager ordered his men to their quarters to "fall in" under arms, and off went generals and orderlies double quick to the front. The cannonading continued until nightfall, when it ceased. I know not what it was, but it is reported that we have a battery at U.S. Ford to keep the rebels from crossing and it is supposed that there was a skirmish there.

Another storm is in prospect today, but of one thing you may rest assured. The Army of the Potomac, still over 100,000-strong, will advance across the Rappahannock River just as soon as the roads permit, which time will not be far distant.

All talk about Suffolk, the Peninsular, etc. is prima facie improbable because if the army had been going to change its base, it would have done so when the 9th Corps left. Yet I do not think we shall cross at Fredericksburg because the fortifications there are much stronger than in December. But above, below, or in front, that river has got to and will be crossed, and the inland route to Richmond will be tried until it is found utterly impracticable. And you know I have always thought via Fredericksburg the way to Richmond on account of good roads, water, wood, etc., and the fact that the southern bank of the river once held, you gain two bases of supplies—the Aquia Creek railroad and the river itself, navigable to gun boats up to Port Royal. Thence it is a good wagon road to Bowling Green and you have a depot of supplies only 40 miles from Richmond. Rush supplies over the railroad to Fredericksburg and up the river to Port Royal. Send them by rail and teams to Bowling Green and you have a depot of supplies only 40 miles from Richmond. Then cut your way to that city and take it, or, be sent reeling backward to the Rappahannock.

Now I don't know anything about it, of course. But see if the next campaign of this army is not something like it. There is one bad thing about it, vic: that the small pox has been very prevalent between Fredericksburg and Richmond, but the whole army was vaccinated some two months since.

There are many very pleasant acquaintances left "in the line." Acting Adj't Doten is a gentleman and very profitable companion. Lt. Nichols of Norwich (gone home on furlough) and Simpson of Waterbury are very pleasant fellows. Beyond these three I have no intimate friends left in the regiment. Yet the others are good officers. In fact the regiment is pretty well officered as far as drill, etc. goes. But there is not so much interest taken in drilling companies of 40, 30, 20, and 10 men as of old in 80 and 90. Co. D has 2 lieuts., 5 S'gts., 6 corporals, and 11 privates for duty, more officers than men and no captain, and 2 corporals absent at that. Still what there is in the regiment now may be depended upon. Seven months hard service throws out the sick, shirking, and skedaddling drones, and of our 225 for duty, I think nearly all will go into battle and do as well and better than many of your fancy regiments 800 strong.

1st Lieut. Miles S. Wright, Co. E, has been dismissed from service for absence without leave since Dec. 6. We are well rid of him.

Have you read the article on "Women" in the March Atlantic?

Love to all. Yours ever, Harry

Falmouth, Va., March 21, 1863

My darling sister May,

We have heard cannonading almost every day this week—one day up the river, the next down. Our cavalry have done splendidly. Col. [Alfred N.] Duffie of the 1st Rhode Island Cavalry, our old Harris Light major, has distinguished himself, among others.

Today we have orders to turn over all superfluous articles to the Quartermaster and to draw all that the men need in the next campaign. Transportation again reduced. Only four wagons to a regiment. One shelter tent for each officer—probably to be carried on his back with his blankets—and only one small valise for each officer in the wagons. In this event I must get rid of the big blue blankets Julia gave me and only carry my light ones. I wish Negroes were more easily to be had but they are as scarce as specie. You see we expect a speedy movement.

The Rappahannock River seems to be getting identified with my history the way I cross and re-cross it in my army life.

Leaves of absence are "played out." God alone knows whether you will see me again or when.

You tell me that Bromley is at home recruiting for the 18th Conn. Recruiting, when they only lack 50 of a maximum! To think that the 18th has been out 5 days longer than we. Aw well, our history is forever engrossed on the hearts of the people of Connecticut, its pages dripping blood are soiled by tears, but through it all, you learn the old, old story that "Dulce et decorum est pro patria mori." But the 18th, what has it done? I will not be uncharitable for a know that stout hearts and eager hands in that regiment are biding their time, and I am glad for the sake of old Norwich that it has yet escaped bloodshed.

Let me tell you the things of which I am proud: First, my mother. Second, by brother and sisters. Third, our regimental colors. It is hard to imagine how dear these inanimate pieces of silk and bunting are to all of us. When you hear that the 14th colors are captured, you may make up your mind that the regiment is annihilated.

We have a long, earnest and terrible campaign before us. Many will be taken. The sowers are many—the reapers will be few. But the harvest, oh how great—liberty and union or slavery and secession! May God defend the right.

Your loving brother, Harry

Falmouth, Va., March 24th, 1863

Dear Mother,

The secret of "immediate action" letters is that whenever the weather is fine and the roads begin to dry, we get orders that look like a move, or else rebel cavalry threaten our rear. Then comes a heavy storm and it doesn't look so much like a move. So we may stay here two weeks and may not stay 24 hours.

Lt. Nichols is a very fine fellow. He has risen from 1st Serg't of Tubb's Co. to 1st lieut. of Coit's. He brought me your letters just 48 hours from home.

Capts. Davis and Bronson were both under arrest. One week since Bronson was released with a reprimand in general orders. He has since been in command till Saturday, when Davis was released, having been "honorably acquitted."

Last night we had a reunion in Davis's tent. Every officer was present. The band serenaded Davis and he made an excellent speech. He has the hearts of all—officers and men—now and his court martial will be a good lesson to him. If he lives, he will make his mark on the political world yet.

Very much obliged for that excellent tobacco. Thanks for the copy of "T'Ouissant L'Ouverture."[1]

Furloughs have been stopped. It has been very pleasant, but today rains very hard, which will delay us a little longer.

Our next campaign will be tough. Four wagons only to a regiment—one for field and staff, one for line officers, and two for rations.

The Quartermaster will carry for each officer one small valise and what blankets will make up 40 lbs in all for each officer, and one cracker box mess chest for the officers of each "division" (2 companies). I shall "back" one rubber and one woolen blanket, and shall put my blue blankets and shelter tent in the wagon. (The rain falling through the tent is what blots this sheet.)

So you "think of me at twilight." Thanks.

I was on picket day before yesterday down at the Lacy house. It was a lovely day and I lay on the banks of the Rappahannock, gazing at and musing over Fredericksburg, watching the rebs playing ball and pitching quoits. The city is sadly changed since I first saw it in April 1862 and the beautiful Lacy plantation is ruined. Hardly a tree is left in it and the buildings are going to ruin. The rebs have three lines of rifle pits now between their artillery and the river. It is said that Lacy's daughter never <u>walked</u> across the river in her life—always rode and yet the bridge was not an eighth of a mile from her residence. Once every week she went to Washington or to Richmond. Now her father is a rebel officer [Maj. J. Horace Lacy] and her house occupied by the sanitary commission.[2]

Thank God this war is waged <u>south</u> of the Mason-Dixon line.

We have lived well this winter. We buy goods of the commissary cheaper than you can at home. But what we get of sutlers costs double. I will give you a sample of each.

Commissary: Ham, 9 cents per lb.; sugar, 12 cents per lb.; white sugar, 15 cents per lb.; tea, 55 cents per lb.; coffee, 41 cents per lb.; bread, 7 cents (big loaf); beef, 10 cents per lb.

Sutler: Butter, 50, 55, 60 cents per lb.; eggs, 60 cents per dozen; cheese, 40 cents per lb.; condensed milk, 75 cents per lb.; sausage, 30 cents per lb.; cod fish, 20 cents per lb.; oysters, $1.00 per quart.

So you see, while we gain on one, we lose on the other. Coffee we never have to buy. The companies actually throw it away. Good coffee too.

Fighting Joe is the man.

The 14th C.V. has issued an "Address to the People of Connecticut." Be sure to read it.

Thanking you for your prayers of which I feel unworthy, and hoping that I may be as good as you wish and as I ought to be.

Your loving son, Harry

1. Toussaint L'Ouverture (born between 1739 and 1746, died 1803) was self-educated slave who led a successful slave revolt against French rule in Haiti after the French Revolution. His ragtag slave army defeated French forces as well as the invading British and Spanish forces.

2. Today the Lacy mansion is the headquarters of the Fredericksburg National Military Park.

Headquarters, 14th C.V., Falmouth, Va., April 2nd, 1863

My dear Mother,

On the 30th March I was detailed to command Co. G, Capt. Fiske having been detailed as assistant inspector general, 1st brigade.

March 31—Officer of the Guard.

April 1—An alarm at 2 A.M. led us to be turned out under arms till sunrise.

Charley Tubbs went up to White Oak Church and brought from my cask for me—one pair trousers (beauties, just fit), one box cigars, one box cranberries, one currant jelly, 2 boxes sardines, six papers tobacco, six pair socks, one loaf cake.

I am more than delighted.

April 2nd. Capt. Davis and Adjt. Doten went on 10 days leave and I am acting adjutant. I send my big Colt revolver home by Davis—it's too large for infantry service.

So you think my letter to *The Bulletin* too bloodthirsty. It's liked in the regiment for when one takes up the Northern papers and reads tales of "Copperhead outrages," it makes the blood boil, I can assure you.

James L. Townsend of New Haven is captain of my company—a man of undoubted pluck, very obstinate in decision whether right or wrong, of little education but good principles. All in all we get along very well. We have no 2nd lieutenants.

Yours lovingly, Harry

Camp, 14th C.V., April 6th, 1863

My dear Mother,

Today is Election Day in Connecticut and we are anxiously awaiting the news.

We have but three of the old ten captains left. First is Carpenter, absent wounded; second Davis; third Bronson. This is as they rank.

Will hereafter send money to you for my own use and if <u>you</u> prefer, the household expense fund.

I want nothing save a new vest with infantry buttons. I have the pants you sent and a pair I got of the Q.M. I can also get shoes whenever I want at the Q.M. and any government articles.

Those Woolseys are splendid girls. Ask them if they know Miss Harris of New York, who is now at the Lacy House in Falmouth—right under rebel guns. She's a noble woman. Makes gruel for the pickets daily. Nurses the sick ones. Has the officers to prayer meetings, etc.

I see the burglaries are becoming very frequent in Norwich of late.

That poem on McClellan's advance on Manassas was very good.

I acted as adjutant general at brigade guard mounting this morning. I do wish you could see me at that or dress parade. Dark blue coat with elegant bullion straps, handsome pants, neatly blacked top boots (paid ten dollars for them to a sutler), white cotton gloves. My sash has been turned and is as pretty as new, and a very neat cap. Don't think I am conceited but one does like to look well.

We are ordered to have a general muster April 10th to see "how many troops are necessary to be drafted to fill up the regiments in the field." I quote the order.

Capt. Bronson is in command. We get along "swimmingly."

Love to all. Your loving son, Harry

Headquarters, 14th Regiment C.V., April 11th, 1863

My dearest Mother,

All hail Connecticut! Nobly do your words of cheer, "3,000 majority for William A. Buckingham" greet the ears of your eager listening children on the banks of the historic Rappahannock! Your children thank you for your determination to stand by them and renew their vows to stand by you and never let your blue banners be profaned by rebel hands.

April 7th. Two brigade drills. Got news of the Connecticut election.

April 8th. Marched five miles to the grand review of four army corps by President Lincoln; a magnificent sight. He rode past us accompanied by "Fighting Joe," his two little boys on ponies, and hosts of lesser "stars." We then marched in review past him (Mrs. Lincoln and numerous ladies being near him in an ambulance). It was a sight never to be forgotten. Was acting as adjutant of the regiment.

April 9th. Adj't Ellis returns. Ellis likes me and wishes me to remain in the Adj't's office till Lt. Doten returns, which I shall do. Lovely spring weather.

April 10th. Another lovely day.

April 11th. Acted as Adj't at brigade guard mounting. Had received no letters from home for some days when my clerk, being at brigade headquarters found yours of the 6th for me kicking about with other waste papers. If they treat your letters so, I will prefer charges against the general.

Was much surprised to hear that Alf has come home.

Don't, don't, don't let him enlist. It would grieve me beyond all else. If I should never return and he should too be a soldier, what would become of you? As you love me, don't let him.

Thank Kemp Abbott sincerely for those cigars. Don't send me any more stockings. I shall have to throw away some clothing when we move and have all I can carry.

Lieut. Nichols is a very intimate friend of mine. He is on picket today. It is actually so hot today that my fatigue clothes feel oppressive.

No, I do not think I shall ever go to the Pacific. I want to live in Connecticut always, provided I come out of this war alive. I love Norwich more than you seem to fancy and flatter myself I can earn a living there, or at least come there to live after I have earned one.

Somehow these spring days give me a sad feeling. I do wish I could get home for some of your counsels and advice and love, before a new campaign. I am growing older, sadder and I hope wiser daily, and feel as if I ought to see you before we go into another hot campaign. But may I learn to say "Thy will be done" in sincerity. I am happier and feel in better spirits just from writing you.

Your loving son, with lots of love for weather-beaten Alf

and sweet sisters. Harry.

Falmouth, Va., April 15, 1863

Dear Mother,

On the 13th, Adjutant Doten returned and I went back to Co. G. Adjutant Ellis received his commission as major and 2nd Assistant Surgeon [Frederick A.] Dudley his as surgeon vice. Rockwell resigned. The same day old "Robe," Capt. Coon's servant, made me a pleasant visit. He was quite affectionate. His regiment and 28 other cavalry regiments, and artillery to the number of 84 guns, moved past us up to the right today. They are to attack in the rear while our infantry goes in hereabout.

April 14. Lt. Simpson and I went on picket. All the 2nd Corps got orders to march tomorrow with eight days' rations. Stragglers to be <u>shot</u>, roads splendid, day very sultry, indications of a movement on one side and much commotion in Fredericksburg. Regiments of reinforcement pouring in on their side. Saw a rebel dress parade.

April 15. At 2 A.M., a terrific rain-storm commenced and continued unabated till now (2 P.M.). The roads are seas of mud. We come in drenched from picket to find everything packed up in obedience to yesterday's orders. Hence I write with a pencil. If this storm continues all night, the move will be "knocked." Just as soon as the roads permit, we expect to "sail in" again. The battle will, as far as the 2nd Corps is concerned, apparently be nearly at the same spot as Dec. 13th. [the battle of Fredericksburg] Many of us may be slaughtered as we, of course, have the ugly work to do. But if I fall it is with a prayer, in which you will join me, that it may be as a Christian soldier should. If I should, I wish to will all my small earthly goods to May, save my sabre, sword, etc., which are for you. My Bible and cyclopedia to Alf. My watch and ring to Jule. Don't let Alf enter the army anyhow. I don't feel half so blue about the coming fight as about the last. I feel that we shall win.

Capt. Davis says that he saw Alf. I am glad after all that, Ellis is major. I am writing on my knee with the rain drizzling on my paper and, as I want to hit the mail, will close.

I have no hopes of a leave till after the battle. Then perhaps I may get one if alive. You were right about "Little Mac." "Mother knows best."

I wish Alf could have seen us coming in from picket—swimming in mud, drenched to the bone, loaded with haversack, canteen, and sword. With much love to the dear old boy and all of you.

Your lovingest son, Harry

P.S. I think the rain must postpone a move unless Hooker has gone so far that he can't stop. If I should be wounded, don't start for me till I telegraph you where I am. H.P.G.

Falmouth, Va., April 17th, 1863

My dear Mother,

As I predicted in my last letter, the storm has delayed our moving. However, the expedition on the right, having laid their bridges, we expect hourly to get orders unless another storm, of which there is some prospect, interferes.

Capt. Broatch and Lieut. Lucas have at length returned for duty. Broatch is a particular friend of mine. He is of Middletown, Lt. Simpson of Waterbury and Nichols are my particular "chums."

By the way, I lost my chance to see Juli and John [Goddard's older sister and her husband, John Piatt] the day I came in from picket when I wrote last. It happened thus. The regiment had orders to take five days' rations in their knapsacks, with one shirt, one drawers, one pair socks. All other clothing had to be put into sacks and marked with the company letter and headquarters regiment, and sent to headquarters to be sent to Washington.

In the afternoon, General French's adjutant general sent to this regiment for Capt. Tubbs' 2nd lieutenant to come over there. The only officer in Tubbs' company is 2nd Lieutenant Pelton on detached service in the ambulance corps. The company is commanded by Lieut. [Charles] Lyman of Co. K. So Bronson sent him over. The adjutant general, hearing that he was in command of a company, told him that he would not do and that he should have to get a lieutenant from another brigade to take the sacks to Washington. In the evening, Adjutant Doten of our regiment was there and the adjutant general said that the officer he wanted from this regiment was the one who had been in the Harris Light Cavalry. "Ah," said Doten, "that is Lieutenant Goddard. That's the man." Said the A.G., "Lieut. French, the general's son, recommended him." "Is he in command of a company?" "No," said Doten, "he has a captain." The A.G. said he was sorry, and if the other lieutenant whom he had sent for didn't suit, he should send for me. It was probably too late as I have heard nothing of it since.

I should not fret much about the Catholics. They are Christians as well as anybody. It does not speak well for Mr. Gulliver, whom I never can admire, to get so rampant about them. I don't believe you will find them such an annoyance after all, even if they do locate so near us.

With much love to all, your loving Harry P. Goddard.

Camp 14th C.V. April 19th, 1863

Dear Mother,

We had an inspection this A.M. in which I acted as adjutant. Lt. Doten, who has been promoted from 1st lieutenant of Company F to be adjutant defacto, being sick. Went to church this P.M.

Things again look like a move tomorrow. The pontoon train encamped near us is now (9:15 P.M.) Reported to be hitching up. This is the train that we are to follow and to cross upon. It is also reported that the 1st Conn. Artillery have orders to shell the city tomorrow. It has been lovely ever since the day I came in from picket, but tonight we had a new moon and the sky is very cloudy. We may have another storm. If not, I should not be surprised if we started on tomorrow. Yet as I said before, it is impossible to tell certainly whether you are going to move till you <u>do</u> and it is better so. We have turned over our Sibleys and live in shelter tents. I was fortunate enough to get the log house built by Capt. Fiske so I am all right while we do stay.

A deserter swam the Rappahannock the other night to the pickets of our brigade. He said the rebs have scarce anything to eat.

My leave of absence is the next in order on the return of Capts. Bronson and Townsend on the 27th inst., but if we move it will knock that. So I do not expect to see home in a long while unless wounded or sick.

I like the idea of selling the Oneco Street lot to the Catholics. I don't think they will prove such a nuisance as Norwichians fear. You know we once feared the establishment of the Methodist Church and now little of an annoyance it proves.

About 7 P.M. I saw the new moon over my shoulder. Immediately after, a brilliant meteor started from the north, ran the length of the heavens and seemed to burst over Fredericksburg. Are not these good omens?

Major Ellis is a good officer though a very strict one. He will command respect, never love. Perhaps he is the best man for our regiment after all.

Gen. Harland's[1] offer is good, but I don't want Alf in either army or navy. I had rather to be a private than an officer <u>appointed into</u> a regiment from outside. I know too well from experience the galling treatment such officers receive. For your sake and my sake keep Alf out of the army or navy.

I do not care particularly to <u>act</u> as adjutant. Would rather like to <u>be</u> adjutant on account of horse, though the work is hard.

I am glad May is learning to paint, that Jule is enjoying herself in Washington, that Alf is in good spirits and hopes. Thank you for that report of the investigating committee [Congressional Joint Committee on the Conduct of the War, 1861–65] and the Tribune with the Sumter anniversary meeting.

Lt. Col. Perkins is the idol of the 14th Regiment C.V. We all respect and love him. We do not want him to resign but greatly fear it. My dear Mother, I only wish I was half as good as you would make me.

Hoping and praying that we may meet again—on earth if He wills—if not, in Heaven if He wills.

Your most loving Harry

1. Harland, former commander of the 8th Connecticut Volunteer Infantry, was then commanding a division of the Army of the James.

Camp 14th C.V., April 21, 1863

My dear Mother,

Lt. Col. Perkins is here in citizen's clothes, having resigned his commission and been discharged, to the great sorrow of all.

The storm has again delayed us and we cannot say when we shall move, though now all expect the order daily. Pontoon trains move off every day.

I am detailed as judge advocate of a regimental court martial. Have been relieved of command of Company G and returned to my own, B.

I was much amused the other day to see an ammunition train of pack mules—some 100 mules with boxes of ammunition strapped on each side were drawn up towards the cavalry expedition, of which we hear nothing, on our right. I presume they await good weather. It has been quite hot, but today is cold and a nor'easter blowing.

Col. Perkins looks pretty well but his soldiering days are over. We hate to lose him, but hope to meet him again in Connecticut. He _made_ the 14th C.V. So it has ever been in this regiment. We lose our best friends and the best officers.

The 14th C.V. will always be a good fighting regiment, but never much on drill and discipline. Sometimes I think it would be better for us to all give our lives away and let the name and colors of the dear old regiment go down in glory together.

Weather bad, roads awful. Some pontoons returning. Some of the cavalry across the Rappahannock, some returning. A big fight soon or else another long stretch of quiet.

Yours ever, Harry

Camp near Falmouth, Va., April 25, 1863

Dear Mother,

<u>April 22.</u> Officer of the Guard today. Was a witness at the trial of 2nd Lt. [Charles W.] Galpin at a general court martial.[1]

<u>April 24.</u> Rained hard all day. Regimental court martial wound up. Was busy till late at night preparing the records to go to corps headquarters. Pride myself that it's very neatly done. Wish my dear father could have seen it. The first legal papers I ever prepared.

Received yours of the 19th with a photograph of father, which I was delighted to get. Received Anne Proctor's poems in "Blue & Gold" from Jule last night.

There are current rumors that Maj. Gen. Hooker is to be relieved by Maj. Gen. Fremont. I hope it's untrue. I admire Burnside, Hooker and Fremont but do not like this constant changing.

Have you seen Burnside's general order, No. 8, which the President did not allow him to publish, in which he <u>dismisses Hooker from service, as unworthy to hold a commission</u>? That will make a row if it's true. I see by the report of the committee you sent me that Burnside was <u>not</u> "relieved at his own request" though the President's order was so needed.

Our generals can fight, as Lincoln says, <u>among themselves</u>.

Many think we shall not move soon. I think we shall <u>very</u> soon. Today is lovely and will fast dry up the roads.

I am confidant I shall never marry. I love mother and sisters too well to want any body to come between us.

We like Major Ellis better daily. He is the man to discipline this regiment. My own Company B is much better than G. It was raised in Middletown by poor Gibbons and is composed of the best young men of that town.

We shall have some promotions soon. I expect none and want none this time. I am perfectly suited where I am.

Your most loving, Harry P. Goddard

1. Galpin was dishonorably discharged December 20, 1863.

Falmouth, Va., April 25, 1863

My dear Jule,

Yours of the 19 received with Anne Proctor's poems. Ten thousand thanks for them.

I would like to see Alf before we go into another fight, but do not think it likely.

My beard is flourishing fast under a southern sun.

Thank you for visiting the hospitals.

Many think we shall not move for some time. I think when we move it will be very suddenly, perhaps in 24 hours, perhaps not this month. It's a big job to move the Grand Army of the Potomac.

Do you know that a secret telegraph wire has been discovered in a house in Falmouth running across the Rappahannock to Fredericksburg?

The rebel pickets already call out, "How are your 8 days rations?"

Gov. [William] Cannon of Delaware, a right noble man, is here on a brief visit to the 1st Delaware of our division. They will come in our brigade next month to take the place of the 130th Pennsylvania (nine months).

Six regiments of two years and nine months-men go out of this division shortly. It will weaken the army so much that I expect a move before they go.

With much love, your loving brother, H.P. Goddard

Camp 14th C.V., April 27th, 1863

My dear Mother,

We have orders to be ready to move at 8 A.M. tomorrow. Wither we know not, troops have been moving towards the right all day. Wherever we go, you may depend a fight will follow. God defend the right.

So you see my "leave" is probably played out, as of course they won't be approved while we are in motion.

If I never see Alf on earth, don't let him feel that I did not do him justice. I feel him to be true and noble as a brother and son. As you love me, keep him out of the army.

Your loving son, Harry P. Goddard

Excerpt from *14th C. V.: Regimental Reminiscences of the War of the Rebellion*, by Henry P. Goddard (Middletown, Conn.: C. W. Church, 1877)

What a winter it was that followed in camp at Falmouth with no field officer, and with Capts. Davis and Bronson alternating in command of the regiment, for the former could not hold command a week without getting into some scrape that usually led to his being put under arrest. But it was no use to court-martial him, for his legal training and his habit of getting the whole court on a spree the night before the verdict, led the judge advocate of the Division to say that it was easier to catch a weasel asleep than to convict Capt. Davis. Ah, what punches Fred Doten used to mix in that winter, as we gathered in each other's Sibleys: "When every officer seemed a friend, and every friend a brother."

It was at some of these gatherings that Capt. [Henry] Lee used to give swan-like imitations and that G's officers used to trot out little "Uncas," the stuttering teamster as a spiritual medium, who used to go into trances and therein deliver addresses on didactic subjects, but who got mad when Lt. Fred Seymour asked him to take a drink in his spiritual, not material, character. Qr. Mr. [Charles F.] Dibble used to say that when Uncas got mad at his mules, he could swear in the most unspiritual manner without stuttering at all (12).

14

Wounded at the Battle of Chancellorsville

On May 2nd, the second day of the six-day battle of Chancellorsville, while "rallying the men" in the wake of a daring surprise attack by Gen. Stonewall Jackson, Goddard is struck down by a piece of shell. He is soon transported to Washington to recuperate from his wounds. "The fight was horribly mismanaged by somebody . . . that reflects no credit on Gen. Hooker," he writes (152).

Hooker's "perfect" plan was, in fact, an excellent one; the fault lay in its execution. Avoiding the type of frontal assault that cost Burnside his job, Hooker's plan of attack involved an elaborate flanking maneuver to force Lee either to attack a numerically superior and well-positioned army or to retreat toward Richmond. Leaving part of his army at Fredericksburg under Maj. Gen. John Sedgwick, Hooker crossed the Rappahannock upstream with more than seventy thousand men. Lee, leaving a small force of men to defend Fredericksburg, marched the bulk of his army—with fewer than sixty thousand men—a few miles west to confront Hooker near the Wilderness, a heavily forested tract of land choked with undergrowth. Hooker grew uncharacteristically cautious and, against the advice of his commanders, abandoned a strategic piece of high ground and ordered the army to take up a defensive posture around a crossroads called Chancellorsville. Lee, seeming to sense his opponent's indecisiveness, split his army in two, sending Jackson with some thirty thousand men around the right flank of Hooker's army. Union scouts detected the movement, but instead of preparing for an attack, Hooker convinced himself that Lee's forces were retreating. Stonewall Jackson in the afternoon of May 2 struck through the thick woods, which Maj. Gen. Oliver O. Howard had left unpicketed, taking the 11th Corps by surprise and routing the panicked soldiers. Scouting the terrain for a possible follow-up attack that evening, Jackson was mortally wounded in the darkness by his own pickets. With his death, Lee lost his best commander, his right arm. Hooker, a successful and victorious commander until Chancellorsville, made this comment about his poor tactical decisions: "I lost confidence in General Hooker."

～

Excerpts from *History of the Fourteenth Regiment, Connecticut Vol. Infantry,* by Charles D. Page (Meriden, Conn.: Horton Printing Co., 1906)

The grounds about the Chancellor House, the scene of the battle, were low and swampy, and covered with patches of woods, with deep and thick underbrush, being almost impenetrable. There seemed to be little work for the regiment on this first day of the battle. About eleven o'clock it was called to arms and marched down the plank road to the Chancellor House, the headquarters of General Hooker and his staff. Heavy firing along the front indicated that the Confederate forces had opened an attack. The regiment then turned to the right through a young growth of pines. There were no skirmishers thrown out and at one time it was discovered the regiment was in dangerous proximity to the enemy. After remaining here two hours, the artillery fire seemed to slacken, and the regiment retraced its course, halted and stacked arms in an open lot adjoining the plank road on the west side, perhaps a half a mile from the Chancellor House. . . . In the evening the regiment was formed in line of battle on the extreme right and threw out pickets for the night (118).

On the morning of the 2nd. the regiment was relieved and returned to the camp previously occupied. Toward nightfall a serious charge by Stonewall Jackson on the extreme right of our line, which was farthest from the river, and was occupied by the 11th Corps, caused a panic and disastrous rout. It was under the command of General O. O. Howard. The generals had neglected to picket their front and the men of the division were busily engaged in cooking supper in the dense thicket, having previously stacked their guns, when they were surprised by the enemy (119).

During this pandemonium caused by the fleeing Eleventh Corps, the attempt to resist it by the Union troops and the demonstrations of the attacking enemy, the band of the Fourteenth Regiment, which was now considered the best in the Army of the Potomac, did its most heroic work. We cannot resist copying Colonel Frederick L. Hitchcock, who gives a beautiful tribute to this band in his sketch of the One Hundred and Thirty-Second Pennsylvania Regiment, entitled "War from the Inside." He says: "One of the most heroic deeds I saw done to help stem the fleeing tide of men and restore courage was not the work of a battery, nor a charge of cavalry, but the charge of a band of music! The band of the Fourteenth Connecticut went right out into that open space between our new line and the rebels, with shot and shell crashing all about them, and played 'The Star Spangled Banner,' 'The Red, White and Blue' and 'Yankee Doodle' and repeated them for fully twenty minutes. They never played better. Did that require nerve? It was undoubtedly the first and only band concert ever given under such conditions. Never was American grit more firmly illustrated. Its effect upon the men was magical. Imagine the strains of our great national hymn, 'The Star Spangled Banner,' suddenly bursting upon your ears out of that horrible pandemonium of panic-born yells, mingled with the roaring of musketry and the crashing of artillery. To what may it be likened? The carol of birds in the midst of the blackest thunder-storm? No simile can be adequate. Its strains were clear and thrilling for a moment, then smothered by that fearful din, an instant later sounding bold and clear again, as if it would fearlessly emphasize the refrain, 'our flag is still there.' It was a remarkable circumstance that none of them were killed. I think one of two of them were slightly wounded by pieces of exploding shells, and one of two of their instruments carried away scars from that scene" (120–21).

[Excerpted by Page from the after-action report to the brigade commander by Maj. Theodore G. Ellis, commanding 14th Conn.] About sundown of the 2nd. we were advanced to the front, and formed to the left of Gordonsville road, near the Chancellor House. From this position we were moved along the plank road leading to Spottsylvania Court House, and formed the line of battle facing to the south-west on the right of the road. The regiment was on the right of the brigade in the second line of battle and was unsupported on the right. This position was somewhat altered during the night, but was substantially that occupied on the morning of the 3rd. About sunrise on the morning of the 3rd instant, the first line of battle having been forced by a terrific assault of the enemy, this regiment became engaged, the enemy appearing on our front and right flank almost simultaneously. We were forced to retire, principally on account of there being no troops on our right to prevent the enemy, which had engaged the front line on our right, from passing through the unoccupied interval and attaining our rear. After withdrawing, the regiment joined the remainder of the brigade and was placed behind rifle-pits to the left. Here we remained from the evening of the 3rd, to the morning of the 6th, being occasionally under a slight fire, but meeting with no loss. About 2 A.M. on the 6th, this regiment was withdrawn and re-crossed the river to the camp. The strength of the regiment on the morning of the 3rd was 219 (128).

While there were none killed, the regiment suffered largely from wounds. Captain Bronson of Company I received his fatal wound, dying June 3, just a month later. The total number of wounded was 3 commissioned officers, 34 enlisted men; missing, 2 commissioned officers, one of whom was Captain Samuel Fiske ("Dunn Browne")[1] who was at the time supposed to be killed; enlisted men, 17 (123).

1. Dunn Browne was the pen name of Fiske, a Massachusetts clergyman who was pastor of a Congregational church in Madison, Connecticut, when he enlisted in the 14th Connecticut Volunteers and whose wartime letters to the *Springfield Republican* were published posthumously as *Dunn Browne's Experiences in the Army.* Fiske was wounded May 6, 1864, in the Wilderness campaign and died May 22.

Near United States Ford, Rappahannock River, May 4, 1863

My dear Mother,

The regiment was engaged about 6 A.M. yesterday in the woods near Chancellorsville. While rallying the men I was struck in the head by a piece of shell which knocked me flat. I was picked up by Sg't [Robert] Russell of my company and a private and stayed with the boys a half hour, but the blood flowed so as to make me faint, and then Major Ellis sent me to hospital in the field, whence I was sent over on the north side of the river, where my wound was dressed. I was pretty faint last night but feel much better today, and am strongly tempted to rejoin the regiment, which has not yet re-crossed the river. But the surgeons here say they shall send me to Washington as I am not strong and have a bad cold, beside being very weak from loss of blood.

Poor Capt. Bronson is mortally wounded. He behaved nobly in the fight. I was near him, as I was to Davis, and both fought like lions—the one from religious confidence, the other from devil-to-pay recklessness. A strange contrast, those two men. We lost some 40 wounded, none killed as yet reported. Our Brigadier Gen. William Hays [commanding 2nd Brigade, 3rd Division, 2nd Corps] was captured, as was Lt. Jim Simpson.

The fight was horribly mismanaged by somebody. I know less about it than any fight I was ever in. We were hurled here and there in a higglety-piggety way that reflects no credit on Gen. Hooker.

This is the 4th days fight. Don't be anxious. We shall win yet.

Your own, Harry

Goddard's Addendum, 1887.

To the above letter let me add from memory 24 years later, some facts.

On the night of April 29, our regiment moved from our camp at Falmouth to Bank's Ford, where we chopped wood and made much noise all night, by order, evidently to mislead as to our real crossing point. Next day we hurried up to United States Ford, where we crossed without opposition.

The day we crossed we lay for hours on the roadside a little in rear of the Chancellorsville Tavern, not engaged though under fire of the rebel shells all day. After sundown we marched out on the pike and then were sent off a road at right angles to the pike in great haste, encountering heavy artillery fire. We were halted and ordered to take to the woods on the right of the road on which we had started. This brought us on the third side of the square of which our first position was the base.

Here we lay all night, May 2nd-3rd, with skirmishes (all around us). I well remember the difficulty with which I got a smoke that night, lying on my belly behind a tree with my soft hat over my pipe to hide the smoke, lest it draw a rebel bullet.

In the late afternoon of the 2nd, Sigel's corps[1] driven in by Jackson, came flying pell-mell through the woods, followed by showers of bullets. Ere we could perfectly form our lines thus broken, we were forced back to the open ground behind the woods near our original position. It was while exposed in aligning my company that a shell burst near me, a small fragment hitting me in the head as stated in the letter.

On the 3rd, I was sent in an ambulance from U.S. Ford to Aquina creek military post of Sedgwick's fight in his brave retreat from Fredericksburg by Bank's Ford. At Aquina creek I was put in a stretcher with hundreds of other wounded— our wants being most fondly ministered to by the ladies of the U.S. Sanitary Commission. I remember that one was afraid that over ten spoons of whiskey might be too much for me. Alas she little knew our capacity for whiskey at that era of our lives.

I reached Washington May 9th and after calling on my sister Julia and her husband next to the Ebbitt House, to breakfast. I was tired and hungry and had a soiled bandage on my head. Hurrying into breakfast, I am at the next table to the charming Woolsey family[2] who had been so kind to me on my first visit to Washington, and who all through the war devoted themselves to nursing us wounded. In my condition I pretended not to see them, but in a moment felt a hand on my shoulder, and looking up heard the words, "My poor boy," from Mrs. Woolsey, whose eyes were full of tears. It was <u>too much</u> for me. God bless her memory and all their family evermore.

After examining my wounds, the Surgeon gave me a sick leave and I returned to Connecticut, where I remained until June, when I started for the front. The letters following complete the story.

1. In fact it was Maj. Gen. Oliver O. Howard who took command of the 11th Corps from Sigel in February 1863.

2. Geogeanna Woolsey, in particular, young and single when the war began, was among a hundred women selected by the U.S. Sanitary Commission to be trained as a nurse. She worked at a hospital for wounded soldiers in Washington, D.C.

Excerpt from *14th C. V.: Regimental Reminiscences of the War of the Rebellion*, by Henry P. Goddard (Middletown, Conn.: C. W. Church, 1877)

The thick woods and bloody carnage of Chancellorsville next sweep past in the review with the figure of Capt. Bronson bravely dying from his wounds in the fierce fight, showing courage that, as he once told me, overcame his natural timidity solely from his faith in the Lord of All (12).

15

Staff Duty with General Tyler
as Gettysburg Turns the Tide

Recovering from wounds received at Chancellorsville, Goddard goes on leave to Washington and then to his home in Norwich. On his way back to his regiment, he visits Baltimore, where he networks with some influential relatives, friends and connections, including Gen. Dan Tyler of Norwich, who asks him to join his staff. He crosses paths with a "red-faced" Gen. Joseph Hooker just after the general was replaced by Maj. Gen. George Meade as army commander. He also meets up with his older brother, Alf, who has left the Sandwich Islands to join the army despite Goddard's entreaties to stay out of harm's way. As Tyler's aide-de-camp, Goddard is absent from his regiment as it plays an important role at Gettysburg, which, he reports, it "was just my luck to miss" (160) after the gut-wrenching defeats at Fredericksburg and Chancellorsville. Although not present at Gettysburg, Goddard interviews members of the 14th Connecticut and writes a moving narrative of the decisive third day on Cemetery Ridge, which was published in *Harper's Weekly*. Bored with his staff assignment, he is eager to return to his regiment.

Encouraged by his rout of Hooker's army at Chancellorsville, Lee decided on a second invasion of the North. Scraping up an army of nearly seventy-five thousand men, Lee—using Maj. Gen. J. E. B. Stuart's cavalry to keep Union observers from determining his whereabouts—moved north into Pennsylvania, most likely en route to the state capital of Harrisburg. Hooker, constantly at odds with chief of staff Maj. Gen. Henry Halleck, tendered his resignation in late June. To Hooker's dismay, it was quickly accepted. Lincoln appointed Maj. Gen. George Meade, a longtime corps commander, as the fifth commander of the Army of the Potomac in ten months. Stuart's long ride around the Union army took him into central Maryland, and Lee was handicapped by the unexplained absence of his renowned cavalry commander, his "eyes and ears." The opposing armies finally converged at the crossroads town of Gettysburg, Pennsylvania, where the bloodiest battle in American history was fought July 1–3. The first two days were inconclusive; then

Lee, against the advice of his chief lieutenant, Maj. Gen. James Longstreet, decided to risk all on a frontal assault on Cemetery Ridge, the center of the Union line which stretched for a mile along Cemetery Hill. More than half the twelve thousand courageous Confederates in Pickett's charge on July 3 were casualties of Union rifles, muskets, and cannon. Lee accepted blame for the defeat as the remnants of his loyal army staggered off the battlefield. On July 4, seeing that Meade was not going to follow up his victory with an attack, Lee began his escape to Virginia across a swollen Potomac River. Lee lost over twenty-eight thousand men at Gettysburg—more than a third of his army was killed, wounded, captured, or missing—a crushing blow. The Army of the Potomac's losses totaled more than twenty-three thousand.

~

Excerpts from *History of the Fourteenth Regiment, Connecticut Vol. Infantry,* by Charles D. Page (Meriden, Conn.: Horton Printing Co., 1906)

The regiment at this time numbered one hundred and sixty men, about forty of whom were doing picket duty in front of its line. Somewhat to the right and about 2,500 feet away were the farm buildings, house and barn, of William Bliss. Mr. Bliss was like many other farmers who gave more attention to the architecture and pretentiousness of their barns than they do to their houses. This barn was a rambling structure seventy-five feet long and thirty-five feet wide. It was a solid oak frame incased by a stone wall one story in height, and then of brick. It was plentifully supplied with doors and windows and hastily made apertures. It was indeed a veritable fort. . . . The Confederate sharp-shooters were not long in seeing the advantage of this improvised fort and soon every window, door and crevice showed the protruding muzzles of long-range rifles ready to do their deadly work. During the latter hours of the 2d. of July, it was found that these rifles were picking off officers and men along the skirmish line which it commanded. Consequently the First Delaware Regiment was sent out to capture the buildings and took the ground and some prisoners, but were obliged to return. The four companies of the Twelfth New Jersey were detailed for the duty of capturing the grounds and buildings. They charged in good style and captured them, taking a large number of prisoners and losing some of their own men. They were withdrawn after dark. . . . On the morning of July 3rd., about half past seven, five other companies of the Twelfth New Jersey again captured the barn, taking more prisoners, and returned again to the line. And again this military eel-pot was set to catch a fresh batch of slippery Confederates. Finding the firing intolerable, especially to men of Arnold's Battery on the crest, as well as those on the skirmish line, General [Brig. Gen. Alexander] Hays ordered the Fourteenth Regiment to capture the buildings "to stay." Captain

S. A. Moore, with four companies of the regiment, numbering some fifty or sixty men, was sent down to capture the brick barn. To reach the barn was a perilous task and no man coveted the work. After passing up toward headquarters and down a lane across the Emmettsburg road, it was then necessary to cross a field, a distance of nearly 1,800 feet. Reaching this field, they were given orders to break and each man reach the barn as best he could. In doing this, the desperate character of the undertaking was realized, as they were open to the fire of the skirmish line and the sharp-shooters in the barn, together with a flanking fire from the brigades of [Brig. Gen. Edward Thomas, Maj. Gen. William Pender's division] Thomas and [Brig. Gen. Samuel McGowan, Maj. Gen. A.P. Hill's division] McGowan located in "Long Lane," but such was the dash and the wild fury of the approach that the Confederates left the barn in haste, giving only parting shots. Captain Moore was the first to enter the barn and the Federal soldiers were soon in full command. Several prisoners were taken. The Confederates, however, took possession of the house about one hundred and fifty feet away, and sheltered as best they could in that and the peach orchard adjoining, where from these two sources they continued the firing. Some of the men were wounded in the run to the barn, and soon after they occupied the barn, a shell struck it, killing Sergeant [Nathan C.] Clement and wounding others. . . . Finding that the capture of the barn did not remedy the trouble, orders were given Major Ellis to take the remaining four companies of the regiment, the other two companies being out as skirmishers, and capture the house. Leaving the colors and the color-guard at the wall, the route of Major Ellis to the house was much more exposed to the Confederate sharp-shooters' firing than was the first detail, but on they went, with a vim of determination which characterized the men of the command. It was like dodging ten thousand shafts of lightning. They soon reached the house, but lost some men on the way. The Confederates left the house as precipitously as they did the barn, some of their parting shots killing Sergeant [George W.] Baldwin of Company I. . . .

Things now began to look serious for the brave men who had driven out the Confederates, now posted in the rear. The house proved a shallow protection and most of Major Ellis' detail went to the barn. As there were no windows or opportunities to fire in the rear of the barn, it looked as if the men were at the mercy of the enemy. . . . General Hays sent instructions to burn the buildings. Captain Postles, of Colonel Smyth's staff, was dispatched with the order to Major Ellis to burn the buildings. Captain Postles[1] bounded off his magnificent charger, going over the ground like a hurricane, fully aware of the dangerous character of his mission. He, however, reached the barn, delivered the order and returned to headquarters to safety. . . . The barn was set afire in different places, and a straw bed in the house proved a convenient dispenser of flame. Then the men, taking up the dead and wounded, started back for the wall, running the same gauntlet as when they went to the barn. They had done their work well and when they reached the Emmetts-burg road both buildings were in flames. . . . The Fourteenth acquitted itself hand-somely, losing ten killed and fifty-two wounded (143–48).

Accounts [of Pickett's charge against Cemetery Ridge, where the 14th C.V. was positioned] seem to agree that the Confederate line broke quicker in the immedi-ate front of the Fourteenth than any where else, and seeing this a shout went up from the regiment, which was taken up and echoed and reechoed along the whole Union line. In vain did the Confederate commanders attempt to reform their bro-ken columns, colors were dropped and the men fled in confusion. . . .

Another incident connected with this remarkable record of the Fourteenth was the capture of a flag by Major [then sergeant major William B.] Hincks. The Con-federate color planted about ten rods in front of the center of the regiment still stood. There were no rebels standing near it, but several were lying down, waiting for the men to advance. Major Ellis called for volunteers to capture the flag and instantly Major Hincks, Major [then captain John C.] Broatch and Lieutenant [George N.] Brigham leaped the wall. Brigham was shot down by a retreating rebel, but the other two sped on, Hincks finally outstripping Broatch ran straight and swift for the color, amid a storm of shot. Swinging his saber over the prostrate Con-federates and uttering a terrific yell, he seized the flag and hastily returned to the line. He was the object of all eyes and the men cheered him heartily as he reached the ranks.[2] It was the flag of the Fourteenth Tennessee Regiment (152–54).

A number of the field and line officers surrendered their swords to Major Ellis and Adjutant Doten. About two hundred prisoners were captured, two for every man in the regiment. . . .

Those of the prisoners who were able to walk came in after which the boys of the regiment went out and brought in the wounded, although under a heavy fire from the skirmish line which the Confederates had been able to reestablish. These Confederate wounded were tenderly treated and cared for, even portions of the previous stone wall being removed so that they could be taken in without jolting. Coffee was made and the meager rations shared, showing that "One touch of sor-row makes all the world akin" even in the horrors of war (158).

The colors captured belonged to the following regiments: 14th Tennessee, 1st Tennessee, 16th North Carolina, 52nd North Carolina, 14th Virginia.

. . . The list of the killed and wounded in the above engagements: Killed, enlisted men, 10; wounded, commissioned officers, 10; enlisted men, 42; missing, enlisted men, 4; total 66 (166).

1. Capt. James P. Postles, Company A, 1st Delaware Infantry, was among sixty-three men awarded the Medal of Honor for heroism at Gettysburg.

2. Hincks was awarded the Medal of Honor for his daring capture of the flag. Two other members of the regiment, Corp. Elijah W. Bacon and Corp. Christopher Flynn, also received the Medal of Honor for deeds of bravery at Gettysburg.

Eutaw House, Baltimore, Md. June 28, 1863

My dear Julia,

I reached New York safely on Friday from Norwich and spent the day there.

I found Col. Donn Piatt at our table and gave him your letter. Soon in came all Gen. [Maj. Gen. Robert C., commanding Middle Department at Baltimore] Schenck's daughters and Miss Ella Kirby—sister of Mrs. Donn Piatt. I was much embarrassed by being encircled by such an array of damsels, but Miss Kirby (bless her) soon came to the rescue and took me under her protection. I gave Miss Schenck your letter.

After tea I called on the Misses Schenck, who presented me to Gen. Schenck, who was very kind. Found Ned Tyler there. I then called on Mrs. Piatt, who is loveliness personified. I would like to know some girl just like her of about 17.

Mrs. Piatt and Ned Tyler asked me if I would like to be a staff officer. Answer, "Yes."

Today Col. Piatt tells me that I had best get a horse as Gen. Dan Tyler of my own dear Norwich wants me on his staff and that Gen. Schenck will detail me. As I belong in another than Gen. Schenck's department, this can only be done—so Col. [William H.] Cheeseboro A A G says by Gen. Schenck's ordering to remain here under medical treatment—when Tyler can detail me as "fit for light duty." This done, Gen. Tyler will apply, with Schenck's approval, to the War Department, who can make the detail permanent if they see fit.

You see I have found friends, here at the hotel. Besides Schenck and Tyler and their staffs are [Brig Gen. Robert H.] Milroy, [Brig. Gen., commanding defenses of Baltimore] E. B. Tyler and their staffs. Yet I fear that I may not suit Gen. Tyler, but I will try.

Love to all, Harry

Baltimore, Md., June 29, 1863

Dear Julia,

Having been examined by Dr. [Willard, surgeon in charge of the Armory Square Hospital in Washington] Bliss, U.S.A., I am ordered to remain here under his treatment, mainly cod liver oil, and I am detailed as A D C to Gen. Dan Tyler. Col. Piatt has put me in the way of getting a horse. (Note: I seized one at a secesh livery stable and used it all the while I was on staff duty. It was a lovely little mare.)

Will Lusk is on Tyler's staff as captain and assistant adjutant general.

Poor Gen. Hooker has "gone up" or rather is "let down" from the command of the Army of the Potomac. He came here after his relief and looked red-faced.

Yours, Harry

Headquarters, Middle Department, 8th Army Corps
Baltimore, Md., June 29, 1863

My dear brother Alf,

Col. Piatt tells me you wanted a place on Tyler's staff. Now I have probably supplanted you unknowingly, and if you still wish the place, I will withdraw from it at once and return to my regiment. I am only temporarily detailed while here as "fit for light duty." It depends on Secretary Stanton, Gen. Tyler and <u>you</u> whether I remain. If you want the place just say the word and I will use all in my influence for you.

P.S. "Fighting Joe" is played.

Your affectionate brother, Harry

Baltimore, Md., June 30, 1863

My dear sister,

To my great surprise Alf arrived today. Your and mother's letters were duly read and considered.

This morning I wrote four copies of an order for Gen. Tyler, and then with Ned Tyler rode to all the camps in the city.

We had an alarm last night. Ned Tyler and I were at the Holiday St. Theater. The Webb sisters were acting when somebody entered the theater and shouted, "The rebels are coming." It didn't take long to clear the house. It's said one of the actresses fainted on the stage. We ran eight blocks to the hotel and got there just as Gen. Tyler was calling for his staff officers. A close shave with "Crazy Dan," as some old soldiers used to call him when he got mad.

We have forts commanding every road into the city and some very poor barricades in the streets. The troops were all under arms all night, but the alarm was a foolish scare as no rebels were near enough to be dangerous, though [Major, commanding the Maryland Confederate cavalry] Harry Gillmore is said to be along the line of the PW&B railroad.

Mrs. Piatt is quite ill from the excitement. Her sister stays by her.

The surgeon here says that I am threatened with "pulmonary phthisis" even though it is "incipient." Hence he doubts my ability for active field service. This makes it hard for me to give up my post to Alf as I really ought to do.

Your loving Harry

Eutaw House, Baltimore, Md., July 2nd, 1863

My dearest Mother,

Still here serving on Gen. Tyler's staff. I rode some 15 miles on duty yesterday and have written a great deal for the general today. I like the duty much and have decided to stay with Tyler till my 20 days under medical treatment expire, and then try to get on staff duty in my own army corps—doing all I can to get Alf my place with Tyler.

I meet friends and see distinguished people here constantly. Among the latter, whom I have been close to, are generals Hooker, [Maj. Gen. Ethan Allan] Hitchcock, Sigel, Schenck, Milroy, [Maj. Gen. Julius] Stahel, D. Tyler, E.B. Tyler, [Brig. Gen. Thomas F.] Meager, [Brig. Gen.] T.L. Kane and numerous others.

Hooker is a splendid looking man, but just now "none so poor as do him reverence."

Yours as ever, Harry

Harper's Weekly, November 21, 1863

"The Fourteenth at Gettysburg"

"Come, Fred [Capt. Frederick B. Doten, adjutant], tell me all about that glorious fight which, you know, it was just my luck to miss. If it had been such another whipping as we had at Fredericksburg, the fates would probably have let me be there. I have heard several accounts, and know the regiment did nobly; but the boys get so excited telling me about it that I have not yet a clear idea of the fight."

"Here goes, then," said the Adjutant, lighting a fresh cigar. "It will serve to pass away time, which hangs so heavy on our hands in this dreary hospital.

"We were not engaged on the first day of the fight, July 1, 1863, but were on the march for Gettysburg that day. All the afternoon we heard the cannonading growing more and more distinct as we approached the town, and as we came on the field at night learned that the First and Eleventh Corps, suffered much, and been driven back outside the town, with the loss of Maj. Gen. [John] Reynolds[1] who, it was generally said, brought on an engagement too hastily with Lee's whole army. We bivouacked on the field that night.

"About nine o'clock the next morning we moved up to the front, and by ten o'clock the enemy shells were falling around us. Captain Coit had a narrow escape here. We had just stacked arms and were resting, when a runaway horse, frightened by the shelling, came full tilt at him; 'twas 'heavy cavalry' against 'light infantry,' but Coit had presence of mind enough to draw his sword, and bringing it to a point, it entered the animal's belly. The shock knocked Coit over, and he was picked up senseless with a terribly battered face, and carried to the rear."

"By the way, Fred, is it not singular that he should have recovered so quickly and completely from such a severe blow?"

"Indeed it is. He is as handsome as ever; but to go on. At four o'clock in the afternoon we moved up to support a battery, and here we lay all night. About dark, Captain Broatch went out with the pickets. Though under artillery fire all night, we were not really engaged, as we did not fire a gun. Some of our pickets, unfortunately going too far to the front, were taken prisoners during the night.

"At about five o'clock on the morning of the 3rd, Captain [James L.] Townsend went out with Companies B and C, and relieved Broatch. As soon as he got out, Townsend advanced his men as skirmishers some three hundred yards beyond the regiment, which moved up to the impromptu rifle-pits, which were formed partially by a stone wall and partially by a real fence. Just as soon as our skirmishers were posted, they began firing at the rebel skirmishers, and kept it up all day, until the grand attack in the afternoon. Before they had been out twenty minutes, Corporal [Samuel] Huxham, of Company B, was instantly killed by a rebel bullet. It was not discovered until another of our skirmishers, getting out of ammunition, went up to him, saying, 'Sam, let me have some cartridges.' Receiving no answer, he stooped down and discovered that a bullet had entered the poor fellow's mouth, and had gone out of the back of his head, killing the brave, Chancellorsville-scarred corporal so quickly that he never knew what hit him.

"Presently Captain [Samuel A.] Moore was ordered down with four companies into a lot near by, to drive the rebel sharpshooters out of a house and barn from whence they were constantly picking off our men. Moore went down on a double-quick, and as usual, ahead of his men; he was the first man in the barn, and as he entered, the Butternuts were already jumping out. Moore and his men soon cleared the barn and then started for the house. Here that big sergeant in Company B (Norton) sprang in at the front door just in time to catch a bullet in his thigh, from a rebel watching at the back; but that reb did not live long to brag of it, one of our boys taking him 'on the wing.' Moore soon cleared the house out, and went back with his men. Later in the day, the rebs again occupied the house, and Major Ellis took the regiment and drove them out, burning the house, so as not to be bothered by any more concealed sharpshooters in it.

"Yes, I know the Major don't like to do a thing but once, so he always does it thoroughly the first time. It was in these charges for the possession of that house we lost more officers and men than in all the rest of the fight.

"About one o'clock in the afternoon, the enemy, who had been silent so long that the boys were cooking coffee, smoking, sleeping, etc., suddenly opened all their batteries of reserve artillery upon the position held by our corps, the Second. First, one great gun spoke, then, as if it had been the signal for the commencement of an artillery conversation, the whole hundred and twenty or more opened their mouths at once and poured out their fire. A perfect storm of shot and shell rained around and among us. The boys quickly jumped to their rifles and lay down behind the wall and rail barricade. For two hours this storm of shot and shell continued and seemed to increase in fury. Good God! I never heard anything like, and our regiment has been under fire 'somewhat,' as you know. The ground trembled like an aspen leaf; the air was full of small fragments of lead and iron from the shells. Then the sounds—there was the peculiar 'whoo?—whoo—whoo?'—of the round shot; the 'which one?'—'which one?' of that fiendish Whitworth projectile, and the demoniac shriek of shells. It seemed as if all the devils of hell were hold-ing high carnival.

"But, strange as it may seem, it was like many other 'sensation doings,' 'great cry and little wool,' as our regiment, and in fact the whole corps, lost very few men by it, the missiles passing over beyond our position, save the Whitworth projec-tiles, which did not quite reach us, as their single gun of that description was two miles off. Had the enemy had better artillerists at their guns, or a better view of our position, I cannot say what would have been the final result; but certain it is, noth-ing mortal could have stood that fire long, had it been better directed, and if our corps had broken that day, Gettysburg would have been a lost battle, and General Lee instead of Heintzelman the commanding officer in the District of Columbia today.

"At about 3 P.M., the enemy's fire slackened, died away, and the smoke lifted to disclose a corps of the rebel 'Grand Army of Northern Virginia,' advancing across the long plain in our front, in three magnificent lines of battle, with the troops massed in close column by division on both flanks. How splendidly they looked! Our skirmishers, who had staid at their posts through all, gave them volley after volley as they came on, until Capt. Townsend was ordered to bring his men in, which he did in admirable order; his men, loading and firing all the way, came in steadily and coolly—all that were left of them, for a good half of them were killed or wounded before they reached the regiment.

"On, on came the rebels, with colors flying and bayonets gleaming in the sun-light, keeping their lines as straight as if on parade; over fences and ditches they come, but still their lines never break, and still they come. For a moment all is hushed along our lines as we gaze in silent admiration at the brave rebs; then our division commander, 'Aleck Hays' [Brig. Gen. Alexander Hays], rides up and, pointing to the last fence the enemy must cross before reaching us, says, 'Don't fire till they get to that fence; then let 'em have.'

"On, on come the rebs, till we can see the whites of their eyes, and hear the offi-cers' command, 'Steady, boys, steady!' They reach the fence, some hundred yards in front of us, when the order 'Fire!' rings down our line; and, rising as one man, the rifles of the old Second Army Corps ring a death knell for many a brave heart in butternut dress, worthy of a better cause—a knell that will ring in the hearts of many mothers, sisters and wives, on many a plantation in the once fair and Sunny South, where there will be weeping and wailing for the soldier who never returns, who sleeps at Gettysburg. 'Load and fire at will!' Oh Heaven! How we poured our fire into them—a merciless hail of lead! Their first line wavers, breaks and runs; some of their color sergeants bolt and plant their standards firmly in the ground; they are too well disciplined to leave their colors yet. But they stop only for a moment, then fall back, colors and all. They fall back, but rally, and dress on other lines, under a tremendous fire from our advancing rifles; rally and come on again to meet their death. Line after line of rebels come up, deliver their fire, one volley, and they are mown down like the grass of the field. They fall back, form, and come up again with their battle flags still waving, but again they are driven back.

"On our right there is a break in the line, where a battery has been in position, but, falling short of ammunition, and unable to move it off under such a heavy fire, the gunners have abandoned it to its fate. Some of the rebels gain a footing here. One daring fellow leaps upon the gun and waves his rebel flag. In an instant a right oblique fire from 'ours,' and a left oblique from the regiment on the left of the position, rolls the ragged rebel and rebel rag in the dust, rolls the determined force back from the gun, and it is ours.

"By-and-by the enemy's lines come up smaller and thinner, break quicker, and are longer in forming. Our boys are wild with excitement and grow reckless. Lieut. John Tibbetts stands up yelling like mad, 'Give it to 'em! Give it to 'em!' A bullet enters his arm—that same arm in which he caught two bullets at Antietam; Johnny's arm drops by his side; he turns quickly to his First Lieutenant, saying, 'I have got another bullet in the same old arm, but I don't care a d—n!' Heaven forgive Johnny; rebel lead will sometimes bring rebel words with it. All of 'ours' are carried away with excitement; the sergeant-major leaps a wall, dashes down among the rebs, and brings back a battle flag. Others follow our sergeant-major, and before the enemy's repulse becomes a rout, we of the Fourteenth have six of their battle flags.

"Prisoners are brought in by the hundreds—officers and men. We pay no attention to them, being too busy sending our leaden messengers after the now flying hosts. One of our prisoners, a rebel officer, turns to me, saying, 'Where are the men we've been fighting?' 'Here,' I answered, pointing down our short thin line. 'Good God!' says he, 'Is that all? I wish I could get back.'

"All through the fight Gen. Hancock might be seen galloping up and down the line of our bully corps, regardless of the leaden hail all around him, and when finally severely wounded in the hip, he was carried a little to the rear, where he lay on a stretcher and still gave his orders.

"The fight was now about over; there was only an occasional shot exchanged between the retreating rebel sharp-shooters and our men, and I looked about me and took account of stock. We had lost about seventy killed and wounded, leaving only 100 men fit for duty. We had killed treble that number and taken nearly a brigade of prisoners, six stands of colors, and guns, swords and pistols without number.

"Hardly a man in the unit had over two or three cartridges left. Dead and wounded rebels were piled up in heaps in front of us, especially in front of Co's A and B, where Sharp's rifles had done effective work.

"It was a great victory. 'Fredericksburg on the other leg,' as the boys said. The rebel prisoners told us their leaders assured them that they would only meet the Pennsylvania militia, but when they saw the ace of clubs—the trefoil badge of the second Corps—a cry went through their lines—'The Army of the Potomac, by Heaven!'

"So ended the battle of Gettysburg, and the sun sank to rest that night on a battle field that had proved that the Army of the Potomac could and would save the people of the North from invasion whenever and wherever they may be assailed."

1. Reynolds was killed at Gettysburg by a Confederate sharpshooter July 1, 1863.

U.S. Hotel Wilmington, Delaware, July 4th, 1863

Dear Julia,

Here I am with Gen. Tyler, who is military governor of the "new Department of the Delaware." The post is more honorable in that the general commands a department, but I fear we shall have little to do and not many troops to handle, whereas in Baltimore I was getting into the good graces of many prominent officers.

Col. Piatt had Gen. Schenck put me on full pay as under medical treatment and Tyler has applied for my permanent detail.

Wilmington is a city as large as Hartford, Conn., noted for the numerous hogs that run at large in its streets, the best ice cream, and in this part of town the worst liquor and cigars, homely girls, and half-naked Negroes. Ned Tyler says that uptown the city is beautiful, but I have not been there yet.

My horse is a beauty. He cost his secesh owner $100 two weeks ago. He cost me "thank you" to Col. Piatt.

This is too dull soldiering; I really want to get back into the field now and relinquish this post to Alf. Cod liver oil is curing me. I now weigh 130 pounds and hope to gain ten in a month.

I get along with Gen. Tyler far better than I had dared to hope. Bishop [Alfred, first Episcopal bishop of Delaware] Lee, Gen. Tyler's brother-in-law, is in the room but I have not yet been presented. We shall hear him preach tomorrow.

Poor Joe Hooker. I cannot help admiring him. In my opinion, he is one of nature's noblemen. He was first to praise Gen. [Maj. Gen. George] Meade, who has just fought the Battle of Gettysburg. How splendidly Meade has done.

Did you read how old [Maj. Gen. Winfield Scott] Hancock took our corps, the 2nd, in with their old yell and how it took 22 stands of colors. The field is the place for a soldier, and the army will fight now as never before as it has at last a leader whom it can trust.

God grant that before another 4th July our old Union shall be restored.

Excerpt from *14th C. V.: Regimental Reminiscences of the War of the Rebellion*, by Henry P. Goddard (Middletown, Conn.: C. W. Church, 1877)

Gettysburg comes next, with its grand reputation as the battle where at last the tide of invasion was finally and forever stayed, and where, as a Southern friend put it, the fight was "Fredericksburg over again but with the boot on the other leg." How grandly Gen. Hancock rode up and down the lines that day with his stockings down over his shoes; how nobly Sgt. Major (now Major) Hincks labored as he captured prisoners and battle flags; and how faithful unto death was Corporal Huxham of Middletown, shot dead in his tracks on the picket line; how coolly Lt. Sam Scranton shot a rebel in the doorway of that troublesome house as he would have shot a squirrel on his father's farm; how well Capt. [Samuel A.] Moore and Lts. [Wilbur D.] Fisk and [John A.] Tibitts fought "F" Company, and how the latter swore at the Johnnies for wounding him in the sound arm. But the story of "How the 14th fought at Gettysburg" is a matter of history (13).

16

Staff Duty, Hospital Stay, Draftees, Substitutes, and Deserters

Now aide-de-camp to Brig. Gen. Dan Tyler at Wilmington, Delaware, Goddard visits Fort Delaware, where he learns to get along with the cantankerous Tyler and enjoys fine dining with general officers and prominent citizens. Visiting with friends from "the glorious old 14th," he vicariously basks in their heroic role at Gettysburg and hopes to recover sufficiently from his wounds at Chancellorsville to rejoin them. He learns of his brother's appointment as a first lieutenant in the 8th Connecticut Volunteer Infantry and comments, "He has been very lucky to get at one jump what took me two years toil" (176). His physician clears him to return to his regiment near Warrenton Junction, Virginia. With a military draft now in force, he decries "the state of things now in the North—everybody trying to avoid the draft, when if we had only 300,000 more men we could settle this business in pretty quick time" (174). He is angered by his neighbors back home who pay the required $300 or pay substitutes to escape military duty. Still in poor health and now beset with scurvy, he is sent by ambulance to the officers' hospital at Georgetown, Washington, where the patients get a visit from the renowned Dorothy Dix. In mid-October, he learns from the newspapers that the 14th was engaged at Bristoe Station, and is "nearly sick with vexation at myself for being away from another fight" (185). He is discharged from the hospital and, returning south, is appointed ordinance officer of the 2nd Corps artillery brigade after turning down a captaincy of Company K because his health would not permit the rigors of an infantry foot soldier's life.

∼

Description of the New Conscripts and Substitutes: Excerpted from *History of the Fourteenth Regiment, Connecticut Vol. Infantry,* by Charles D. Page (Meriden, Conn.: Horton Printing Co., 1906)

While experience proved that many of these men, who were for the most part conscripts and substitutes, did very valiant service and were an honor to the brave old regiment, a large percentage were not only conscripts, but nondescripts. Perhaps no occurrence brought to the minds of the original men of the regiment, now reduced to about eighty, the great loss they had sustained by battle and disease since their departure from Connecticut as did the advent of these new recruits. The character of this addition, mostly foreigners from New York City, left little in common between the men. These new men had scant sympathy with the cause for which they were fighting; they lacked the bond of state pride and the tie of companionship, made not only by kinship in many instances, comrades and school-mates of old, but by the experiences of the days and weeks since they entered the service. This motley array of new recruits, representing fifteen or twenty nationalities, presented strange types of character with manifestations at times ludicrous and at other times provoking and disgusting (175).

The presence of a large class of men of this character made it doubly difficult for the old and trusted men in the regiment. A constant watch had to be kept that they did not desert and very few of them could be trusted to do picket duty (180–81).

Sergeant Benjamin Hirst says of this [October 14, 1863] engagement:—"This affair at Bristoe Station was one of the most brilliant little battles that occurred during the whole war and came about in this way. General Lee, whose army was rapidly recruited after its return to Virginia, began to get tired of inactivity and so resolved upon a new campaign with the object of driving the Union troops out of Virginia and taking advantage of any errors that might be committed on the Union side. How near he succeeded is told in the battle at Bristoe Station where the Second Corps, through some mistake of General [Maj. Gen. George] Sykes, was left without support in front of General [Jubal] Early's Division, who was thrusting his brigades in the gap between Sykes' rear and Warren's advance. Both sides were taken by surprise. Early supposed he was following the Union rear when he was attacked by Warren, and Warren supposed the road was clear in front until the head of his column was assailed by the rebels. In the mutual surprise, Warren displayed the best judgment by seizing the railroad cut and embankment a moment or two before the rebels could get there, and when the rebels did get there, they were driven back with great loss. After this repulse, Early was more cautious than was his habit and waited too long before renewing the attack, when he had at least one-half of the rebel army under his command while Warren had but the Second Corps, containing about 12,000 men only."

[Sergeant E. B. Tyler:] ". . . Hardly deserving to be called a battle in all that implies, yet for a short, sharp and promptly decided little fight, it was a rare specimen. The rebel attack with artillery, cavalry and infantry on our Second Corps, who were acting as rear-guard that day, was spirited enough, but they ought to have known better, and the short time it took the old Second Corps to capture one of their batteries and about five hundred prisoners was probably a surprise to some of them. It was not a trifling lesson to us, however, and was the first time that some of our recruits were under fire. In the main they acted creditably, some being wounded and others taken prisoner."

The following is the list of casualties to the regiment returned by Colonel Ellis: —Killed, enlisted men, 4; wounded, commissioners officers (1st Lieutenant Wilbur D. Fiske) 1, enlisted men, 17; missing, 4; total, 26 (192–94).

Wilmington, Del., July 8, 1863

My dear Jule,

Yesterday General Schoepf[1] sent a steamer up from Fort Delaware for General Tyler, who taking Ned and myself proceeded down the Delaware River to the fort, an hour and a half's sail. The trip was delightful, especially as we had the news of the taking of Vicksburg at starting.

Arriving at the fort, which is located on a beautiful island, General Schoepf received the general in a most affectionate manner. They served together with Halleck at Corinth [the Siege of Corinth, Mississippi, June 1862] and were both on the Buell courtmartial.[2]

We then proceeded to the general's residence inside the fort—a neat, lovely cottage surrounded by shrubbery, with a garden full of every kind of flower, fruit and vegetable.

Entering the house, a charmingly pretty little woman rushed up and embraced General Tyler, who was delighted to see her, who was introduced as Mrs. Schoepf. Then her mother and sister and children came down into the parlor. Several officers came in. The general brought in a box of real Havana's sent him by Admiral Dupont [Samuel Du Pont]. Mrs. S. had several bottles of fine Catawba brought in and we did have a splendid time.

We took tea, took a glance at some of the 4,000 rebel prisoners, and took the boat for Wilmington. All along our homeward route, the people were celebrating the capture of Vicksburg, and the view of the rockets, etc. was delightful from the water.

Have you read how the 14th C.V. took four stands of colors at Gettysburg; how Dr. Dudley, Capt. Coit, Lts. Seymour, [Frank E.] Stoughton and Tibbets were wounded? This is the third bullet that the latter has received in one arm. Did you read how when the rebels were hurled back our boys would rise and howl, "How do you like Fredericksburg now?" How Meade and his lines were formed so that supports were always ready. How we licked them and how we charged and are charging them. Yours, Harry

1. Albin Schoeph, an officer in the Austrian army, emigrated to the United States in 1851. In September 1861 he was appointed brigadier general of volunteers; commanded a brigade at the battle of Mill Springs, Kentucky; commanded the 1st Division, 3rd Corps at Perryville, Kentucky; and then commanded a prison at Fort Delaware for the remainder of the war.

2. Maj. Gen. Don Carlos Buell, commanding the Army of the Ohio, was court-martialed after the battle of Perryville, Kentucky, October 8, 1862, for his failure to pursue retreating Confederates.

Wilmington, Del., July 8, 1863

Dear Mother,

Have you seen in the papers how the old 14th took four stands of colors and our division 11? How Coit was wounded in the face and Dr. Dudley in the arm? How Hancock gloriously fighting was wounded and how our noble old Army of the Potomac has at last flogged the rebels in a fair stand-up fight. Wasn't it glorious?

Don't fret about me, any of you. I am better daily and my only grief now is that I was not with my regiment in the late row; also pity for poor Alf, who I fear will think I "chiseled" him out of a place. I feel very sorry about it and hope all will come out right yet.

Yet I can but think it best that we should not serve in the same department. I prefer not, decidedly for many reasons. I would not like to be in the same battle as other would fret about the other. It's always best for brothers not to be business associates. No, let each take his own course. That's best.

Again, I don't think Alf would like Gen. Tyler, although I like him better daily. He is a gentleman, with all his faults, and all one need do is to obey his orders without questions. If you don't understand them, don't say so, but find out by the connection and by outside enquiry. Think quick and find out somehow what the old man wants or means. Then fly and do it. That's all, and the old man will never trouble you.

Your loving Harry

Wilmington, Del., July 11, 1863

Dear Mother,

I ran down to Baltimore Saturday afternoon, with my mind about settled to return to the regiment. Arriving there, Col. Piatt said I must not do it, at any rate not without seeing the surgeon-in-chief.

On Sunday I called upon Dr. Bliss, who said I certainly looked much better than I did 20 days ago, but must not return to the 14th yet. So he made another 20 days certificate for me. I told him that at the end of that term, if I did not hear from the War Department, I should go to the front nolens, volens. "We will see," he replied. "Come here again at the end of that time."

At the Eutaw House found Major [William H.] Mallory, late of the Harris Light. Walked with the major and his father to Federal Hill. The major was very pleasant, but awfully down on Kilpatrick.

On Monday I met here under medical treatment Col. Ellis, Lieuts. Simpson and Fiske, all of my regiment.

Major Ellis, Lieuts. Simpson and Fiske called and spent the evening. They say the fight was glorious. Hays and Morris arrived a day too late. Officers and men covered themselves with glory. Capt. Moore of Co. F and Lt. John Tibbits of the same company are particularly mentioned. John got another bullet in his arm (No. 3). The hard marching and fighting and hunger have reduced the number of officers present to six. Capt. Davis commands the regiment.

The regiment has got to be so admirably drilled that it was selected in Maryland to show off "evolutions of the line" in Uniontown.

So you see, if I don't hear from the War Department ere August 9th, I shall then go to the glorious old 14th. So you can write me at Wilmington for the present.

I bought a jacket in Baltimore—new style, braid on arms, etc., which with straps cost me $20.

When I get my next pay, we'll have that stone to father erected. Thank uncle Charles and George, but tell them that you have two sons, one of whom at least loves his mother and his father's memory better than all else on earth.

Yours lovingly, Harry

Wilmington, Del., July 16th, 1863

My dear Julia,

On the 14th took a long ride on the other side of Christina Creek. The rides are most beautiful all about here. There is a long, level plain south of the city and it is planted with maples for miles, making it a charming ride.

North of the city the country is rugged and steep so you have every variety of scenery. Looking out of our office window, the eye sweeps across plains, hills and valleys till it loses itself in the Delaware.

Called on Dr. [J. Frank] Vaughan, president of the Union League. He and some dozen or more gentlemen have a private billiard room where Ned Tyler and I have a standing invitation and play a great deal. Yesterday the general, Ned and I (Lusk has gone to New York to volunteer his services against the draft rioters wherever he can be of use. Noble fellow, that Lusk.) dined at Mr. Lamont's—one of the bon ton. His sister is wife of one of the Duponts. His own wife is a Spanish lady and without question one of the handsomest women I ever saw. Her sister is very beautiful also, and they all are very patriotic. Mrs. Lamont and sister, as indeed all the ladies in Wilmington, are at the depot daily as the wounded soldiers pass through, with all manners of delicacies. This is one of the most hospitable places I ever got into, and more loyal than Norwich. Why, the ladies have all torn McClellan's picture out of the "Rebellion Record."

The dinner was recherche—six kinds of wine, and such wine. Not champagne nor such "stuff," but first muscatel—a Cincinnati wine far ahead of all champagne.

Then California "golden ladies wine." Then a Connecticut wine said to be equal to Madeira in its palmiest day. Then sherry, port and whiskey.

Last night, more billiards and more riding. Then two hours reading [the 1862 novel] "The Pearl of Orr's Island," of Mrs. [Harriet Beecher] Stowe. Then sweet sleep.

I am copying a great deal for the general of late. Can read his writing easier than any other member of his staff and surprise myself at the neatness of the documents I have copied.

I know the old general likes me and wants to keep me on his staff, but of this anon.

Now, then, about the "bird in hand vs. bird in bush." First, I have not the bird in hand. Here is the case. Gen. Schenck ordered me to report to the surgeon in Baltimore. The surgeon certified that I would not be able to travel for 20 days, ending July 19th. Then Schenck gives me permission to serve with Tyler as acting aide during that time. Meantime, Tyler applies to Piatt to have me detailed by the War Department. The application comes back to Gen. Tyler, endorsed by Halleck that "the application must come through the regiment commander." Gen. Tyler sends it to Piatt again with a letter requesting him to procure the proper endorsements. Since then I have heard nothing of it.

Yours, Harry

Wilmington, Del., July 22nd, 1863

Dear Jule,

I enclose a little document that settles the staff question hereabout. The adjutant general <u>refuses</u> the detail. Don't think I am disappointed, as it was like Paddy and his pig, viz:

"How much did your pig weigh, Pat."

"Not as much as I expected. <u>I never thought it would</u>."

The general is in New York. Upon his return I shall go to Baltimore and, as soon as pronounced fit for duty, to the regiment with the other officers.

Now if Alf wants to serve with Gen. Tyler, let him. Apply at once and he can get it. I am totally out of the question.

I got a letter from mother this morning. I am glad Alf has one place sure, but if he does go into the army, he had better go into the 18th. It will cause less growling. I wish Alf would get into the Navy. I think he would enjoy that.

I shall leave my saddle, halter, blanket, spurs, etc. with Ned Tyler, and if Alf gets a staff appointment, he can get them of Ned.

I am pleased that a stone has been selected for father's grave.

So poor purblind cousin George Goddard of New London has been drafted. A pretty looking "sojer boy" he would make, with his defective eyes.

Yours ever, Harry

Wilmington, Del., July 23rd, 1863

My dear May,

Yesterday, as you know, I received notice that the War Department "couldn't see" detailing me.

We dined at Mr. Milligan's [Delaware Superior Court justice]—Lusk, Ned and I—Judge Milligan and wife are fine people of the country style. Their son, a gentleman of 42, late an officer in Rush's Lancers [6th Pennsylvania Cavalry], retiring for disability. Their daughter, a very pretty woman of 26.

The dinner was excellent, but I am wearying of this Wilmington-English custom of sitting two or three hours over wine.

Do you know that I shall be 21 on the 25th? To take time by the forelock, you might like to know that I have made up my mind to see how long I can go without smoking or drinking. I am not afraid that I shall break my resolution on the last point, but fear that when I get to the regiment, I shall have to take to smoking again.

I shall go to Baltimore and go on to the 14th when Major Ellis goes. I shall turn my horse in to the general and leave my saddle, etc. here where I can call for it or sell it as occasion may require.

In accordance with your advice, I am reading Timothy Titcomb's works, Hepworth Dixon's "Personal History of Lord Bacon," etc.[1]

I have enjoyed Wilmington much. Like the general and esteem Capt. Lusk more than almost any man I ever met.

Love to all, H.P.G.

1. Timothy Titcomb was the pseudonym of Josiah Gilbert Holland (1819–1881), American author, poet, and moralist. Hepworth Dixon (1821–1879) was an English historian and author.

Baltimore, July 28, 1863

Dear Julia,

I took Major Ellis of our regiment to call on Miss Ella Kirby, and he is very badly in love with her—shot at first sight. Why, there is a grand ball at Governor [Edward G.] Bradford's tonight and he has bothered my life nearly out to induce me to get cards for myself and for him, inasmuch as Miss Schenck hinted she could procure me one. I would not permit it for three reasons. One, don't like to be rung in. Second, got no suitable clothes. Third, an invalid officer has no business dancing and flirting.

The Piatts go to Cape May Thursday with Miss Kirby, and Ellis vows he will go also. I have to tell him yarns by the dozen of the number of distinguished men Miss K has refused, but the major is from Boston and, like Dr. [Oliver Wendell Holmes Sr.] Holmes, holds that Boston omnia vincent. It's funny, but he will be sure to offer himself if he gets a living chance.

Called on the Perkinses last eve with Ellis. None of them are the earnest unionists we find at home.

Alf was here Sunday, running about like a chicken with its head cut off—so nervous, poor boy. I wish he could be cooler. He got me pretty warm and the weather itself is awful hot, so I fear I was not very fraternal.

I met a scout the other day who served under Gen. Sigel. He was captured, taken to Richmond, tried, and liable to be condemned to be executed as a spy. Sigel by the underground railroad hired a Richmond lawyer to bribe witnesses not to testify, and he escaped. Naturally he adores Gen. Sigel.

I am tired to death of Baltimore, and as soon as I am rid of a beastly cold which has been troubling me, but shows signs of disappearing, shall gladly turn my face to the southward and the dear old boys.

Yours, Harry

Baltimore, Md., July 31, 1863

Dear Mother,

Was much grieved to hear of the death of my old friend and school-mate, Lt. Harvey Jacobs, 26th Conn.

I am anxious to return to the regiment as soon as possible. The company business needs to be straightened. My health is better in the field and I am a better man there morally as well as physically. I mean by that that I am not afraid of ordinary temptations, such as drinking at a bar, etc. but these incessant invitations out to dinner, such as we had at Wilmington with all hands sitting by the hour wine guzzling thereafter is more tempting than the routine of the regiment. Again, if I am not fit for duty <u>now</u>, I never shall be, and I want to try it. Besides, the regiment is my post of duty and the post of duty is the post of honor.

As for smoking, I have not given it up entirely, but smoke very little—not one-fourth of what I did.

Gen. Tyler was right in saying that his staff "doesn't like the peace establishment." Since he has been in service, over a dozen officers have been on and off his staff.

Yes, Mother. I believe in every way it's best for me to be with the regiment.

With love to all, Yours, Harry

Baltimore, Md., Aug. 2nd, 1863

My dearest sister,

My dear, don't talk to me about "lords of creation." Mrs. Donn Piatt and I were discussing that today. I tell you that <u>she</u> wields more influence than many men and she says, and I concur, that <u>you</u> will and can do so yet.

Do you know that your and Mother's visit to me in camp at Hartford is perhaps the pleasantest recollection of my life. That "weeping fit" was the outburst that had to come out of a long-covered grief [over the death of Goddard's father in April 1862]. It did me good and I turned a smiling face on the morrow. I have wept but once since—then at Fredericksburg when I fancied Col. Perkins was dying.

How nobly the 6th, 7th and 10th [Connecticut regiments] fought at Charleston.

I can truly say that drinking is not a habit with me. I drank a glass of claret with Alf last week at the Eutaw House in a private room, and that was the last. I smoke a cigarette every time I take that horrid cod liver oil and one cigar after dinner.

I should have gone to the front last week but for a bad cold that set me back a little. Hope to get off with Major Ellis this week.

I find in a newspaper that Alf is appointed 1st lieutenant Co. B, 8th Conn. It's rather singular that each should hold same rank in same company of two regiments. I hope for his success yet in his aspirations for the Navy.

Of course I prefer a staff position, but I have made up my mind to take whatever I can get and not to leave the army "while I can stand and see," as says Tom Brown of rugby. I have "been lucky." No, I really think God has been very kind to me all my life. Not yet 21 and I have been prospered in all my undertakings. I have always got the position I sought and have seen a great deal of the world and of kindness. I will trust in Him and believe I can really say whatever He ordains is best.

Poor Alf. I have been too hard on my noble brother. He is more generous than I. His is by far the nobler nature and he has shown it in this staff matter.

Your list of drafted pleases me much. I can already see them coming down with their $300.

My health is improving daily. I am half through my cod liver oil bottle and so fat I can hardly get around. I suppose we call it 200 pounds.

Your Harry

Baltimore, Md., Aug. 9th, 1863

Dear Julia,

At last I am once more in a fair way to see service again. I have reported for duty and expect orders to start for the regiment tomorrow.

I send you Sidney Dobell's[1] poems. Read his "Evening in War Time." It's excellent.

I should not be surprised if the Army of the Potomac should go the Falmouth soon—the Warrenton line is so long and hard to protect.

I am losing confidence in Rosecrans;[2] why does he let [Maj. Gen. Braxton] Bragg reinforce Charleston, as it's admitted he has done?

It makes me mad to see the state of things now in the North—everybody trying to avoid the draft, when if we had only 300,000 more men we could settle this business in pretty quick time. "Oh, vat a peeples, vat a country."

I send you one of dear old Joe Rockwell's photographs to keep for me. I hope he will yet get out of Libby prison.[3]

Col. Morris is sick at Washington. I wish Lusk could be made Lt. Col. of our regiment.

Your loving bro, Harry

1. Sidney Dobell (1824–1874), the English poet and critic, wrote sonnets on the Crimean War.

2. Maj. Gen. William Rosecrans was defeated at battle of Chickamauga in September 1863 while commanding the Army of the Cumberland.

3. A Confederate prison for Union officers in Richmond, Virginia.

Camp-in-the-Woods, 12 miles from Warrenton Junction, Va., and apparently 1,000 miles from civilization. August 13th, 1863.

Dear Mother,

Left Baltimore Monday, reaching Washington that evening. Saw Capt. Townsend, who is quite ill, J.J. Piatt and Frank Whiting, dining with the latter. Heard that Col. Morris has been recommended for discharge on account of his health.

Tuesday left Washington via the Orange and Alexandria R.R. Reached Warrenton Junction at 5 P.M. by the courtesy of Mr. Gordon, commissary clerk to Gen. R. O. Tyler. I was invited to spend the night at Gen. Tyler's headquarters—headquarters of the reserve artillery, to which we rode on horseback. The general was very kind and invited me to dinner. Had a charming evening with the general and his staff, and a good bed.

On Wednesday Mr. Gordon had an express wagon hitched up, and we started. After a six-hours ride, found my regiment stretched out in a two-miles line, on permanent picket duty. Corps headquarters is 15 miles away; division headquarters is 10; brigade headquarters 5. Find 185 conscripts here and more to come. An awful hard set.

I find on duty three captains, two 1st lieutenants, three 2nd lieutenants, two surgeons, the chaplain, adjutant and quartermaster. I am not well and this duty is awful dull work. The conscripts have no guns, and we really do nothing, but to watch them and send out pickets hourly.

On reporting for duty, was detailed to command Co. G. I called them out, addressed them as a whole, and then drilled the conscripts in saluting. I have the biggest "rough" in the regiment in this company. He has a scar 6 inches long, where the mate of a vessel knocked him down with a marlinspike. He has been discharged from the Army and Navy for the reason that he could not be handled. I think he and I have got to have a row yet, and only wish now that I had kept my Colt revolver (given me by Mr. Green) as it may be necessary for him to get shot some day. A pleasant prospect—having such men to handle.

Yours as ever, Harry

Camp near Bristonburg, Bristol Station, Catletts Station, or Warrenton Junction, in-as-much-as it is so termed by being as far as possible from any of the above places. Aug. 16th, 1863.

Dear Julia,

Don't think me too much in earnest when I growl, as above, for you know my bark is worse than my bite, but "<u>now</u> is the summer of our discontent." Truly did Will Lusk say that "city soldiering is not the post of honor, but that it is perhaps a lesser evil than the dullness of an infantry regiment after staff duty." He has been there and knows.

We have got the regiment together again, camping in the woods, throwing out pickets, and having two drills daily. We had our band last night and had a good dress parade. The <u>old</u> 14th C.V. numbers just 141 muskets. We have about 180 unarmed conscripts.

My health is very poor indeed and I have been to Dr. Dudley and told him all about it from first to last. I am glad that I did as I have been striving to keep on full duty and find I have very little strength. Dudley says I look very weak and he will do what he can to get me well here, and if he fails will try to send me to the officers' hospital at Georgetown till the hot weather is over, when he hopes that I will pick up.

Have had a splendid letter from Will Lusk, also one from Alf, whose prospects brighten as mine grow cloudy. He has been very lucky to get at one jump [being commissioned as a first lieutenant] what took me two years toil.

Yours truly, H.P.G.

Washington, D.C., Aug. 23rd, 1863

Dear Mother,

One year ago we were mustered in. Only two years to serve now.

Last Sunday I was examined by Dr. Dudley and the division surgeon, and recommended to be sent to the officers' hospital at Georgetown on account of "incipient phthesis." That night we had a visit from Capts. Hale and Tubbs. We had music by our band in the still Virginia moonlight in our woodland camp with two Virginia ladies, from 20 to 25 years old, for auditors. If I had a sister seven years old as ignorant as they, I should be ashamed of her.

I was officer of the guard the next night and arrested the big ruffian in Co. G, of whom before I wrote, for slapping a first sergeant in the face. Was about to tie him up by the thumbs when he agreed to beg the orderly's pardon before the field and staff, and I let him off, telling him I had my eye on him and that he had <u>got</u> to behave. At 2 A.M., with a sergeant arrested two drunken conscripts whom we caught gambling and drawing knives and pistols. At 3 A.M., put a drunken 2nd lieut. to bed.

Tuesday we marched ten miles to division headquarters and camped under a hot sun. I suffered from weakness. Gen. [Brig. Gen. Joshua T. "Paddy"] Owen, who commands the division, told Capt. Moore, commanding the 14th, that if any conscripts escaped, he should go under arrest, and that all the old men would have to do would be to guard conscripts.

Wednesday we had to send 60 men on picket duty and 30 on guard, leaving but about 40 muskets for duty (the conscripts were unarmed). I was acting adjutant at dress parade but had a pretty weak voice for the duty.

Thursday Maj. [John T.] Hill of the 12th N.J. Vols., our bitterest rivals, was put in command of our regiment, leaving his own in command of a captain. Our poor old regiment felt awfully insulted. Capt. Moore cannot get a definite explanation and has demanded a court of inquiry. Our officers don't speak to the Jersey major except on duty and the men openly show dislike. Old Gen. Hays says "the 14th is the sassiest regiment in the service," that they have "nicknames for every body and don't hesitate to bestow them." Received notice that Col. Morris is discharged for disability. Our officers signed a petition to the governor to promote Lt. Col. Perkins, if he will return to the service. Every body but Adjt. Ellis prays for this. 2nd Assistant Surgeon [Charles] Tomlinson of New Haven reported for duty. He is a new appointee and already seems worried as to "where he can get a good dinner." Friday got my order to proceed to Washington.

Saturday left camp in an ambulance at 7 A.M. Left Warrenton at 10 A.M. and reached Washington at 3 P.M. Went to the Ebbitt House, bathed and took dinner. Found Capt. Carpenter of the 14th, Lt. E. W. Whitaker of the Harris Light, now A.D.C. to Gen. Kilpatrick. He was very cordial; gave me the particulars of his brother's death at Aldie [the battle of Aldie, June 17, 1863, in Loudoun County, Virginia, part of Gen. Lee's campaign leading up to Gettysburg].

We also met Maj. Ellis on his way to the regiment to straighten out matters and enable poor Moore, who is sick, to get away honorably to a hospital. It appears that the Lt. Col. of the 12th N.J. commands the brigade and sent his major to us, that his own regiment might be commanded by a captain who is his intimate friend. Ellis wants to be our colonel, but we of the line hope not.

Capts. Davis and Broatch and Lieut. [Newell P.] Rockwood are ordered on duty at conscript camp, New Haven, Conn.

Capt. Fiske has sent in his resignation "As his church only gave him a year's absence." He says that if it is not accepted, he shall leave the staff and return to his company, which certainly needs him, as poor Co. G has both lieutenants absent wounded and is the only company in the regiment that has never had a promotion. The poor boys were almost ready to cry at my leaving them, and if Fiske's resignation[1] is accepted, want me to be captain of that company.

Capt. Townsend is still here suffering from scurvy. I report to the medical director and to Georgetown tomorrow. The division surgeon says that my symptoms are not alarming and that good treatment may bring me around all right after this enervating weather is over.

Yours truly, Harry

1. Capt. Samuel Fiske, Company I, decided not to resign and return to Madison, Connecticut, where he was the minister of a Congregationalist church. A native of Shelburne, Massachusetts, Fiske's voluminous wartime correspondence was published in the *Springfield Republican* under the pseudonym of Dunn Browne. Fiske was mortally wounded in May 1864 at the battle of the Wilderness. *Mr. Dunn Browne's Experiences in the Army*, edited by Stephen W. Sears (1866; repr. New York: Fordham University Press, 1998).

Georgetown Hospital, Georgetown, D.C., Aug. 26th 1863

Dear Julia,

Here I am incarcerated in Georgetown "jail," as we term it. A large, roomy building with plenty of air, good beds, good care, pretty volunteer nurses, etc. The building is historic, having been once the most fashionable Southern ladies seminary. Here on a certain evening years ago a young adventurer with the rank of lieutenant of engineers, eloped with the daughter of a distinguished Southern statesmen, much to the father's ire. The adventurer is now Maj. Gen. [John C.] Fremont, the lady Jessie Benton Fremont. These walls have also echoed to the tread of another pupil now known as Varuna Davis, wife of Jeff Davis.

The surgeon in charge of our ward, Dr. [David, a cousin of Secretary of War Edwin Stanton] Stanton, is a gentleman and sensible fellow. He scoffs at my lungs being seriously affected—says that I am only suffering from prostration from the heat and a slight cold. He will give my lungs a most careful examination soon, but thinks the trouble has been much magnified.

I got my baggage all right at regimental headquarters, but had to throw away all the underclothing, as vermin infested.

Lt. Whitaker of Kilpatrick's staff and I are now very good friends. You see, time works wonders.

Here I am only "No. 27, ward 2." How <u>mighty</u> is a man.

Love to all. Yours affectionately, Harry

Seminary Hospital, Georgetown, D.C., Aug. 30th, 1863

My dear Mother,

Yesterday Maj. Clark, Capts. Carpenter, Moore and myself, all of "ours," hired a hack and rode over to Virginia. There we called on the officers of the 1st Conn. Heavy Artillery, and went over and examined the five forts which they garrisoned, namely forts Richardson, Berry, Bernard, Blenker, and Ward.

Being very courteously received by the officers at all of them, we dined at Fort Ward, where we witnessed the finest dress parade I have ever seen by a volunteer regiment. Capt. Joe Perkins of Old Lyme was very kind; he looks more like a military and less like a literary man. We had some punch with him and his lieutenant, Charley Bulkley of Hartford, Conn. It was served on a marble table which Joe had put up in his tent. On my expressing my surprise at such luxury in camp, Joe suggested that I look on the reverse side of the marble slab. In so doing I found an inscription thereon, showing that the slab was a grave stone "confiscated" from a neighboring grave yard; Joe's excuse being that the deceased was probably a rebel, or would have been had he lived till now. Joe is a sybarite if ever there was one.

We drove back by moon-light over the historic heights of Arlington, which Lee was fool enough to forfeit by his treason, over the memorable long bridge back to the nation's capital. The dome of the capitol is nearly finished, half of the goddess of liberty now being visible.

Visited the Smithsonian again the other day and heartily wished that you were with me as I rejoiced over birds, eggs and the entire natural history collection which you would so much enjoy.

Dr. Stanton, surgeon in charge of this ward, after a thorough and careful examination of my lungs, pronounces them not diseased at all, and that I "may live fifty years for all consumption will prevent." He says that one may have a consumption tendency, which great trial or exposure may bring out in any man, and seems to agree with me in my theory that my long sickness after Chancellorsville was the crisis of my case, since which I have been gaining, but that my return to the regiment with overwork and exposure under an August sun gave me a cold and diarrhea from which the autumnal breezes and good care here are bringing me to a better state of health. I sincerely hope to be able to return to the regiment in a week or so.

Yours affectionately, H. P. Goddard

Seminary Hospital, September 2nd, 1863

Dear Julia,

Monday went into Washington and called on John J. Piatt, who had twice called here and missed me. He promises to take me to see his charming wife, Sallie M. B. Piatt.

You must remember that I am under government orders. I am getting so much better daily that I expect soon to be ordered back to my regiment.

I believe sincerely that the surgeon is right about my lungs. I have no hemorrhage, no sweats, no pain in breathing, and am far better than before I went under treatment here.

I am glad mother saw <u>our</u> old state flag. We have a new one with four little words engraved upon it that tell their own story: Antietam, Fredericksburg, Chancellorsville, Gettysburg.

Yours, Harry

Seminary Hospital, Georgetown, D.C., Sept. 10, 1863

My dear Mother,

A letter from Charley Arms speaks very highly of Alf and says "he will make a good officer." Both on Harland's staff.

Sorry you didn't like my photographs—the 14th officers think them excellent. It's not my fault that I am not handsome and sickness has much reduced me. I shall increase what I send home for household expenses to $30 per month, as Alf cannot lay up much. No staff officer can.

Congratulate Charles Dyer on his marriage. If he has sent a "substitute," he is likely in our regiment, as are most of the Norwich substitutes—and about the worst in the regiment.

Dr. Stanton has just made his morning call. He is one of the handsomest men I ever saw. He is very much taken with May's picture and wishes me to promise that "if ever badly wounded and get sent here, to send for her to take care of me." That's the beauty of this hospital—there are so many rooms that several ladies are here looking after <u>their</u> wounded sons. The proudest looking woman I ever saw is here with her son, a cavalry officer full of bullets. He is slowly recovering and I verily believe she loves those scars better than she would so many diamonds.

Miss [Dorothy] Dix was here the other day. She is good, but <u>so</u> homely.

Lt. Simpson is really entitled to promotion before me, so I do <u>not</u> wish any influence brought to bear in my favor.

Your loving Harry

Georgetown, D.C., Sept. 11th, 1863

Dear Mother,

We disagree as to my photograph. I had my hair cut short to be rid of the "animals" I brought home from Chancellorsville. I shaved close so that when I get where I cannot get shaved, my beard will grow the faster. I don't wear a garotte because I can't make a cravat stay around it.

Yours sincerely, Harry

Sept. 11th, 1863

Dear Julia,

Drew my pay yesterday. It only amounted to $202, as the paymaster takes out the hospital board bill. I send home $100.

All the troops of the Army of the Potomac which were sent to New York during the draft riots are on their way back to the front. Many of them left Alexandria yesterday.

Yours affectionately, Harry

Georgetown, D.C., Sept. 17th, 1863

My dear Julia,

One year ago today, Antietam fairly inducted the undersigned into the <u>pleasures</u> and mysteries of warfare. In that year he prides himself that he has learned something, met a few Southern "friends" he did not before know, and learned that <u>fighting</u> will end this war and nothing else will. I hope he is duly impressed with the sense of the constant protection which has been afforded him by divine Providence through trials that he never dreamed of in years gone by, and of the supreme kindness which has favored nearly all his plans and made the years so pleasant to him in all respects. Three big battles, two slight wounds, one long visit home, two months' staff duty in two of the loveliest cities in the Union, full views of nearly all the leading men of the nation and unbounded kindness everywhere is probably a more pleasant experience than most officers have experienced.

Dr Stanton will not let me go this week. I cannot say when. Adjt. Doten reached here yesterday, leaving the regiment quietly in camp at Culpeper.

Give my best love to the Misses Schenck. They are real splendid girls tho they did take me by storm when I was dropped down among the trio at the Eutaw House. You see I cannot decide which to fall in love with. I think now it is Miss Julie.

Ned Stedman has resigned his post here and gone to New York to become a broker. He publishes a new volume of poems soon.

Have bought me a great Burnside hat that covers me. It will answer to get behind when under artillery fire.

Harry

Georgetown, Sept. 18th, 1863

Dear Mother,

Adjutant Doten has arrived here on sick leave from Culpeper where he thinks the army liable to remain for some time. He brings news of Capt. Carpenter's transfer to the invalid corps. Doten tells me Lt. Jim Nichols is to have the vacant captaincy. Well, that jumps Lt. Simpson and myself, but Jim Nichols deserves it if ever man did. Simpson and I have both been absent from the regiment nearly all the time since Chancellorsville, where he was captured and I was wounded while Nichols was away but 20 days. Yet Simpson was at Gettysburg, which Nichols missed, but that is an accident of war.

Don't talk about "my hard earnings." Unfortunately for me, for the last three months I have had such easy work it shames me.

Your loving Harry

Seminary Hospital, Georgetown, Sept. 22, 1863

Dear Mother,

Charles Lanman,[1] the author, called the other day and courteously invited me to his house here any evening for supper.

May's picture is very sweet. She will be a great belle yet.

Am very sorry to hear of the death of Gen. Will Lytle—the Ohio soldier poet.[2]

Yours lovingly, Harry

1. Charles Lanman (1809–1894), travel and history writer.

2. Lytle, a brigadier general of the Army of the Ohio, was killed in the battle of Chickamauga, September 1863.

Georgetown, D.C., Sept. 23rd, 1863

Dear Mother,

I have no cough nor any symptom of lung trouble and should have been at the "front" ere this were it not that within the past ten days I have been suffering severely with boils, a complaint just now very common in Delaware, Maryland and the District of Columbia.

When I said that $30 per month of the money I sent home was for household expenses, I <u>meant</u> it. If you complain at me for sending it, I will invest that amount in whisky and send the whisky home. That will not be acceptable, I know, so you had best let me do as I please.

Yours, Harry

Georgetown, D.C., Sept. 23rd, 1863

Dear Mother,

The evening paper contains the following in a list of dismissals by the War Department: Capt. Samuel Davis, 14th Conn. Volunteers (dishonorable) for gross neglect of duty as officer of the day, and while in charge of a detachment of drafted men, allowing 70 out of 117 to escape, and for general indifference to his duties and to the interest of the service.

This makes four captaincies vacant in the regiment and Capt. Coit, who came out junior 1st lieutenant, is now senior captain, who says a double-breasted coat is hard to win.

Brigadier Gen. [George Armstrong] Custer, "the boy general with golden locks," is a younger looking man than I. He has long yellow curls, almost effeminate in appearance, but is a knight errant in war.

The Army of the Potomac is on the eve of another campaign, in which I think they will show the western armies that if they who are used to winning are getting flogged now, we who always get whipped will give Lee the biggest whipping he ever got. For the first time since Williamsburg [the battle of Williamsburg, May 5, 1861, first battle of Peninsular campaign] the Army of the Potomac is really anxious for a fight. I know this and only hope I shall get well soon enough to be in it.

Army surgeons are not like those draft surgeons. If they were, we should not have any soldiers at all. The patriotism of the North is at a discount just now. I wish that every man drafted who had four limbs and could walk had to come. No $300, no substitutes, nothing but hard fighting. A sweet lot of substitutes they send us from New Haven, Hartford and Norwich. All New York roughs. Of the 380 who reached us, 92 have deserted, four have been shot, and I almost wish they would send them with or in their coffins after this if they are going to send us such men when 200,000 could clean out the rebellion in three months. To hear of this constant "how shall we get rid of the draft" makes me despair of my country. Men say, "T'is sweet for one's country to die, but much sweeter to live for it." I am sorry to growl so much in this letter but I am mad clean through.

Yours, Harry

Georgetown, D.C., Sept. 26th, 1863

Dear sister,

I walked out yesterday for the first time in several days. I have had calls from Charles Lanman and Capt. Broatch. The latter has been for two months on duty at the conscript camp in Connecticut. He took 200 conscripts for the 14th down last Thursday and is on his way home. He says that the army is on the eve of a move.

I hope to go down next week, but I am afraid I cannot get away until the end of the week. I am very anxious to get to the regiment now that it is to be filled up and the vacancies in the commissioned offices filled. I want no influence exerted for me, but one must be on the ground to expect promotion. There is great jealousy and contention among the officers in view of the large number of promotions to be made.

Yours truly, Harry

Georgetown, D.C., Sept. 26th, 1863

Dear Mother,

Equinox has brought with it cold dismal days and we poor fellows shiver in these large, and as yet stoveless, halls, halls that have rung to the tread of Mesdames Fremont and Davis in their girlish innocence; halls where youth, grace, beauty and deviltry probably once reigned supreme in the persons of some 300 daughters of the then "fair and sunny" South. All, all is changed; now the long row of white cots, the silent tread of slippered nurses, the monotonous ticking of a Connecticut clock are, to coin a word, home-sicky, in their effect upon a patient, from which much longer hospital life, "spare us good Lord. In his mercy we hope to change our base this present week, a change either to front or rear were better than this feeling of being a minute fraction of a wheel in a government machine laid up for repairs. If one were seriously ill, this would be a good place in which to recover, as the care is admirable, but to just lie here, ordered to keep quiet until the doctors get through blistering and poulticing me is very annoying, especially as one <u>cannot</u> keep quiet as he ought. Yet I think this week will make me fit for duty as the cool autumn breeze makes one really anxious for the fray.

We are to have 200 more conscripts in the 14th, making about 800 in all. Won't we have <u>sweet</u> times with these Dutch, Irish, Poles, <u>Chinese</u>, Danes, half-breed Canadians and the Lord knows what else—thieves, murderers, incendiaries, gamblers and men whose only active service has been as rioters in the "Battle of New York." [New York City draft riots, July 1863] These are the men sent to us by the representative business men of Connecticut as their substitutes. The 14th Conn. is a thing of the past, with its 140 men and tattered colors. With 800 new men, new guns, new colors, etc., we shall set out on a new campaign. Not one of the ten captains who came out with us 13 months ago is with the regiment. The present lieutenant colonel and major came out 1st lieutenants.

Yours, Harry

Georgetown, D.C., Sept. 29th, 1863

Dear Mother,

Dr. Stanton says that he cannot let me go to the front yet—that my lungs are sound now, but my blood not in a good condition, hence these boils and just now an eruptive skin disease from which several other officers of the 14th have suffered. Lovely days now, a comfortable stove to warm us nights, good spirits and a kind surgeon, good reading matter, and a resolve to accept <u>His</u> verdict as to when to go to the front—makes me happier than for a long time.

Yours, Harry

Georgetown, Oct. 1st, 1863

Dear Sister,

I thought Will Ripley wanted <u>to go to war</u>. You said he cried about it because he was exempt. Now he pays $300 to be exempt. It is all humbug when men say they "want to go but can't." Uncle Sam will take all who will come. <u>Cold</u> lead—that is what is the matter.

Yours, Harry

Georgetown, D.C., Oct. 8th, 1863

Dear Mother,

You mistook my last complaint. It was not vermin but a kind of scurvy showing itself in little red eruptions with an itching tendency. It arises from a bad state of the blood. I shall leave here Saturday or Monday <u>sure</u>.

It is raining hard today and I shall devote my time to [John] Crowley's "Salathiel" or Eugene Sue's "Wandering Jew," which I am now reading. I have read more in six weeks than in two years before with the regiment.

Yours, Harry

Georgetown, D.C., Oct. 13th, 1863

Dear Mother,

Against all expectations, I am still here. This eruptive disease has troubled me awfully. You have no idea of the pain it gives me nights. I often think that it will drive me crazy. The doctor has however lately given me a lotion which checks the pain.

They cannot keep me here much longer as the War Department has ordered that all officers away 60 days must be sent to their regiments or mustered out, and I don't think they will do the last with me. Hardly anything but loss of limbs will produce <u>that</u>.

Yours, Harry

Georgetown, Oct. 15th, 1863

Dear Julia,

Correct that article of mine on "How the Fourteenth Fought at Gettysburg" on all points you have mentioned, except that I prefer that the dialogue form should be retained. Send it to Uncle Don with a request from me that he will—if he seems it worthy—send it to Harper's Weekly with a note from himself. In that way I can probably get a better price for it and that is what I wish. If you prefer, send it direct to the publishers yourself.

Captain Townsend says that my description of the Gettysburg fight in my article could not have been better had I been present.

By the evening paper I see that a portion of our corps were engaged at Bristoe Station yesterday. I am full of anxiety for the regiment and nearly sick with vexation at myself for being away from another fight. I will, however, hope for the best for the regiment and for my speedy return.

Your loving brother, Harry

Georgetown, D.C., Oct. 16th, 1863

Dear Julia,

Our regiment was engaged at Bristoe yesterday. We lost about 20 wounded, one killed. Lieut. Fiske is here slightly wounded. He says that the conscripts fought splendidly, that we won a brilliant victory—our brigade taking a four-gun battery. The army is now near Centreville.

The governor has commissioned Ellis as colonel, Moore as lieutenant colonel, and Coit as major, and they have all been mustered. The latter appointment is very unpopular with the line officers. They say he "knows less upon military matters than any other officer in the regiment and is too conceited to learn."

Col. Ellis has promoted Lieutenants Simpson, Nichols, [Henry] Snagg and Adjt. Doten to be captains and Sergeant Maj. Hincks to be adjutant. This last appointment is an excellent one, as Hincks won his commission by his behavior at Gettysburg.

Two of my old friends in the Harris Light were killed the other day—Captains Grinton and Griggs. "Kill Cavalry," as the boys in the regiment call him, uses up his men very fast.

Your loving brother, Harry

Washington, D.C., Oct. 20th, 1863

Dear Mother,

I have been discharged from the hospital and ordered to my regiment.

My eruptive skin disease is still very troublesome, but not dangerous. Attended the theater tonight and saw Maggie Mitchell. She is charmingly simple and childlike. The play was an illustration of a mother's love and made me feel as watery about the eyes as did my first reading of Uncle Tom's Cabin and of David Copperfield.

Your loving son, Harry

Camp near Turkey Run, five miles from Warrenton, Va., Oct. 23rd, 1863

Dear Mother,

Left Washington on the 21st in the afternoon after having, with much trouble, straightened up both quartermaster and ordnance returns and got certificates of non-indebtedness to both departments.

Stopped that night at the Marshall House in Alexandria—the house where Col. Ellsworth was shot in 1861. Tried to get a piece of the stair balustrade for a relic, but gave it up when the clerk told me that this was the fifth balustrade since the shooting, the others having been carried off by relic hunters.

Left Alexandria yesterday via the Orange and Alexandria R.R. to Manassas Junction. There were about 100 officers on the train and we all had to wait at the junction about two hours. When some growled at this, a bright young Sixth Corps staff officer said, "Remember, gentlemen, your pay is going right along." This changed the current of feeling and we voted to have a "picnic" on the spot, each one contributing something out of his store. The result was a very jolly time. As the O & A R.R. is torn up below Manassas, we took the Manassas Gap R.R. to

Gainsville (five miles). I got out there and found two baggage wagons of our train about starting for the corps. Threw in my haversack and footed it behind the wagon. Regretted much that I had not brought my valise. At Greenwich, six miles from Gainsville, we all got a splendid supper at a house on the road. The people were very inquisitive as to how many wagons were behind. We were the only two wagons on the road, but suspected the males, of whom there were five or six about, of guerrilla inclinations, and felt ourselves justified in lying, saying that a whole train was behind. We made lively time after supper and were quite relieved from anxiety when about 9 P.M. we joined the regiment at Auburn, 12 miles from Gainsville. I had a warm reception from Capt. Townsend. We have no second lieutenant yet, our old one having been promoted.

This morning we marched to this place where we have a nice camp and expect to stay a few days. It rains this afternoon, but I am quite comfortable, though somewhat "itchy" as always in bad weather.

Dr. Dudley thinks it doubtful whether I can stand field service, but advises me to make the trial.

Yours, Harry

Camp 5 Miles From Warrenton, Va., Oct. 25, 1863

To my great surprise, I am better daily and begin to think that field life is the best for my health, after all. I still suffer nights, but begin to think that the best way to get over this "camp itch" (for that's what it is), is to let it cure itself. My lungs I believe in better condition than ever.

Our new adjutant, Hincks, is the best we ever had. We are hoping for the return of glorious old Hancock. Gen. Warren is liked as an officer, but Hancock has been identified with the corps from its formation. His "charge, gentlemen," is still a battle cry of the corps, now pronounced the fighting corps. "Reb" prisoners say they would rather fight the rest of the corps together than the wearers of the "ace of clubs" singly!

Yours as ever, Harry

Camp Near Turkey Run, Va., Oct. 26th, 1863

Dear Julia,

I have just learned that through the influence of Captain Elliot (late of our brigade commissary) and of my friend Lt. Pelton of the 14th, now commanding the division ambulance train, that Col. [Orlando] Smith, our brigade commander, will nominate me for "ordnance officer and A.D.C." to fill a vacancy on corps staff. Hurrah, hurrah, hurrah. A horse, extra pay, gentlemanly associates, etc., etc.

Also, Lieut. Col. Moore tells me that a few days ago Col. Ellis said he wished that "Goddard would come back so that he could fill the vacant captaincy." If both these positions are offered me, I shall take the place on Warren's [Maj. Gen. Gouverneur Warren] staff as it is so much easier to ride than to walk.

With much love, yours, Harry

Camp Near Warrenton, Va., Oct. 30, 1863

Dear Mother,

I have accepted the position of ordnance officer of the artillery brigade, 2nd corps, in preference to the captaincy of Co. K, 14th C.V. This brigade is independent of all but corps orders, is commanded by Lieut. Col. J. A. Monroe, a Rhode Islander and a very pleasant gentleman. My idea is that the place will be much easier and the duty more pleasant than in the line. I shall have a government horse, a wall tent, good mess, can draw my pay monthly, and have much less responsibility than I had supposed. My duty as ordinance officer will be to supply the batteries with shot and shell and to account for them quarterly to the Ordinance Department at Washington. My other duties are those of any aide-de-camp. Col. Perkins, who has made a short visit here, and Captain Hale, both of whom have had experience, have advised me to take the post by all means.

Col. Ellis was very kind, saying that if he had known I was coming back, he should certainly have given me the captaincy of K company or any that may become vacant. It is my health, however, that makes me accept this staff duty as I am very sure I cannot stand foot service.

The cars reached here last night for the first time since the railroad was destroyed.

Yours ever, Harry

Near Warrenton, Va., Nov. 1, 1863

Dear Mother,

A special order from Headquarters, 2nd Corps, dated Oct. 31, 1863, just received by me is as follows: "First Lieutenant H. P. Goddard, 14th Conn. Vols., is hereby detailed as acting ordinance officer to the artillery brigade, 2nd Corps, and will report without delay to Lieut. Col. J. Albert Monroe for duty."

A week's hard trial has rendered it certain to me that it was impossible for me to longer perform infantry duty, as I find I cannot stand the long marches, on account of short breath, and sleeping on the ground on guard and picket duty, with no shelter in camp but a shelter tent, with no meat but ham, which made my "scurvy" much worse. Hence I am delighted at this appointment which secures me a horse, a good mess, and a wall tent.

The expense will be heavier at the outset, and large all along. For this reason I hated to take the place, instead of a regimental captaincy worth $120 per month. Here I shall only get $108 per month, with horse and forage furnished by "Uncle Sam." I feel that I can stand this duty as my lungs give me no trouble and I really think Dr. Dudley is curing the "scurvy" with potassium. I should lay up <u>some</u> money on staff duty, and can draw my pay monthly, can get leaves of absence easier, and have little to do, except when the artillery is in action.

If I get well I shall be happy to go back to the regiment for a captaincy, and if I get worse I shall have to resign.

Yours ever, Harry

Excerpt from *14th C. V.: Regimental Reminiscences of the War of the Rebellion,* by Henry P. Goddard (Middletown, Conn.: C. W. Church, 1877)

What a crowd of officers was scattered through the North in the following summer, with but six on duty and twenty-one absent—sick, wounded or detached—while the Qr. Mr. was reading "Queechy" with those pretty Misses George, at Warrenton, and Col. Moore having the band serenade them with their favorite, "Blue Juniata." A crowd of us at Baltimore with Lieut. Fiske at our head, used to tell the Baltimoreans that the 14th C.V. on our caps meant 14th Cherokee. Here it was that one of our boys got so sweet on a Baltimore belle that he grew irregular at his meals, so one day Capt. Simpson sent all his luggage by an express over to his sweetheart's, excusing himself by explaining that he thought our comrade had changed his boarding house, as he was there so much and at his hotel so little. At the same time Capt. Carpenter was masquerading on crutches at Washington, and Capt. Townsend running a German hotel on Pennsylvania Avenue in the same city; Capt. Snagg was on provost duty in Baltimore, charged with arresting officers out after 9 P.M. who didn't have the countersign. Whenever he overhauled a 14th man, he would halt his man with great show of authority and then demand the countersign, which he at the same time whispered *soto voce* to his friend, who then of course found it easy to give it.

Then came the campaigns up and down from Washington to the Rapidan, which Captain Sam Fiske (Dunn Browne) used to call the trips of Meade and Lee's express line (13).

17

Another Change of Duty—Pleasant
Living as an Artillery Officer

S till physically unable to resume his duties in the infantry with its long marches
and other rigors, Goddard again reinvents himself, this time as a brigade
artillery officer. He quickly learns his new duties, and lives in relative luxury compared to the spartan existence of a regimental officer. Still in poor health, he takes
a twenty-day leave to rest back home in Connecticut and returns in late December
1863. On the way back to Virginia, he dines in Washington with Col. Theodore
Ellis, his regimental commander, Senator Charles Sumner of Massachusetts,
Senator James Dixon of Connecticut, and the French ambassador and his wife. He
writes glowingly of Maj. Gen. Winfield Hancock, 2nd Corps commander, who is
contrasted with acting commander Maj. Gen. Gouverneur Warren, who is a "a very
good engineer, but inspires less enthusiasm" (200).

$\sim$

Headquarters, Artillery Brigade, 2nd Corps, Nov. 3rd, 1863

Dear Mother,

I like my new position very much, but am hard to work at present and somewhat bothered by having no ordinance sergeant—the old one, who understood the
business thoroughly, being away under arrest. As a move is imminent I have to
work hard to understand things, having to keep six batteries supplied with ammunition. I shall get a sergeant today but shall have to teach him, and that will be
hard—both green.

I saw Gen. Warren for the first time last night. He seems very young and looks
very much like Joe Bromley, brother of Ike.

Yours, Harry

Headquarters Artillery Brigade, 2nd Corps, Nov. 4th, 1863

Dear Uncle,

You make think me foolish, but my reasons for accepting this post instead of
the captaincy are that here I am mounted (by the government too), sleep in a wall

tent, live like a fighting cock, have plenty of gentlemanly associates, make acquaintance with staff officers from all sections of the army, and see and know all that goes on. At the regiment I had a shelter tent, ham and hard tack to live on, bad ground to sleep on, guard and picket duty twice a week, and always on the march. But the great trouble is that I am so weak that two hours battalion drill or a five miles march left me so faint and out of breath that I could not move another step.

The army is moving towards Catlett's Station today. Gen. Bob Tyler and staff have just passed with the reserve artillery. We expect to move tomorrow.

Our staff is as follows: Brigade commander, Lieut. Col. J. A. Monroe, 1st R.I. Artillery; Asst. Adjt. Gen., 1st Lieut. G. Lyman Dwight; 1st R.I. Artillery; Ordinance Officer, H. P. Goddard, 14th Conn. Infantry; Commissary Subsistance, Capt. J. Thomas Elliott, U.S. Vols.; Quartermaster, Capt. Dunn, 19th Mass. Infantry; Brigade Surgeon, Dr. Merrill, 1st R.I. Artillery.

There are six batteries in the brigade, namely, "G" 1st N.Y., Capt. Ames, Light 12 pounder, six guns; "B" 1st R.I., Capt. Hazzard, Light 12 pounder, four guns; "C" 5th US, Lieut. Weir, Light 12 pounder, four guns; "A" 1st R.I., Capt. Arnold, Rifle D 10 pounder, six guns; "F & G" 1st Pa., Capt. Ricketts, Rifle D 10 pounder, six guns; "C & F" 2nd Pa., Capt. Thompson, Rifle D 10 pounder, six guns.

Yours affectionately, H. P. G.

Headquarters, Artillery Brigade, 2nd Corps, Nov. 6, 1863

Dear Mother,

My health is improving though I am not strong and the eruption on my skin is very slow to disappear. The duties of ordinance officer are not arduous, though responsible, and unless some unforeseen accident happens, I shall have no trouble.

I like Col. Monroe very much. Acted as his aide today on the artillery drill in which I was much interested. The artillery service I already think preferable to cavalry or infantry.

While on drill there was a big fire in the woods near my ammunition train. I tell you I was excited till I got the train moved, as had that caught—horses, wagons and men would have been blown to atoms, and had I escaped myself, a doubtful chance, the loss of a million dollars worth of property would have been a bad beginning for a new ordinance officer.

We are hoping for glorious old Hancock daily.

Your loving Harry

Berry Hill, south of Rappahannock, Nov. 11, 1863

Dear Mother,

We left Warrenton on the 7th and marched through Warrenton Junction, Bealton and Morrisville to Kelly's Ford—about 20 miles. I was completely tired out and could hardly keep in my saddle. Had I been an infantryman, I could not have marched 5 miles. The destruction of the railroad by the rebels was the most complete work of the kind I have seen. All the sleepers were torn up and burned and the rails thrown on the fires and then twisted and bent—while in some places the embankment had actually been shoveled over where the road had been. We heard heavy firing all day, and on our arrival at the ford, found that the 3rd Corps had crossed the river there while the 5th and 6th had crossed at Rappahannock Station. On the 8th, we again crossed the Rappahannock and marched to this place.

Berry Hill [plantation], late of the property of Col. [John Watson Triplett] Thom of Baltimore, Md., a soldier of the War of 1812, is three miles from Kelly's Ford and two-and-a-half miles from Brandy Station. The rebs are supposed to be across the Rapidan. We shall remain here until the railroad is rebuilt to the Rappahannock—it is not destroyed this side—and think an advance will then be made across the Rapidan, but whether that way or down toward Fredericksburg again is problematical. The latter route is more easily guarded and a better place to winter while the Gordonsville route is more exposed to attack.

Gen. Meade is very popular again with the army. The late advance was rapid, brilliant and totally unexpected to the rebs, who were building winter quarters all along the Rappahannock. The prisoners we took were well clothed and shod and had plenty to eat. They receive bountiful supplies from England.

Our soldiers are, as Hooker said, not men but knights errant. Could you see them bravely plodding 20 and 30 miles a day with guns—equipments, 60 rounds of ammunition, and 8 days of rations, you would be astounded as I am at the small amount of straggling.

My own health is poor. My arms trouble me much with the "scurvy" and I hope soon for 20 days leave as the surgeon fears he cannot cure it here. Yet I dread New England so far as my lungs are concerned.

Your Harry

(Note: Took 20 days leave at this time. Went to Connecticut and returned much improved.)

Washington, D.C., Dec. 30, 1863

Dear May,

Arrived here at 10 o'clock today. I spent some hours in Philadelphia with your friend Blake. He took me to see Edwin Forrest [(1806–1872), American actor] as "Rolla" in "Pizarro." I got here tired, sleepy and hungry, four hours late. I go to the front tomorrow.

Your affectionate brother, Harry

Camp near Brandy Station, Va., Dec. 31, 1863.

Dear Julia,

> "Full knee deep lies the Virginia mud,
> Blow ye the tattoo call sad and slow,
> And tread softly and speak low,
> For the old year lies a-dying.
> Old year, you must not die;
> You came to us so readily,
> You lived with us so steadily,
> Old year, you shall not die."
> —*Tennyson, revised by a soldier.*

Arrived tonight in a drenching rain. Rode over here in an ambulance with the surgeon of the Harris Light Cavalry, who I was lucky enough to meet at Brandy Station. Col. Monroe and all hands were very glad to see me.

In Washington last night, I called with Col. Ellis (who is on court martial at Washington) at Senator Dixon's, Mrs. Dixon, Bessie and Clementina were all delightful. Senator Sumner and Count Mercer (the French minister) called and I was presented to each. Mrs. Dixon, the senator and the count all conversed in French most of the evening.

Col. Ellis tells me Capt. Townsend has been <u>dismissed</u> and intimates his willingness, but I am very reluctant to leave the staff for anything the 14th can offer. That ill-fated regiment has just had to leave the just-completed winter quarters and go 6 miles to the front to do picket duty on the Rapidan.

We have delightful quarters here. Col. Monroe has his headquarters in the dwelling house, and his wife comes tomorrow. I now tent with Adjutant General Dwight, whose darkey is also going to work for me <u>pro tem</u>.

We are only a slight ways from Gen. Kilpatrick, whom I hope to see shortly, that I may get from him material for a Harper's Weekly article.[1] General K. dearly loves newspaper notices.

Tell May[2] that Blake doesn't amount to much. He was very civil to me and is as good as most men, but she deserves something better than "most men."

Yours affectionately, Harry

1. Brig. Gen. Judson Kilpatrick, known as "Kill-Cavalry" for his aggressive and often reckless use of the cavalrymen under his command, had played an important role in engagements in Virginia leading up to the battle of Gettysburg, in the three-day battle itself, and in pursuing General Lee's army back to Virginia. The "Richmond ride" Goddard mentions later in the chapter refers to a daring but unsuccessful raid in which Kilpatrick led his cavalrymen to the outskirts of Richmond in an attempt to free Union soldiers imprisoned at the Confederate capital. Kilpatrick was repulsed by Confederate cavalry commanded by Maj. Gen. Wade Hampton.

2. May, or Mary, Woodbridge Goddard (1850–1884), his younger sister, became the first wife of Louis Comfort Tiffany, a family friend, in 1872. The couple had two children before May died at age thirty-four.

Camp near Brandy Station, Va., Jan. 2, 1864

A happy New Year to you, Mother dear,

On New Year's Day, I rode down to the old camp of the 14th. I found the regimental surgeons and Lieut. Eddy Hart, the latter very ill with dyptheria. He greeted me pleasantly but sadly. I fear he will not live. He was Fred Ward's nearest friend when both were corporals in Company G and both were very fond of me. Hart has missed Ward sadly.

Dr. Dudley and I then rode down to the present camp of the regiment near Morton's Ford on the Rapidan—a six miles ride on an awful muddy road. Arriving there found more officers present for duty than ever before since Antietam. Dined with Lieut. Col. Moore commanding and the regimental staff. I found poor Capt. Townsend sick bodily and mentally. He has received no notice of his dismissal and hopes it may be an error, but is going to be sent to Georgetown sick, where he will soon find out. I do fear that he has no chance of getting restored. The second lieutenant, [Robert] Russell, brave, good and a hard-working old Scotsman, begs me to come back, as do all the non-commissioned officers and the "old" men in the company. I tell them that I won't go back as first lieutenant, and hope that Col. Ellis will make no nomination until Townsend has used every effort to be reinstated. If then Col. Ellis offers me the captaincy, I will give an answer.

Col. Monroe's very pleasant little Virginia wife arrived at headquarters last night and we all passed a very pleasant evening. She will be here 20 days.

Last night was without exception the coldest I ever saw in the service and all the officers say the same. I slept but very little as I could not keep my feet warm. The thermometer was but 16 above inside the tent. What makes it so cold here, the inhabitants say, is the snow which we see on the summit of that cold, gloomy blue ridge only 16 miles distant, though no snow has fallen here.

I expect that the poor old regiment in its only half-finished log houses must have suffered fearfully. The pickets of both armies stood a good chance of freezing to death.

Find my ordinance in capital condition. I shall have no trouble with my first quarterly returns.

Yours, Harry

Camp Hancock near Stevensville, Va., Jan. 8th, 1864

Dear Mother,

My health is perfect during the day, but at nights I suffer a little. My elbow still itching a little from scurvy, but the worst is that the sores on my shoulder feel very sore at night, especially if it is stormy.

Our staff has, I am sorry to say, been a very quarrelsome one. I have avoided taking sides, but two days since it came to a point where Lieut. Farrell and I (both neutrals) were called upon to sign a paper requesting part of the staff to leave the nest, being threatened with the enmity of the others if we did not. Farrell and worked like beavers and finally restored peace to the extent that two of the staff who had not spoken for six months shook hands and made friends. Enclosed find extracts from my dairy since I last wrote.

Jan. 4th. It snowed. Got into our new log house, one third larger and as wide and high as your dining room. A desk, two bedsteads and a table with a red blanket tablecloth, a brick fire place and chimney make it very neat, warm and cozy.

Jan. 5th. Rode over and called on Dr. Dudley of the 14th where learned of the death of 2nd Lieut. Hart of Co. G. Wrote an obituary notice for the New Haven Journal and Courier.

Jan. 6th. Made calls among the battery officers, one of whom is to teach me cribbage. Big row in the staff mess.

Jan. 7th. At work on returns. At 2 P.M., with three ambulances started for the camp of the 14th C.V. at Stoney Mountain. Lost the road twice, but got there at 6:30 P.M. Saw Capt. Nichols and Townsend—the latter has scurvy ten times worse than I did. Having secured permission, got our regimental band into ambulances and started back to headquarters. Lost the road repeatedly and last found myself in the camp of the Harris Light Cavalry, where I was profanely greeted, but joyously received, by my old comrade Capt. Cook, who gave everybody a drink and gave me directions as to the right road, so I made my way here by 10 P.M. It was the worst night I was ever on the road and I was almost frozen to the saddle.

We gave the band a good supper, and then they serenaded Col. and Mrs. Monroe till 1 A.M. When we sent them to bed, they were pretty full of whiskey.

Jan. 8th. The band breakfasted, played three or four tunes when we sent them home.

Yours, Harry

Camp Hancock, Jan. 10th, 1864

Rode over to the camp of the Harris Light Cavalry. Called on Majors [Edward W.] Cook and [John E.] Naylor, Capt. [Francis M.] Plum, and Lieut. [Robert] Loudon, who are about all of my old acquaintances now in the regiment. Dined on roast turkey, oysters and cod fish with Capt. Plum, who then accompanied me to Gen. Kilpatrick's. I was cordially received by the general, who referred me for information about his "Richmond ride" to Capt. [Henry] Grinton, H.L.C., who kept a diary on the expedition. The general told me to get my facts and then come and talk with him. I presume he wishes to read the manuscript to see whether I puff him sufficiently.

Gen. H. E. Davies, my old major in the H. L. C., was present and greeted me cordially, saying, "I hear very good accounts of you, Mr. Goddard," where I cannot imagine. Lieut. Whitaker is away with the Connecticut Squadron, who have reenlisted. Capt. Coon[1] has been dismissed from the service.

Got my first reprimand today from Col. Monroe. He told me to make a requisition for a traveling forge for my train. I thought that belonged to the Quartermaster's department as some of the battery commanders so advised me. I told the colonel what they said, when he gave me a sharp and deserved reprimand for questioning an order and said that there was altogether too much interference on the part of battery commanders, which is true, owing to jealousy.

I do not think the colonel bears me any ill will for this incident, as he invited me to spend the evening in his room, which I did, he playing the guitar and his wife singing little ballads, we passed a very pleasant evening.

Our mess is a fearfully extravagant one, but there is no help for it. What do you think of 58 pounds of beef bought Saturday noon, gone Tuesday evening. These Providence boys have been very luxuriously brought up and want the best of everything.

Yours affectionately, Harry

1. Capt. Marcus Coon's "dislike" was a primary cause, in addition to the death of his father back home, for Goddard's resignation from the 2nd New York Volunteer Cavalry in May 1862 after less han three months' service.

Camp Hancock, Jan. 13th, 1864

Dear Mother,

I extract from diary as follows.

Jan. 11th. Rode to Brandy Station and thence to the headquarters of the Army of the Potomac, where I had my ordinance requisition approved by Brig. Gen. [Henry] Hunt, chief of artillery, a queer old codger, wearing a private's blouse and trousers and without any insignia of rank. On the whole I was very well treated at army headquarters.

Drew two loads of ammunition from Brandy Station.

Jan. 12th. Rode down to the 14th camp and saw all the officers and Capt. Fiske, wife and child. Only think Mrs. Fiske is living in her husband's hut in the camp, which is at a point only about a mile from the Rapidan. In fact she probably is in range of the enemy's heavy guns.

Jan. 13th. Rode over to the camp of the Harris Light and saw Capt. [Henry] Grinton, who tells me that to his utmost sorrow, he has recently lost in a skirmish his diary, containing a full record of events since he has been in service, including his Richmond ride.

Then rose over to Lieut. Pelton's ambulance train where I had taken a picture of myself on horseback.

In today's Washington Chronicle is an intercepted letter from the rebels written from the headquarters of Lee's army to a Baltimorean. It states that Longstreet's forces are with Lee, and that the latter has returned and is about to consummate a series of maneuvers and all be it bloody battles too. The writer says, "The day cannot be far off when we shall embrace each other in Maryland in the old homestead in Baltimore, beneath the victorious flag of the free and recognized South."

Gen. Meade has gone to Philadelphia and Sedgwick is in command of the army. My health is now quite good as I have facilities for plenty of bathing and can get my clothes washed. We have on the whole a very pleasant staff and the life is very enjoyable.

Jan. 14th. Rode over to the camp of Pelton's ambulance train, where was introduced to Mrs. Gen. Alex Hays, wife of the commander of the Third Division, an elderly, but very sensible, motherly kind of lady.

Jan. 15th. Spent the morning with the surgeon, adjudicating charges against our headquarters Negroes of stealing money from a sutler. I think them innocent, but if guilty they were very shrewd.

The owners of the place where we reside, Colemans by name, who, according to Mrs. Monroe, herself a Virginian, are very aristocratically connected, insist upon asking if I am not connected with the Taliaferros of Virginia, whom Mrs. Coleman declares I resemble. She says she is going to send for one of them to make her a visit—a young niece about my age. Doubtless it will be pleasant, but it does seem funny to fall into the hands of match-making mothers out here.

I gave mortal offence to Mrs. Coleman when I came here by tracking mud over her floor one cold stormy night before our log house was built, when I sought refuge in her house from the cold. Regarding her as one of the poor whites of the South who are not apt to be very cleanly, I made a convenience of her kitchen, which is a parlor and bed room also. Her Southern pride being aroused, she complained to Mrs. Monroe, and it has been a standing joke on me since among the staff. Since I heard it, I have devoted myself to Mrs. Coleman, who now speaks of me in the highest terms and is very anxious that I should meet and surrender to the charms of her niece, Miss Maggie Taliaferro.

Yours affectionately, Harry

Camp Hancock, Jan. 16th, 1864

Dear Mother,

I have been to corps headquarters today to see Lieut. Col. Frank Walker, A.A.G. of the corps. He says that I can take a commission and be mustered as captain in the 14th and retain my present position without any new detail, provided my colonel is willing. Will write Ellis as to this at once as I hate the captaincy of "B" to slip through my fingers. The regiment will gain a first lieutenant if I take a captaincy and so will really lose nothing. When I refused "K" company, my second lieutenant got it and was immediately after detailed on staff himself. My ordinance sergeant is an attorney at law at home and is a very smart fellow.

Acted as adjutant at the brigade guard mounting this afternoon and was complimented by Col. Monroe. You see, these artillerists don't know half as much about such matters as the infantry and it is hard work to teach the men to do it prettily, as they have no arms but sabres, but my Harris Light experience helped me out there.

The camps are filling up with ladies, who are arriving by every train.

Yours affectionately, Harry

Camp Hancock, Jan. 22nd, 1864

Dear Mother,

Was much surprised but glad to hear of Alfred's visit home with his regiment. Tell him not to leave the staff for the line. I have grown so used to riding that I don't walk even to our guard mounting, one-sixteenth of a mile, but ride down and have an orderly hold my horse. I would not go back to the regiment for $200 a month. I am happy as a clam at high tide, although there is very little to do now but to ride about, read, write and superintend the building that is going on to furnish quarters for the ladies expected. I extract from my journal as follows:

Jan. 21st. Attended a supper given by Capt. [John G.] Hazard of Battery "B," 1st R.I., to the Rhode Island officers and Col. Monroe and staff. Mrs. Col. Monroe and Mrs. Capt. [William A.] Arnold were also present. Mrs. Arnold is much more of a woman than Mrs. Monroe, who is a thoughtless, little young Virginia girl, naturally a secessionist, but bound up in her husband. The party numbered 14, which crowded the room (wall tent) so much and the table was so heavily loaded that Capt. [Charles B.] Elliot and myself edged back and ate but little so as to make room.

Over the table hung a wooden chandelier with eight adamantine candles. The bill of fare, served in two courses, was as follows: Broiled fish, roast turkey (a monster), broiled partridges, quail, woodcock; roast duck; (vegetables) mashed potatoes, celery, cranberry, onions; (desert) canned peaches, almonds, raisins; coffee, champagne.

A good supper, considering that all the articles had come 100 miles. The ten who drank (Mrs. Monroe, Mrs. Arnold, Capt. Elliot and myself not joining) consumed a dozen bottles of champagne—that single item cost $35. We came home about mid-night, having had a delightful time.

There were some indications of a move on Lee's part the other day at Germania Ford, but a heavy storm came up and now the mud is <u>awful</u>.

Your loving son, Harry

Camp Hancock, Va., Jan. 24th, 1864

Dear Mother,

Have been looking at the rebs today from one of the mountains this side of the Rapidan. They look all right but have three lines of pickets—one to watch our forces, two to keep their own men from deserting. New style of outpost duty, that.

Your loving son, Harry

Camp Hancock, Va., Jan. 31st, 1864

I shall not go to see Miss Taliaferro unless accompanied by other officers. She lives within our lines, nearer Rappahannock Station than I had supposed, and I may stop there some time when I go to visit the 5th Corps in camp, not otherwise. I continue my journal to date.

Jan. 26th. Rode over to the Harris Light camp where had a glimpse of Maj. Cook's wife—the prettiest woman here yet.

In the evening, I attended a darky "banjo picking" in the woods near headquarters. It was a lovely moon-light night and the scene was very picturesque—the best fun I have yet seen in Virginia.

I am going to send you a picture of "Dick," a handsome little mulatto boy, now the colonel's servant, who used to work at the Lacy House in Falmouth, where he often saw my old admiration, Miss Herndon of Fredericksburg. He says that Miss Lacy prided herself on never walking across the bridge to Fredericksburg. Although it was but a few rods from her house, she always rode.

Jan. 27th. Col. and Mrs. Monroe attended a review of the cavalry and then a dance at Gen. Kilpatrick's. Their horses broke loose and ran home, and they had to follow in an ambulance.

Jan. 29th. Visited Kilpatrick's headquarters and dined with his staff. The general was superintending the erection of a theatre in Stevensburg. Have had most oppressively sultry weather for a week.

Jan. 31st. Rain and fog. Wrote my ordinance report.

Yours affectionately, Harry

Camp Hancock, Feb. 6th, 1864

Dear Mother,

I received a letter from Joe Rockwell written from Libby prison [in Richmond] Jan. 4th. As it had to undergo rebel inspection, it bore on purely personal matters. I am delighted tonight to hear of the escape of 100 officers by a tunnel under Libby prison. I only hope Joe is among them.

Gen. Hancock is now on recruiting service. We want no better leader than our dear old swearing, dashing, rushing (on the march or in the fight), courteous, calm, dignified (in camp) Hancock. He is a knight in whom we all believe and I think one of the best generals in the service. Gen. Warren is a very good engineer, but inspires less enthusiasm.

Yours affectionately, Harry

<u>Feb. 6th, 2 A.M.</u> Have just got out of bed in response to an order to march at 6 A.M. with half of our brigade. I know not how extensive the move is to be, except that we are to attempt to cross the Rapidan.

Excerpts from *14th C. V.: Regimental Reminiscences of the War of the Rebellion*, by Henry P. Goddard (Middletown, Conn.: C. W. Church, 1877)

That winter we spent in camp at the foot of Stony Mountain. It was here that the 3rd corps ran a picket line between us and the rest of the 2nd corps, till Gen. Warren sent Gen. French word that if he didn't withdraw it, he would give the job to the whole 2nd corps. Gen. French withdrew it. Here the ladies (God bless them always) gladdened our hearts, and all of us envied the happy married officers who had their wives in camp. One of these ladies, I think Mrs. Captain Wadhams, who is with us today, said to me at her departure that she could bear this testimony to the men of the 14th—that she had not seen an offensive act nor heard an offensive word in the six weeks she had spent in their camp. Here Colonel Ellis established his West Point Academy, which the officers deemed a hard old spot at first, but long since have confessed its usefulness.

Mrs. Wadhams has told me today another story of the camp in Stone Mountain. She was awakened one night by the groans of a prisoner, whom Capt. [Newell P.] Rockwood (officer of the day) had tied up for some offense; while peeping out of her tent to learn the cause of the sounds, she saw Mrs. Rockwood issue from her tent and untie the man. When the captain discovered her at it and demanded the reason, Mrs. R. replied, "That man has been tied up long enough," and Rockwood succumbed. What a pet we all made of little Jessie Wadhams, the four year old daughter of Lieut. [Henry W.] Wadhams, who losing her own father in battle a few months later, was adopted by the regiment, and is right welcome here today, as its "daughter," who we shall take care, shall never want a protector while any 14th veteran survives (14).

18

A Gauntlet of Bullets
at Morton's Ford

G oddard, now in charge of artillery, twice runs a gauntlet of bullets from Confederate sharpshooters, racing on horseback with urgent messages for Union batteries along the Rapidan River. He describes Gen. Alexander Hays leading the charge across the river and calls Hays, habitually drunk on the field, "the rashest soldier I ever saw, ahead even of Kilpatrick" (204). Although Union artillery fire drives the rebels back with only one artillery brigade casualty, Goddard criticizes individual commanding generals for missing an opportunity to seize the rebel battery on the heights, even though the operation was just a "reconnaissance." As for the 14th Connecticut, the regiment suffered "one-fourth of the 204 casualties of the battle," and "held their ground until the rebs gave it up in despair" (204).

~

Excerpts from *History of the Fourteenth Regiment, Connecticut Vol. Infantry,* **by Charles D. Page (Meriden, Conn.: Horton Printing Co., 1906)**

About this time it was the evident design of the commander in chief of the Union army that General Butler should attempt the capture of Richmond. To attract the attention of Lee and hold his army from Richmond a show of active operations was proposed at this point on the Rapidan. . . . The Second Corps, under command of General Warren, was ordered to move to Morton's Ford, which it did, moving through a belt of woods to a broad plain and formed line of battle on the north bank of the Rapidan opposite Morton's Ford. . . . Standing on this broad plain and looking across about a mile the Confederate troops could be seen moving toward the breastworks from all directions, until it was evident that the enemy had many more troops than the Union. The course of the Rapidan at this point was like a bended bow or crescent. The Confederate entrenchments about a mile distant followed the course of this bend, its concave side toward the river and its extreme right and left coming down nearly to the river. The Confederates also had a line of rifle-pits in which were planted about eighty men between the bank of the river and the entrenchments. Shortly after crossing the river was a ridge extending along in front, near which stood the house of Major Buckner. Still farther on stood the house of Dr. Morton, from whom the ford took its name. . . . About one o'clock the order was given to move forward. The First and Third Brigades were the first to ford the stream and the Second Brigade [including the 14th Connecticut] brought up the rear. The water was icy cold, mixed with snow and ice. . . . On reaching the opposite shore, they ascended the bank and advanced at the double-quick across an open space which was raked by the fire of a rebel battery, fortunately aimed too high, and thus none of the men were hit. The men were here massed with their comrades in a ravine where they were protected from the enemy's shot and shell and remained all day. . . . The position of the Union men was a hazardous one, being exposed to an attack from the right, left and front or from all three quarters combined by a greatly superior force, and such an attack could hardly have failed to dislodge the Union forces from the shallow ravine and drive them back in confusion upon the river. General Hays rode back and forth upon his galloping steed, his reckless manner and incoherent language indicating that he had added two or three extra fingers to his morning dram. . . .

It was nearly dark when there was a lively firing from the enemy's batteries, responded to by the Union guns across the river, and the firing across the skirmish line assumed the proportions of a volley. The Thirty-ninth New York, known as the "Garibaldi Guards," was brought up to the support of the skirmish line. These were probably the most unfit troops in the whole corps to take up the duty. They were mostly foreigners, could not understand the language of the orders as they came over the crest of the hill and encountered the enemy's fire, they became confused and instead of keeping their line, recoiled in confusion and huddled together in groups, upon which the enemy's shot made sad havoc. Finding these men could not be depended upon the Fourteenth Regiment was ordered up and the sharp, clear voice of Lieutenant-Colonel Moore was heard "Fall in Fourteenth" and the men went forward, stepping over the prostrate forms of the Twelfth New Jersey, who lay directly before them. The Fourteenth Regiment moved swiftly up to the brow of the hill when the order was given to deploy as skirmishers, the men being four or five feet apart. The bullets fell thick and fast and the noise was indescribable. Lieutenant-Colonel Moore with the right wing and center of the regiment marched down the slope on to the broad plain toward the enemy, while Adjutant Hincks took the left. A couple dozen of the recruits clustered behind one of the buildings, but were soon dislodged and forced into line through the proddings of the sharp points of Adjutant Hincks and Sergeant-Major [William] Murdock's sabers. The darkness was intense, the artillery had ceased to play and the sharp flashes of the musketry were the only indications of the whereabouts of the enemy. Above the shouts and clatter of the musketry could be heard the sharp tenor voice of Lieutenant-Colonel Moore, directing his men and encouraging them to proceed. The advance was rapid and the line had now reached the Morton houses in a cluster of trees, the men shielding themselves behind the garden fence. Just before reaching this house Major Coit was wounded and left the field. Captain Broatch, senior captain of the regiment, while advancing sword in hand was struck by a bullet which shattered his fingers and threw his sword twenty feet into the air. Picking it up and grasping it in his left hand he swung it over his head, at the same time guiding his men with his voice until his wound proved so painful that he was obliged to retire from the field. . . .

With the serious losses which the Fourteenth had met in its advance, it was not able unsupported to dislodge the Confederates from the strong position which they had formed behind the Morton house and among the outbuildings. The contest had become fierce and in many cases it was a hand to hand fight with bayonets in the darkness. . . . Seeing this General Hays ordered up the 108th New York and the 10th New York Battalion in line of battle. Halting them just a little before reaching the house, in front of which stood the Fourteenth, he ordered the 10th New York to fire. An officer of the 10th replied, "General, those are our men in front of us." General Hays replied, "They are rebels," preceding his order to fire by an oath. Crash went that dreadful volley and how many of the brave Fourteenth fell by that stupid drunken order will never be known. There was a loud cry of dismay, and the two advancing regiments approached the house. The line was further strengthened, the attempt to flank was foiled, the Confederates were routed and the battle of Morton's Ford was at an end (216–23).

The Battle of Morton's Ford

Camp Hancock, 11 p.m., Feb. 7th, 1864

Dear Mother,

Since my last, we have been to and across the Rapidan, fought a little fight and come back—all in 40 hours. Of the corps, only Gen. Hayes' division was much engaged and our batteries but slightly. We had only one man slightly wounded in the brigade. The 14th loses heavily: of the 202 casualties of the fight, one third are in that regiment. Maj. Coit is slightly wounded in the leg (Call on his mother right away and tell her, as my letter will be from 24 to 48 hours ahead of those of the regiment.) It is a very slight wound. Capt. Broatch had his sword shot twice all to pieces and loses one or two fingers. Capt. Snagg and Lieuts. [Frederick E.] Shalk and [George A.] Stocking are slightly wounded. My dear friend Capt. Fred Doten, to whom I was talking only the other day, and four of his men were taken prisoners by thirteen rebels whom Doten was trying to capture.

I got under heavy fire from rebel sharp shooters early this morning while carrying orders to an exposed battery. But rode down and back like the wind and none of the bullets had my name on them, so I escaped unhurt, for which I assure you I am profoundly thankful to Him who has always been kind to me.

As I have been in the saddle since dawn, I am tired to death. Will write at length Monday. We entirely accomplished the object of the reconnaissance.

Your loving son, Harry

Feb. 6th. Got marching orders at 2 A.M. and was off with our command by 6:30 A.M. We reached Morton's Ford by 10 A.M.

Gen. Aleck Hays, followed by Gen. [Brig. Gen. Joshua] Owen's brigade of the Third Division, 2nd Corps, waded the river and drove the rebs out of the rifle pits on the southern bank, Hays himself being the first man among the rebs. They took 27 prisoners. The rest of the division, including the 14th C.V., followed and advanced to Morton's house when the rebels commenced shelling and we brought our batteries to the north bank of the river while the Third Division massed in close column behind the house, where they lay all day skirmishing. Our batteries (we only took three with us) did not cross nor did the other two divisions.

About 3 P.M., Col. Monroe, Lieut. Dwight, Dr. Carroll and myself forded the river and rose along our lines on that side, inspecting the rebel works. Fortunately, we did not draw fire and I had a chance for a few words with the 14th boys. Returning to the north bank, we opened on them from Arnold's battery, Gen. Hunt showing us where to place it, but could get no response.

About 6 P.M. the rebs commenced shelling the Third Division furiously and then made a sortie, attempting to drive them across the river. The division fought splendidly, the 14th having one-fourth of the 204 casualties of the battle, and held their ground until the rebs gave it up in despair.

As we could not fire from our batteries without injuring our own infantry, we just stood still and watched the fight from the north bank. It was a magnificent sight and old Aleck Hays held his ground splendidly. He is the rashest soldier I ever saw, ahead even of Kilpatrick. (By the way, we saw "Kill" on our way to Morton's Ford and I saw Lieut. Whitaker, who is to tell me all about that famous "ride to Richmond" in which he was lately engaged.)

During the night the Third Division quietly re-crossed the river without discovery.

Although some of the rebel shells almost reached us, we were not really "under fire" the whole of this day. We slept in a house on the river bank, expecting to be shelled out all night, but they left us alone.

Feb. 7th. As I had posted two guns of a battery a mile down the river yesterday, the colonel sent me at dawn to tell the commander to withdraw it out of range, as our troops had re-crossed the river.

I rode quietly until within a quarter of a mile of it, when I saw the opposite bank covered with reb skirmishers, and that was not the worst of it—they saw me.

Zip, zip, zip came their bullets. Down goes my head under the horse's neck, in the spurs go, and I <u>ride</u> for it. Reach the battery and in an instant find that most of our men here have run away, having supposed that our troops held the other bank, they were completely surprised, and worst of all, all the horses had run away with one of the limbers so that the gun could not be hauled off.

Finding that the officer in command had gone after the limber to bring it back, I galloped off to him, running the gauntlet of bullets ahead, but being safe out of range when I reached the limber. He said that if I would get the limber back, he would ride to the nearest regiment and get infantry support and then haul off the guns. So he rode to the adjacent regiment, whose colonel sent it down in front of the cannon. The battery commander went to his guns and right bravely fastened both guns to one limber just as I came up with the other limber, as it had taken me some time, threats and the necessity of drawing my sabre to make the driver mount and start. Only one man was wounded in all this—the only man hurt in our brigade in the move.

As soon as the lieutenant got his guns back to a safer position, he opened fire on the rebs and with a few rounds drove them back from the river to the hills, minus some half dozen killed and wounded. As they were taken off on stretchers, I heard him say, "There, damn you, take <u>that</u> for spoiling my breakfast."

Nothing more of interest occurred till 6 P.M. when we got orders to return to our old camp. I rode back ahead of our command, by order of Col. Monroe, with Gen. Warren and his staff arriving here an hour ahead of the colonel, in time to assure his wife of his safety and get almost kissed for my pains.

Capt. Elliot's sister is here, just from Philadelphia. I tell you it was right pleasant to have two ladies at the tea table to question us about the fight and crown us with laurels.

The ladies in the army were in a terrible state while we were gone, as every cannon shot and volley of musketry could be heard clear to Brandy Station.

As to whether we accomplished our object, I <u>know</u> we did, as our headquarters were at corps headquarters all through, and I heard the consultation between the three division commanders—Gens. [Brig. Gen. John] Caldwell, [Brig. Gen. Alexander] Webb and Hays—and Col. Monroe during the whole day. It is merely a reconnaissance. Still I think a golden opportunity was thrown away to carry the heights and take the rebel guns early in the morning of the 6th. In truth I do not think much of any of our division commanders. Gen. Caldwell is too fearful of risking his men to accomplish anything; Gen. Hays is too rash and was drunk all day on the 6th. Gen. Webb is a very clever fellow and a charming gentleman, but a better fellow to show you around New York than to command troops on a battle field.

Maj. Gen. Warren, commanding the corps, did not arrive on the field till 5 P.M., having been either sick or drunk (reports differ as to which). He is a splendid soldier, but we all miss Gen. Hancock, who will have things his own way when he returns to us next spring.

Feb. 8th. At 11 P.M. completed my ordinance returns. Thank heaven that job is over. Miss Elliot is very pretty and interesting. Intellectually she is superior to Mrs. Col. Monroe. The wife of Capt. Arnold was also up here today and we youngsters on the staff had a very jolly time with the ladies.

The Connecticut Squadron of the Harris Light has returned reenlisted for the war.

Yours ever, Harry

Excerpts from *14th C. V.: Regimental Reminiscences of the War of the Rebellion*, by Henry P. Goddard (Middletown, Conn.: C. W. Church, 1877)

Then came that too little known fight at Morton's Ford, where the 14th under Lt. Col. Moore covered itself with laurels, and where Capt. Fred Doten was immensely disgusted to find himself started for Richmond alone, and we were all sorry to lose our handsome little captain with the golden locks, braided staff jacket and sombre hat that made him look like one of Prince Rupert's cavaliers (14).

19

Goddard Reluctantly Resigns from the Army

Goddard predicts "a long and bloody campaign" come spring, not a "walk" as some predict (208). He renders his opinion of generals Robert E. Lee, George Meade, George McClellan, Ambrose Burnside, Joseph Hooker, and a new army commander, Ulysses S. Grant. He defends the Army of the Potomac, "abused and decried as it is," and speaks of military service as building gentlemanly character (208). He describes the attitude of mortally-wounded soldiers toward death. He attends a "grand ball" at 2nd Corps headquarters, where he sees Vice President Hannibal Hamlin, several senators, and a host of generals. His confidence now seems strong: "With a Lieutenant General [Grant] at our head," coming reinforcements, and "a determined purpose on the part of the officers and men to <u>this</u> summer achieve . . . Richmond, death or glory" (212). Grant, he writes, "has pleased the army by his first official step—in pitching his headquarters with his troops in the field" (213). He thinks it fitting that his brother, Alf, has left his staff position to join the 8th Connecticut Infantry as a line officer. Following the directive of General in Chief Grant, Maj. Gen. Winfield Hancock orders all brigade artillery officers back to their regiments, prompting Goddard, shortly after being promoted to the rank of captain, to resign from the army with a certificate of disability from the brigade surgeon. "It was <u>very hard</u>, he writes his mother, but I am heartily convinced that I have done my whole duty under all the circumstances" (216).

In early March 1864 Lincoln appointed Ulysses S. Grant as general in chief of all Union armies, now composed of more than 500,000 troops. With Grant's victory at Vicksburg, Mississippi, splitting the Confederacy in two and with the states of the Upper South falling to advancing Union troops following Lee's defeat at Gettysburg, the fate of the Confederacy looked rather bleak in early 1864. However, the Southerners appeared willing to continue fighting in the hope that growing war-weariness in the North, punctuated by draft riots in New York and other cities, and the likelihood that Lincoln would be defeated by a "peace" Democrat in November would bring a negotiated peace favorable to Southern independence.

~

Camp Hancock, Va., Feb. 9th, 1864

Dear Mother,

Col. Ellis says that in accord with my request, he will leave the captaincy of "B" vacant until Townsend has exhausted every request for reinstatement. He says that as a senior first lieutenant I am entitled to it, the only trouble being about my staff detail, and that he will talk the whole thing over with me at the corps ball, for which I have procured an invitation. Our corps ball will be on Washington's birth day, the 22nd. It is to be a grand affair, tickets $10 a piece to officers of the 2nd Corps, and none but invited guests admitted.

Yours, Harry

Dear Mother,

Lieut. Col. Moore was in command of the 14th during the late fight, having arrived from home that morning. Col. Ellis has been away since Nov. 7th, as a member of a court-martial sitting in Washington.

I am not one who believes that we are going to have a "walk" over the course of the coming campaign. I believe the Confederacy will have a large and powerful army this spring and that we shall have a hard fight, a long fight and a stout fight to go through. I believe in my heart's core that the Army of the Potomac—abused and decried as it is—is the only army on this continent that could have success-fully foiled and resisted the plans of the truly master mind of Robert E. Lee. I believe too that Gen. Meade is one of the few leaders who can comprehend and foil these plans. Meade is capital in defense, cautious and perhaps a trifle too wary in his attacks (though this is not yet proved), not quite enough of an enthusiast to gain the entire love of his army, but who commands their respect as he has no commander save McClellan, and perhaps not he. Gen. Burnside was unlucky and Hooker too. I dislike that man more and more.

As you love me, don't join in the cry against the Potomac army. Several officers who have lately come to us from the West have revealed facts that show me that the western army is not half so well drilled and disciplined, nor have they had such hard battles nor a Lee to encounter.

A long and bloody campaign will soon open here and many of us will fall, but I have chosen and remember:

> "Whether on the scaffold plank, or in the battles van,
> The noblest death for man to die is where he dies for man."

Feb. 13th. With Lieut. Col. Moore, rode over to a horse race at Gen. Kil-patrick's. There were nearly 100 ladies present. The 2nd Corps horse won. Rode home and on my way met an ambulance containing Capt. and Mrs. W. W. Coit of Norwich on their way to visit their son at the regiment.

Feb. 14th. A most lovely Sunday. Had lots of callers. There are some indications of another move. The moon tonight had a halo of the seven colors of the rainbow, making a perfect ring about it. It was a beautiful phenomenon. Did you see it? We took it for a good omen.

Feb. 15th. Very busy having my light 12 pounder ammunition condemned by Capt. Thompson, an expert. We got one-third through when we were stopped by a snow storm as we were afraid of getting the ammunition wet. Col. Ellis writes from Washington with great enthusiasm as to the coming ball to which he will bring a bevy of ladies.

Yours affectionately, Harry

Camp Hancock, Va., Feb. 24, 1864

Dear Julia,

From my diary I extract as follows:

Feb. 22nd. No salute fired in the army today—the first time I ever knew it omitted on this date. With Capt. Brownson (son of Orestes A. Brownson, a noted Catholic) and Lt. Pelton rode over to Brandy Station and received Col. Ellis and the seven young ladies he brought from Washington to attend the ball, and escorted them to corps headquarters in an ambulance where Dr. Dudley had pleasant quarters provided for them.

The 2nd Corps Ball. Attended the grand ball at corps headquarters in the evening, escorting one of Col. Ellis' friends, a Miss Richards, whom we have already adopted as "La Fille" of the 14th C.V. The ball room was an immense frame building covered with canvass. It was decorated with the corps, division, brigade and all the regimental flags, while two light 12-ponder guns and several stacks of muskets added to the effect. The floor was perfect for dancing. Supper was furnished by Gautier of Washington at an expense of $2,000.

Among the notabilites present were Vice President Hamlin, a jolly old New England farmer in appearance, showing to advantage in the supper room his wife (pretty, quiet and very proud of the vice president), his daughter (a gay, dashing, rattling, teasing brunette, not very pretty but full of life and fond of dancing)—rather the belle of the ball with a dozen flirtations on her hands at once. Kilpatrick and his staff rather had the lead with the girl (she wore the crossed sabres in her hair) but the artillery came next and several of our officers had their hearts smashed, myself among them. No, I was not introduced, tho two staff officer friends who know her promise to present me yet. Others there were Gov. Andy Curtin [of Pennsylvania] and daughter, [New Hampshire] Senator John P. Hale's daughters, [Rhode Island] Senator [William] Sprague and his beautiful wife, with whose appearance I was charmed. They say that Sprague is very much in love with his wife and is less rowdy than of old. Orestes A. Brownson, the great reviewer (a venerable-looking man who resembles Secretary Welles), Secretary of Interior [John] Usher, Gen. Meade, whom I am ready to swear by, I so admire him, Gens. Sedgwick, [Brig. Gen. Alfred, commanding Cavalry Corps] Pleasanton, [Maj. Gen.

Andrew, Meade's chief of staff] Humpheys, [Brig. Gen. William, commanding the 22nd U.S. Colored Infantry] Birney, Warren, Kilpatrick and a host of brigadiers were all present.

Owing to Col. Ellis, I had plenty of partners, beside Mrs. and Miss Elliot of the artillery and the 14th ladies. I danced till 4 A.M., when I gave out, cancelled the remaining engagements and hastened home to bed, fondly hoping for a good sleep.

Feb. 23rd. What was my vexation to be aroused at 8 A.M. to go to corps headquarters for a corps review at 11 A.M. I begged and protested, but old Capt. Thompson, temporarily commanding the brigade, is too old a soldier to let up on his "boys" as he calls his staff, and I had to go.

What with preparing, marching and waiting, it was 2 P.M. before Gen. Meade, Pleasanton and their staffs rode down our line and those of Kilpatrick's division of cavalry. Several ladies rode with Meade's staff and escort. You would have enjoyed that. Then Gen. Meade took his post, and the cavalry and 2nd Army Corps passed in review.

It was a cloudless day and the prancing steeds, flashing sabres and gleaming bayonets, the dipping colors and steady tramp of horses and men in solid columns, with a host of officers and ladies on horseback and in ambulances, made the scene truly brilliant.

I noted Col. Ulric Dahlgren,[1] with his one leg present, on horseback. He is very handsome. I met him the other night at Kilpatrick's and spoke to him. He sent his regards to you. He was at the corps ball. He walks with a crutch, but is on duty.

At 6 P.M., I threw myself on a couch, tired to death of dancing and with galloping.

Feb. 24th. Rose at 9 A.M. with reluctance. Visited the corps hospital today, calling on the officers and ladies there.

Lieut. Dwight goes north on ten days leave tomorrow, and I have got to act as assistant adjutant general in his absence. Dwight is a brilliant fellow—one of the most remarkable men I have ever met. He is very intellectual and a great student. Carries more books than any major general, is brave to a fault, yet dearly loves his own comfort.

Yours affectionately, Harry

1. Dahlgren, who had lost a leg at Gettysburg, was killed March 1, 1864, during Kilpatrick's Richmond raid.

Camp Hancock, Feb. 25th, 1864

Dear Mother,

Completed my inspection today, and am now ready to turn over all my business in good shape. If the reorganization of the army costs me my place, in which case I shall in all probability resign, as it is better to leave now honorably, in fair health, than to rejoin the regiment, and probably be compelled shortly to resign in wretched health.

Yours affectionately, Harry

Feb. 28th, 1864.

Dear Mother,

My army experience teaches me that our New England ministers make mistakes. I never saw a soldier die uneasy—that is, never yet saw one die fearing death after being mortally wounded, and many surgeons will confirm this. They all seem to trust in forgiveness. If their trust is false, it is sorrowful, but I cannot believe it to be such. Many preachers here try to <u>scare</u> men into the service of God. It's not the way for soldiers.

Journal.

<u>Feb. 25th.</u> Lt. Dwight has gone north, leaving me acting assistant adjutant general. Finished inspecting the ammunition train.

<u>Feb. 27th.</u> The 6th Corps and 2nd Division of cavalry started to flank Lee's army on the extreme right, hoping to make him think it was our whole army, that he might attack in front. We are under marching orders.

<u>Feb. 28th.</u> Lt. Col. Francis A. Walker, A.A.G. of the corps, dined with us today. Gen. Hancock is expected this week to commence re-organizing the corps.

<u>March 2nd, 1864.</u> Dear Mother, Ere this reaches you, Gen. Kilpatrick will probably be in Richmond, either as a victor or prisoner. He left three days since with a picked command, and was last heard from as having safely passed Lee's entire army, in which movement he was assisted by the 6th Corps, Merritt's cavalry division, and the 1st Division, 3rd Corps. The infantry returned to camp today, having bothered Gen. Lee much. This morning Lee is said to have thrown a force across the Rapidan, driving in the 2nd Corps pickets. This whole movement is said to have been part of the plan to make him think our main army had moved while we were keeping merely a shell of pickets in his front. Gen. Kilpatrick is <u>par excellenz</u> the bold rider of our army.

<u>Feb. 29th.</u> A heavy storm arose, lasting till the night of March 1st, making it very muddy.

With best love to all, Harry

Headquarters, Artillery Brigade, March 22, 1864.

Dear Mother,

Reached here yesterday after a pleasant trip to Washington. My face is about well and I am quite comfortable. A tremendous snow storm prevails—six inches of snow at 7 P.M.

Yours, Harry

212 THE "FIGHTING FOURTEENTH"

Norwich Bulletin, **April 1, 1864**

"Correspondence of the Bulletin

From the Army of the Potomac"

Camp Hancock, Culpeper, Va., March 26, 1864

After a long silence, during which time your old correspondent has been knocking around with the Army of the Potomac as of old, I again address you. Last year was spent by that army in the old way, marching and countermarching; across the Rappahannock to Chancellorsville, where, somehow, we got whipped without knowing it, how and why, most of us have never found out; back across the river again to Falmouth; then our chase after Lee, up, over the old Bull Run ground across the Potomac, into Maryland, then on into Pennsylvania; then Gettysburg, with its glorious repulse of the rebel invasion; then we chased after Lee to Williamsport; then again across the Potomac into Old Virginia once more, down to Warrenton; then a new advance across the Rappahannock, to Culpeper this time; then Lee's chase of us up to Bristoe, where the old Second Corps again gloriously repulsed him, and to the old Bull Run ground again; then back to Warrenton; then again across the Rappahannock to find Lee across the Rapidan; then across the Rapidan to gaze at his works at Mine Run; then (most sensibly, too, in spite of newspaper critics) back across the Rapidan to this ground; then winter quarters with the excitement of a reconnaissance and fight across the Rapidan at Morton's Ford; than back here once more; then Kilpatrick's raid—glorious, grand, but unsuccessful in its main object, and then a quiet settling down to inquire, what next?

What next? Why, a grand reorganization into three corps, a Lieutenant General at our head, plenty of reinforcements (we hope) and a determined purpose on the part of the officers and men to this summer achieve, as Gen. Kilpatrick has well expressed it, Richmond, death or glory. And with God's help, it shall be Richmond and glory.

The dull and dreary winter has been enlivened by the ladies bringing balls, races, concerts, lectures, etc., etc., where the brave old soldiers of this army here proved that they can turn their hands to any and everything, and have not forgotten how to be gentlemen in being soldiers.

Apropos of this an incident is told of Fitz Green Halleck [(1790–1867), poet], the talented son of Connecticut. During the dark closing days of Buchanan's administration, he was met by a friend on Broadway, who, speaking of the war cloud that hung over the land, was responded to by the poet, "Yes, the era of soldiers is coming when, thank God, we shall be ruled over by gentlemen."

A handsome tribute to a class of men who ought by the very nature of their profession, and who have proved, in the main, true gentlemen. A military education tends towards this happy consummation, in teaching firmness, gentleness, and kindness towards our inferiors, with due respect to and consideration for our superiors, while it teaches us all one great point of good manners, viz.: how little we ourselves are as a minute fraction of a grand whole.

Our new Lieutenant General has pleased the army by his first official step—in pitching his headquarters with his troops in the field, away from that most famous (or infamous) city of Washington. We firmly hope that the first city where he establishes his headquarters will be Richmond.

But let me caution your readers on one point, namely, in believing that Lee's army is "totally demoralized," and that all we have to do to get into Richmond is to march there. We have these same "demoralized" yarns every winter, and every spring proves their fallacy. Robert E. Lee is a great general, as well as a great traitor, and undoubtedly has the confidence of his army and of the so-called Confederacy as no other general on this continent has the confidence of his army or people; and his men will fight, as they always have fought, desperately.

Hard marches, hard fights, and able strategy is necessary to enable us to accomplish the grand end of this army, viz.: the capture of Richmond; for whatever might be said about the unimportance of the place, its probable evacuation, etc., the capture of Richmond will be the virtual end of the war; and heavy battalions and a trust in Divine help are all that will enable us to accomplish that end.

But we all firmly believe that we shall accomplish it gloriously and completely, for we believe that

> "Behind the dim unknown
> Standeth God, amid the shadows,
> Keeping watch above His own."

Omega

Easter, March 27, 1864.

Dear Mother,

I am delighted to read that Joe Rockwell is exchanged. Tell him that he must write me all about his experiences in Libby. I also rejoice at Will Lusk's success. He is the best staff officer I ever served with.

Yes, General Grant will set the army at work soon and it is anxious to begin. We have now four divisions in the 2nd Corps under Generals [Brig. Gen. Francis] Barlow, [Brig. Gen. John] Gibbon, [Maj. Gen. David] Birney and [Brig Gen. Joseph] Carr, getting rid of timid Caldwell and drunken Hays, the latter is given only a brigade. The 14th C.V. is now in Col. [S. Sprigg] Carroll's brigade, of Gen. Gibbon's division. We are to have two more artillery batteries and probably a regular army officer as brigade commander. The reorganization is a good thing.

My captain's commission came today and I was mustered for three years more in the 14th C.V. Townsend dismissed. [George N.] Brigham becomes my first lieutenant, and Sergeant [Robert] Russell second lieutenant. Both good men. Lieut. Pelton is promoted to a captaincy.

I have just finished writing my account of Gen. Kilpatrick's first raid and shall run over to his "theatre" tonight. The 1st Conn. Cavalry are with him now. They will not remain 800 strong if they remain under <u>him</u> long.

Have been reading Robert Browning's new book. Have enjoyed the poem "Easterday" very much. Its theology of love would please you as it does me.

Much official business renders letter writing hard.

Yours affectionately, Harry

Camp Hancock, Va., April 1, 1864

Dear Mother,

Col. [John C.] Tidball, 4th N.Y. Heavy Artillery, assumes command of our brigade tomorrow. His regiment, 2,200-strong, just from Fort Ethan Allen, where it has been two years, joined the corps today. The regiment is armed and will act as infantry, but furnish all guard details, fill up the batteries, etc. Col. Tidball, a captain of artillery in the regular service, is said to be "a Tarter <u>on</u> duty, a gentleman <u>off</u> duty." Supplying the ordinance for this regiment and the new batteries will keep me very busy.

April 3rd, 1864

Dear Julia,

Col. Tidball assumed command today. I like his appearance. Our brigade has now 8 batteries and one heavy artillery 21-strong. Col. Tidball has just sent for me to come in and "mix some whiskey punches." Don't be alarmed as the Fourteenth and I drink nothing but beer.

Yours, Harry

Headquarters, Artillery Brigade, April 5, 1864

Dear Mother,

Col. Tidball, 4th N.Y. Artillery, now commands our brigade. Lt. Dwight is still AA.G. and I am captain and ordnance officer. This big 4th N.Y. Artillery, 2,000-strong, trebles my work. My train has now 43 wagons and my pecuniary responsibilities large. I have plenty to do and hence am happy.

Yours, Harry

Mountain View, Culpeper County, Va., April 7, 1864

Dear Mother,

Alf is a right noble fellow anyhow. He is naturally now experiencing some of the discomforts of service, but is learning as he never could have done on the staff. To be a good staff officer, one should serve in the line first. He is nobler, truer and better than I in every way.

The "Army of the Potomac ring" is very pretty. It has all the corps insignia set in it in silver. We are about to change our artillery badge from silver to gold-crossed cannon.

Col. Tidball lets each department run itself, apparently without influence, but if aught goes wrong, we hear from him, I assure you. As a regular officer, he secures us far better equipment than ever.

Col. Ellis made a long and pleasant call and dined with me. Capt. Pelton and I were mustered same date.

I am to deliver a speech in behalf of Battery B, 1st R.I., on Sunday when they present a sword to one of the lieutenants.

Your loving Harry

April 13th, 1864

I like Col. Tidball very much. He is a thorough gentleman in camp, though they do say he is a Tartar in action.

I have run the staff mess for thirteen days, and am happy to say, finish tonight. As I have made it cost each man $2.86 per day, they think I have run it long enough, and so do I, as it shoves me back pecuniarily. Tomorrow we split into smaller messes, which will be cheaper and better.

Yours, Harry

Headquarters, Artillery Brigade, April 17th, 1864

Alf Goddard did well in returning to his regiment. I may yet have to do the same, as General Hancock is trying to send all infantry officers back to their regiments.

Hancock reviewed the Second Division yesterday. He was received with rapturous cheering by his old fighting men, who had not seen him since Gettysburg. He is the best soldier, but the biggest swearer in this army, except Sedgwick, who I think as a good soldier. Of Warren I think less.

Yours, Harry

April 20, 1864

On Monday an order was issued from 2nd Corps headquarters that "all officers of infantry now serving with the artillery brigade, be at once relieved and sent back to their regiments." This order is in accordance with Gen. Grant's program, and all the enlisted men from the infantry have already been sent back.

As I have a surgeon's certificate of disability from the brigade's surgeon, and the corps medical director will approve it, this will probably involve my resignation. But there is a new order requiring one in such cases to go before a board of three surgeons of the brigade. This I shall do, and their decision will be final.

Gen. Hancock reviewed our brigade today, after which I had the pleasure of shaking hands with him at our headquarters.

Yours, Harry

Ebbitt House, Washington, D.C., April 28, 1864
Dear Mother,

I have resigned and been honorably discharged and am here settling with the Ordinance Department. A long and complicated series of accounts.

It was very hard, but I am heartily convinced that I have done my whole duty under all the circumstances.

Yours affectionately, Harry

Ebbitt House, Washington, D.C., May 1, 1864
Dear Mother,

I am hard at work straightening my ordinance returns. I cannot leave until this is done, as discharged officers are not allowed to leave the city with unsettled accounts. Oh hear, I have just got the "hang" of this ordinance business. When I was relieved, the surgeon certified that I was "unfit for infantry duty." Don't think that I love the service or the cause any less, as had I the strength of an ordinary man, I would have enlisted as a sergeant of artillery before leaving.

I trust that the Providence, always so kind, will provide for me in the future, as I mean to work, not to loaf.

With much love for all, ever your affectionate Harry

Excerpt from *14th C. V.: Regimental Reminiscences of the War of the Rebellion*, by Henry P. Goddard (Middletown, Conn.: C. W. Church, 1877)

Here was held that brilliant 2nd corps ball, to which Col. Ellis brought six blooming young ladies, keeping the prettiest of the lot for his own partner in every dance, to the immense disgust of the two young staff officers who had furnished transportation for the party—Captains Pelton and Goddard. But in view of the fact that the Colonel's partner that night is now his partner for life, we have forgiven him and have each of us gone and done likewise, leaving Captain Frank Morgan—if I mistake not—the only bachelor out of the whole line and staff. May he too soon see the error of his ways.

The night of that ball Captain Nichols sought permission to essay the capture of a small band of rebels who used to cross the Rapidan and have dances at a little white house on the north bank of Morton's Ford. Alex Hays, "always spoiling for a fight," said "Go," but General Warren refused permission, lest a general engagement might ensue.

As the writer's immediate connection with the regiment closed by his assignment to other duty ere the summer campaign of 1864–65, he will here drop his personal reminiscences, leaving to the future historian of the regiment the tale of that tremendous battle-summer of 1864, where seed was sown that was not fully reaped till the spring of 1865, when under the apple tree of Appomattox, the sword of the great Southern leader was tendered to our commander-in-chief, whom we all love to remember as the great soldier of the war, U. S. Grant.

The 14th was finally mustered out on the 31st of May, 1865, when it numbered but 234 officers and men on the rolls, out of the 1,726 who had served under its banner.

Comrades: the great drama of the war, in which we had the high privilege to be among the actors, is ended. Our record is made up; and, I say it in all reverence, we have reason to thank God for permitting us to have had the opportunity to serve in such a regiment as the Fourteenth Connecticut, and in such a cause— a cause that has its fruition at last in a fully restored Union and in the enfranchisement of four millions of human beings. Let us thank Him that so many of us survive to clasp hands together here today; thank Him for health and happiness; thank Him for the noble record that our dead left behind them as an heritage to us and to all free peoples. Over and above all, let us thank Him that at last those who wore the blue and those who wore the grey carry the same grand old banner of the Union, acknowledge the same chief magistrate, and while each tenderly cherish the memories and decorate the graves of their own loved ones who fell on either side, whether the graves be in the South land or in the North land, under the palmetto or under the pine, both now acknowledge a common country, a common government, "of the people, by the people, for the people," and a common God who ruleth over all (14–15).

Part 3

FIGHTING FOR PRINCIPLE BEFORE AND AFTER THE WAR

Goddard Recalls Candidate
and President Lincoln

Norwich Bulletin, July 4, 1903

[author unknown]

In his address at the dedication of the Hubbard Gates at the Norwich Town ceme-tery, Henry P. Goddard of Baltimore indulged in a flow of most interesting remi-niscences of old Norwich.

About the first notable event that I recall was a memorial service for President Taylor,[1] held upon the Little Plain in 1850. I recall that we small boys all carried lit-tle white flags with a black border containing these words, "We mourn our leader."

Upon the platform with the speakers of the day sat several venerable gentle-men, veterans of the war of 1812, who I remember ascended the stage with some difficulty and seemed to suffer from the rays of the summer sun.

The next public event of political character which I recall was the great Repub-lican clambake, held at the lot opposite the Big Plain in October 1856. This was when I made my military debut as one of the company of "Liberty Boys off '56." We were all young lads, wearing white shirts and a blue sash upon which was inscribed 'Fremont and Freedom,'[2] with the picture of the "Pathfinder." Our fun was greatly lessened by the news that came to us in the midst of our hilarity that "Pennsylvania had gone Democratic" in its October state election.

Far deeper was the impression created upon my mind by the great bicenten-nial celebration of 1859. Never shall I forget the procession in which I rode. I remember ex-President [Millard] Fillmore [president, 1850–53] and other notable men. It seemed to me that the procession was larger and the decorations of the town more beautiful, and the enthusiasm of the town greater than on any occasion of my life, although I have since witnessed some half dozen presidential inaugura-tions and two or three great army reviews. But the ball that night, who can describe its delights? Even now I do not believe that there were as pretty and attractive women at any ball ever given in this or any other country or that there have been any better music or more enthusiasm. I still possess a faded blue silk badge that I wore that night and an engagement card, showing that out of the sixteen dances I danced four times with a young lady still living and still attractive.

In the fall of 1860 I was a member of Capt. Joe Starkweather's famous company of "Wide Awakes,"[3] who carried torches and enthusiasm wherever we went, and it seemed to me we went almost everywhere in eastern Connecticut, "shouting the battle cry of freedom" and working and praying for the election of **Abraham Lincoln of Illinois.**

Close following this was the stirring outbreak of the civil war, when our mothers and sisters were working hard day and night, on Sunday included, in Breed hall, helping to get needed articles ready for the companies which Capt. Frank Chester and Henry Peale were leading to the front. Of what that war cost my own mother you can read in a little mound in another cemetery by the side of the fair flowing Yantic that he loved so well.[4]

1. Zachary Taylor, a hero of the Mexican War, was elected president as a Whig in 1848 and died in office on July 9, 1850.

2. John C. Fremont (1813–1890), famous for his exploratory expeditions to the West and who later became an unsuccessful Union general in the Civil War, ran for president in 1856 as the candidate of the newly formed Republican Party on the slogan of "Free Soil, Free Men, Fremont." He lost to Democrat James Buchanan.

3. Starkweather was a leader in Connecticut of the Wide Awakes, political clubs of young men in northern states who marched and rallied in support of Republican candidates in the 1850s and watched polls to guard against voting irregularities by Democrats.

4. This is a reference to his older brother, 1st Lieut. Alfred Mitchell Goddard, 8th Connecticut Volunteer Infantry, Army of the James, who was mortally wounded near Petersburg on May 7, 1864.

Harper's Weekly, February 13, 1909

"Remembering Lincoln—a Glance Backward at the Tragic Life of the Martyred President Which Is Stirringly Recalled by the Centenary of His Birth His Droll Side"

On the night of March 9, 1860, while still in my teens, I was sent to the old town hall at Norwich, Connecticut, to report the speech of one Abraham Lincoln, of Illinois, for the local newspaper of which I was a reporter. Mr. Lincoln was on a brief political tour of the State and was to address the Republicans of Norwich and the vicinity on the issues of the hour in the spring election, now close at hand. The story of the Lincoln-Douglas debate of the preceding year was of course known to me, and I knew that a stalwart orator had dared confront the 'Little Giant' of Illinois, and in a contest for the United States Senatorship, in which the latter had won the coveted prize, but the former had sprung into national prominence.

Of Mr. Lincoln's personality I had only a vague anticipation. Accustomed to the carefully dressed and, as a rule, polished speakers of the East, it was quite a surprise to find the orator of the evening a tall, lank, raw-boned son of the soil, which an ill-fitting coat, limp shirt, collar and black tie that was way out of its place when he had finished. Although at the time I pronounced him the homeliest man I had even seen upon the rostrum, long ere he had finished his speech I was convinced that here was a man novel and interesting, a strong, powerful child of a civilization that we of New England hardly understood; a man who spoke the truth and knew that he spoke it, and was worth listening to as one who was a thoughtful and wise adviser on the great problem confronting us.

After Mr. Lincoln had finished his speech he was entertained at the local hotel by several prominent Republicans. Next day the town was full of reports of his amusing stories and the cheery Western manners that had won him many friends. Some months later I heard from the lips of the Hon. John F. Trumbull of Stonington, Connecticut, the story of an incident that has never been published.

It appears that after the callers had all bidden good-by to Mr. Lincoln, Mr. Trumbull recalled another story (he had told many) that he thought would amuse Mr. Lincoln, so he went back to his room, knocked, and was told to enter. He found Mr. Lincoln disrobing and was about to withdraw, but on explaining his errand he was told that he must stay and tell the story. He did so, Mr. Lincoln listening and laughing heartily. Some time next year, during Lincoln's first administration, Mr. Trumbull was aroused by the ringing of his door-bell at his home at Stonington about one o'clock in the morning. Putting his head out of the window, he asked who wanted him, and was much surprised to hear a caller reply, 'Mr. Trumbull, this is Mr. Anson Burlingame'—the Massachusetts Congressman [House of Representatives, 1853–61; minister to China, 1861–67] who had been an active campaign orator the previous year. Mr. Burlingame explained that he had called to ask Mr. Trumbull to tell him the last story that he had told Mr. Lincoln at Norwich in 1860. As a reason for this late call and strange request he stated that, as Mr. Trumbull knew, he had been appointed by Mr. Lincoln Minister to Austria, but that the Emperor of that country had pronounced him *persona non grata* on account of the active interest he had manifested in the House of Italy in the Austro-Italian War in 1859. When Mr. Lincoln was advised of this he changed the appointment to the Chinese court, at which Mr. Burlingame did distinguished service.

Mr. Burlingame said that he had been on to Washington to thank Mr. Lincoln for his appointment, and when he saw him, the President said, "Burlingame, my sending you to China instead of Austria reminds me of a little story. I have no time to tell it now, as I am going into a Cabinet meeting, but the story was told me last year in Connecticut by Mr. John F. Trumbull of Stonington, and my first official order to you is to stop at Stonington on your way home to Boston and have him tell you the story." Hence Mr. Burlingame had taken the New York steamer to Stonington, and when he found that the steamboat train did not leave till an hour after the boat got in he seized the occasion to rush up to see Mr. Trumbull, who thereupon told him the story from his window. Mr. Burlingame laughed heartily, thanked Mr. Trumbull, and hurried to the train.

"What of the story, Mr. Trumbull?" exclaimed one of the auditors. Just then, "In there broke several people of importance," as Browning puts it, who carried off Mr. Trumbull from the city. I went into the army shortly after and never saw him again. And so the tale remains untold.

The second time I saw Mr. Lincoln was when he was attending the funeral of Gen. Fred W. Lander [brigadier general, died March 2, 1862 of "mortal chill" in Paw Paw, Virginia] from the Church of the Epiphany at Washington early in March 1862, I being present as an officer of the Harris Light Cavalry. The third time was after he had visited Antietam battlefield with General [Maj. Gen. George] McClellan on October 3, 1862. He passed so near our regiment at the time that I noted well the marvelous sadness of those eyes that seemed even then full of the foreknowledge of death.

On April 1, 1863, not long before the battle of Chancellorsville, Mr. Lincoln visited General [Maj. Gen. Joseph] Hooker's headquarters and reviewed the Army of the Potomac, when I again had a good view of him.

It was in connection with this last review that [Maj. Gen.] Dan Sickles told us an amusing story at the reunion of the Society of the Army of the Potomac at Fredericksburg, Virginia, in 1900.

General Sickles said that during this visit he gave a reception to Mr. Lincoln at his headquarters, to which the President brought his son Tad, but not Mrs. Lincoln, who sent regrets and remained at army headquarters. Mr. Lincoln seemed at this time dispirited and depressed to such an extent that General Sickles told the ladies present (mainly the wives of staff officers) that they must do something to cheer him up. "Let's all kiss him," said the vivacious Princess Salm-Salm, wife of a dashing foreign officer serving under Sickles. The question then arose who should be first to do that, but when the fair princess consented to "bell the cat" and lead off, the others all followed suit. Mr. Lincoln brightened up after the incident and was quite jolly, but Tad sat by, watching all that was going on, but said nothing.

Next day General Sickles had occasion to go to Washington by the steamer from Aquia Creek and found on board the President, Mrs. Lincoln, and Tad. He found Mrs. Lincoln very stiff and even gruff, and nothing either General Sickles or Mr. Lincoln could say seemed to mollify her. Finally, when the party went into the cabin to dine, Mr. Lincoln suddenly said, "General Sickles, I have made an interesting discovery on this visit to the army."

"What is that, Mr. President?"

"I have discovered that you are a very religious man."

"Indeed, Mr. Lincoln, that does surprise me. I have been called a good many things in my day, but never that. What led you to that conclusion?"

"Well, General, I have discovered that you are not only a Psalmist, but a Psalm-Psalmist." At this Mrs. Lincoln burst into laughter and for the rest of the voyage was cheerful and entertaining.

Lincoln's Remarks on the Question of Slavery in his March 6, 1860 Campaign Speech in Norwich, Conn., as reported by Goddard in the *Norwich Bulletin*

For, whether we will or not, the question of Slavery is the question, the all-absorbing topic of the day. It is true that all of us—by that I mean, not the Republican Party alone, but the whole American people, here and elsewhere—all of us wish this question settled—wish it out of the way. It stands in the way, and prevents the adjustment, and the giving of necessary attention to other questions of National housekeeping. The people of the whole nation agree that this question ought to be settled, and yet it is not settled. And the reason is that they are not yet agreed on how it shall be settled.

Again and again it has been fondly hoped that it was settled, but every time it breaks out afresh, and more violently than ever. It was settled, our fathers hoped, by the Missouri Compromise, but it did not stay settled. Then the Compromises of 1850 were declared to be a full and final settlement of the question. The two great parties, each in National Convention, adopted resolutions declaring that the settlement made by the Compromise of 1850 was a finality—that it would last forever. Yet how long before it was unsettled again! It broke out again in 1854, and blazed higher and raged more furiously than ever before, and the agitation has not rested since.

These repeated settlements must have some fault about them. There must be some inadequacy in their very nature to the purpose for which they were designed. We can only speculate as to where that fault—that inadequacy, but we may perhaps profit by past experience.

I think that one of the causes of these repeated failures is that our best and greatest men have greatly underestimated the size of this question. They have constantly brought forth small cures for great sores—plasters too small to cover the wound. This is one reason that all settlements have proved so temporary—so evanescent. (Applause)

Look at the magnitude of this subject! About one sixth of the whole population of the United States are slaves! The owners of the slaves consider them property. The effect upon the minds of the owners is that of property, nothing else—it induces them to insist upon all that will favorably affect its value as property, to demand laws and institutions and a public policy that shall increase and secure its value, and make it durable, lasting and universal. The effect on the minds of the owners is to persuade them that there is no wrong in it.

But here in Connecticut and at the North, Slavery does not exist, and we see it through no such medium. To us it appears natural to think that slaves are human beings—men, not property; that some of the things, at least, stated about men in the Declaration of Independence apply to them as well as to us. (Applause) We think Slavery is a great moral wrong, and while we do not claim the right to touch it where it exists, we wish to treat it as a wrong in the Territories, where our votes will reach it.

Now these two ideas, the property idea that Slavery is right, and the idea that it is wrong, come into collision, and do actually produce that irrepressible conflict which Mr. Seward has been so roundly abused for mentioning. The two ideas conflict, and must conflict.

There are but two policies in regard to Slavery that can be at all maintained. The first, based on the property view that Slavery is right, conforms to that idea throughout, and demands that we shall do everything for it that we ought to do if it were right.

The other policy is one that squares with the idea that Slavery is wrong, and it consists in doing everything that we ought to do if it is wrong. I don't mean that we ought to attack it where it exists. To me it means that if we were to form a government anew, in view of the actual presence of Slavery, we should find it necessary to frame just such a government as our fathers did; giving to the slave holders the entire control where the system was established, while we possess the power to restrain it from going outside those limits. (Applause)

Now I have spoken of a policy based on the idea that Slavery is wrong, and a policy based upon the idea that it is right. But an effort has been made for a policy that shall treat it as neither right nor wrong. Its central idea is indifference. It holds that it makes no more difference to us whether the Territories become free or slave states, than whether my neighbor stocks his farm with horned cattle or puts it into tobacco. All recognize this policy, the plausible sugar-coated name of which is popular sovereignty. *[Typewritten copy of the remarks sent to Goddard by the* Norwich Bulletin *in 1908]*

Norwich Bulletin, October 14, 1904

My own connection with the Bulletin as local reporter began in the fall of 1859, when to my great surprise Mr. Bromley [Ike, Bromley, publisher of the *Norwich Bulletin*] offered me the position after the suspension of the Norwich Courier, on which I had a brief experience in the same capacity, in course of which the Bulletin had frequently satirized my work, but Mr. Bromley explained to me then a principle in which he always believed, that it was a good thing for a young newspaper man to receive hard knocks in order that he might become "thick skinned," which he held was an indispensable quality of a newspaper man.

Our old sanctum on Franklin Square was always crowded, and was the center of political and local gossip. In the early days of the civil war it contained so many military critics that for one, I decided that it was better to take part in the war as a soldier of the Union than to stay at home and criticize the armies in the field. Mr. Bromley soon came to a similar determination, and wrote a stirring editorial entitled "Come On," just before raising a company in the Eighteenth Connecticut, a few months after the writer had gone out as an officer in the Harris Light Cavalry of New York.

Nov. 1, 1861

[Letter to his brother, Alfred Mitchell Goddard]

I resume my pen at this late date to say that I have just returned from helping Kemp recruit in Windham and New London Counties. Bromley has just returned from Washington in no happy frame of mind. I have as yet no conversation with him but have little hope that he has done everything for me as I understand that he was trying to get a place for himself and has probably failed. I now think that I shall get his consent to a furlough of two weeks to recruit for Kemp in Salem, Lyme, etc. If so and I can raise enough men, I shall try to get a lieutenancy in the company. If I can not do that, I am almost resolved to enlist under Kemp as sergeant or corporal.

The truth is Alf that I am heartily sick of the Bulletin for the reason that Bromley and the Ass't Editor, Campbell, are both drunkards and I cannot stand it much longer. If you ever breathe this to a living soul I shall never forgive you, but you would get as sick of it as I am, when you dare tell no one and have all their shortcomings charged to you.

If Bromley and I were alone we could do well enough, and I think one of the editors will leave soon on account of hard times. If Campbell leaves, I will stay. If Mr. Bromley leaves, I won't stay anyhow.

All your old friends are getting places. John Piatt is Adjutant of an Ohio cavalry regiment, Charley Farnsworth of a Connecticut cavalry battalion, Ned Harland Colonel of the 8th Connecticut, H.W. Brige Major 4th C.V., John and Oscar Dennis Captains.

Ellen Fisher, Martha Ripley and Hattie Lester are all unmarried yet.

Good Bye my dear brother,

Yours ever, Henry P. Goddard

Baltimore Sunday Record, **February 22, 1903**

"Maryland Men Who Helped Make History." [—**Hugh L. Bond; first in a series**]

In the gray of an early morning of July 1863, Hugh L. Bond,[1] at the time judge of the Criminal Court of Baltimore and one of the most pronounced Union men of the city, was on duty in Mount Vernon square as a private in the Union Minute Men, an organization of citizens that only turned out on extraordinary occasions when the city was supposed to be in imminent danger of a Confederate attack.

There had been an alarm the night before, and Judge Bond was patrolling his beat, armed with a gun that, as he said, "could not have been fired even with a hammer," when a Union brigadier general rode past with an orderly in attendance.

The judge presented arms, whereat the general sent the orderly to say that this ceremony could be omitted at that hour. The orderly added: "You hold that gun wrong—with the barrel out instead of in, as it should be at present arms."

The judge replied: "No, that is all right. I see that is [Brig.] Gen. Dan Tyler of Connecticut. He was a guest at my house yesterday at dinner, and he and his companions drank up everything we had in the house. So I hold the gun in this fashion in order that he may see that the barrel is out."

When this message was reported, the stately old general inquired the name of the sentry, and when it was ascertained he rode away, smiling grimly.

The writer had served as an aide-de-camp on the staff of General Tyler at the time of the incident described . . . and upon taking up his residence in Baltimore in 1882 was very glad to renew his acquaintance with Judge Bond, and during the next ten years of his life had ample opportunity to listen to his entertaining talks, full of reminiscences of the civil war and many of the great actors connected with the national government during its progress.

A CALL ON LINCOLN

In discussing the events of the memorable 19th of April 1861, when the Sixth Massachusetts Regiment was fired upon at Baltimore,[2] Judge Bond gave an interesting account of a council held at the house of Mayor [George William] Brown on the evening of the 19th, at which were present Gov. [Thomas] Hicks, the mayor, Judge Bond and three or four other gentlemen. Although Mayor Brown had bravely marched at the head of the Massachusetts regiment during part of the time at which they were under fire, yet he and most of the gentlemen present were anxious that President Lincoln should be requested to send no more Northern troops through Baltimore. Judge Bond was the most radical Unionist of those present at the council, but finally consented to go to Washington with two other gentlemen present and present such a request to President Lincoln in a modified form.

The party arrived at Washington quite late at night and sent their names to the President, who said he was glad to meet some gentlemen from Maryland, and wanted to know "What in the name of Heaven is the matter with you over there." He would have no extended conversation with the delegation then, but asked them to call at the White House at 7 A.M. on the 20th. The party were promptly on hand next morning, when Mr. Lincoln came down in a wrapper, saying, "We must wait for [Maj. Gen. Winfield, commander in chief of the army, retired October 1861] General Scott."

In a few minutes the old general limped into the White House and into the room in which the delegates were gathered. The President said: "These gentlemen have come over from Baltimore to tell us about the trouble there."

GENERAL SCOTT'S PROFANITY

At this General Scott rose to his feet, and, said the judge, towered over us and seemed to me about ten feet high, as he thundered out, "What in —— and —— are you —— scoundrels in Maryland doing down there?" Judge Bond replied that he represented Gov. [Thomas H.] Hicks, who was a loyal man, "and not the rabble who had attacked the Massachusetts regiment." . . . The party went to the cabinet room where, said Judge Bond, in relating the incident, it was suggested by General Scott, who was very impatient in his manner, that the proper way was to land troops at my house, on the Northern Central railroad, and March them over to Mount Clare, a mile or two away, without going through the city. President Lincoln suggested that then the *rabble* from Baltimore might march out to attack them in the fields. He was told that this was very likely, but that then the troops could shoot back without accidentally killing women and children. This proposition was agreed to, and we returned to Baltimore.

After the return of the party to Baltimore Judge Bond was very unpopular with the anti-union men, but his fearlessness and grit were well known, and although many threats were made he was never personally attacked. The troops were finally sent from Havre de Grace to Annapolis by water, until a few weeks later, when General [Maj. Gen. Benjamin] Butler took possession of the city by a night's march from Annapolis Junction.

STANTON'S STOCK IN TRADE

Judge Bond was an intimate friend of Secretary [of War Edwin] Stanton, and frequently visited his private office in the war department. He was there on one occasion when Ex-Governor Hicks, then United States senator from Maryland, came in with an order from President Lincoln for the release of a Confederate prisoner on Johnson's island.[3] The prisoner was a Marylander, and some Eastern Shore neighbors of the senator induced him to secure the order from the President. This was written on a small card—Judge Bond said that Mr. Lincoln often wrote on little cards, and once he saw him write a commission for a governor of Louisiana upon one. As soon as Secretary Stanton read this card he tore it in two and said: "Senator, you ought to know better than to come stumping in here seeking the release of rebel prisoners." What followed I quote verbatim: The governor, who had lost a leg by accident, limped out in high dudgeon, and I told the secretary that, in view of his infirmity he ought not to have so addressed him and that he had best follow and apologize. We followed him, but he refused to reenter the war office and went back to the President. We followed him thither and entered the White House just as he told his story. The President said, "Mr. Stanton, why did you disobey my orders?" The secretary replied, "Mr. Lincoln, I can't lose my stock in trade. Those rebel prisoners are my stock to trade for Union soldiers, and for everyone you release unconditionally some poor fellow is compelled to remain at Belle Isle [the Confederate prison for enlisted men and noncommissioned officers west of Richmond] or Andersonville, [the notorious Confederate prison in Georgia where nearly thirteen thousand Union soldiers died of disease, exposure, and malnutrition] and I won't have my stock so reduced."

Mr. Lincoln turned to Senator Hicks and said: "Senator, what can a man do who has such a secretary as that." The prisoner was not pardoned.

On one occasion Judge Bond was sitting with Mr. Lincoln when the latter was signing commissions, among which was one for Brigadier-General [Alexander] Schimmelfening. "There," said Mr. Lincoln, "if the Johnnies ever capture that fellow he will be held until the end of the war, if they keep him till they learn how to pronounce his name."

COULDN'T GET RID OF BOND

My last interview with Judge Bond was on September 17, 1893. . . . On this occasion Judge Bond talked of Gen. John E. Wool [seventy-seven years old when the war began, Wool was the oldest officer to exercise active command on either side during the war; retired August 1863], saying that when he was in command at Baltimore he was a weak, vain old man, easily hoodwinked by Southern sympathizers. If invited to a good dinner he would accept and be blind to the fact that a Confederate flag might be attached to the chandelier. This grew so annoying to Bond and other Union men that Bond went to Washington and demanded of President Lincoln his removal. A cabinet meeting was about to be held and Mr. Lincoln asked the judge to attend and make his complaint. When the cabinet assembled, Mr. Stanton alone was absent.

The judge stated his grievance, and as Stanton entered the room he asked, "What is the matter?" The President replied, "The fact is, Mr. Stanton, that Judge Bond and General Wool cannot get along together, and we have to get rid of one of them. We can't get rid of Bond, so I suppose we shall have to get rid of Wool." The matter was talked over by the cabinet, when Mr. Lincoln turned to the judge and said, "Bond, can't you get along with him until after next Tuesday?" He replied, "No."

"I noticed, however," said Bond, "that Secretary Welles began to make signals to me to reply in the affirmative, which, after some hesitation, I finally did. As the cabinet meeting broke up Mr. Welles joined me, and when I asked why he had signaled me to consent to the President's wish not to act until next Tuesday, which would be some five days later, he replied, 'Why the New York state election will be held next Tuesday and the President does not wish to act until after that day, as General Wool is a New Yorker.' I saw the point; and just after the election General Wool was relieved of the command."

1. Hugh L. Bond (1828–1893), a Baltimore native was a judge of the Criminal Court of Baltimore, 1860–70, and following his appointment by President Grant, served as a circuit court judge of the Fourth Judicial District, 1870–93.

2. In Baltimore on April 19, 1861, a mob of Southern sympathizers surrounded and jeered, then started throwing bricks and stones at the 6th Massachusetts Infantry on its way to defend Washington, D.C., from a feared Confederate attack. Several soldiers fired into the crowd, killing twelve and injuring many others. Four soldiers were killed in what is called the Pratt Street riot—the first bloodshed of the Civil War. Maryland and Baltimore officials demanded that no more federal troops be sent through the city. But on May 13, 1861, federal troops occupied Baltimore and martial law was declared, squelching pro-Confederate activities for the duration of the war.

3. Johnson's Island was a prison for Confederate soldiers and disloyal civilians in Sandusky Bay, Ohio, on Lake Erie.

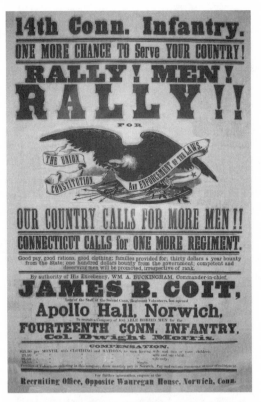

Recruitment poster for the 14th Connecticut. Courtesy of Company G, Fourteenth Regiment, Connecticut Volunteer Infantry, Inc. 1862–1865

Henry Perkins Goddard after moving from Hartford to Baltimore in the early 1870s. From the collection of the editor

Harriet Beecher Stowe, author of *Uncle Tom's Cabin* and Goddard's friend and neighbor in Hartford. From Nolman Photo Company, *Hartford* (Boston: Nolman Photo Company, 1885)

Samuel L. Clemens, Goddard's neighbor and dinner companion in Hartford. From Nolman Photo Company, *Hartford* (Boston: Nolman Photo Company, 1885)

Maj. Gen. Dan Sickles, feature of anecdotes about Lincoln related by Goddard. From the collection of the editor

Maj. Robert Anderson, commander of Fort Sumter, who surrendered the fort following the Confederate bombardment that triggered the war. From the collection of the editor

UNION VETERAN CORPS,

1ST CO.,

DECORATION DAY,

THE CORPS WILL GO TO

FREDERICKSBURG, VA.,

On May 30th,

To Decorate the Graves of their Fallen Comrades in the National Cemetery at that place.

TRAINS will leave the BALTIMORE & POTOMAC DEPOT, 6th Street, at 8, A. M., and arrive in Washington on return at 8, P. M., same day.—Giving SIX HOURS to go over the BATTLE FIELDS of **Fredericksburg and Chancellorsville.**

ROUND TRIP, - $2,00,

Tickets for sale at the Depot.　　　　Special Cars Reserved for Ladies and Families.
Pistorio's Celebrated Brass Band will accompany the Corps.

ON TO BROOKLYN!
DO NOT FORGET THAT THE
CELEBRATED FAY TEMPLETON OPERA COMPANY

Will give a series of LIGHT COMIC OPERA at Ford's Opera House during the week commencing May 26th, for the benefit of the fund to pay expenses of the Corps to Brooklyn, N. Y., to attend the REUNION of the SOCIETY OF THE ARMY OF THE POTOMAC.

TICKETS now for sale (usual prices) by Active and Honorary Members of the Corps, and the Ladies' Auxiliary Association.

Poster inviting Union veterans to a reunion of the Army of the Potomac in Fredericksburg, Virginia, among many reunions that Goddard attended. From the collection of the editor

THE PARAMOUNT ISSUE

"AN HONEST ELECTION LAW"

For House of Delegates

HENRY P. GODDARD,

Third Legislative District.

Comprising Wards 10, 11, 14, 16, 19 & 20,

ELECTION, TUESDAY NOV. 5th, 1907.

Polls open from 6 A. M. to 5 P. M.

Goddard's first and only campaign for political office, in which he lost his bid for the Maryland legislature. From the collection of the editor

(*left*) Alfred Mitchell Goddard after joining the 8th Connecticut Volunteer Infantry. From the collection of the editor; (*right*) Brig. Gen. Edward Harland, who commanded a brigade that included the 8th Connecticut during A. M. Goddard's service. From the collection of the editor

THE AMERICAN TELEGRAPH COMPANY.
NORTH, SOUTH, EAST AND WEST.
CONNECTING WITH ALL THE SOUTHERN, WESTERN, EASTERN AND NORTHERN LINES OF TELEGRAPH.

Terms and Conditions on which this and all Messages are received by this Company.

In order to guard against and correct as much as possible some of the errors arising from atmospheric and other causes appertaining to telegraphy, every important message should be REPEATED, by being sent back from the station at which it is to be received to the station from which it is originally sent. Half the usual price will be charged for repeating the message, and while this Company in good faith will endeavor to send messages correctly and promptly, it will not be responsible for errors or delays in the transmission or delivery, nor for the non-delivery of REPEATED MESSAGES, beyond TWO HUNDRED times the sum paid for sending the message, unless a special agreement for insurance be made in writing, and the amount of risk specified on this agreement, and paid for at the time of sending the message. Nor will the Company be responsible for any error or delay in the transmission or delivery, or for the non-delivery, of ANY UNREPEATED MESSAGE, beyond the amount paid for sending the same, unless in like manner specially insured, and amount of risk stated hereon, and paid for at the time. No liability is assumed for errors in cipher or obscure messages; nor is any liability assumed by this Company for any error or neglect by any other Company over whose lines this message may be sent to reach its destination, and this Company is hereby made the agent of the sender of this message to forward it over the lines extending beyond those of this Company. No agent or employee is allowed to vary these terms, or make any other or verbal agreement, nor any promise as to the time of performance, and no one but a Superintendent is authorized to make a special agreement for insurance. These terms apply through the whole course of this message on all lines by which it may be transmitted.

CAMBRIDGE LIVINGSTON, Sec'y,   E. S. SANFORD, Pres't,

145 BROADWAY, N. Y.

No. 4 2

Dated _____ Fort Monroe _____ 186 4

Rec'd, Fonmeh May 9 1864 _____ o'clock, _____ min. M.

To _____ Lems Mitchell

Tell mother to Come Am badly wounded & at Chesapeake General Hospital

A. M. Goddard

A. M. Goddard's telegram to his mother after he was mortally wounded during his first engagement near Petersburg. From the collection of the editor

21

Stories of Confederate and Union Friends and Reunions after the War

Hartford Evening Post, September 17, 1872
"Of the Fourteenth C. V., at Madison"

Madison, Conn.

Editors *Post*

The eighth annual reunion of the Fourteenth Connecticut volunteers was held in this town today, about one hundred and fifty of the old regiment being present.

Under the supervision of Mr. S. H. Scranton, superintendent of the Shore Line railroad, who was actively engaged in the organization of the Fourteenth regiment, in which both his son and son-in-law held commissions, the town was decorated with flags and a general holiday was observed.

The regiment formed in column about 1 P.M., and under escort of company G (the Madison company in the Fourteenth), paraded through the principal streets. Rendezvousing at the Methodist church, Lieut. J. S. Scranton, vice president of the union, took the chair, in the absence of the president, and a business meeting was held.

The usual annual reports were presented of the necrological committees, recording five, viz: Privates Charles Kraft and Wm. Gorham of Co. I, Ransler Goodale of Co. G, F, C. Bowman of Co. A, and James P. Alcott of Co. F. The following named were chosen officers for the following year:

Major W. B. Hincks, Bridgeport, president; Sergeants L. A. Spencer, Waterbury, and John Meigs, Madison, vice presidents; Lieut. J. W. Knowlton, Bridgeport, recording secretary; Sergeant E. L. Goodwin, New Britain, corresponding secretary; Rev. H. S. Stevens, chaplain; Capt. G. N. Brigham, Rockville, treasurer; Chaplain Stevens of Cromwell and Capt. H. P. Goddard of Hartford, necrological committee.

It was voted that the next reunion be held at Waterbury, Conn., Sept. 17, 1873. A copy of the diary of Capt. S. F. Willard, of Madison, comprising the last entries therein, before his gallant death at Antietam, having been presented to the regiment, a vote of thanks was extended to his widow therefor. The vestry adjourned to the Congregational church, where a sumptuous collation had been provided. Rev. Mr. Gallup of Madison delivered an address of welcome, after which the boys fell to with a will and partially succeeded in clearing the heavily laden tables. After dinner Chaplain H. S. Stevens delivered an eloquent reply to the address of welcome, and Capt. Goddard read E. C. Stedman's poem on "Gettysburg," written for the last reunion of the Army of the Potomac. (May 7, 1872, Cleveland).

Lieut. W. D. Fiske then delivered a bright and witty address. He was followed by Gen. Theo G. Ellis of Hartford, the last colonel of the Fourteenth, who gave an admirable account of the battle of Antietam, of which this day was the tenth anniversary.

Messrs. Bradley and Lawton, two venerable gentlemen who gave their sons to their country, having been cheered by the regiment, Capt. Goddard made the closing speech. In closing he begged the members of the regiment to remember the gratitude we owe to those at home who sustained us during the war. Whatever perils, griefs or woes time brings us in its flight, we must never forget our duty to that country that called us into this organization ten years ago, and for whose salvation we must pledge our lives, our fortunes and our sacred honor.

With rousing cheers for Madison and its good people, for our flag and the country, the regiment marched to the depot singing the John Brown chorus. At the depot ranks were broken and the men departed with many pleasing memories of the day.

Springfield Republican, July 23, 1875
"Our Hartford Letter
From Our Special Correspondent"

The events of the current week have been the general reunion of Connecticut veterans of the late war, and the final adjournment of the state Legislature. In this instance, Hartford was certainly true to the old precept to "Welcome the coming and speed the parting guest," for a right hearty greeting she gave the one or two thousand soldiers who gathered at Charter Oak park, and no regrets were heard at the departure of the Legislature that spent its last hours in investigating itself, finding, as I predicted, that nobody had been bought, though whether anybody was anxious to buy is decidedly doubtful. . . . .

The notable instances of encampment were the approach toward amalgamation of the different regiments, which, while each is proud as ever of its individual record, are now free to confess (as they were loath to do of old) that others did equally well, the good speech of Gen. Hawley [Maj. Gen. Joseph Hawley, postwar Connecticut governor and U.S. senator] and the presence of ex-confederate soldiers in the ranks at the grand parade. Gen. Frank Pargond [commanded 3rd Louisiana Cavalry] of Louisiana, who was the great and special pet of the 14th Connecticut, was a magnificent specimen of a man, standing over six feet in his stockings, with dark hair and complexion, looking as the confederate generals used to look, when we were fortunate enough to catch them, or unfortunate enough to be captured, yet accepting the situation with greatest good feeling, marching in our ranks, and smoking the great pipe of peace, presented by Lieut. Fiske, which went round the regiment.

In camp, there was felt the lack of a definite program and a lack of discipline, unavoidable where nobody had any real authority, there was "lots of fun." Especially this was true, the last night, when no one was allowed to sleep, and when a big express wagon was driven from street to street by a lot of "bummers," who searched every tent for those who were intoxicated, and, piling them into the wagon, drove them to a spot at one end of the camp, where the tail-board was pulled out and the whole crowd dumped in a confused heap. But after all I inclined to the belief that, for some years to come, the best and most orderly plan is the old one of separate regimental reunions of a single day, with business meeting, dinner, and an hour or two's fun.

Baltimore Sunday Herald, December 20, 1903
"Henry Kyd Douglas"

> *Once in the gray—now in the blue,*
> *But in either and always "tender and true."*

These lines are inscribed on the back of a photograph which lies before me as I write. The picture is that of [Col.] Henry Kyd Douglas [(1838–1903), on Stonewall Jackson's staff beginning in June 1862] taken when he was adjutant general of Maryland [1892–96], and sent to me with his kindest regards about the time of the Spanish war. It is a superb likeness of one of the handsomest men, and one of the most distinguished soldiers that I have ever had the pleasure of knowing, and whom (now that he is gone) I am most proud to remember as one of the warmest personal friends it has been my pleasure to have made in Maryland.

Forty years or more ago Colonel Douglas and myself were soldiers in opposing armies in the civil war. Somewhat of his brilliant war record was known to me at the time, and I have heard ladies who saw him riding up and down the Shenandoah valley fighting single-handed half a dozen federal cavalrymen, describing him as at that time a striking picture that suggested Prince Rupert of the Rhine as he dashed through Winchester with bullets flying about him like hail, but bowing and smiling to the Southern ladies who knew him as he passed their houses.

My personal acquaintance with Colonel Douglas began when I was returning from a reunion of federal soldiers on the battlefield of Antietam, about twenty years ago. We rode to Baltimore on the same train and there began a friendship which I can but hope will never cease, although he has for a while gone out of our ken.

In 1888 we began a correspondence which was kept up with considerable regularity until his health failed him a year or so ago. The packet of letters that I have from him will always be preserved among my choicest souvenirs of the friends that I have had among the men with whom on one issue we had differed at sword's point. His letters were always bright, crisp, witty and interesting. The first one was called out by a letter which I had printed in the *Springfield* [Mass.] *Republican*, in which I had commented very favorably upon Colonel Douglas as a public speaker. In the same letter I had been very enthusiastic over the talent and beauty of a certain Virginia lady just then coming into national distinction as an author. In his letter Colonel Douglas said that if he possessed all the good qualities which I had attributed to him, and this lady all the beauty and charm that I had assigned to her, he felt that it would be his duty to seek her out and throw himself at her feet. As a matter of fact, he told me afterward that later on he met the lady at a summer resort and used by *Republican* letter as a fitting introduction, which the lady took in very good part.

In 1888 Colonel Douglas ran for Congress [as a Democrat in Hagerstown, Maryland] in his district against the Hon. Louis McComas [Republican congressman, 1883–91]. Mr. Cleveland was president at this time, and was being bitterly assailed for his vetoes of private pension bills, in which vetoes I felt that he was fully justified. Mentioning this to Colonel Douglas, he suggested that I might be willing to come into his district where there were a good many Union soldiers, and make some speeches in his interest. I was but too glad to accept this invitation, especially as it had been charged that none but ex-Confederate soldiers were among his supporters. My speeches had but little effect, as Mr. McComas was elected by a large majority, but I was more than repaid by the thanks that I received from Colonel Douglas.

Not long after Colonel Douglas delivered an address in Boston, Mass., as one of a series delivered alternately by Union and Confederate officers. He told his audience in opening his lecture that this was his first public appearance in Boston since the civil war, and he had felt that perhaps he should perform some act of repentance for having rebelled against the United States government before appearing in Boston. Hence he had that morning climbed Bunker Hill Monument; but, he added, 'as between repeating that performance and rebelling again, you may rest assured that I will rebel every time.' The remarks so delighted the audience that they secured him a written invitation from a lineal descendant of Gen.

Joseph Warren, a dear old lady, asking him to come and take tea with her the next night, which he did to his great enjoyment.

In 1898 Colonel Douglas was nominated by President [William] McKinley as a major and adjutant general of the United States Volunteers during the Spanish war. He was not at all pleased with being tendered a commission of such low rank after his brilliant civil war record and wrote me freely and frankly upon the subject. In the course of a letter he wrote me: "Things have their compensation, and I know the newspaper clippings sent me have taken the place of any subordinate commission in the pleasure they gave me—especially from the North."

Miss Julia Marlowe, the actress, was a warm personal friend of both of us and was kind enough to ask each of us to see her "Barbara Fritchie" and pronounce judgment, especially upon its historical possibility, as, of course, she did not claim that it was historically correct. I saw it first and wrote Douglas urging him to see it. He did so, and wrote a delightful letter concerning it under date of January 3, 1900, from which I quote some interesting passages: "I saw the new Barbara Fritchie. It is a curious jumble, with nothing in it but Julia Marlowe, and she is in it up to the eyes and heart. When I called upon her I found her as fascinating off as on the stage. I told her that since you had asked me once to dine with her I had great desire to meet her. The new Barbara Fritchie was interesting and amusing to me for reasons that did not appeal to you. I failed to recognize the semblance of Stonewall Jackson, who marched across the stage on foot, but I did have to shudder when Barbara was shot and fell backward across the railing, for I was afraid she would sprain her back or ruin her corsets. I have a picture of this Barbara and one of the old. I think I will put them together in a frame, congratulating myself that I have had greater luck than Jackson in that I did see the new and beautiful Barbara, while he never saw even the old one."[1]

Of lofty and aristocratic bearing, it has been said that Colonel Douglas never drew the masses to him, but those who knew him best knew that no tenderer or more gentle heart ever breathed in a more soldierly frame. Those who knew him best loved him best, and in his own household he was worshiped by those of his own blood, to whom he gave the devotion of a lifetime. As I throw my little wreath upon his grave on this December day I think of the dying scene of "Cyrano de Bergerac," where that fearless soldier and most unselfish of lovers rises to his feet as death approaches and with drawn sword faces the grim tyrant and utters those striking lines as he falls dying at the feet of his lady love:

> *One thing is left in spite of you,*
> *Which I take with me, and this very night,*
> *When I shall cross the threshold of God's house,*
> *and enter, bowing low, this I shall take*

Despite you, without wrinkle, without spot—
And that is—my stainless soldier's crest.

1. Fritchie was ninety-five years old when Maj. Gen. Stonewall Jackson's corps paraded through Frederick, Maryland, in October 1862. Although an American flag may have flown from the window of her home in that city, she was probably sick in bed that day, and it is unlikely that she and Jackson confronted each other over the flag as legend would have it.

New York Sunday Times, January 3, 1904
[Letter to the editor]

Gen. Henry Kyd Douglas, who died recently at Hagerstown, Md., was not only one of the most brilliant officers who served in the Confederate Army during the civil war, in which he achieved great distinction, first upon the staff of Gen. "Stonewall" Jackson and later as a regimental officer. He was one of the brightest and wittiest of companions, always ready with a story of his army life.

One day he was speaking of the style assumed by the wealthy young men of the South when they first went into the Confederate army. Plenty of handsome clothes and a colored body servant were not at all uncommon. After a year or so there was a great change in this respect, and Gen. Douglas narrated an incident of his life as a regimental commander. Seeing one of the wealthiest and most aristocratic young Virginians of his regiment in a shabby old uniform, carrying a bucket of slops from the company kitchen on one occasion, he commented: "Tom, I never expected to see you carrying slops." The young soldier promptly replied: "D—n it, Kyd, this isn't slops; it is patriotism!"

Baltimore Herald, December 31, 1903
"These Had Standards"

To the Editor of *The Herald*:

The closing year has taken away from beyond mortal ken the four dearest friends the writer had left among civil war veterans. Two of them served in the Union Army and two in the Confederate. Of the former one was an officer closely associated with me in the old Fourteenth Connecticut Infantry, the other a brigadier general of volunteers from my own New England city. The two Confederates were [Brig.] **Gen. Bradley T. Johnson** and **Col. Henry Kyd Douglas**. Their war record is too well known in Maryland to need comment here. All four of these men were of undaunted courage, and the heroes of distinguished exploits during the civil war, but today what comes to my mind concerning them first and foremost is that each and all were gentlemen in the truest sense, and all of them magnanimous to a degree, not only during, but after the war.

I think of **Major [William] Hincks** and **General [Alfred] Rockwell**, not only on the field of battle, but in the lofty lives and moral courage which each repeatedly exhibited in civil life. I think of General Johnson not as leading a charge of his beloved First Maryland Confederate Regiment, but as calling upon Colonel Kenly, of the First Maryland Union Regiment, after that terrible fight between the two regiments at Front Royal, in which Kenly was left a wounded prisoner upon the field, and tendering him all the aid and comfort in his power. I think of Colonel Douglas not on his wonderful night ride of 100 miles around the Federal Army, but as standing in the sunlight at Druid Hill Park on a lovely afternoon and presenting the Stars and Stripes to the Fourth Maryland Infantry, commanded by Col. Willard Howard, an old soldier of the Union, but ever since his devoted friend.

Bridgeport (Conn.) Standard, **January 10, 1907**

"Tribute to Major Hincks—Captain Goddard, His Companion-in-Arms, Writes Feelingly"

It was with inexpressible sorrow that I received the news of the death of my old war comrade, Major William B. Hincks. It was my rare good fortune to be a fellow member with him of the old Fourteenth Connecticut Volunteers during the Civil War, and to form during that connection a friendship that has but just terminated—that is if such friendships ever terminate, which I greatly doubt.

Looking back over all these years, it seems to me that Major Hincks was, all in all, the best officer the regiment ever had, and it had some excellent ones upon its roll. I never knew a braver man physically, and his moral courage was equal to his physical courage.

The story of his bravery at Gettysburg, when he captured the battle flag of the Fourteenth Tennessee for which he deservedly won the medal of honor awarded by congress to very few men, is an old story known to all familiar with the history of the dear old Fourteenth Connecticut, but, to my thinking, a braver, more daring, more dangerous and nobler action was that of Major Hincks, when regimental adjutant in August 1864, when after the battle of Ream's Station [August 25, 1864, during the siege of Petersburg] he found that Captain James R. Nichols was severely wounded and left upon the battlefield, where he had been stripped by the Confederates, who left him, not dreaming of his surviving the night. During the night the casualty was reported to the regiment, when Hincks with Privates [Thomas] Goff and [Edward] Rigney sought Nichols out on the abandoned field and bore him through the darkness eight miles into our lines. The battle flag at Gettysburg was captured in the full sight of the regiment, and was a splendid act of courage, but this toilsome night search for, and bearing of the heavy burden of a wounded comrade was done in darkness, and known only to his two brave assistants.

Here is this Southern city [Baltimore] we are sometimes told that most of the Northern soldiers were hirelings, and that all too many of them are now pension grabbers. Thank God, this reproach would never be bestowed upon William B. Hincks. He entered the service as a private, and in two well deserved promotions became adjutant and then major of a regiment whose history is written in the hearts of the people of Connecticut. Such men as he served from patriotism and never sought pensions for doing their duty.

Baltimore Sunday Herald, March 15, 1903
"Maryland Men Who Helped Make History
Gen. John R. Kenly"

On the afternoon of May 23, 1862, a party of boys from the town of Front Royal, in Virginia, were swimming in a creek that enters the Shenandoah river near that place.

They were having a very jolly time, when they heard shouts and cries and, looking up the road, saw the Union soldiers who had held possession of the town for a few weeks previous running in various directions. The boys hastily put on their clothes, and one of them, who is now a well-known Baltimore physician (Dr. Thomas A. Ashby) tells me that he hastened to the village, hearing cries that "the rebels are coming!" which greatly rejoiced him, as, in common with most of the inhabitants, his family were Southern sympathizers. He was hurriedly hastening home on the outskirts of the village, when he heard bullets flying about him, and decided to take shelter for a while. Later he ventured on the streets again and found a young Confederate cavalry officer, who told him that it was no place for boys and he best hurry home. Before he could get home, however, the Union forces, who had been driven out of the town, began to shell it vigorously, and young Ashly again had to hide himself until the shelling was over. Hurrying home, he found that several shells had struck near his home, but had done no harm except to a cow.

That night he learned that the Union forces under command of Col. John R. Kenly, of the First Maryland (Union) Infantry, who had two companies in the town and the rest of the regiment about a half a mile in reserve, in all not much over 1,000 men, had been worsted and defeated in action by Gen. Stonewall Jackson's Confederate division of some 12,000 men, headed by the First Maryland (Confederate) Infantry, under command of Col. Bradley T. Johnson. In fact, General Jackson, when he discovered that the troops in front of him were Marylanders, had sent word back to Colonel Johnson to bring up his regiment in order that the Maryland Confederates might attack the Union regiment from the same state.

Dr. Ashby's father owned a large and beautiful place in the town, and within the next twenty-four hours entertained and fed nearly 500 Confederate soldiers. But the next morning, when Mr. Ashby learned that Col. Kenly had been wounded in the fight and was a prisoner in a small house in the village, he sent his son with ample food and drink for the Union officer, to whom not only he, but nearly all the citizens of Front Royal, felt most kindly, owing to the fact that while his troops had occupied the town, he had permitted no thefts or outrages of any kind upon the inhabitants, but had treated them most courteously and kindly.

Col. Kenly was grateful for the refreshments sent him, but was suffering severely from a saber cut in the face received in the battle and apparently even more from chagrin at having been wounded and captured by a non-commissioned officer, who had demanded the surrender of his sword, which Colonel Kenly had refused on account of his inferior rank. It so happened that his assailant was himself killed later in the fight, but Colonel Kenly, with a punctiliousness that marked his whole life, could not get over his vexation at being captured by a non-commissioned officer.

According to Dr. Ashby's account, Colonel Kenly had made a most gallant fight, and only gave up the contest after being flanked on both sides and to largely superior forces. While he himself was wounded, and with nearly all his command captured, his fight had delayed Stonewall Jackson's advance up the valley, and for the time saved General [Maj. Gen. Nathaniel] Banks' army from a similar fate, as General Banks testified repeatedly during his life.

UNREWARDED HEROES

Few Maryland men of note have had full justice done them by their posterity in the way of historical memorials. Neither with pen, brush or chisel have her great men been honored as they should. We are just beginning to erect proper memorials to our revolutionary heroes, but have put up none to her distinguished sons who strove to save the Union during the civil war. Personally I should welcome monuments to the brave Marylanders who fought on either side during the war of the rebellion, if erected by their surviving comrades, but it cost something to be a Union soldier in Maryland during the early days of the civil war, and the state owes something to the memory of the men who bore the burden in those days.

It is Emerson who said that "It is easy in the crowd to live in the world's opinion; it is easy in solitude to live after our own; but the great man is he who in the midst of the crowd keeps with perfect sweetness the independence of solitude." Judging by this definition, Gen. Kenly was a great man.

Although small of stature and in the years when I knew him (1882 to 1891), always quietly dressed in garments that bore the marks of age, though scrupulously neat, yet he had an innate dignity of presence, combined with an airy looseness of manner, that made it a pleasure to meet and receive his greeting. It was this, combined with his perfect fairness and justness of view, that made him, although an unfaltering Unionist, so highly esteemed and even beloved by the brave men who fought on the other side during the war. In fact, I have heard none speak in higher terms of the man than such gallant ex-Confederates as Gen. Bradley T.

Johnson and Col. Charles Marshall [aide-de-camp and military secretary to Gen. Robert E. Lee].

When the Mexican war broke out in 1846, he raised a company of volunteers (the First Baltimore Battalion) and was commissioned by the Governor as captain in the same. He served with his battalion in General Taylor's army in the campaign in Northern Mexico. . . . He was actively engaged in the three days' battle which resulted in the capture of Monterrey, and on the fall of Colonel [William] Watson, he rallied the command and kept it in action until the battle ended.

Returning to Baltimore with his command he was at once commissioned major of the Second Baltimore Battalion and started back to Mexico in July 1847. He served with his command in General Scott's army until the close of the war in 1848.

In a story published in the *Century*, he says of the Mexican war that "it was a tidy, comfortable little war, not without picturesque aspects. Out of its flame and smoke leaped two or three fine names that dazzled men's eyes awhile, and among the fortunate was a silent young lieutenant of infantry (Grant), a taciturn but not unamiable young lieutenant, who was afterward destined to give the name of a great general into the keeping of history forever."

On the outbreak of the civil war our hero at once tendered his services to Governor Hicks and was appointed brigadier general of the Maryland Militia, and was assigned to the duty of raising and organizing the Maryland Volunteers for the Union Army. As soon as the First Regiment was raised and mustered into the service, President Lincoln appointed Kenly colonel of the First Maryland.

REJOINED HIS REGIMENT

In June 1861, he was appointed provost marshal of Baltimore, a position which he filled with rare tact and discretion, but which was most distasteful to him, and July 16 he rejoined his regiment. The regiment was then at Williamsport, Md. Early in the spring of 1862 the First Maryland crossed the Potomac into Virginia and took part in the marching and counter-marching in the Shenandoah Valley until May 23, when he fought in the battle of Front Royal, described in the opening paragraph.

Concerning this Front Royal fight, Gen. Bradley T. Johnson, who never was ought but a chivalric foe, and who led the attack upon General Kenly, furnished me at my request at the time of General Kenly's death the following brief account:

"He was attacked at 8 A.M. by the First Regiment Maryland line—the advance of Jackson's army—who were moving to cut Banks off from Winchester. Kenly had a selection of a battery and a squadron of Pennsylvania cavalry and held his position until the afternoon, when I flanked him and got an enfilading fire down his line and rear. From his position from a high hill he could see our cavalry moving around him and retreated across the Shenandoah. Before dark the cavalry caught him and broke him after he had inflicted heavy loss and killed Captain Shields of a Virginia regiment, which then captured his command. In this melee and rout Kenly got a saber wound over the head.

"The next morning I called on him with my staff in form and offered him any assistance that was proper for him to receive and me to afford. With the most stately courtesy he thanked me and said he needed no assistance and declined help. This was not churlishness, but extreme sensitiveness. He was a knight and lived 300 years too late."

WHEN MARYLANDER MET MARYLANDER

Our Maryland Historical Society has always dealt rather gingerly with the civil war, and although it had among its members distinguished Marylanders who took an active part in the contest on one side or the other, never encouraged papers from them upon the subject of which they were best informed. Would it not be a matter of congratulation if that society possessed in its picture gallery—to supply the omission of papers from Generals Kenly and Johnson—a painting of this scene at Front Royal, where the dashing young Confederate general, in full gray uniform, accompanied by his brilliant staff, is calling to tender any services in his power to the wounded and bleeding veteran of his own state, clad in his dust-covered blue, in command of the opposing forces—all Marylanders. Such a picture properly executed should be dramatic in its power, touching in its lessons, and full of patriotic and well as pathetic suggestions to every son of Maryland, whether his father fought under the Stars and Stripes or under the Stars and Bars.

General Kenly was thrice wounded in this battle, twice by saber cuts, once by a bullet, each time in the head. The last wound knocked him from his horse, and while almost senseless from the loss of blood he was made a prisoner, and it was in this condition that General Johnson found him lying upon a bed of straw.

Col. Frank Markoe of Baltimore, who was in this fight, tells us an amusing story to the effect that as the Union prisoners of Kenly's regiment were led to the rear, he, with other Maryland Confederates, were watching them, when one exclaimed: "I must get out of sight."

"Why?" said Colonel Markoe.

"Because I see among those Yankees the man who made me a pair of boots just before I entered the Confederate service, and I have never paid him, and am afraid that he will dun me if he sees me here."

REPAID THE LOAN

From the memoranda found among the papers of General Kenly I learn that while he was in captivity, a Confederate orderly came to the tent where he was confined and handed him $100 in greenbacks, which General Kenly assumed to have been sent him by Captain White, of the Louisiana Tigers, an old Mexican war comrade, who was at the time serving in the vicinity. On June 25, 1864, General Kenly writes:

"Received letter today from Captain White, of the Louisiana Rifles, prisoner at Fort Lafayette, [Union prison on a small rock island between Staten Island and Long Island] saying that he was a prisoner himself, and if it would be convenient he would like to have me return the money loaned me at Front Royal. Wrote to Colonel Coffman, commissary general of prisoners, enclosing a letter to Capt. Alexander White, of the Tigers Rifles, Wheat's battalion, a prisoner at Fort Lafayette, and a draft on New York for $100, drawn on McKim & Co. This was the money loaned me at Front Royal."

It was such incidents as these—not uncommon—that tempered human passions in the red whirl of our civil war; that help us now to forget the sorrow and anger of those days, and to rejoice in the valor and chivalry of both parties to the strife.

KENLY BADLY WOUNDED

Capt. Frank X. Ward, formerly of Baltimore, now of Philadelphia, who was adjutant to the First Maryland Confederate Regiment, advised me that he was told by Col. John L. Thomas that before he went though the lines to go South, General Kenly, then provost marshal, was requested to arrest him and some of his friends as Confederate sympathizers, but that he refused to do so on the ground that they were entitled to their beliefs.

THEIR LOYALTY DOUBTED

Lieut. Col. Fred C. Tarr, who is still living in Baltimore, in an interview shortly after Kenly's death, said, "I was adjutant of the First Maryland Union Regiment and afterward A. A. G. to Kenly's Brigade. The Maryland regiments always suffered from a certain distrust felt of their loyalty, and I think it was unfortunate for Kenly and for the regiments that they were brigaded together for this reason. Each would have had better opportunities had they been with troops of other states. Our regiment was given the poorest arms that were to be had. At Front Royal we had old smooth bore buck and ball muskets, the load consisting of three buckshot and one bullet. This was the same arms used by the Americans in Mexico.

"When [Brig. Gen. James] Shields' Cavalry attacked us at Front Royal, I was in the road with General Kenly and the major. Most of our men were in a field on the other side, whence they poured a volley into the Confederate cavalry that emptied some thirty-seven saddles. In an instant they were upon us, and Kenly and I were wounded at the same time by saber cuts, and I fell unconscious. Except at brief intervals I continued so for two days, at the end of which time I found that owing to the kind suggestion of Captain Ward, I had been removed from the hospital to a private house, where I was kindly cared for. There I remained when the troops retreated, and was recaptured by General Shields, of our Army, and sent home, whence I returned to the front as soon as I recovered."

PAROLED AND AT HOME

Colonel Kenly was soon paroled and returned to Baltimore, and as soon as exchanged, on August 22, 1862, promoted to be "Brigadier General United States Volunteers for gallant services at Front Royal." He subsequently commanded a Maryland brigade and later division in the First Army Corps, and in the later part of the war held several independent commands requiring legal and judicial as well as military ability.

At the time of both Lee's invasion of the North and later at Early's advance upon Washington in 1864, General Kenly handled the troops under his command so as to render efficient service to the Union cause. In helping to block the movements of the invaders, Governor [Andrew G.] Curtin of Pennsylvania always said that General Kenly saved him "from being scooped up at Hagerstown by the Confederate advance in 1863." On March 13, 1865, General Kenly was breveted a major-general "for gallant and meritorious services during the war." He was mustered out with an honorable discharge August 13, 1865.

The later years of his life General Kenly lived very quietly, practicing law a little and rarely appearing on public occasions except at occasional military reunions, such as that of the Army of the Potomac, in Baltimore, when he was chief marshal of the parade, when the writer first made his acquaintance and served upon his staff. He was several times elected president of the Maryland Association of Union Veterans, and held that position at the time of his death.

His most notable utterance in these post-bellum years was an address before the Grand Army reunion at Camp Carroll, in 1884. From this I quote a paragraph which attracted then and deserves now the thoughtful consideration of all students of the history of the civil war:

WHAT MIGHT HAVE BEEN

The military leaders of the rebellion were much abler men than its statesmen. If Col. Jefferson Davis, of the First Mississippi Regiment in the war with Mexico, had been put at the head of the Confederate armies in 1861 and General R. E. Lee at the head of state, the war would have been prolonged and something might have been saved from the wreck. Lee, while a great soldier, was, nevertheless, a civilian by nature. Davis, with great mental power, great personal courage, and the embodiment of the advice given by Danton to the French army on the Rhine, "toujours l'audace!" Would have kept the Southern heart on fire, while there was a man, a gun, or a cartridge. Lee would have temporized in unlucky times, kept down or smothered the personal antagonism of his generals, and by the great weight of his character perhaps have effected what alone could saved for the time the Southern Confederacy—men and money through a foreign alliance.

One who was with Mr. Davis has told me that a week ere Richmond surrendered, Davis told him that it was the regret of his life that he had not served the Confederacy in the field, and some one else been President.

General Kenly was a Quaker and attended the Friends meetings. The services at his grave, attended by many old war comrades and some dear friends from among his old opponents, were conducted by the Rev. Dr. Hodges, of St. Paul's Episcopal Church.

Among the books and papers left by General Kenly, now in the possession of his brother, Maj. William L. Kenly, to whom I am indebted for much material in preparing this paper, is a history of the First Maryland Infantry, published in 1871, compiled by Charles Camper and J. W. Kirkley, both members of the regiment. . . .

Springfield Republican, May 15, 1873

"Connecticut Topics—Scenes and Incidents

How the Officers Were Received by the Men, 'Little Phil,' Sherman and Hancock the Favorites"

. . . As the numerous general officers and persons of note took their seats on the platform at Music Hall on Wednesday afternoon, at the meeting of the society of the Army of the Potomac, it was astonishing to note the various degrees of attention with which they were greeted by the veterans below. The president and Gen. [Maj. Gen. William Tecumseh] Sherman were received with very general applause, which was higher for [Maj. Gen. Ambrose] Burnside, [Maj. Gen. Irwin] McDowell, [Maj. Gen. William] Franklin and various lesser lights, but the entrance of Gen. [Maj. Gen. Winfield Scott] Hancock, who had not attended any previous reunion, drew down a great storm of applause that seemed very acceptable to the general, who has grown stout and full of face since he used to be the terror of young staff officers, rousing us out at early dawn, in the old war days. He acknowledged the compliment with one of his old-time, graceful bows, and not seeming to notice the president, seated himself by the side of Gen. Hawley, with whom he had once entered into conversation. A moment later entered Gen. [Maj. Gen. Philip] Sheridan, with his rosy face and bullet head, when the whole assembly of soldiers rose *en masse*, with rousing cheers for "Little Phil." Evidently he was, par excellence, the soldiers' pet, as was repeatedly indicated during the day, for while Grant was always applauded and Sherman drew cheers, as did every mention of Hancock, the enthusiastic spirit of the hour was poured lavishly over Sheridan as not only the dashing soldier but gay comrade, who, as he said himself, "had come here on a bum, and did not know where he should bring up." As this was the plan of a very large number of the vets, they heartily echoed the sentiment. It was doubtless for this reason that, while the president, Gen. Sherman and many of the notables were the guests of private citizens, Sheridan positively refused to go anywhere but to a hotel. As Hancock was not seen to speak to Grant, so I observed that Gen. Hawley did not look up to Vice President Wilson [Henry Wilson, vice president in Grant's second term] nor to Postmaster Sperry, [Nehemiah Sperry, appointed postmaster of New Haven by President Lincoln] yet I noted that Hawley was almost the only general officer who applauded with any enthusiasm the allusions to Grant.

The oration by Gen. Devens [Brig. Gen. Charles, postwar U.S. attorney general] of Worcester was a most suitable production, admirably well written, and delivered with great force and effect, and without any reference to his notes. It was a tribute to the memory of Gen. Meade, the last president of the society, with a brief sketch of his life and eloquent description of the battle of Gettysburg. It was received with great favor by the soldiers, who, I think, are themselves conscious that, like the public at large, they have never done full justice to the abilities of Gen. Meade, whose fame is certainly growing since his death.

Of the poem of Gov. Van Zandt of Rhode Island it is not necessary to say much, though some of his personal hits, in wretched verse, at the peculiarities of the various generals seemed vastly to amuse those gentlemen, as it did the soldiers in the body of the house. The applause with which his ridicule of [Maj. Gen. Benjamin] Butler was received showed the contempt in which that worthy is held by the veterans of the army of the Potomac. The allusion to Gen. Butler was as follows:

> Ben Butler's great head, like a billiard ball shining,
> He caromed on Bethel, and pockets himself;
> But the maids of Orleans his fair laurels are twining,
> And he always rolls off when he's laid on the shelf.

At the business meeting after the literary exercises, there was quite a strife over the election of the president for the year to come. Gen. Hancock was nominated by enthusiastic friends, but he declined, urging the election of Gen. Franklin, but Gen. McDowell's friends, however, nominated and pushed that officer's claims, so that, after an exciting ballot, he was elected over Franklin by a small majority. It was a little singular that the friends of both these candidates intimated pretty plainly that the chief argument for the election of their favorite was that they had not been quite well treated by the government.[1]

In the evening, after a great concert by Gilmore's band, a banquet was given in Music hall, at which were present all the notabilities of the day and some 500 members of the society, filling the long tables which occupied the body of the hall, while the galleries were crowded with New Haven ladies and gentlemen, the former turning out in great numbers and sitting through the entire regular program of toasts and speeches apparently with great interest. The supper was fine and the wine plenty, but I am pleased to say that during the entire regular program it led to little or no disturbance. Of the speeches of the evening the best were those of Gen. Sherman, who responded to "The Army and Navy" in a sensible, telling manner, avoiding all claptrap, and of Gov. Ingersoll, [Charles R. Ingersoll, governor of Connecticut, 1873–77] who, in reply to the toast, "The State of Connecticut," made a very graceful, handsome and dignified address of welcome to the officers and soldiers present. Gen. Hawley's speech disappointed and Vice President Wilson's disgusted me, the former because he said nothing worth remembering, and the latter from its obsequiousness.

But Gen. Sheridan carried everything before him in response to "Our Wives and Sweethearts." In compliance with a general demand, the little fellow climbed up on the table and for ten minutes kept the crowd in a roar. Gen. Sheridan is no speaker, but the sight is one that I shall not forget in a life-time of the little red-faced, jolly-looking "puss in boots," in full-dress uniform, with all the badges and decorations of the day upon his person, standing on a supper table trying to talk to the "fellers," all of whom worshiped him, and enjoying the petting he was receiving, and yet wondering how he should get out of it.

After the regular business was over, most of the ladies left the galleries, and Gen. Sherman and many others the hall. Those who remained then fell in for the annual reunion of "the bummers of the army," and with speech, song and revelry had "a high old time" of it for a couple of hours longer.

1. Franklin was blamed by Major General Burnside for the fiasco at Fredericksburg, harming his reputation. McDowell commanded the Union army at the first battle of Bull Run, another disaster for the Union.

Springfield Republican, December 13, 1874
"A Trio of Heroes—Gen Robert O. Tyler, Lieut-Col Sanford H. Perkins and Lieut-Col Robert Leggett
Representative Officers of Connecticut Regiments, Who Have Recently Died From Our Special Correspondent."

Hartford

Within a month past three of the finest soldiers that Connecticut produced during the war of the rebellion have passed away. As these three men were all field officers and in many senses representative men of what I think may be fairly called our three representative Connecticut regiments in that struggle, I do not think that a brief resume of their careers will be altogether profitless.

The three men were Gen. Robert O. Tyler, who died suddenly of neuralgia of the heart at Boston Dec. 1; Lieut-Col. Sanford H. Perkins, who died at the Middletown insane asylum Dec. 9; and Lieut-Col. Robert Leggett, who died at a public hospital in New York City in the latter part of November. Gen. Tyler was colonel of the 1st Connecticut heavy artillery—which he transformed from the original

4th Connecticut infantry—from August 31, 1861, to November 19, 1862, the date of his promotion to a brigadier-generalship. Lieut-Col. Perkins, originally a captain in the same regiment, was made a major of the 14th Connecticut infantry, June 7, 1862, and quickly promoted to the lieutenant-colonelcy, which position he held till forced to resign, April 20, 1863, on account of wounds received at Fredericksburg. Lieut-Col. Leggett was commissioned captain in the 10th Connecticut infantry, August 1, 1861, and rose to be lieutenant-colonel of the same, which post he was compelled to resign, August 15, 1864, owing to the loss of a leg from wounds received in action.

I have termed the regiments in which these men served and in whose reputations and histories their own are closely interwoven *representative* regiments, and I do it without disparagement to the history and brilliant record of any of our other volunteer organizations, simply because I think their respective records will bear out my claim. The 1st artillery represented the height of military discipline, *esprit du corps* and regular army modes of thought and action, and that "Bob" Tyler was its creator is the universal testimony of every officer and man who served with it, who was present on that doleful August evening at Hagerstown, Maryland, in 1861, where the utterly demoralized 4th Connecticut—first of our three-years regiments—lay in a dirty camp, half dressed in the rags to which their shoddy uniforms were crumbling. Their companion Connecticut three-month regiments had all gone home; the defeat at Bull Run had dampened their military ambition; of their three field officers one slunk in his tent, a sulky, half-hearted soldier, with a "secesh" wife demoralizing his ambition; a second was always full of patriotism, but also full of whisky, while the junior of the three desired and strove to bring up the tone of the men but was utterly without military experience.

To this demoralized command came this young captain in the regular army with a commission as colonel, superseding the half-hearted soldier. Taking in the situation at a glance, he secured a temperance pledge—faithfully kept all through the war—from his next in rank, and to his major gave such advice and aid as soon enabled that officer to take command of another regiment for himself, where the lessons of "Bob" Tyler were so faithfully carried out that the major general's stars were in due season the reward of the faithful young soldier. To the almost mutinous men of the 4th, Col. Tyler first showed an unconquerable determination to be obeyed at all hazards, quelling a half-mutiny by pointing artillery upon his own camp, and then showed a determination to care and provide for their comfort by a peremptory refusal to take them into a campaign till he had secured new and proper clothing. Then he marched them to the forts opposite Washington, converted the organization into heavy artillery, weeded out incompetent commissioned officers, promoted competent non-commissioned officers and privates, added two companies of recruits and inaugurated a system of drills and inspections that in less than a year made his command the model volunteer regiment of the army of the Potomac and one that the regular army inspectors were compelled to confess was in no whit inferior to their own. When the time for campaigning came, to this regiment was assigned the siege train of the Potomac army in McClellan's Peninsula campaign, where the guns thundered in the siege of York-town and woke the echoes of Malvern Hill, where with the gunboats the heavy artillery saved our retreating army; yet, despite the almost fathomless slough of the Chickahominy swamps, the men saved every single gun and lost not a single man. Returning to the Washington forts during the summer of 1862, the regiment lost its colonel, promoted to a brigadiership, but never lost the character that he had made for it and in it, but in all its subsequent service during the war did credit to its organization and founder. Its line officers were so continually drawn upon for promotion to field officers in other Connecticut regiments that Col. Tyler once stoutly remonstrated that his regiment ought not to be deemed a yeast-pot from which to draw material to "raise" other regiments.

Gen. Tyler's own career after his promotion involved more of active service in the field than his old regiment was called upon to furnish. Commanding the reserve artillery corps of the army of the Potomac, he won brevets innumerable in the volunteer service, for his services at Fredericksburg, Gettysburg, Spotsylvania and Cold Harbor, and, March 18, 1865, was breveted major general in the regular army "for gallant and meritorious service in the field during the rebellion." At the battle of Cold Harbor, Va., he was severely wounded in the leg, and would surely have suffered amputation of the limb had he not pointed a pistol at the head of the surgeon who was making the preparations, and threatened to shoot him if he essayed the operation. As a result he saved the limb, but underwent much of suffering and was lame for life.

During the war thousands of anecdotes were in circulation about Gen. Tyler, many of them purely fictitious, yet some of which that have more foundation only serve to illustrate his stern discipline combined with patriotic ardor, love of his own command and the quickness of retort and ready wit that mark the blood which flowed in his veins. Such was the nature of his response to the chaplain who, besetting him when much occupied with duties, with a complaint that the men were not fond enough of listening to sermons, "whereas in the Massachusetts regiment (whose camp adjoined that of the 1st artillery) six men had just been baptized"—met the quick retort, "Then let the adjutant detail twelve of our men for the same purpose, for surely we must not be outdone by any Massachusetts regiment."

Since the war, Gen. Tyler has served in his army rank of lieutenant colonel in the quartermaster's department as chief quartermaster at New York, Louisville, Charleston, San Francisco and lately at Boston, where he died. He was a son of Mr. Frederic Tyler of this city, a nephew of Gen. Dan Tyler, who commanded our three-months troops, and a descendent on the other side of Israel Putnam

[(1718–1790), major general in the Continental Army)] and of Jonathan Edwards [(1703–1758), Calvinist preacher and theologian].

That the 14th Connecticut was of different type from the 1st artillery may seem strange when it is remembered that to its dashing little lieutenant-colonel, who "learned how" as a captain under "Bob" Tyler, it was indebted for its first instruction in the military art. Dropping suddenly into the recruiting camp of the regiment on Wethersfield Avenue in Hartford, one June afternoon in 1862, the little fellow, who had traveled night and day from the moment he had received his new commission, and a reluctant permit from Col. Tyler to leave the 1st artillery, then on the Peninsula, touched his hat to Col. Morris with the words, "I am Capt. Perkins and report for duty." "*Major* Perkins, I am very glad to see you," said the colonel, "but have you not been home?" "No, sir; my orders were to report at the regimental headquarters, and here I am." The colonel insisting on his taking a brief leave, he came back in 48 hours, to find himself promoted to be lieutenant-colonel, in which position he served with untiring zeal and tremendous efficiency, until his serious wound at Fredericksburg incapacitated him for field service. It was owing almost solely to his persistent drill that the 14th, which was hurried into action within three weeks of the date of leaving the state, made so good a record at Antietam—its first great battle. As Col. Morris had a brigade, his command there and at Fredericksburg fell upon Lieut-Col. Perkins, whose coolness and bravery in action completed the victory over the heads and hearts of the regiment for which his previous labors had prepared the way. At Fredericksburg, twelve years ago this very 13th of December, the colonel was urging the regiment forward in its final charge up Marye's heights [the battle of Fredericksburg, December 13, 1862] on whose slopes our men were falling like autumn leaves, when a bullet struck him in the neck. He fell into the arms of the writer, who, with three other members of the regiment, succeeded in bearing him off under a very heavy fire. A coincidence may be mentioned, that, twelve years later lacking a single day, two of us, who, that day, bore his living body to a place of safety, were of the group of four of his old comrades who bore his dead body to its last resting-place in the New Britain cemetery.

Sanford Perkins gave the impress of his own character to the 14th, and, had he stayed with us, might have made it a better-drilled regiment, but its constant series of battles—35 in all—and consequent frequent change of commanding officer gave it a reputation rather for dashing, fighting qualities rather than for spotless muskets or perfection of drill. It had all the *verve* of its lieutenant-colonel, but as officers and men felt that the chances for death or promotion were both constant, they did not devote themselves to the routine duties of the camp for the sake of the credit to be gained therefor, as did regiments less constantly at the front. Four months after his wound, Lieut-Col. Perkins found that it was useless to hope to return to duty in any reasonable time, and resigned. Later, he served awhile as a state allotment commissioner, and since the war has been in business in New Haven and Springfield, Mass.

His wound has always troubled him, and, two years ago, epileptic fits resulted in insanity, so that he had to be sent to the state asylum at Middletown, where, last week, he died. The blow to his old comrades came in discovering that their friend and loved leader had sacrificed his mind to the country to whom he had freely given his body, so that when death came we could not look upon it as other than a blessed release to the worn-out soldier. New Britain, that had honored him living, mourned his death, Rev. Mr. Dennison delivering a most tender and appreciative little address over his body, while, to sound of martial music and the rattle of musketry, his old comrades laid him in the grave, and left him to rest at last,

> "—rest from the two-fold strife,
> the battle-field of armies and the battle-field of life."

Lieut-Col. Leggett did not *make* the 10th Connecticut, but, though a man of much individuality, was so good a soldier that, when he rose from his captaincy through the majority to be lieutenant-colonel commanding, which he was for a long season, he kept up the prevailing tone of the regiment. An Englishman by birth, Leggett had served as a private soldier in the British army in China, and later as a private in the United States Marine Corps. With very thorough ideas of drill and discipline he had also acquired in these fields of service the habit of hard drinking that too often prevails therein. Yet he was so good a soldier that after a night of revelry he would come out fresh and vigorous at drill and dress-parade. Not a professor of religion, he at first was disposed to ignore the chaplain, but after the latter had been six weeks with the regiment, Col. Leggett dropped in at a prayer-meeting held, one evening on the line of march, at the close of which he called Capt. Trumbull to him and thanked him for the good he was doing in the regiment. He then added that he had determined to introduce prayers at the daily dress-parade, which he inaugurated, next day, and which were ever after kept up in the 10th. When some of the Romanists remonstrated at having to remove their hats at this service, Col. Leggett replied in his prompt, military way: "When I say attend to prayers by the chaplain, it's a military order that you *must* obey."

Lieut-Col. Leggett was in command of the 10th in its famous charge at Kingston, N.C., December 14, 1862, where nearly a third of his men were placed *hors du combat*, and where he won great commendation for his services. Later he led the regiment in the South Carolina campaign, where, during the siege of Charleston, he was struck in the leg by a rebel shell. Amputation at the upper third of the limb was performed. In the sweltering summer heat and amid the discomforts of the rough army hospital, the wounded veteran could not have survived but for the tender nursing and gentle care of Miss Clara Barton, the famous army nurse. Thanks to her, he recovered, got a wooden leg and returned to duty, but in the Virginia campaign of 1864 he found that he could not do full duty with his wooden limb. But he was so proud a soldier that he would stand in no man's way of promotion, and so resigned.

After the war he married, had one daughter, whom he named Clara Barton, and then lost both wife and child. After this, the broken-down soldier wandered about working at his trade as a journeyman-tailor at Great Barrington, Mass., and elsewhere, till at last he drifted into a New York hospital, weary, sick and worn, and soon passed away from life to find a pauper's grave in the Potter's field.

To the credit of New London let it be said that her citizens, who had presented the soldier a with sword while living, no sooner heard of his death than they at once raised funds to remove his remains to that city, where, last week, they received honorable burial. Brave-hearted and faithful Bob Leggett, with his one fault, leaves a good record of service for his adopted country that one can but hope that his single serious error of conduct was pardoned him in consideration of his service for others.

Of the three heroes I have herein mentioned, there were some things in common; each loved his country, each received wounds that finally cost him his life, each died away from home and relatives; only the general died in full possession of his faculties, while each of the others were but wrecks of their old selves.

If I were to seek to draw any lessons from their lives, it would be that each should use the talents given him to the best advantage. Each of these men gave theirs; the one who had the most received the greatest reward, but the others were duly honored for their services. It cost all of them their lives, but won them friends and honors. What soldier hopes for more than these? "Greater love hath no man than this, that a man should lay down his life for his friend," and even in this world such sacrifice never fails to be honored.

Springfield Republican, June 6, 1878

"After-Notes of the Reunions.

From Our Special Correspondent."

Hartford, Ct.

You must permit me to say how heartily we enjoyed your city and its hospitality. It makes more dim the remembrance of any discomforts in the old war days, and gilds the past as well as present to have such ample reward showered upon us.

A few notes of the reunion from an insider may also be worth recalling. You have already noted how warmly Fighting Joe was greeted everywhere, but you can hardly express how dear he is to the veteran men now that they see him in his badly crippled condition that strikingly appeals to the sympathies of those of us who remembered him as we used to see him in the full prime of health and manhood, mounted on his magnificent black horse, which, he tells me, ended his days peacefully on a farm where he had no work to do, was buried with military honors and has a monument to his memory. No staff or orderlies could keep up with the general when he was on that horse, and it used to be very amusing to us infantrymen to see them try.

You remember, by the way, the oft-quoted remark attributed to Hooker in 1863, "Who ever saw a dead cavalryman?" The general denied yesterday having made it, but explained with a merry twinkle of the eye that when he took command of the Army of the Potomac, he found the cavalry in very poor condition—rather ornamental than useful, and did then remark that he personally had not had the fortune to ever come across any dead cavalrymen. He certainly did increase the utility of that branch of the service, and gave it the impetus that made it of equal value with other branches during the balance of the war.

Two more anecdotes of Hooker, of whom I could tell you dozens, and I am done. You have noted how tenderly he received Col. Thompson's beautiful children during that delightful reception at Highland Place, where the music, the fair women, the brave men—did you note how many disabled ones there were? Hooker, Sickles, [Brig. Gen. Selden] Connor, etc.—the good cheer all combined to make a not-soon-to-be-forgotten picture. There in the big chair sat the old hero of Lookout [the battle of Lookout Mountain, November 24, 1863; Hooker commanded the force that captured the 1,200-foot peak rising above the Tennessee Valley] with a child on his knee, while the sunlight and shade fell in alternate ripples on the floor and the music rose and fell on the air. When one of us said to the lovely seven-year-old girl as the general embraced her, "You must remember this. Ten or fifteen years hence you will be very proud of having been kissed by Fighting Joe Hooker," the general wittily retorted, "I should not mind it either, my dear, if you were ten or fifteen years older now."

The second story is of the point made by that inimitable and untiring of flowery impromptu speakers, Gov. Van Zandt, when, in denouncing the attempt in Congress to cut down the number and the pay of the army, he said that he did not envy the men "who should seek to curtail the provender of this old Eagle of Lookout who sits in front of me with one disabled wing that incites tears whenever I gaze upon it. Would God that I could bathe it in such tears and restore it to its pristine splendor." How the boys shouted and how the general alternately laughed and cried then.

The Potomac veterans have done wisely in making Gen. Franklin their next president, and in doing it unanimously, thus demonstrating that it is not a partisan organization, for Franklin, Hancock and one or two other notably good officers of Democratic proclivities have kept away for two or three years past. Possibly some of the rather extravagant "gush" over Grant has had something to do with it, and Burnside's prominence last year doubtless had still more, for all the old army quarrels have not entirely died out, though I think the masses of the organization wish them to do so.

Baltimore American, May 22, 1886

"A Visit to Antietam by One Who Was There in 1862

Interesting Spots on the Old Battlefield, the Burnside Bridge, the Famous Lost Dispatch, South Mountain, Why Hooker Was Removed"

On the night of September 17, 1862, the writer slept, an unexpected and uninvited guest, upon the farm of Mr. Wm. Roulette, of Sharpsburg, Md. Upon the night of May 17, 1886, he had the pleasure of sleeping upon the same farm, this time as an invited and cordially welcomed guest of Mr. Roulette, whom he found a most courteous and hospitable host. In 1862, sleeping was rather a difficult task upon the plowed field upon which it was sought, owing mainly to the fact that a party of gentlemen in gray suits, who were lying upon the other side of the little lane in our front, had a very disagreeable way of shooting carelessly, or perhaps I should say very carefully, in our direction.

In 1886, sleep was easy upon a good bed in Mr. Roulette's house, although some of the very same gentlemen who sought to disturb our rest in 1862 were not far distant, yet now, like myself, resting easily, equally welcome to the hospitality of the good people of Sharpsburg, whose homes and property were both greatly damaged twenty-four years agone. Surely, it adds to one's pride as an American when in less than a quarter of a century the wheel of time has made such things possible.

As one of a visiting party of old soldiers of both armies who were making a trip to these two Maryland battlefields in which they had been engaged, the writer was able to discover some new facts of historical interest to the many readers of The American in the state in which are located these battlefield which have an abiding interest to traveler and historical student.

Owing to the fact that but little, in any, entrenching was done at Antietam, and that the battle was waged over an extensive surface of country, which was but for a very days occupied by either army, it is far more difficult to trace the battle lines than at Fredericksburg or Gettysburg. The fences destroyed have all been rebuilt, the injured buildings all repaired or replaced, some new roads laid out, the bridges built and old forts abandoned, while the thrifty Maryland farmers talk of closing up the famous "Bloody Lane" [where Goddard and his regiment spent several hours under fire] and throwing it into the adjacent farms, in order to avoid the expense of two sets of fences, as the peculiar confirmation of the lane, which abounds in angles and curves and runs "every which way," has led to no end of controversy as to the position of different troops; and as some of the severest fighting was done across this lane, it should either be bought by the state or general government, and the position of different commands marked, as has been done at Gettysburg, even if necessary to do as was done there, gather a concourse of commanders of each army to point out their positions. If the land is thrown into adjacent farms, as threatened, it will be very difficult for future visitors to understand the battle, as it was only by close study and comparing notes that many of us could identify our old positions on this trip.

The Most Interesting Spots

to general visitors are the National Cemetery, where are buried the Union soldiers who fell in the two battles [the battle of South Mountain, September 14, 1862, and Antietam three days later], the "Dunker" Church, which stood at a point about which the waves of battle ebbed and flowed on the Union right, and the "Burnside bridge," the scene of contest on the Union left on the afternoon of the 17th. The cemetery contains several thousand graves of Union soldiers, is beautifully laid out, and affords an excellent view of the whole scene of strife.

The Confederate dead were all subsequently removed to Hagerstown, and there buried in a cemetery devoted to that purpose by an association of which Colonel H. Kyd Douglass of Hagerstown, who served on Stonewall Jackson's staff, is president. The funds for the removal of the bodies of the dead Confederates were raised throughout the South, and it is a curious instance of how much cheaper work is done when paid for from private sources than when "Uncle Sam" foots the bill, to note that while the cost of burying the Confederate dead was but $3 each, the contractors who buried the Union dead received about $13 for each body.

The Dunker Church was and is used for religious worship by the sect after which it is named, who have still quite a following in that part of Maryland. Although nearly ruined during the battle, it has been so renovated as to show scarce any marks of the shot, shell and bullets by which it was riddled.

A Visit to the Burnside Bridge

and surrounding country can but convince everyone of the desperate bravery of the Union troops, who finally captured and crossed it, at the same time that a study of the official reports of the battle and the admissions of ex-Confederate officers engaged equally convince that had Burnside attacked in the morning of the 17th, when the other Union commanders were fighting on the right and center, he could have much more easily won the bridge, and been in a position then that would have ensured a decisive Confederate defeat. It is also generally admitted now that had McClellan sent in Porter's [Maj. Gen. Fitz John, commanding the 5th Corps] corps to Burnside's support even late in the afternoon of the 17th, the Confederates could have been driven into the Potomac and badly worsted.

Among the Union officers engaged on this excursion trip were General [Brig. Gen. William] Dudley, late pensions commissioner, of Indiana; Gen. [Brig. Gen. Edward] Bragg, member of Congress from Wisconsin, who commanded the old "Iron Brigade," and Col. Joe Dickinson, of the Pension Office, who served as adjutant general to Gen. Joe Hooker when he commanded the Army of the Potomac. All three of these gallant officers still suffer severely from wounds received in battle, but three more interesting or jovial traveling companions cannot be found.

From Col. Dickinson I learned the facts, before never made entirely clear, as to

Hooker's Removal from Command

of the Army of the Potomac. Col. Dickinson states that when he started to pursue Lee on the Gettysburg campaign, Gen. Hooker sent Gen. [Brig. Gen. Daniel] Butterfield, of his staff, to Washington to demand of Gen. [Maj. Gen. Henry, army general in chief] Halleck that French's [Maj. Gen. William, commanding the 3rd division, 2nd corps] division on Maryland Heights and other detached troops in Washington and Baltimore should be attached to the Army of the Potomac. Gen. Butterfield was unable to secure this, and telegraphed Hooker to that effect, begging that Col. Dickinson be sent up to aid him in securing the end from President Lincoln, of whom he (Dickinson) was a warm personal friend. Col. Dickinson was sent, but during his and Butterfield's absence, Gen. Hooker had a sharp telegraphic correspondence with Halleck on the subject, ending by Hooker demanding the troops *immediately,* or else that he be relieved from command. Had his staff officers been present, that dispatch would probably not have been sent, as they had great influence in restraining the fiery temper of "Fighting Joe." But sent it was, and Halleck was but too glad to seize the opportunity of relieving Hooker of command.

Mr. Roulette—in whose spring house the regiment with which the writer was connected (Fourteenth Connecticut) captured some two dozen prisoners in the battle, and on whose farm we all Friday fought—gave a vivid description of events prior to, during and subsequent to the fight. In fear of the strife, he had sent his family away a few days before, but remained to guard his property. When he came into the meadows the night of the 16th, he found the Confederate pickets, who told him he might come in, could remain or go to their rear, but could not return to the Union lines if he came in. He consented, went to his house, and had a pretty restless night, knowing that he was between two armies, though neither bothered him personally.

Next morning, when he heard firing on his right, he saw his neighbor's (Mona) barn set on fire by shells, he went out and tried to lead a young horse of which he was fond into the cellar, in hope to save him. The frightened horse refused to be led, and as the noise of the battle grew near, Mr. Roulette let go the halter, when the frightened animal galloped off, never to be found by its owner. Mr. Roulette then took the collar himself, while shot and shell flew over his house—one big shell coming through, but fortunately not exploding. In a few moments, bullets flew about the house like bees; then he heard the Yankee cheers, and then came out to find the few Confederates about the house captured, and the Connecticut regiment go charging by, as it swept up into the famous corn field where it battled for three long hours, losing some 150 men. As the Yankees came in, Mr. Roulette decided now was his time to get well inside our lines, and he started, naturally, at a pretty lively gait as he heard the Confederate bullets whistling by his ears till he reached a place of safety.

He returned the 19th to find his house, barn and buildings all hospitals, where he and his family rendered all possible assistance till all the wounded were removed. Many soldiers were buried on his farm, but all have since been disinterred and removed to the Union and Confederate cemeteries, save one Connecticut lad, whose body Mr. Roulette disinterred and sent North to his relatives in Connecticut, who most gratefully acknowledged the kindness, and with whom he has since kept up an interesting correspondence.

Although a pronounced Union man, Mr. Roulette was never mistreated by soldiers of either army. He is profoundly grateful to Gen. Hancock who, when his troops camped on Roulette's farm in the next year's (Gettysburg) campaign, forbid the men to tie their horses to the young apple trees, lest they girdle them.

My comrade on this trip, the chaplain of our old regiment, Rev. H. L. Stevens, of Washington, and I were quite fortunate in being enabled to pick up many bullets on the field of our old position, the late heavy rains having washed up the lately plowed land so as to make it easy to find them, even after twenty-four years. Some of the rail fences that were in Hooker's front are still standing, showing the bullet holes with which they were riddled in that hot fight. Evidently your Maryland farmers build their fences of endurable wood. In all accounts of these Maryland battles much is said of

The Famous "Lost Dispatch"

sent by General Lee to General D. H. Hill, which fell into General McClellan's hands just before the battle of South Mountain. In the *Century Magazine* of May, 1886, General Hill explains, and Colonel Kyd Douglass, of Jackson's staff, assures me this is true, that two copies were sent him, one from Lee's and one from Jackson's headquarters. General Hill argues that no great harm came from the loss of this order, but the general opinion is that it gave McClellan a decided advantage, and one that might have caused a decisive Confederate defeat had his troops been more promptly moved. Be that as it may, I was fortunate enough on this trip to gather from General C. S. Colegrove of Washington, who at the battle of South

Mountain commanded an Indiana regiment, the unpublished details of the discovery of this dispatch.

On the night of September 13, 1862, Colonel Colegrove's regiment went into camp near South Mountain on the very ground occupied that morning by Gen. D. H. Hill. A little before sunset a corporal and sergeant of the regiment found on the ground a bundle of cigars wrapped in paper. Examining the paper, the sergeant discovered it to be from Confederate headquarters, and at once took it to his colonel. Col. Colegrove, on reading it, found it to be an order from Lee to Hill, designating the course of the different Confederate corps during the campaign. Realizing its importance, he mounted his horse and immediately rode to Gen. McClellan's headquarters and gave him the paper. General McClellan read it, pronounced it authentic, thanked Col. Colegrove heartily, and proceeded to make his plan of campaign conform to the situation.

Excerpt from Capt. Henry P. Goddard's Address, as Vice President of the Baltimore Life Underwriters Association, to the National Life Underwriters Convention at Baltimore, October 13, 1903

The State of Maryland has just placed on the field of Chickamauga [the battle of Chickamauga, Tennessee, September 18–20, 1863, a Confederate victory] a monument to the memory of its dead who fought on both sides during that bloody and eventful contest. I am told that on one side of that monument is the figure of a Federal soldier, with an appropriate inscription, and on the other of a Confederate soldier, with fitting words beneath it; but that the mechanics who built the monument at first accidentally placed the wrong inscriptions under each figure. When the sculptor discovered the error and remonstrated, the reply given him was, "They all look alike to us." The statue was properly completed, but perhaps the blunder may teach us a lesson, and my friend, Colonel Markoe, of the Penn Mutual, who once wore the Confederate gray, as I once wore the Federal blue, unites with me and our whole Baltimore association in welcoming you to our Maryland.

22

Maryland's Notable
Confederate Sympathizers

Baltimore Sunday Herald, March 15, 1903
"Maryland Men Who Helped Make History—Gen. John R. Kenly" [Excerpt]

There is no question that at the outbreak of the war, the most fashionable society of Baltimore as a rule was Southern in its sympathy. A good illustration of this condition of affairs is pictured by General Johnson [Brig. Gen. Bradley Johnson, Confederate] in a paper upon Maryland that he wrote for a Confederate military history published in Atlanta, Ga., in 1899, from which I quote a characteristic passage:

"In one of the parlors of one of the greatest houses of the town, blazing with every luxury that wealth and culture could buy, one or twoscore beautiful woman would meet—doors and windows sealed—to see the messenger and to hear the news from Dixie. Every story of a Maryland boy who had died in battle for the right, every exploit of a Marylander that had thrilled the army, every achievement of the First Regiment of the line, was recited and repeated and gone over, until human nature could stand no more, and 'In Dixie's land I'll take my stand, and live and die for Dixie' would burst from the throng and make indistinct vibrations on the outer air. At one of these mystic meetings of the faithful at the Winns' house, on Monument street, the messenger produced James R. Randall's grand war song—'My Maryland.' It was read aloud and reread until sobs and inarticulate moans choked utterance. Hetty Cary was then in the prime of her first youth, with a perfect figure, exquisite complexion, the hair that Titian loved to paint, a brilliant intellect, grace personified, and a disposition the most charming. She was the most beautiful woman of the day, and perhaps the most beautiful that Maryland has ever produced. (An opinion fully shared by the present writer.) . . . While this little coterie of beautiful women were throbbing over Randall's heroic lines, Hetty Cary said, 'That must be sung, Jenny, get an air for it!' and her sister Jenny, at the piano, struck the chorus of the college song, 'Gaudeamus igitur,' and the great war anthem, 'Maryland, My Maryland,' and was born into the world. It went through the city like fire in the dry grass. The boys beat it on their toy drums, the children shrilled it at their play, and for a week all the power of the provost marshal and the garrison and the detectives could not still the refrain."

Baltimore Sun, March 26, 1911

"Hetty Cary—a Baltimore Heroine of the Lost Cause" [Excerpts]

It was a hot afternoon in the spring of '63. The Adjutant-General of the Department of Maryland looked at the thermometer, wiped his brow and swore thoughtfully. Major General [Robert] Schenck, the Department Commander, entered.

"From the reports that have come to me, Colonel [W. H.] Cheeseboro," he said, "I think that if Miss Hetty Cary continues to be so active in communicating with her Southern friends, we shall have to send her South."

"Yes," said the Adjutant-General, "you will be fully justified."

"But if I do, I shall have to forbid the officer who escorts her through our lines to look at her, much less speak to her, for that woman could bewitch the Angel Gabriel."

And truly, Hetty Cary was, in those days, a name to conjure with. She was the most elusive will-o'-the-wisp that ever troubled the brains of Federal forces, from the department commander to the humble sentry on picket duty. She hated to have her movements restrained by the burdensome restrictions that the blockaded condition of her State had placed upon them, and she threw off these restrictions as the spirit moved her. Wherefore ask for a pass through the lines and be safely conducted in a tiresome and prosaic fashion, when one might have all the fun of eluding pickets and dodging gunboats and be spared the disgrace of having to ask a favor of a hated enemy in the bargain. And so Miss Cary fixed her comings and goings to suit herself and not the Yankees. Naturally the Yankees were not exactly pleased. They decided that if Miss Cary didn't see fit to make them a party to her proceedings, they could get along very well without her. Hence the previously quoted conversation. . . .

LIONIZED BY THE SOLDIERS

During a visit to the Army of Northern Virginia, the ladies [Hetty and her two sisters] were literally overwhelmed with attentions, and, after attending a grand review of the Maryland Line held in their honor by Generals [Maj. Gen. Jeb] Steuart and [Maj. Gen. Arnold] Elzey, and a handsome banquet given them by General [Maj. Gen. Richard] Ewell, they beat a hasty retreat to Richmond to escape complete inundation.

Here, during the winter of 1861–62, the three misses Cary (Hetty, Jenny and Constance) were entrusted with the making of the first three silk battle flags of the Confederacy. The ladies set their best stitches upon them, hurrying them through to completion, and sent them to the forces in the field. Jenny's went to Gen.

Bradley T. Johnson, of Maryland; Constance's to Gen. Earl Van Dorn, while Hetty's, which was made entirely of her own and her sister's silk dresses, was sent to Gen. [P. T. G.] Beauregard. All three of the flags have been preserved.

Not till the summer of 1862 was Hetty able to compass her return to Baltimore, which she did with the aid of the Confederate Signal Corps on the lower Potomac, her sister Jenny accompanying her. But she was not destined to remain long at home. Her outspoken expressions of sympathy with the Southern cause became so obnoxious to the Union element in the city that the authorities finally thought it necessary to imprison her. A detail was sent to her home to place her under arrest. Just in time she received warning. Hastily borrowing some old clothes from a neighbor and covering her tell-tale auburn hair in a gray wig, she sat with composure while the house was searched. "Who was she?" "Why, Mrs. M, of course, an old friend of the family." And so the disappointed soldiers were left empty-handed, taking it for granted that the elusive Miss Cary had once more slipped through their fingers and their lines. And this was what she immediately proceeded to do, recognizing that Baltimore was not, just at that time at least, a healthy place for her. But this time her experiences in running the blockade were not so commonplace as before.

PERILOUS TRIPS BY WATER

Awaiting a favorable opportunity, she made a hasty flight to the Eastern Shore of Maryland. Here, with the help of a Dr. George Dennis, of Kingston, Md., she secured a small canoe with a sail and undertook, under escort of two of the doctor's employees, the 40-mile passage across the bay. Setting out from Richmond, on the Pocomoke river, they made Tangier Island before nightfall. Nosing their way into the tall grass of the salt marshes, they lay in hiding overnight, and started out at daybreak next morning to complete their trip.

When less than halfway across, they were horrified to see Yankee guard boats bearing down upon them. A fearful storm was coming up at the time, and capture seemed inevitable. To attempt to weather the storm in such a craft seemed madness, and both men became completely demoralized. Hetty remained calm as ever, and they ran the boat into the face of the wind. Stirred by the bravery of their comrade, the men regained their spirits and managed by a miracle to keep the canoe afloat until the storm abated. Searching the horizon, they were overjoyed to find that the guard boats had been blown off the scent and were nowhere in sight. Before them loomed the hospitable Virginia shore, which they made in safety and with devout thanksgiving.

Once safe in Virginia, Hetty wrote her father a long letter giving a thrilling account of her passage. Enclosing it in a lead packet, she entrusted it to her two companions, who were about to make the return passage. The men, believing themselves in danger of capture, threw it overboard when near the Maryland shore.

The packet was later dredged up and taken to the Federal authorities, and Dr. Dennis only escaped imprisonment for his part in the affair through the intercession of powerful Union friends. . . . .

FAITHFUL TO THE LOST CAUSE

[In Baltimore after the war] Her love for the old Confederacy remained as true as ever and she took an active interest in all the bazaars and benefits that were held for the soldiers of the Lost Cause. This she gained as many admirers after the war as she had during the struggle, and many a broken-down old veteran came to consider her his fairy godmother.

There is hardly an old Confederate soldier of any distinctions now living in Baltimore but has some story to tell of Hetty Cary's devotion to the Southern cause and some anecdote reflecting credit upon her. One tells of how she found him wounded and neglected in a hospital, took him some delicious birds, and had him removed to a private house, where he received much better treatment. . . .

It was not until 1882, that coming here to live, I came to know the lady and to hear from her own lips her story of her Civil War experiences.

I first met the lady at a Confederate fair. She was still very beautiful and attractive, and after I told her of what General Schenck had said about his order to whoever took her through our lines, she laughed heartily and we became good friends, and continued such to the day of her death.

Springfield Republican, June 30, 1909
"Various Notes from Baltimore: Visiting the Grave of Mrs. Martin, Who Helped Maryland Confederates in the Civil War—'Beautiful, Brilliant, Brave'
Correspondence of *The Republican.*"

Baltimore

In a letter which began this Baltimore correspondence of *The Republican* in 1882, comment was made on and a brief sketch given of the remarkable and interesting career of Mrs. Hetty Cary Martin, a famous Baltimore belle and beauty of the civil war days, who probably rendered more efficient help to the Maryland soldiers of the confederacy than any other woman of her day and generation. Descended from an old Virginia family (she was a grandniece of Thomas Jefferson) she naturally sympathized with the South, and when the civil war broke out and during its entire progress, did all she could in getting supplies through the lines to the large number of Maryland boys who had joined the confederate army. After successfully running the blockade across the Potomac on several occasions, she at last decided that it was unsafe to make Baltimore longer her home, and fleeing to escape probable arrest, took up her residence at Richmond. There early in 1865 she married

[Brig.] Gen. John Pegram of the confederate army, a brave and accomplished soldier, who was shot in battle in front of Petersburg within three weeks of his wedding day and was buried at the same church (St. John's, at Richmond) in which he had been wedded. After the war Mrs. Pegram returned to Baltimore and assisted her mother in a famous girls' school here for some years, but about 1880 married Prof. Harry B. Martin, the distinguished young English professor of biology in the Johns Hopkins University. After this marriage Mrs. Martin was for several years prominent in literary and social circles here until both she and her husband failed in health, and she died in 1892.

No Maryland woman of her day was more beautiful or attractive or had a more interesting history. This and a profound personal regard led me last Sunday to visit her grave at Garrison Forrest churchyard in Baltimore County. The remains rest under a slab of marble which has a somewhat florid inscription, ending, however, with the three truthful words: "Beautiful, brilliant, brave." The churchyard is one of the most beautiful in Maryland, and St. Thomas church adjoining—one of the oldest in the state, having been built in 1742—is picturesque and interesting. The day was perfect, and standing by the grave of this beautiful and devoted hero of the South, who had lived long enough after the war to win the respect and regard of old foes as well as the lifelong devotion of all the old soldiers of the South, one could but recall some of the closing lines of Mrs. Browning's "A Rhyme of the Duchess May"—also suggested by a visit to a churchyard:

> *Beating heart and burning brow, ye are very patient now!*
> *And I smiled to think God's greatness*
> *Flows around our incompleteness,*
> *Round our restlessness, His rest.*

Baltimore Sun, February 13, 1911

"A War-Time Belle

Loyal Legion Hears Interesting Paper by Capt. Goddard" [author unknown]

An interesting paper on 'A Maryland Belle in War Time' (Miss Hetty Cary, of Baltimore) was read by Capt. Henry P. Goddard at a meeting of the Maryland Commandery, Military Order of the Loyal Legion of the United States, held at the Belvedere last night. . . .

He related many instances in which the beautiful and accomplished young woman aided Maryland soldiers serving in the Confederacy. Her brother, Mr. Wilson M. Cary, who was in the Confederate Army, was among the guests of the evening and listened with great interest and attention to all Captain Goddard said, frequently nodding his head as if in approbation of the incidents. Mr. James Hewes, who served in the First Maryland Regiment, Confederate States of America, was also a guest and read a short paper giving some recollections of visits the belle paid to the command, cheering and aiding the men. Mr. Joseph Packard, who had charge of the ordnance department of the Army of Northern Virginia, was another guest and made a short address.

The meeting developed into a reunion of the Blue and the Gray, as the veterans of the opposing armies sat at individual tables or stood at a buffet and exchanged experiences as they partook of a delightful luncheon.

Captain Goddard told of how Miss Jennie Cary, who lives in Baltimore, and is a sister of the subject of the paper, was the first person to set 'Maryland, My Maryland' to the familiar tune. She was the first to sing the popular hymn, and with her sisters, Miss Constance Cary and Mrs. Martin, frequently made the camps of the Maryland soldiers ring with its melody. In his address, Mr. Packard said he remembered the visit of the three young ladies on one such occasion, after which the bands took up the tune.

Baltimore Evening Sun, October 3, 1912

"A War Play That Arouses No Animosities."

To The Editor of *The Evening Sun.*

Sir—It is now nearly 30 years since, at a dinner given by Hetty Cary Martin, the famous Confederate sympathizer, Lawrence Barrett [(1838–1891), actor] was asked whether he thought that Mr. Gillette [William Gillette (1853–1937), actor and playwright] would succeed in Baltimore with his play, "Held By the Enemy," the first by the series of plays on the subject of the Civil War. Mr. Barrett was decidedly of a negative opinion, holding it would be impossible to produce a play bearing upon the Civil War, which would be presented both North and South, without awakening sectional animosities. Seeing the play the next week, both Mrs. Martin and myself, were delighted with the performance and were convinced that Mr. Barrett erred in his judgment.

The latest play of this order to be produced here is "The Littlest Rebel," by Edward Peple [(1869–1924), playwright] which is running here this week, and the author solves the problem as successfully as did Mr. Gillette. In this play William Farnum is excellent as the Federal Colonel, and David Landau even better as Captain Cary, a Confederate scout. His daughter Virgie, played by Miss Boots Wooster, is a very remarkable rendition for a child. . . . The minor characters are all well conceived and executed, except that of the General, United States Army, who was made up for and supposed to be Gen. U.S. Grant, but whose appearance and actions in the play were as about unlike that doughty and silent warrior as is possible of conception.

Baltimore Herald, **August 22, 1903**

"She Got the *Gazette*"

To the Editor of the *Herald*

There is a dear old lady living in the vicinity of Baltimore who rarely comes to town. Before and during the war she was a Southern sympathizer and a devoted reader of the *Baltimore Gazette*—a paper which ardently advocated similar views. She came to town last week, and when she got on a street car the newsboy who came to the car called out, "Want a daily paper?" She hailed him and said, "Have you a *Gazette*?" He said: "Oh, yes," and proceeded to sell her a newspaper, at which she did not look until she got home, when she was horrified to find that she had bought a copy of the *Police Gazette*.

Moral: Buy the *Herald* next time.

23

Post–Civil War Politics and Race Relations in Maryland

Springfield Republican, March 24, 1909
"Gov. Swann's Work in Maryland"

Baltimore, Md.

To the Editor of *The Republican*

In a recent paper written for the Maryland historical society upon "Some distinguished Marylanders I have known," I quoted that excellent newspaper, *The Springfield Republican,* as having editorially stated that "the South had by far the most romantically interesting history of any portion of our country." The paper was an attempt to demonstrate that the study of the lives of distinguished Marylanders of the last 30 years went far to prove *The Republican* correct in its statement. Further evidence to the same effect is given in a pamphlet just issued from the Johns Hopkins press. . . .

This particular pamphlet is by William Starr Myers, now preceptor in history at Princeton, but a Baltimore man and Johns Hopkins graduate. It is entitled, 'The Self-Reconstruction of Maryland, 1864–1867,' which covers an interesting period of Maryland history and tells with accuracy and fairness the story of how Maryland repudiated its radical constitution, adopted by a very slim majority in 1864 and reversed its action toward old confederate soldiers and sympathizers by restoring their political privileges under the constitution of 1867.[1] This was a very delicate task and was chiefly manipulated by Gov. Thomas Swann, who was elected governor by the union party in 1864, but who led the revolt against the radical constitution, and as many thought, against the party that had elected him to power.

As to Gov. Swann's motives there has been great difference of opinion, for as Mr. Myers truly says: "At that time and even to this year of grace, 1908, the mention of his name in conversation is often sufficient to call forth torrents of abuse or extreme praise." . . . Although I have known many very severe critics of Gov. Swann, and am not inclined to believe that he was altogether unselfish, I fully concur with Mr. Myers that the new constitution was a good thing for Maryland and that in adopting it "a large majority of the people of Maryland showed the characteristic restraint of the strong American stock from which they had sprung. They never forgot that the corner-stone of a democratic government is after all the rule of law as made by the will of a majority. They were willing to submit when beaten, and turned their attention to repairing the losses caused by the civil war, and to advancing the prosperity and future well-being of the state of Maryland."

1. During the war the Republicans had gained power in the state; after the war, power shifted back to the Democrats and support for the 1864 constitution shrank. The new constitution of 1867, approved by 54 percent of the state's voters and still in effect today, resembled the 1851 constitution. While reapportioning the legislature on the basis of population —not counties—gave greater power to the freed slaves, the document undid many of the benefits that the previous constitution had given to the state's African American population.

Springfield Republican, October 23, 1885
"The Reform Fight in Maryland
From Our Special Correspondent" [Excerpts]

Baltimore, Md.

Students of American politics will find in the present contest in Maryland one of the most interesting of studies. Ever since 1867, when Confederate sympathizers, disenfranchised during the war, were re-enfranchised, the Democratic party have had full swing here, and a machine system has been so thoroughly perfected that its power seems almost unconquerable. There have been repeated attempts at revolt, with more or less success, but, owing to the power of the local bosses, none has been sufficiently successful to rid the city of their rule.

But in the fall of 1882, an entering wedge was made, in the election of a reform judiciary by some 14,000 majority, that bids fair to result in a complete defeat of the ring in the coming municipal election, and victory therein will be very apt to eventuate in the overthrow of the "arch boss," Senator Gorman,[1] at the state election a few days later. If this is the case it will be another instance of the manner in which the schemes of the unrighteous end in their own destruction. In order that he might stab his old enemy, ex-Senator Pinckney Whyte, in the back, by defeating that gentleman's brother and other political friends of Whyte, Senator Gorman secretly lent all his political power to the success of the reform judiciary ticket.

In consequence, Baltimore has now for the first time in many years a judiciary and a grand jury willing and able to take proper care of men who tamper with registry lists, stuff ballot boxes, destroy ballots and tamper with returns—all very common tricks in our past elections and tricks that have been successful and unpunished. Now the case is different, and already two or three ward heelers and corrupt registers have been indicted *before* election for dropping the names of voters from the list, and a court presided over by an honest and brave judge is in daily session to hear complaints and reinstate names dishonestly dropped from the lists.

1. Arthur P. Gorman served as U.S. senator from Maryland, 1881–99 (defeated by Republican Louis E. McComas) and 1903–6, and as Democratic Caucus chairman and leader of the conservative Bourbon Democrats. He was also a member of Maryland House of Delegates, 1869–75, and Maryland State Senate, 1875–81.

Springfield Republican, November 20, 1903

"Recent Baltimore Happenings—Relating to Politics and Things Which Bear Thereon

Correspondence of The Republican."

The recent political victory of the Democratic Party in Maryland will put in the gubernatorial chair for the next four years Edwin S. Warfield [Maryland governor, 1904–8], a typical Southern gentleman with many charming qualities and much business ability. If he is able to resist the sinister influence of the Gorman ring, which for many years has controlled the party in Maryland, he has a great opportunity before him. The most regrettable thing about the campaign was the prominence in the canvass of Senator Gorman, and the fact that in all the speeches of that gentleman he took great pains to make the race question an issue, and to severely criticize President Roosevelt for the manly and straightforward course he has taken on that issue.[1] Many persons think, however, that the senator won for his party by this program. . . .

Last year our school board, composed of men of all parties, including some of the wisest and best men in Baltimore, and some who had served in the Confederate army, had ordered the discontinuance of a white school in a certain section, and that it be turned over for a colored school, owing to the fact that the colored people were in a large majority in the district. Indignant protests from the white people of the district, who said they could not bear the proximity of so many rude colored children, induced the board to change its action.

Not long since some one wrote to the *Baltimore Sun* that he was on a train from Philadelphia on which were several negroes, when "a Baltimore lady passenger" loudly objected to the presence of 'niggers' in the same car. A colored man sitting near her rose and said: "Madam, there are no such people as niggers. You probably mean negroes," whereat the lady drew a revolver upon the speaker and told him to "Mind his business, and keep still," that she knew what she was talking about.

1. This is a reference to the invitation to visit the White House that President Theodore Roosevelt extended to Booker T. Washington (1856–1915), educator, author, and the most

prominent leader of African Americans in the late nineteenth and early twentieth century. Many whites, especially Southerners, strongly criticized Roosevelt for the invitation, which was the first visit to the White House by an African American since Frederick Douglass's visit to the Lincoln White House.

Springfield Republican, October 30, 1903
"Baltimore Life and Politics
Notes about the Campaign—the New and Improved City
Correspondence of *The Republican*"

Baltimore, Md.

This is a state in which politics are always interesting, and they are especially so this year, when our two United States senators, although of the same political party, are arrayed against each other in a bitter fight over the proposed constitutional amendment,[1] a pet scheme of our senior senator, Gorman, who is supposed to have had a hand in its exact wording. This wording is thoroughly characteristic of Senator Gorman in that it is evasive and misleading, and while nominally designed to prevent only negroes voting, really gives very dangerous powers to the election judges, under which they can easily throw out a very large proportion of the foreign vote, or, in fact, of the native American vote. At any rate, it has excited the indignation of the best and ablest men in the democratic party in Maryland, including our excellent and popular Gov. Warfield, Attorney General William S. Bryan, and last, but not least, United States Senator Isadore Rayner, who, elected only last winter, in defiance of the wishes of Gorman, has had the moral courage as well as political wisdom to throw down the gauntlet, and not only to come out against the amendment in a ringing letter, but has challenged his colleague to publicly debate the question with him. To this challenge Gorman has yet sent no answer, but there is little hope he can be induced to accept it, as in the only public speech he has made since he received it, he ignored it, contenting himself with a few side blows at his colleague by insinuation, not even mentioning his name. This is characteristic, as Gorman has never fought in the open in all the years in which he has been the marplot of Maryland politics. . . .

The campaign is very interesting, and it is pretty generally believed that the amendment will be snowed under here in Baltimore, where not only almost the entire republican and independent democratic vote, but a very large foreign vote will be cast against it. The only chance of its success lies in the intense anti-negro prejudice in the counties, and the fact that the ballots in many of these counties have, under sanction of democratic boards of supervisors, been prepared in a manner designed to confuse the negroes and all illiterate voters. It cannot be carried on a fair vote and honest count, but we do not always get these in the state of the Lords Baltimore. If Gorman is whipped this time, it will be a body blow, as southerners do not admire a man who is afraid to accept a challenge to debate, and who always prefers to fight under cover.

1. The Poe Amendment, proposed by Maryland Democrats and defeated in a 1905 state referendum, was intended to restrict the voting rights of African Americans.

Springfield Republican, **December 6, 1905**
"Notes on Baltimore Affairs
What the Maryland Election Result Means—Personal—the Southern Section
  of the State
Correspondence of *The Republican"*

Baltimore, Md.

The results of the state election in Maryland were, on the whole, eminently satisfactory in that, by the defeat of the so-called "Poe amendment," by a tremendous majority, a knock-down blow was given to Senator Gorman and the old democratic "ring," who had hoped not only to disenfranchise the negroes, but to perpetuate themselves in power. This is not a republican victory, but a victory for Gov. Warfield, Senator Rayner and the better element of the Democratic Party, who can, and probably will, make a wise use of it. The Legislature has a small democratic majority, but it is thought that enough of its members are independent democrats, who will stand by our excellent governor in his efforts for good legislation, to foil the schemes of Gorman and his retainers. Senator Rayner has a splendid opportunity to become a real leader if he will only "paddle his own canoe."

Baltimore is developing some excellent literary and dramatic critics in its local newspapers. . . . On the Herald, the dramatic critic, Henry L. Mencken[1] is only 27 years old, but is writing dramatic criticisms of a very high order that are attracting much attention. He is a native Baltimorean, whose verses have been printed in the magazines often under pseudonyms, and a published collection of them has been well received. J. W. Luce and Co. of Boston have just published his latest book, 'George Bernard Shaw: His Plays,' a vigorous and candidly written account of this meteoric Englishman and his plays. The book shows Mr. Mencken's strong vitality, and his friends believe that he will make for himself a name in literature. He has had offers to remove to New York, but so far the Herald has succeeded in keeping him here, where just such fearless critics are much needed.

A recent visit to southern Maryland, once the section where more negroes were held in slavery than anywhere else in the state, finds many sections still sadly in need of moral culture. People are courteous and kind to a fault, but it is almost impossible for the state's attorneys to convict any white man of crime in the local courts, owing to the fact that the people are so closely bound by family ties that it is very hard to get a jury on which is not some relative of the accused who will never find him guilty. The climate is delightful, the soil fruitful, but immigration is sadly needed to infuse more diversity in the population.

1. H. L. Mencken (1880–1956), known as the Sage of Baltimore, was a renowned and controversial journalist, satirist, linguist, and literary and social critic. Goddard, who reviewed plays for the *Baltimore Tribune*, recommended Mencken for a job at the newspaper.

Springfield Republican, April 6, 1910
"Affairs in Maryland
Sins of the Late Legislature, the Negrophobe Law the Chief of All
Correspondence of *The Republican*"

Baltimore, Md.

We in Maryland have just got rid of a Legislature that goes out of existence with maledictions well deserved for the most part, for its sins of omission and commission—almost its only work being the establishment of a public utility commission. . . . This and the passage of a pure food law are on the credit side, and that this much was accomplished is due very largely to the Baltimore Sun and Baltimore News, each of whom fought manfully for these measures. Per contra the Legislature refused to pass a "loan shark bill," which was prepared by the counsel employed for the people by the *Baltimore News*, and which was a much-needed measure for relief of the poorer classes from the extortions of the little corporations which make small loans on chattel mortgage and personal property. But a far worse offense than this was the passage of the so-called 'Digges law,'[1] which, taking its name from the obscure country member who introduced it, reopens the question of endeavoring to suppress the negro vote, despite the 15th amendment. The plan of openly challenging the constitutionality of that amendment was originally devised by some Baltimore lawyers of high standing, who are negro haters, and whatever their legal acumen, show mighty poor judgment in again raising this unfortunate issue. So many good democrats of cool judgment here are satisfied that this renewed agitation is most unwise, that I sincerely believe that this third attempt to suppress the negro vote in Maryland will be snowed under at the polls when the voters get a chance at it.

1. The Digges Amendment was an amendment to the state constitution proposed by the state Democratic Party that would have used property requirements and other provisions to effectively disenfranchise many African Americans, immigrants, and workers. The amendment was passed by the Maryland General Assembly and approved by Gov. Austin L. Crothers, but it was rejected in a 1910 state referendum.

Baltimore Sun, **April 9, 1910**

"Captain Goddard Praises Those Who Announced to the Sun Their Opinions of the Digges Bills."

Baltimore

Messrs. Editors:

Now that the fight is won and Governor Crothers has risen to the occasion, it is not well to prolong the controversy over the Digges bills, but it can do no harm to give a little praise for some of the good work done in this matter not only by The Sun but by its correspondents.

To my thinking, those life-long Democrats who expressed themselves so courageously in your columns all deserve much praise, and I think especial credit is due to Secretary of State Winslow Williams [Maryland secretary of state, 1908–12, Democrat, appointed by the governor], who was in a very delicate position in the matter, and to Miss Florence Mackubin [(1866–1918), portrait artist and writer of historical papers]. Mr. Williams rose above partisanship and Miss Mackubin, a representative of one of our oldest and best Maryland families, showed such breadth of view and moral courage in her recognition of what is due to colored men of character and intelligence that she almost converts me to the cause of women's suffrage. Whether or not she is an advocate of that cause I do not know, but I do know that she showed by her letter to *The Sun* that she had more good sense and good judgment than had some of our prominent lawyers, who let their prejudice run away with their brains.

Springfield Republican, **November 23, 1910**

"Affairs at Baltimore

Election Results and Trickeries—Old Prejudices Still Linger

Correspondence of *The Republican*" [Excerpt]

Baltimore, Md.

In the recent election Maryland went "with the swim" and the Democrats gained two congressmen, electing only one Republican, Thomas Parian, in the 5th district, and he certainly ought to have been elected, for, in the first place, he is an abler man than his opponent; and secondly, in that special district the Democrats resort to every possible species of trickery to defeat a Republican, owing to the fact that this special district has a very large negro vote, and the Democrats think themselves justified in using "trick ballots," so that it is almost impossible for a man of average intelligence to vote correctly. They allege that the whites must not submit to negro domination; yet it is a fact that in no part of the state is there so good a colored element. For example, in Charles County, where the negroes are in a majority and almost all Republicans, no colored man has ever yet been tried for rape, and very many of the darkies are property owners and well-behaved citizens. But the old prejudices in Maryland are so strong that our city papers are even now printing protests against including *"Uncle Tom's Cabin"* in our public libraries, and men who should know better write of dear old Mrs. [Harriet Beecher] Stowe[1] as if she was animated by a virulent prejudice against the people of the South, which assertion, as one who knew her well, I can emphatically deny. Mrs. Stowe was a good woman and felt in her heart that slavery was a curse to our country, and wrote *"Uncle Tom's Cabin"* in that spirit. It is not a great book in literary construction, not as good as her later novels, but written as it was for a good purpose, it was a great tract and served its end for, as I heard Gen. Dan Tyler say to her years ago, it did much to bring on the civil war, which was inevitable and ended in the right way. One can say and believe all this, and yet pay high tribute to the South and its gallant soldiers, among whom I count some of my dearest friends. . . .

1. Stowe was a friend and neighbor during Goddard's residence in Hartford, 1867–82.

Baltimore Herald, **November 19, 1906**

Baltimore

To the Editor of The *Herald*

Though there are many persons in this city who consider the presentation of such plays as Mr. Dixon's "The Clansman"[1] ill-advised and in evident bad taste, there are also many who challenge the right and resent the assumption of the *Herald* to either charge directly or by insinuation that the audiences who saw and applauded the performances at the Academy of Music last week were either ignorant or possessed of "debased tastes."

While not doubting the inexpediency, to say nothing of the evident bad taste shown in presenting plays possessing a tendency to awaken animosities or to widen the breach between the North and the South, it is in even poorer taste for a newspaper to indulge in unwarranted editorial travesties upon audiences of intelligent and representative men and women because, forsooth, they fail to agree with some tyro district reporter who is 'assigned' one night in the week to "criticize" the work of men of the intellectual caliber of Mr. Dixon, [and such actors as Richard] Mansfield, [Sir Henry] Irving, [Joseph] Jefferson or even a [Edwin] Booth.[2]

Without knowing who the *Herald's* verdant critic of 'The Clansman' was, it were safe to say that his ability to judge of the element of viciousness in the play was on a par with his good taste and ability in 'sizing up' Baltimore audiences.

I have often questioned, Mr. Editor, the expediency and element of common fairness in the system of some Baltimore newspapers in assigning effervescent boys and intellectual striplings to criticize the dramatic and musical work of artists of conceded strength and merit in their respective professions. But when these bud-ding journalists are accorded carte blanche to place reputable audiences under the ban of their displeasure and brand them as ignorant, vicious and as lovers of the 'bizarre and sensational,' then the snapping point has been reached in the latitude to be given to the jealously guarded fiction of the freedom of the press and the right of intellectual featherweights to sit in judgment on the artistic product of the master thinkers and doers of the world.

Following your editorial idea and the caustic criticism of the Herald's hyper-critical critic of "The Clansman" to this logical conclusion, the negro waiters who, at a local hotel, refused to wait on the advance agents of Mr. Dixon's play because of their disapproval of it, are superior in good taste and in judging of what con-stitutes the common elements of viciousness to the thousands who saw and applauded the performances at the Academy of Music last week.

"The Clansman" has been designated by an editorial writer of no mean repute as "recalling attention to an important chapter of American history, and under the form of a novel tells a true story of the great movement by which the lives and property of the Southern people were rescued from the corrupt domination of carpet-baggers, scalawags and ex-slaves."

Doubtless had the play met the approval of your critic, the audiences that so enthusiastically greeted it would have been reported as "great outpourings of rep-resentative people to learn of conditions prevailing in the South immediately after the war."

Now, Mr. Editor, I am of the decided opinion that the play of Mr. Dixon, like that vicious travesty upon common sense and common decency, "*Uncle Tom's Cabin,*" (though I would not for a minute compare the one with the other, because Mr. Dixon's work is a true picture of past conditions, while Mrs. Stowe's book is not) should be barred from the stage. The tendency is to embitter and keep alive sectional prejudice, things to be frowned upon and checked whenever they appear.

But I must, Mr. Editor, ask for a square deal for the people in all matters where the question at issue is one of purely individual judgment. I was willing to con-done the sin of the boy critic when he launched his broadside of jumbled sarcasm and assumed wisdom against the poor clansman and his benighted, ignorant and vicious audiences, but when I read your editorial in Sunday's paper I was forced to exclaim, Et tu Brute, and made haste to register my feeble protest—and here it is.

—One of the "Vicious."

1. Thomas F. Dixon Jr., angered by the 1901 staging of *Uncle Tom's Cabin*, wrote the novel *The Clansman: An Historical Romance of the Ku Klux Klan* in 1905 and then a play, *The Clansman*, in 1906, in response. Dixon's works attempted to justify Klan violence in restor-ing Southern white supremacy after the Civil War and Reconstruction. D. W. Griffith drew heavily upon *The Clansman* for his classic 1915 film, *Birth of a Nation*.

2. Edwin Booth, a noted nineteenth-century Shakespearean actor, was the older brother of John Wilkes Booth.

Baltimore Sun, **November 13, 1908**

To the Editor:

. . . Many years ago the late lamented Lawrence Barrett [nineteenth-century actor] predicted to the writer in the presence of a lady who was notoriously an active Southern sympathizer in the Civil War, that plays relative to the Civil War or its issues could never succeed all over our country; that in one section or another antagonisms would be aroused that would kill the play. Not four weeks after that utterance, "*Held by the Enemy*" was played here and both the lady with her Southern and the writer with his Northern views, both attended and equally enjoyed the play in which the principal officers of both the Union and Confederate armies never forgot to be gentlemen.

In "*The Warrens of Virginia*," now running at Albaugh's, the sympathy of the spectators is entirely with the old Confederates, not only because of the expert character acting of Frank Keenan and Charlotte Walker, but because the Union officer is guilty of an inexcusable piece of treachery to his Southern host. It is inexcusable under the circumstances, although it leaves open the old, old questions as to whether a gentleman could ever act as a spy and as to how far deceit is excusable in war, and I have heard very gallant, high-minded soldiers of both old armies of North and South justify both the spy and the deceit; but to most men of honor, the duty, if such it be, is obnoxious. Still the play is intensely interesting and exceptionally well acted.

Springfield Republican, **November 19, 1906**
"Matters in Baltimore
Correspondence of *The Republican*"

Baltimore, Md.

. . . Among recent deaths in Baltimore have been those of two men of rather remarkable characteristics, with each of whom I served upon a grand jury where each did excellent service. One was white, the other colored. The first was Col. Mark Alexander, an ex-confederate officer with a fine war record and delightful personality, who died in his 84th year. The second was William H. Bishop, one of the old-time negroes, who was over 70 and who had been a barber in Baltimore for over 50 years. Those who insist that a race issue is inevitable in the South would alter their opinion if brought into personal contact with such representatives of the two races. Col. Alexander never demeaned himself, but was ever and always a gentleman, loved by every man on the jury, and Mr. Bishop carried himself with such propriety of bearing at all times that not once during our four-months' service was there the slightest objection made to his presence at any of our official dinners at the various state institutions by a single member of the jury, although among them were some of the bitterest partisan Democrats in Baltimore. It is curious to recall in this connection that, on our visit to the Maryland house of refuge, one of our white members partook so freely of liquor that he had to be carried to the train on our return.

During our service together Col. Alexander told me an illustrative story of the character of a prominent and well-beloved southern planter whose biography attracted much attention and commendation some 20 years ago. The book represents its hero as almost absolutely free of earthly faults. Col. Alexander's comment on it was that the hero was a dear old gentleman, but an excellent poker player, and said that among his own cherished possessions was a beautiful gold-framed miniature of John C. Calhoun [early nineteenth-century U.S. senator from South Carolina, vice president, fierce defender of slavery and the right of secession], given him by the hero of the book, who knew that Col. Alexander had been a lifelong admirer of the southern statesman, while he himself was a devoted partisan of Henry Clay [early nineteenth-century House and later Senate leader from Kentucky, known as the "Great Compromiser" on the slavery issue]. When Col. Alexander expressed his gratitude he inquired, "How in the world did you come by a miniature of a man you so detested?" With a quiet smile the donor replied: "I won it poker on a Mississippi river steamboat before the war from a gentleman who had nothing else to pay with."

Baltimore News, November 7, 1907

"'One of the Great Defeated' Recites Some of His Pleasant Memories of the Campaign"

Baltimore

To the Editor of *The News*

If *The News* will for once waive its rule of charging for obituary notices, may I trespass upon its space for a few reflections on the late campaign?[1] As one of the great defeated I have no axes to grind, rewards to offer or punishments to inflict, and hence ought to treat of the campaign philosophically and impartially.

Personally, I found the campaign an interesting and moderately exciting affair. It was pleasant to meet and study so many varied types of people, and while one grew tired of hearing his fellow candidates make the same speech at so many different times, they probably were just as tired of hearing me. It was rather amusing, however, to hear one chairman of a meeting say at the close of my speech, "We have been quite entertained with some good logic, and I will now introduce you to a gentleman"—then a long pause and reference to a list of our candidates in his hand—'Mr. Robert H. Smith.'

Of the Republican speakers three impressed me always as not only able and clear, but as always sincere. The three were Mr. [George R.] Gaither, Mr. [Robert H.] Smith and Frank Wachter. The two first named were ideal candidates for the positions for which they were nominated, and Maryland is the loser by their defeat; for, while not all alike, each is a fine specimen of the Maryland gentleman, who is honest in his convictions and fair and courteous in expressing them. Mr. Wachter I heard for the first time in my life, and I now understand his strong personal following, for what he says rings true, and one feels that he is listening to a man who believes what he says and who will keep his word to his auditors. He has his faults, for he is human, but he has won my regard and respect in this campaign as have few Maryland politicians in all the years I have lived here.

Of the Democrats of Maryland the one whose course in this campaign has won my undying respect is Attorney General William S. Bryan. Were I a member of his party and a member of the new Legislature, he is the one man of all others I would vote for United States Senator, for he has shown more pluck and real moral courage than any man prominent in the State since those fearless champions of what they believed right—Henry Winter Davis and S. Teackle Wallis—each of whom made some mistakes, as has my good friend Bryan, but each of whom never flinched from his ideals. Other men in the Democratic and Republican parties in Maryland have fallen in my esteem in my campaign, but Mr. Bryan, as is his want, has proved himself a greater man than he claims to be.

The average ward leader and political managers have impressed me more favorably than I expected. Not one asked me to do ought that seemed unfair or dishonorable. Not one Republican asked me whom I favored for United States Senator nor to grant him a favor if elected. On election night I watched the count at a precinct where I was warned that one of the Democratic judges was a bitter partisan. So he was, but in the seven long and weary hours of counting I did not see him do a mean or tricky thing, and I believe he wanted a fair count. He lost his temper at times, but so did all the rest of us, and it would take a mighty good Christian not to do so when he is a judge or clerk under our present election law.

Personally, I have to thank the hundreds of independents who voted for me, although I was a candidate of the party to which most of them are generally opposed. Notable among these are some very dear old Confederate soldiers, who proved as magnanimous in peace as they were brave in war. The press without exception treated my candidacy kindly, and even if one old friend wrote me that 'It gave him positive pain' not to support me, I recognized his honesty of purpose and kindness of heart. But 'all's well that ends well' and it's up to our Democratic friends now to prove themselves worthy the powers with which they are again entrusted. For me, I resume business at the old stand.

1. Goddard had just been a Republican candidate for the Maryland legislature. The campaign, his first and last for public office, was run on the platform "An Honest Election Law" during the Progressive era, when Theodore Roosevelt was president. Goddard, along with his GOP running mates from Baltimore, lost.

Springfield Republican, November 10, 1907
"Election Results in Maryland
Some Features of Its Conduct—Gov. Warfield—the United States Senatorship
Correspondence of *The Republican*"

Baltimore, Md.

The state election in Maryland resulted in a democratic victory for the whole state ticket by some 8,000 majority. To the casual observer here this seems a deplorable result, as the Republican candidate for governor, George R. Gaither, was not only infinitely superior in almost every respect to his Democratic opponent, the successful candidate, Judge Crothers [Austin L. Crothers, Democratic governor of Maryland, 1908–12], a comparatively obscure country politician, ever a sub-servient follower of the leaders of our bourbon democracy, but was pledged to give the state a new election law. That such a law is sadly needed is evidenced by the fact that while Judge Crothers is given some 4,000 majority in Baltimore alone by the returns, it is said that the official count will show that in the same city some 5,000 ballots were thrown out as defective. As one who watched the count from 5 P.M. to midnight in one precinct where but 226 ballots were cast, of which some 15 were thrown out, I do not claim that one party suffered much more than another in the city at least, but I do claim that a ballot, 19 by 25 inches, containing some 128 names, from which but 27 are to be voted, is, to say the least, undemocratic. These ballots have to be cast in small booths of little more than their own width, lighted by flickering candles, and must have no marks on them other than a small cross after the name of the candidate voted for, and must be folded exactly as when received, else they are thrown out. Is it a wonder then that in some precincts it took nearly 24 hours to count the vote, and that nearly all judges, clerks and watchers (of whom I was one) were in a state of mind that the word "acrimonious" faintly describes.

The new Legislature is democratic by a three-fifths majority, and it is boldly avowed will promptly try to pass some act that will do away with negro suffrage to the greatest degree possible. This has long been the desire of our old bour-bon democratic ring, and now that it is in the saddle it is bound to attempt this result. . . .

Baltimore News, **November 4, 1901**

"The President and His Obligation"

To the Editor of the News

Does not your correspondent, Mr. Alfred W. Gieske, let his impulses run away with his good judgment in his letter to The News of the 21st? Simply because President Roosevelt invited to a private dinner the most distinguished colored man in America [Booker T. Washington], the man who has done more than any other to solve the troublesome race question in the South by his advice and example in teaching the negro to attend to his duties and not be forever bothering about his fancied rights or social privileges, Mr. Gieske advises Marylanders to "vote for so-called corruption, vote for so-called ring rule, vote for bossism, vote for anything—but don't, if you have pride left, vote for the negro!" Frankly, now, Mr. Gieske, is this good logic, or even common sense?

The writer has served on two Grand Juries in the city of Baltimore, each of which was presided over by a strong Democrat, and on each of which were some of the best and ablest business men in the city of Baltimore. On each of these juries was one colored man. He went with us on our visits to all State institutions which are visited by such Grand Juries, at nearly every one of which a dinner was served to which we all sat down. I do not think that any gentleman on those juries ever thought that he had demeaned himself by this act—and we were from all political parties—or that by this act we proved ourselves in favor of general social intercourse between the different races. We recognized an official obligation, as I think the President has just shown that he recognized a moral obligation to the ablest representative of the colored race. Surely, it is unwise "to bite off one's nose to spite one's face."

24

Concerning Booth, Fritchie, Randall—
Setting the Record Straight

Springfield Republican, March 7, 1907
"John Wilkes Booth's Body"

Baltimore, Md.

To the Editor of *The Republican*

Anent the revived discussion of the body of John Wilkes Booth, concerning which mention has been made in your columns, the present writer is able to furnish some corroborative evidence to the letter of Col. Frank H. Phipps [commandant of the Springfield Armory, Springfield, Massachusetts, 1899–1907] in the Army and Navy Journal. Col. Phipps is correct in saying that the body was brought to Baltimore near the close of Andrew Johnson's presidency, at the request of Edwin Booth. It was interred in the Booth lot at Greenmount cemetery. As Col. Phipps says, 'The remains were identified beyond question.' Among those who identified them was the late John W. McCoy of Baltimore, a wealthy philanthropist, who died here several years ago, who told me that he had known Booth well, and was requested by the family to examine the body after it was brought to Baltimore, and did so, satisfying himself beyond doubt. Edwin Booth was a man who had more than his share of 'Fortune's buffets,' but in nothing does he command admiration more than the magnificent manner in which from first to last he bore the crushing blow of his brother's awful crime. Hamlet himself had not so heavy a burden and cannot command our sympathies as does this peerless gentleman who was his greatest representative. . . .

Baltimore Sun, March 9, 1910
"Barbara Fritchie" [Letter to the *Baltimore Sun*]

Despite your warning in your editorial as to the eternal controversy over Barbara Fritchie I must ask a little space in the matter . . . you must let me emphatically deny the assertion of Mr. Connelly [John Robert Connelly, Democratic candidate for U.S. House in 1908, later elected for three terms] of Kansas, that she was not "a patriotic Northern woman."

It is true that her family were Southern sympathizers, but years ago I satisfied myself by conversation with her old friends and neighbors that she was ever devoted to the Union cause and did keep the Stars and Stripes flying from her window all through the Confederate occupation of Frederick. The writer was in Frederick with the Union Army a few days after the alleged incident and has talked it over with Col. H. Kyd Douglas of Stonewall's staff; with Capt. W.G. Fitch of the Fourth Connecticut, and many others who were at Frederick in 1862, and none of them ever questioned Barbara's loyalty to the Union.

Springfield Republican, January 22, 1907

"A Letter from Baltimore

Three Notable Men Who Have Recently Died, 'Father' Stafford, J. R. Randall and E. C. Stedman

Correspondence of *The Republican*"

Baltimore, Md.

Death has been busy at work in the early days of the new year among literary men of distinction known to the writer. Rev. T. J. Stafford, better known as 'Father' Stafford, the eminent Roman Catholic divine of Washington, D.C., for many years a resident of Baltimore, was not only a great preacher but by all odds the most eloquent lecturer on Shakespeare in this country since the death of "Bob" Ingersoll. . . . He was a born orator, and a never-to-be-forgotten incident was at a Loyal Legion[1] meeting at Washington during the McKinley administration when the speakers of the evening were Secretary [of State Elihu] Root, Congressman [George A.] Pearre of Maryland and Father Stafford. President McKinley came in while Father Stafford was speaking, and after we had all risen to salute him, motioned to the speaker to continue his speech. With a graceful bow the orator gave the president in two minutes a condensation of what he had said in 10, and then went on to a strain of lofty patriotism that aroused intense enthusiasm. He could have been a great actor, but preferred to be a faithful servant of God. . . .

A member of the same communion and a devoted member, was the late James R. Randall, author of "Maryland, My Maryland," of which I have long possessed an autograph copy given me by Mr. Randall when literary editor of our Republican organ, the *Baltimore American*, on which he succeeded the late Maj. Inness Randolph, an ex-confederate soldier. It is rather singular that Randolph was also the author of a famous confederate song of which I also have an autograph copy from its author, entitled, "I'm a good old rebel and I do not give a damn." Randolph was impulsive to a fault, and one could easily have a "row" with him, but he had lots of human and a genial temperament, so his little "tiffs" were soon over and he was very popular.

Randall, on the contrary, was less impulsive but brooded over annoyances and grievances and took life hard. He always felt that circumstances prevented his developing his poetic genius and was somewhat sore about it, hence did not make many friends while in Baltimore, although he had some very strong ones, notable our present United States senator, ex-Gov. William P. Whyte, who is just now endeavoring to have published a collection of Randall's poems. As to his famous war song, I have ever felt it owed much to the success of that famous Baltimore belle, 'Hetty Carey' (the late Mrs. Martin) in finding such suitable music for the words. Randall had much of sorrow in his life, but of his devotion to the Christian faith of his historic church there is no shadow of doubt, and his name will ever be associated with that of the Maryland he loved so well. . . .

Last, but by far the greatest of the literary trio who have just left us, is Edmund C. Stedman, whom I have known and loved for half a century, ever since he gave the little Connecticut city of Norwich a clever weekly paper, the Norwich Tribune. In the red days of the civil war he was ever a kind friend and adviser to the young officer on his visits to Washington, when he was in the office of Attorney General [Edward] Bates. . . . As literary critic, as poet, and as a true-hearted gentleman I have ever admired him. . . . He embalmed Norwich with his verses, "The Inland City," years and years ago, and today he is embalmed in the hearts of all who knew and loved the man. . . .

1. The Military Order of the Loyal Legion of the United States, now a hereditary organization, was established by Union officers on April 16, 1865, the day after President Lincoln's assassination.

Springfield Republican, July 12, 1911
"Some Maryland Authors
Correspondence of *The Republican*"

Baltimore, Md.

Dr. Henry E. Shepherd of Baltimore has written, and the Whitehall publishing company of New York has just published, an interesting little volume entitled *Representative Authors of Maryland.* The author is well adapted to his work by his past experience as a professor at the Baltimore City College and the superintendent of public instruction at Charleston, S.C.

One of the longest articles in the book is upon James R. Randall, author of *Maryland, My Maryland,* of whom Mr. Shepherd is a most extravagant admirer. To my thinking, the praise is immoderate, for while *My Maryland* was undoubtedly a brilliant inspiration on the part of young Randall, it has always seemed to me as if its success turned his head. Mr. Randall was a devoted Roman Catholic, and his private life was irreproachable, but to me he never seemed companionable, but rather impracticable and hard to get along with. However, Mr. Shepherd greatly admires all his poems, as do many other Marylanders. To my thinking, Dr. John Williamson Palmer, favorably noticed in the same book, was a more pleasing writer, and his poem, 'Stonewall Jackson's Way,' written to the sound of the guns of the battle of Antietam, is an admirable war poem.

25

Racism and Veterans' Poverty in Hartford

Springfield Republican, May 31, 1875
"Our Hartford Letter
From Our Special Correspondent"

Hartford

Decoration day[1] was very little of a holiday here, today. Barring the national banks and a few of the insurance offices, no places of business were closed, and there was very little of a procession, the Grand Army posts and Colt's band in their elegant new uniforms forming about all there was. At the hall where the flowers were received there were a few workers from the Grand Army and a few lady assistants. To me it seems a pity that the observance of the day is not more general, for I do not agree with the idea advanced by some that the day should cease to be observed, as tending too much to keep up bitter memories of the war. On the contrary, it seems to me that over the graves of our dead old animosities soften, and we none the less honor the memories of our own dead when we acknowledge the honesty and courage of those who fell in the opposing ranks.

That this sentiment is felt in the South is a matter of personal knowledge, for, a few years ago, I witnessed the decoration of the graves of the dead confederates in the beautiful cemetery at Montgomery, Ala. . . . The same night, I heard a southern orator, in the course of his memorial oration, pay a most handsome tribute to the federal dead who fell in the war.

And so I have ever found it, North and South, that those who fought on either side are most free of animosity toward their old opponents, and most heartily approve of decorating the graves alike of friend and former foe. This leads me to believe in "Decoration Day" as a day that should be generally observed North and South in decorating the graves of all who fell on either side, not as a day of partisan rejoicing or of mourning over a "lost cause," but a day sacred to the memory of all who held that

> *"What was worth living for*
> *Is worth dying for too."*

Surely such a day is one that may be very fruitful of good in its suggestions to the rising generations, while it will ever be a grateful task to honor the memories of those who died for us, even though at the same time we throw a few flowers on the graves of our old foes.

    1. Decoration Day originated from the postwar practice of decorating with flowers the graves of fallen soldiers in both the North and the South. It was officially proclaimed on May 5, 1868, by Maj. Gen. John Logan, founder of the Grand Army of the Republic (GAR), and was first observed on May 30, 1868, at a ceremony at Arlington National Cemetery. In 1882 the name was changed to Memorial Day, and soldiers who had died in other wars were also honored. In 1971 Memorial Day was declared a national holiday to be observed on the last Monday in May. However, the Sons of Union Veterans of the Civil War, the successor organization to the GAR, continues to observe Memorial Day / Decoration Day on May 30.

Winchester (Va.) Leader, June 7, 1895

"Address Delivered at the National Cemetery, May 30th, by Capt. H. P. Goddard, Formerly of the 14th Ct. Volunteers" [Excerpts]

In August 1863, Gen. William H. Lytle [major general of the militia, poet], of Ohio, a gallant soldier of the Union Army, who soon after gave up his life to his country on the battlefield of Chickamauga [September 20, 1863] delivered an address to his old regiment, the 10th Ohio, that for the future it would be for the survivors of the Union Army "to heal up the sores and scars, and cover up the bloody footprints that the War will leave, to bury in oblivion all animosities against your former foe; and chivalrous as you are brave, standing on forever stricken fields, memorable in history, side by side with the Virginians, Mississippians, and Alabamians, to carve on bronze or marble, the glowing epitaph that tells us of Southern as well as Northern valor."

    In the winter of 1892–93, Col. Charles Marshall, formerly of the staff of General Robert E. Lee, who was the only Confederate present at the historic interview between Lee and Grant at Appomattox Courthouse, Va., closed his story of the surrender to an audience of three hundred gentlemen at the University Club in Baltimore. His closing words were, "and this was the end of the Army of Northern Virginia, for which, in view of all that has happened since, I can honestly say, let us reverently thank God."

    Standing here today in this historic city which changed hands so frequently during the Civil War that the inhabitants scarce knew from day to day which flag would be floating over the town ere night, I feel that I cannot find better texts than these two utterances, one from the chivalric Northern soldier, whose poem, "I am dying Egypt, dying," has given him literary renown, and his gallant death for the cause he loved has given him patriotic memory, the other from the present leader of the Baltimore Bar, whose war record as a gallant wearer of the gray gave him military fame that is not forgotten in the City in which his brilliant eloquence and sterling patriotism makes him now one of its esteemed citizens. If such devoted lovers of the Union as General Lytle could make such predictions while in the "Valley of the shadow of death," and such brave Southerners as Col. Marshall can now so loyally accept the results of the struggle, surely my comrades and friends under whatever flag you fought, you and I stand here without regret or shame this day when we gather to honor the dead who died for the Union cause.

Memories of a past, now a third of a century gone, rise before me today, as I doubt not the companion pictures can be evoked by all the veterans among my hearers, whether the scene be located with mine in New England, or in the mountains or valleys of your Old Dominion, or elsewhere in one common country.

One such is a patriotic and loving mother standing on her vine and rose-covered porch in the fairest city of Connecticut on an August morning in 1862, pressing to her heart her son as she bids him farewell, fearing that it may be forever, but commanding him to the God whom she served, as thousands of other mothers serving the same God were sending their boys on the same errand in the same spirit.

Another picture is of a seagirt isle in the Pacific [Hawaii], where under the shadow of a lofty volcanic mountain, with cocoanut palms tossing their branches in the air and the soft ripple of the sea breaking on the coral reefs heard in the distance, two northern-born lads just emerging from their teens are parting, one [Capt. John D. Griswold, 11th Connecticut] facing eastward to give his life to his native land, the other [Goddard's older brother, 1st Lieut. Alfred Mitchell Goddard, 8th Connecticut] for the time facing westward to close up his business and then hie homeward on the same patriotic errand. It was the last who wrote that moonlight night at Honolulu these touching words on his parting with a friend whom he never again met on earth, each giving his life on the Southern battlefields in the cause of the Union.

"If God spares our lives, we shall sometimes meet again, and have, I hope, an unblotted story to tell of the years flown by since we parted. In a spirit of honest emulation let us each do the work before us, rejoicing in whatever success the other is blessed with. Such a friendship will be a jewel for us to wear undimmed and unbroken forever and ever."

Ah, my friends of the South, who have sometimes been taught that the armies of the North were composed mostly of foreigners and hirelings, do these words not ring true in your ears as they do in mine, and do not my brother who wrote, and the friend to whom he wrote, commend your honest admiration?

I do not have to wait for your reply. I know the warm hearts of the Southern born too well, and in these years since the war have seen too many proofs of your generous admiration for honest, faithful service in the Union army. In my adopted city of Baltimore, the veterans of the Massachusetts Sixth, fired upon in the streets of that city in 1861, were in 1880 greeted with cheers and welcome by the citizens. Just as in 1885, the R. E. Lee Camp of Confederate veterans from Richmond were the honored guests at a reunion of the Society of the Army of the Potomac, in the same city.

That the women of the South felt, and even now feel, more keenly than the men the passions of the Civil War is true and most natural. It is most of the noblest attributes of woman that she always feels deeply and keenly, and it is harder for her to forgive and forget than for men who can fight out their battles physically, as she cannot do. Your own city of Winchester offered notable examples of devotion to the cause she loved on both sides during the war. It was a Winchester woman, loyal to the Union, who gave General Sheridan such important information upon one occasion as to lead him to seek out and reward her after the close of the war. It was another Winchester woman, now residing in Baltimore, whom today I count as one of my most devoted friends, who gave the Union generals stationed in the Valley more trouble by her secret services in behalf of the Confederate armies than a company in arms.

That brave men honor and respect each other is a well known truth. This it is that enables us to understand Col. Marshall's reply, made at my own table, when talking of the surrender to a distinguished Union officer who asked, "Colonel, how was Gen. Grant's conduct towards Gen. Lee at the time?" His reply was, "Had Gen. Grant and the Union officers present on that occasion rehearsed their conduct in advance, they could not have borne themselves in a manner better calculated to spare the feelings of their conquered foe."

It is because for thirteen years past I have broken bread and eaten salt with those against whom I have battled, that I, a soldier of the Union, still loyal to the old flag and surer than ever that I was on the right side during the Civil War, come to the beautiful Shenandoah Valley today to help you strew with flowers the graves of our honored dead, and at the same time pay a foeman's tribute to the bravery of those who wore the gray.

In the month of May, 1886, I stood on a green hillside in the cemetery at Anniston, Alabama, by the grave of Gen. Daniel Tyler of Connecticut,[1] a gallant commander of the Union army, who lies buried under a granite block that crowns the hillside overlooking the beautiful and prosperous Southern city which it is his greatest honor to have founded [Tyler founded Anniston, Alabama, in 1883] on soil that his sword helped to preserve to the Union. As I gazed upon the lovely prospect before me of a city encircled by green hills and smoke of whose furnaces, the rattle of whose looms evidence its material prosperity, while its handsome school house, its picturesque inn, its beautiful church, its stately homes bore witness to its moral and mental growth, I thank God that out of the red flames of the Civil War, He had in His own time and way brought peace and prosperity to the Southern people.

In the fall of the same year I attended a political meeting at Charles Town, West Virginia, in your own Valley, and there in the very building in which John Brown was condemned to death, I heard the present Postmaster General [William Wilson][2] whose honesty no one will dare to impugn, and who is, to my thinking, the most eloquent speaker in his State, speak of "the great curse of African slavery," and at the same time assure his colored auditors that that question and that of their right to suffrage was settled forever. As I listened to this frank and manly utterance of that old Confederate soldier, I felt proud that he was my fellow countryman and rejoiced in the patriotism of a section of the country that could produce such statesmen.

When Connecticut soldiers seek their homes and found cities in Alabama, and when Virginia orators who fought for the "lost cause" can condemn the curse against which John Brown fought and gave his life, the lessons taught are not hard to learn.

1. Goddard served on Tyler's staff during the summer of 1863.

2. Wilson, a Democrat, served as postmaster general 1895–97. He was born in Jefferson County, Virginia, and had been a private in the Confederate army.

Baltimore News, May 29, 1900
"Welcome from Kind Hearts
A Baltimorean's Experience at the Fredericksburg, Va., Reunion."

To the Editor of *The News*

The reunion last week of the Society of the Army of the Potomac at Fredericksburg, Va., was such a notable event and of such historical interest as to justify, in the opinion of the writer, a letter to *The News* from an old soldier of the Union Army that he may pay due tribute to the genuine hospitality and chivalry shown by the inhabitants of that beautiful and historic city to himself and his compatriots. I doubt if there are many instances in history where the veteran survivors of a bloody civil war have been so warmly welcomed and so kindly treated by the people of a city which suffered so much from the effects of the battle fought within its limits and from the constant state of war that prevailed in and around it for four long years.

The weather was perfect during the two days of the reunion, the city was gaily decked with flags and red, white and blue trimmings. Nearly every house in town was thrown open for guests, and in many cases the hosts were those who had been in the Confederate service, or were the descendants of such Confederate veterans.

At the Courthouse on Friday the address of welcome was made by Mr. St. George R. Fitzhugh, the most prominent lawyer in the city, who served in the Confederate Army and was so badly wounded at the time that for weeks he hung between life and death. I have attended many reunions North and South since the war, and have heard many similar addresses, but never one in better taste, in more appropriate language, nor delivered with as much earnestness and sincerity. He conquered the hearts of all the Union veterans in attendance and was equally applauded by the citizens and ex-Confederates. This address should be published in full and in due time find its place in the school books North as well as South.

President McKinley was in attendance with nearly all his Cabinet, and was most cordially received. He seemed deeply impressed by Mr. Fitzhugh's oration. The speech of Gov. Tyler [James Hoge Tyler, Virginia governor, 1898–1902 and private in Confederate army] of Virginia and the response of General McMahon [John E. McMahon, colonel of 164th New York Infantry] in behalf of the Army of the Potomac were in good taste, but the regular oration that followed by Gen. Daniel E. Sickles was far too long and wearied the auditors. General Sickles seemed to realize this and occasionally laid aside his manuscript to tell a good story, and these diversions were more enjoyed than was the oration.

On Friday afternoon the Fifth Corps dedicated a monument on Marye's Heights, the scene of the hottest fighting on December 13, 1862, which is now a National Cemetery. The exercises were interesting and the speech of the Secretary of War, Mr. Root, in accepting the monument, admirable, as are always the utterances of that gentleman. The writer was especially interested in going over the field of Marye's Heights with the Secretary of the Navy [John D. Long, secretary of the Navy, 1897–1902] and a brother officer of his own regiment, Lieut. Charles Lyman, late Civil Service Commissioner, now of the Treasury Department. This was the third time in which Mr. Lyman and myself have been together on that historic field—once during the battle of December 1862; again at a Confederate and Union reunion (when Generals James Longstreet and John Newton were the principal figures) in 1884 and now in 1900.

The writer cannot close this little sketch of a most interesting trip without paying personal tribute to a charming Virginia lady, Mrs. E. J. St. John, the widow of a distinguished Confederate engineer officer, and connected with several prominent Baltimore families, who is now the mistress of the famous Herndon mansion, which is over 140 years old and is one of the handsomest and most interesting houses in Fredericksburg. With that house are associated memories of the gallant Captain [William L.] Herndon of our navy, who went down on the Central America in 1857 after saving all the women and children and many of his male passengers by putting them in small boats. It was his beautiful daughter who became the wife of President Arthur, and it is to her memory that her devoted husband erected that beautiful window in St. John's Church in Washington, as it was there that her lovely voice in the choir first attracted his attention and led to their acquaintance. With this house the writer had most pleasant memories when in Fredericksburg with General McDowell and the Harris Light Cavalry in the spring of 1862. That it was not much injured is a matter of sincere rejoicing, and that it is now in such good hands a matter of congratulation. The present hostess won the hearts of all her guests in 1900, as the fair Misses Herndon were wont to do in the old days before the War.

Springfield Republican, October 28, 1872
"Hartford's Social Problem
A Live Pulpit on the Question of the Hour
The 'Christian Expediency' Dodge—a Generous Plea for Equal Rights
  by Rev. E. P. Parker
Correspondence of *The Republican*"

Hartford

The "Christian expediency" question got into at least three of our city pulpits on Sunday. Rev. Mr. Johnson of the colored church and Rev. Dr. Cone of the South Baptist church animadverted severely upon the unchristian action of the Women's Christian association in deciding that "Christian expediency" prevents their admitting colored women to their privileges. At the South Congregational church, Rev. E. P. Parker preached from the texts: "For there is no respect of persons with God," and, "But if ye have respect to persons, ye commit sin." He declared that the majority of this association, by their action in this matter, had placed it in radical disagreement with God. It had committed what he could not consider other than an inexcusable blunder, which brings great scandal upon the church and cause of Christ. After reciting the facts in the case, he said that the decision of the managers "repeats in its feeble way all that was ever alleged against the notorious Dred Scot decision" [1857 Supreme Court decision that blacks could not be citizens and that Congress could not limit slavery in the territories]. There were not wanting brave women at that meeting who stood up to denounce and oppose the decision. I thank God that I can say that there was not found one woman from this church in the association who did not protest against this decision.

These ladies have all resigned their positions in the association, and the speaker hoped that no lady of this church would accept the vacated posts.... He wished the ladies of this church to keep out of the association as long as it holds its present policy....

The attempted justification of the majority that white women would keep away if colored women were admitted, he pronounced a timid, groundless fear. But even if temporarily this proved the case, a bold, brave persistency in the right would have conquered this prejudice.... Whence the authority or right to discriminate between young women on the ground solely of the blood that is in them, when the fundamental article of faith is that God has made them of one blood, is their common Father, and that in Jesus Christ, whose name the association bears, all the race masks and external diversities are annihilated.

Passing on the show how this shameful prejudice against color is dying out the world over, the speaker said, Christianity takes things as it finds them, not to bend to them and leave them as it found them, but to bend them and make them what they ought to be. Apostolic Christianity scorned this wretched policy of expediency—how Christ and Paul loathed it! This prejudice is a small kind of contempt of Almighty God, who sent these people of color into the world. Admit their humanity and there is nothing more to be said. Their persons are sacred—their place is any place they can deserve—any place they could occupy were they white and not black. They have God for their Father, Christ for their Savior, and unless we can treat them as our brothers and sisters in Christ and put honor upon them and bear their burdens also, we cannot be God's children. . . .

The sermon was listened to with close attention by a large and approving audience. Rev. Mssrs. Twichell of the Asylum Hill and Wines of the Fourth church are in full sympathy with Mr. Parker in his view, as in the main are their churches. Dr. Burton of the First church is now en route from Europe, but his voice will be sure to be lifted up on the same side. It is generally believed here that the association, always heavily in debt, will go down under these needed rebukes, unless it changes its policy.

Springfield Republican, March 15, 1872

"Letter from Hartford

An Afternoon with the Poor—Where and How They Live—Their Hardships and the Measures of Relief

From Our Correspondent" [Excerpts]

Hartford

"But where do your poor folks live?" is the remark attributed to some new-comer, Mark Twain, when he had been shown about the wide streets of our city, and driven through some of its attractive suburbs. Elegant residences, palatial insurance offices, beautiful churches, had passed in review before him, but nowhere had he seen any indications of poverty. The response to this question your correspondent will try to give today, having spent this bleak March afternoon with Father Hawley, our city missionary, who has been a most faithful worker in this city for the past twenty years, and who has done his work so as to win the confidence of all the wealthy and charitably disposed citizens, while the poor people love him like a father. . . .

Our last call was at the home of a soldier—a brave, manly youth, who went out in the 16th Connecticut, leaving a young wife to the care of his country and his

God. Bearing himself modestly, yet gallantly, through the arduous campaigns of his regiment, he was captured with them at Plymouth, N.C. A year at Andersonville and other rebel prison pens ruined his constitution, and though full of grit to the last—he went back to his regiment and came home with them—he has never been well since. He crawls to a factory, where he earns some two dollars and a half per diem, though he is compelled to lose much time from ill-health. His rent is $3 per week, and he has a wife and two children to support. Already the family has begun to consider the question of sending the elder daughter, a pretty and very efficient child just entering her teens, to work in the factory. She delights in her school, and gives much promise there, and greatly dreads factory life. Yet a stern necessity may demand it of her, to help herself and family as her father's health declines. This man is so proudly sensitive that he stays away from Grand Army meetings, and, with his wife, from church, because they cannot appear as he wishes. A false pride, is it? If so, it is but an unhealthy form, growing out of an invalid life, of that delicate sensitiveness which has led so many of the heroes of our late war to sink out of sight in their home life.

... Our two hours' stroll this afternoon has revealed cases of distress within five minutes' walk of the residences of wealthy citizens, such as we believe are scarce conceived of by a very large number of very good and respectable people. Just at this time there is a missionary society being organized by our most prominent ladies to help this very class of people. If this letter shall serve to indicate to any how vast a work such a society may find to do, and to show that we do have some "poor folks" living in Hartford, it will have served its purpose. The field promises rich reward to any desirous of doing God service in doing service to His poor children.

Springfield Republican, October 19, 1906
"A Summer on the Sound Coast
Correspondence of *The Republican*"

Baltimore, Md.

A summer spent in Connecticut by a native of the state who for a quarter of a century has made his home in Maryland has afforded him an opportunity for some comparisons between life and manners in two sections of our country, barely 250 miles apart, that he has found of much interest. *The Republican* once said editorially that the South had by far the most romantically interesting history of any section of our country. This utterance I have frequently quoted and indorsed. In some respects it is true, for the South has had more class and race contrasts, a more genial climate and larger leisured class, yet I am not sure the statement is an absolute truth. It would be difficult to find any section with more picturesque scenery and more interesting history and legends than the country about the mouth of the Connecticut on either side of the river. Familiar with this country from childhood, I divided my time this summer mainly between Lyme and Say-brook. It has been a delight to find that while each town has been rejuvenated, nei-ther has lost its old charms. . . .

Contrasting these old Connecticut towns with the old settlements in Maryland and Virginia, I find in the North infinitely better roads and streets although more cursed with these infernal automobiles, which I agree with the Hindus in Kipling's books in calling 'devil carriages,' much handsomer houses, better laid out and kept-up grounds, and far more evidence of prosperity. One notes without regret the absence of negroes and of any class that seem to be suffering in poverty. Lyme is a temperance town and no liquor is ever sold there, nor did I see any drunk there or any man under its influence in a whole summer. At Saybrook liquor is sold, but not offensively and one sees little evidence of it except at the hotels, and not much there.

In most southern summer resorts a total abstinence town does not draw many visitors. There may be plenty of total abstainers, but such do not look askance at their fellow guests who sample the seductive julep, and far too often too much whisky is consumed, and the effect of its open sale is too apparent. Yet in the South one finds far more uniform courtesy of manner, not only from hotel keepers, but from all public officials. There is no rule without exceptions, but this summer's observation leads me to conclude that in the country towns energy and zeal are more notable in the North, politeness and courtesy in the South. When a public official combines these qualities, he can rest assured he will be popular regardless of his political affiliations.

An interesting incident of my vacation in Connecticut was attendance at the reunion of my old civil war regiment, the 14th Connecticut, at Hartford, September 17. This reunion was especially interesting for the reason that the long-talked-of regimental history had been completed, and the volumes were delivered to the members of the regiment. This work has been well done, but should have been done many years ago, as the official records show that the 14th Connecticut sus-tained the largest percentage of loss of any regiment from the state. It participated in a great many engagements and had some excellent officers and very gallant pri-vate soldiers. I met Capt. William Murdoch, like myself one of four to whom it fell to bear off one of the battlefields of Virginia a very gallant officer [Col. Sanford Perkins, regimental commander, battle of Fredericksburg, December 13, 1862] who had been dangerously wounded, and who never was able to return to duty, but later regained his health for some years, and then became insane and died in an asylum, when Capt. Murdoch and myself were bearers at his funeral, 12 years from the day we took him off the field. We commented on the irony of fate that spared his life from lead, to end it in an insane asylum. "Count no man happy till he dies."

A visit to Norwich called up memories of boyhood days when Donald G. Mitchell, Edmund C. Stedman and Daniel C. Gilman were its literary lights. It is a matter of rejoicing that I have met all these literary veterans this summer, all in good health and all still loyal to the old creed of every Norwich man, that it is the most beautiful city in our country. It certainly would be hard to name one that combines so much that is picturesque with so much that is of historical interest. The Norwich Free Academy reaches its 50th anniversary, October 21. As one of its first class, who tremblingly entered its walls on that October morning in 1856, I can but pay loving tribute to the founders of this splendid institution and to its first principal, Prof. Elbridge Smith, a scholar, gentleman and Christian whom generations of pupils loved and honored. Never could there have been a teacher better qualified to implant literary tastes.

Springfield Republican, **October 5, 1907**
"Connecticut Revisited
Correspondence of *The Republican*"

Baltimore, Md.

. . . Early in September Gen. William A. Aiken entertained at his Norwich home the members of the executive committee of the national civil service reform association, and from Attorney General Bonaparte [Charles Joseph Bonaparte, attorney general, 1909–13] down all were charmed at the loveliness of this city, which seems one great park in which the residents live at peace with God and each other. . . .

. . . At the post office I found that most gallant of civil war soldiers, "Billy" Carruthers, whose whole life is a romance, who was wounded so often and so severely that in 1863 the army surgeons gave him 30 minutes to live, which minutes, thank God, have run to over 44 years. Today he is one of the most active and efficient post-office officials in Connecticut. I wish they had his like in some of their rural towns where courtesy is not always the rule.

The only fly in the pot of cream in my summer at Norwich was an innkeeper, who thought he knew how to make a mint julep. I asked him, and in reply he said, "After your crushed mint, sugar, ice and liquor, put in some soda or seltzer water and a slice of banana." He insisted that he got that recipe from a "Kentuckian." Needless to say, I did not try that prescription.

As we grow older we indulge more and more in reminiscences, but one delightful experience must not be omitted, and that was the reunion of our old 14th Connecticut regiment at Middletown, where Color Sergeant Hirst took from his pocket a fragment of our old colors, which we all kissed with a fervor of passion that is hard to describe. Our old comrade, J. E. Stannard, is telling well the story of this grand old regiment in the columns of the *Sunday Republican*, which should be secured by all its surviving members—all too few.

Norwich Bulletin, March 2, 1908
"Speech to Norwich Board of Trade Dinner"

Norwich, Conn.

. . . The gazetteers speak of Norwich as a manufacturing city, and your cotton and woolen goods and superior firearms are known the world over, yet for me one of the great charms of Norwich has ever been that its factories do not obtrude, as they do in so many Connecticut cities, but are hidden away so that the ordinary visitor sees them not. Instead, he sees your beautiful rivers with their romantic Indian names, your terraced hills, your wide and beautiful streets, your stately elms, and your handsome houses on unfenced green lawns, that give the whole city the aspect of a park. Never have I seen a city of such size, where so many people live in such apparent comfort, with such quiet, well-bred manners, not ashamed of their vocations, but not always "talking shop" as they do in some of your noisier neighboring cities.

As I study its history from the earliest settlement, nearly 250 years ago, I become more and more convinced that the greatest product of Norwich has been its men and women. For this let us reverently thank God.

Without retracing our steps to those earlier days in your notable history, "When Tracy [Paul Tracy (1783–1861), U.S. Navy officer], Griswold [Roger Griswold, Connecticut supreme court judge, 1807–9, governor, 1811–12 (d. 1812)], Huntington[1] and Trumbull [Jonathan Trumbull, governor of Connecticut, 1769–84] were judges in the land," let us pass in rapid review the names of a few of your citizens whom I personally knew and honored. First and foremost is that of the grand and courtly head of the house of Buckingham, your great war governor, whose name and fame are indelibly stamped on the history of Connecticut and the hearts of its civil war veterans.

Of the many good soldiers and sailors that the old town sent forth to battle in those dark days of strife, were my old chief, Gen. Dan Tyler, Generals Henry Birge and Edward Harland (the last name still one of your honored citizens) and that grizzled old sea-dog, Admiral [Joseph] Lanman.

Of the comrades of those days, none were braver or more faithful than your present postmaster, "Billy" Caruthers. . . . Then there were your . . . great manufacturers and merchants, such as John F. Slater (whose benefactions have done so much to help that terrible negro problem). . . .

Your newspapers have had far more than local reputation ever since that December day in 1858 when Ike Bromley founded *The Bulletin*. Of this witty and brilliant journalist, with whom I was closely associated for several years, I could tell you stories by the hour, but it would need his own presence and tongue to make them effective. . . .

I was a local reporter upon *The Bulletin* from March 1859 to February 1862, when I entered the union army. After my return I was local and later night editor till May 1867.

The most interesting experience in retrospect is my reporting the speech of Abraham Lincoln at the old town hall, where he addressed the Republicans of Norwich upon the issues of the day in March 1860. No soldier of the civil war can ever forget the faithful services done for him at home by such women as Mrs. Eliza Perkins and Miss Lizzie Green.

1. Samuel Huntington (1732–1796), of Norwich, was a signer of the Declaration of Independence, 1776; president of the Continental Congress, 1779–81; the first presiding officer of the Congress of the Confederation in 1781; and governor of Connecticut from 1786 until his death in 1796.

26

Impressions of a Changing South— Industry, Charm, and "Savage" Women

New Hampshire Journal, September 17, 1874
"Speech at the Re-union of the 14th Connecticut, Soim Rock, New Haven"

Captain Goddard delivered the following address, which for the excellent sentiment it expresses, we publish in full. The captain addressed his comrades as follows:

On a lovely spring afternoon in the month of May, 1870, I stood in the beautiful cemetery in that fairest of Alabama towns—the city of Montgomery. There was gathered there a large proportion of the entire population for the purpose of decorating the graves of the confederate dead, some 600 of whom repose therein, the city having been the site of one of the confederate hospitals. Over more than one hundred graves grouped together were little wooden head boards with that most touching of inscriptions—the simple word "Unknown."

As the procession filed past, what was my surprise and pleasure to see its leader, the ex-rebel General Clanton,[1] fiercest of confederates, accompanied by the captain commanding the federal forces at that post, the grey suit worn by the former touching the loyal blue uniform of the latter. Together the two soldiers, conqueror and conquered, watched the strewing of the graves.

As the odorous magnolias, spotless camellias, delicate jasmines, and gorgeous roses of every hue were showered upon the graves to the sweet, sad strains of music that filled the air, my heart was strangely stirred, and as my eyes fell upon the long row of "unknown" graves, that had been strewn with nought but blood-red roses, the green mounds were changed to a field of rose-beds, on which the setting sun smiled lovingly as its rays lingered on the sloping hillside, whence the gorgeous color seemed reflected back into the western skies. As I gazed on this scene, I queried whether the time had not come for the north and south to bury ancient animosities as they had buried their victims. This impression was not lessened when the same night I attended a memorial service to the confederate dead, and heard an ex-rebel soldier deliver a finished oration, urging that the remains of the confederate dead at Gettysburg be brought into southern soil, but paying a most handsome tribute to the northern valor displayed on that battle field, and praising the north for building a monument to the memory of its heroes who died there.

Seems to me, my comrades, that it is not an unfitting time for us to consider whether—as citizens—if not as an organization, it is not most meet and proper for us to resolve to do all in our power to bury past hates, and unite heartily with all honest men who seek to foster good government and free institutions.

I know full well that this may seem to some an unpropitious time to urge gentle charity and friendship to old opponents when ill-advised men have thrown one of the loveliest of southern states into apparent opposition to federal authority. But let me tell you that we at the North are not blameless that they have done so. By sustaining a set of wanton adventurers who were no more true Unionists than camp-followers were true soldiers, we have helped to lay upon them a grievous burden.

God knows that on the old issues I am unchanged. An older brother and my dearest friend—our own dear Captain Nichols, God rest his soul—lie in graves to which rebel bullets sent them. When I forget them or the cause for which they died, may my right hand forget its cunning. Yet, from the depths of my soul, I believe that could there be any of our dear dead ones speak, they would say to us "forgive as ye hope to be forgiven."

Comrades: You have proved yourselves faithful men in miles of heavy marches and tiresome labors, enduring sleepless picket duty and rationless bivouac and braved weeks of skirmishes and on thirty-three bloody fields of battle—will you now prove yourselves also generous men by holding out the olive branch to any and all of our old opponents who are seeking, blindly mayhap, but yet seeking, now to secure both in state and nation for themselves and their children that for which we fought and our brothers died—a free, honest and stable government that shall insure for each and all life, liberty and the pursuit of happiness. Let us show them that the brave can be tender, gentle and generous as well as daring, remembering that—

> "They banish our anger forever
> When they laurel the graves of our dead."

After brief addresses by other members of the society, hearty cheers were given for the old "fighting" Fourteenth, good-byes were said, and the comrades dispersed, hoping to meet again on the next recurring anniversary.

1. Maj. Gen. James Clanton was among a group of six Confederate veterans who founded the Ku Klux Klan in Pulaski, Tennessee, on December 24, 1865. Clanton headed the Klan until he was killed in a street duel with a U.S. Army colonel in Knoxville, Tennessee, in September 1871.

Springfield Republican, March 25, 1870

"**Trip Down South**

**The Southern Women Still Savage—Southern Contempt for Carpet-Baggers—
Some Notable Characters**

Correspondence of *The Republican*"

Selma, Ala.

Dear *Republican*: The more one sees of the South the less he feels disposed to express fixed opinions concerning the present condition of the people. There are so many different stand-points from which to look upon affairs here that it is difficult to hit upon that one which affords the most correct view. The writer's present opinion, however, is that the temper of the male population here has improved of late and that were it not for the women of the South a northerner would find a permanent residence here pleasant. As it is, northern men are succeeding in business here wherever they have taken hold of it—but socially, they and their families receive no recognition from the old society here. I was present at a theatrical performance a few nights since, which was attended by more representatives of the old families than I had before seen in public. The utter scorn with which the ladies looked upon the northerners present was as marked as were their shrugs when they looked toward the galleries where sat several mulatto belles in full evening costume, opera cloaks, frizzled hair and all. During the evening the orchestra gave the audience "Dixie," and the burst of applause from below showed that the "lost cause" was still uppermost in their hearts.

For the carpet-baggers and scalawags these southerners assume to have more contempt than for the negroes themselves. It is partly merited, although some of the former are loyal, gallant gentlemen, who did their duty handsomely in the Union army and, settling here, have accepted offices which they alone of the loyal men were intelligent enough to fill. And among the "scalawags," so called, are several ex-confederate officers that the love of office (and office-holding is very dear to a southerner) has drawn over to the radical party. Yet many of the ruling class are demagogues of the worst kind who, like a certain Massachusetts congressman[1] we wot of, are a curse to any party that contains them.

Attending court here a day or two since, I found three negroes on the jury, a white woman in the prisoner's box and a negress on the witness stand. The woman was convicted of being accessory to a rape on a colored woman and was sent to state prison for life. At a political meeting here a few nights since, one of the candidates, a white, in the excess of his radicalism, invited the whole party out to drink, saying, "By G—d, you must all go and all drink before me. I will drink gladly out of the same tumbler—after you." He was most righteously rebuked by an aged darkey, who in reply, said that "the day had passed when that sort of thing would influence the colored men, and that if Mr. —— had no better argument than that, he had best go home."

There are some notable characters resident here. Gen. Joseph E. Johnston resided here till recently and still has an office here, though making Savannah his headquarters. He has the general agency for the southern states of the New York Life and Liverpool, London and Globe fire insurance companies. He is much respected everywhere and is building up an enormous business. Strolling down the road last night with an ex-confederate officer, I saw him tough his cap to gray-haired, spare figure in an old United States officer's overcoat that rode past us on a quiet little mare. "Who's that?" "That's Gen. [William Joseph] Hardee." At once I recalled the man, whose tactics were wont to bore and perplex us in the early days of military life. Hardee's war record was not very brilliant, and he is doing better as a cotton warehouseman than he did as a rebel major general.

Were you to drop into one of our large wholesale stores here, you might notice at the book-keeper's desk a dark-complexioned, very whiskered, thin, sullen looking man. A close look would show that he was evidently in poor health. Rarely speaking to any one, he pursues his usual work with a settled melancholy that leads you to wonder at his history. That man's name is Samuel Arnold, whose name will be remembered as one of the conspirators against President Lincoln. As you remember, the result of the trial was to send him with Dr. [Samuel] Mudd and [Edman] Spangler to the Dry Tortugas[2]—where an attack of yellow fever impaired his constitution. He was pardoned and released some two years since, and leaving Baltimore, his home, has secluded himself here. Though loath to allude to the subject, he still asserts his entire innocence of design on the life of Mr. Lincoln, though he did know of the plot to capture the president, and was an intimate friend of the chief conspirator, Booth. At any rate his part in the affair was such that he has become

> "Lost to life and use
> And name and fame."

1. Probably a reference to Benjamin Butler, the Civil War major general and Massachusetts congressman, 1867–75 and 1877–79, who was a vociferous supporter of Radical Reconstruction.

2. The Dry Tortugas, an island chain off the Florida Keys, housed Fort Jefferson, which served as a federal prison during and after the Civil War.

Springfield Republican, June 25, 1905

"Memorials of the Old South

What to See in Richmond, Va., as Set Forth by a Sympathetic Northern Visitor.

**Correspondence of *The Republican*"

Richmond, Va.

June is not a month in which a northern-born man would usually elect to visit the capital city of Virginia, but if one is called here during that month in the year he cannot fail to find much of interest. Leaving Baltimore by any of the fine large steamers of this line at 5 P.M., one sails down the Patapsco, past Federal hill, historic Fort McHenry (now used only as a supply depot under a small guard), past Fort Carroll in the center of the river—with its two tremendous guns now pointing out to sea, although the fort was first planned during the civil war with its guns to point toward Baltimore—but 'we have changed all that' since 1865; and still on past the two formidable forts, Howard and Armstead, that now guard either short of the Patapsco as it enters the bay. Thence one has a lovely quiet night sail down the beautiful Chesapeake and up York River, with its historic points of interest, such as Yorktown and Gloucester. If one rises betimes he sees the fine monument erected at Yorktown on the site of Cornwallis's surrender, and after a comfortable breakfast on the boat on Chesapeake bay luxuries and Virginia fruit, reaches West Point, so well known in the civil war times, and leaving there by rail at 8 A.M., after a ride through an interesting country historically, finds himself at Richmond at 9:30, ready for a day's enjoyment.

If our visitor is limited in time he best first of all visit the old capitol building, where the confederate Congress sat during the war, although just now it is being thoroughly repaired and partly reconstructed. The superb statue of Washington by Houdon is just now not being shown, owing to the work being done, but on the esplanade just outside the beautiful square which contains the capitol is that wonderful equestrian monument of the father of his country in bronze, executed by Crawford, rising from a pedestal of granite on which stand bronze figures of Henry, Jefferson, Marshall, George Mason, Thomas Nelson and Andrew Lewis—a sextet of notables that would be hard for any other state to match.

Next one should be driven down historic Franklin Street, with its beautiful brick residences all standing well back from the street, and as a rule covered with vines that at this season are beautiful in their verdure. Such names as those of Cabel, Carter, Lee, Wickham, Haxall, Gordon, Poindexter, and other historic Virginia names, are those of the residents on this beautiful street, on the porticos of which sit lovely Virginia women, all in white garments at this season, while numberless black nurses trundling white babies in the baby carriages indicate that 'race suicide' is not one of the dangers in Virginia, for which let us be reverently thankful—for, northern born as I am, I have rarely met as fine a type of manhood as is in evidence among the young men of Virginia at this present hour. No longer the idler, born with a gold spoon in his mouth, the large majority of young men in Richmond work, and work hard, for their living. In fact, to my thinking their office hours and court hours are too long, much more so than in the sister city of

Baltimore, which has of late years grown to be more like the great northern cities in this respect.

Above all praise is the charming courtesy of manner that one finds here at the courts, shops, hotels and wherever one wanders. It enables one to understand that Virginia pride of birth, at which we sometimes have been wont to smile when too loudly proclaimed, but which one finds in Richmond to have behind it a spirit of 'noblesse oblige' that is delightful to find in this rushing, whirling 20th century civilization, and which is too often sadly lacking in the metropolis of the new world.

Next the visitor should be all means visit Hollywood, that most picturesque and entrancing of burial places. Here one wanders among the beautiful hollies that give its name to the place, to find everywhere the graves of and monuments to the great dead of Virginia. Two presidents, Monroe and Tyler, rest here. There is a very handsome statue over the grave of Jefferson Davis, looking over the tawny James to the city where his hopes were finally dashed. Close by is a lovely marble monument to his beloved daughter, Winnie, 'the daughter of the confederacy,' and not far away is the as yet unmarked grave of the gallant soldier of two wars, who honored both the blue and the gray uniforms he wore, Fitzhugh Lee. The writer, standing by his grave, could but be mindful of how he said to me, years ago, when I called upon him as governor of Virginia, with a letter of instruction from Col. Charles Marshall of the staff of his great uncle, Robert E. Lee: "Col. Marshall tells me that in war days you spent years trying to get into Richmond. We will treat you so, sir, that I hope you will wish to remain here for years." J. E. B. Stuart, the other great confederate cavalryman, is buried not far from Gen. Lee, and there is a fine large vine-covered pyramid to the unknown confederate dead; but I think I was more impressed by the graves of two soldiers, side by side, one marked by the stars and stripes, the other by the stars and bars. The same sun and same moon shine on both, and the graves might be, nay, are they not, those of two brothers?

Moreover, there is a confederate museum in the old executive mansion of the confederacy, their soldiers' home, and any number of interesting churches, including St. Paul's, with its fine memorial windows to Lee and Davis, both of whom worshiped there; old St. John's church, where Patrick Henry made his great speech ending, "Give me liberty or give me death;" Belle Isle, with its sad prison memories, but now the site of flourishing iron works in part, and green in verdure elsewhere.

As one drove about the streets of this historic city on the lovely moonlight nights this month, it brought back never-to-be-forgotten memories of the old civil war days, when "On to Richmond" was the war cry, and when after four years of sturdy defense it at last surrendered. As I look up at the heroic equestrian statue of Gen. Robert E. Lee, which commands the admiration that all now yield to his sterling character, whether one fought under or against him, I was minded of a story once told me by a descendant of Gen. [John B.] Magruder to the effect that when a young girl in Richmond, at the outbreak of the war, heard Gen. Lee say to some officers who were predicting the early triumph of the confederacy, "Before that time comes we shall be living on nuts and acorns in the mountains of Virginia." Knowing this, as he must, who can doubt that he was honest in the course he espoused; and, in view of his manly course after his surrender to his magnanimous opponent at Appomattox, who can fail to recognize that America has a right to be proud both of conqueror and conquered in that final strife of the war.

In closing one must pay tribute to the bounteous hospitality shown those who call with introductions by such gentlemen as that famous old teacher and peerless scholar, Col. Gordon McCabe, the lifelong friend of Tennyson, whom he visited yearly the last 15 years of the poet's life, and at the Westmoreland and Commonwealth clubs, each of which occupy one of the stately homes of old Virginia, and at each of which one meets soldiers, scholars and gentlemen so entertaining, and mint juleps so enticing, that it is hard not to yield to the invitation once given by Gov. Lee, "to remain here for years."

27

An Honest Republican
Revolted by the 1876 Election

Times, November 25, 1876
"A Republican Speaks Out"

Hartford, Conn.

To the Editor of *The Times*:

It has not been often that I have had occasion to agree with the editorial views of The Times, but you "hit the nail on the head" when you said, in a recent issue, that if the position of parties were reversed, and the Democrats were attempting to throw out the honest vote of a state and change its footing to elect a President, the opposition would be holding public meetings of indignant remonstrance all over the country. As one who voted for [Ohio] Governor [Rutherford B.] Hayes, but desires to see no man unjustly deprived of his honest rights, I can but compliment the Democratic leaders for their coolness and forbearance at this juncture. Believing, from a careful study of the situation, that [New York] Governor [Samuel J.] Tilden is fairly chosen President of the United States, I can but think that the honest masses of the Republican Party are really desirous that the present period of anxiety and doubt should be ended by a fair declaration of the vote as cast. That "intimidation" and persuasion have been used by both parties, south as well as north, is unquestionable; but that the Democratic Party is wholly responsible therefore is known to be sheer nonsense to any one conversant with the politics even of our own state. Certainly the Democratic Party is not responsible for the intimidation and suasion used in more than one election in the manufacturing districts of eastern Connecticut, or in the Portland quarries.

In the late campaign one prominent Republican stump speaker boasted to the meeting, just before the Indiana election, that the Republicans have "got Indiana all fixed, as there was one thousand niggers in Indianapolis who looked so much alike that no inspectors could tell 'em apart, and that these one thousand could be depended upon for four thousand votes." The speaker justified this intended fraud on the ground that "down South they won't let the niggers vote as they wish to, so they must vote triple and quadruple in Indiana."

I cite the above merely to show that chicanery and fraud in elections is not at all contained to one party, as too many of my good Republican friends seem to believe. Granted much that is claimed by strong partisan Republicans, I have yet to find a fair-minded man who believes that a legal majority of the votes in Louisiana were not cast for Governor Tilden. . . .

In the midst of the anxiety, excitement and doubt that prevail on all sides, and allowing for the disgust that it seems to me all honest men must feel at the legal tricks and subterfuges that the Republican managers are resorting to, it is a comfort to find men like Wade Hampton[1] showing such forbearance, and men like Mr. Hewitt of the National Democratic Committee summing up his advice in such golden words as these: "We have full faith in the justice of the people of the United States, and we do not entertain a doubt of the final verdict which they will pass on the occurrences of the last two weeks. This verdict will surely vindicate their majesty and reestablish this government upon a lasting basis."

If honest-minded Republicans will have courage to express their true sentiments as frankly and consistently, we need never despair of the republic.

1. Wade Hampton, a Confederate cavalry lieutenant general and postwar governor and senator from South Carolina, was known as the Savior of South Carolina for his opposition to Reconstruction.

Times, November 28, 1876
"A Correction by Captain Goddard
The Plan of the Late Campaign"

Hartford

To the Editor of *The Times:*

Please correct a typographical error in the letter published last evening. I wrote that a prominent Republican speaker boasted to the "*writer,*" not "to the *meeting.*" as your compositors made it. As a rule politicians don't say such things in public; yet, lest I should be accused of betraying a confidential communication, I would state that the remark was made in an open and above-board discussion with the gentleman in question, who seemed to fear that I was not a supporter of Governor Hayes because I expressed the honest doubt that I felt as to his success under such auspices as those with which the campaign was conducted. He seemed anxious to convince me that Hayes was bound to be elected, and that no growling at the conduct of the campaign was permissible.

One word more. While I am fully aware that the personal views of a single private citizen are of little comparative consequence, I would say to those who seem to doubt the "Republicanism" of the writer, that I have never yet voted for a Democratic candidate for a national office, nor ever failed to vote for the Republican competitor. In state and local politics, no party ties ever have, nor, God willing, ever shall prevent my selection of (what I deem) the fittest regardless of any party lash.

At this juncture my only wonder is that the honest clergymen and bankers who, like myself, voted for Hayes but assert that they believe Tilden elected, do not say in public what they avow in private. But party ties seem to bind with iron links those whom they enfold.

Hartford Courant, **November 1, 1880**
"For Garfield
An Admirer of Hancock Decides to Vote against Him
The Effect of Forgery as a Campaign Argument"

Hartford, Conn.

To the Editor of *The Courant*:

At the reunion of our old regiment at Rockville in September, I said to my old comrades: "Don't let them make you believe Hancock a secessionist—or Garfield a thief."[1] At that time and until within a week it had been my intention to vote for our old well-beloved corps commander, Hancock. The events of the past week, however, have led me to believe that if General Hancock can permit the circulation of a letter[2] as genuine that General Garfield has pronounced a forgery, he must have succumbed to the influence of men from whom for his own sake he ought to be speedily rid, for I cannot believe that General Garfield is a liar or that General Hancock believes him to be such. However, as a true friend of General Hancock, it seems to me that the kindest act I can do him now is to oppose his removal from the regular army in which he has ever been recognized as a model soldier and gentleman, and rid him of the tricksters who are trying to make base use of his noble name and fame.

1. Goddard's regiment served under the popular 2nd Corps commander Maj. Gen. Winfield Scott Hancock, who ran as the Democratic nominee against the Republican James A. Garfield.

2. About two weeks before the 1880 election, a New York newspaper published a letter allegedly written by Republican candidate Garfield to H. L. Morey of Lynn, Massachusetts, that implied that Garfield favored a liberal policy toward Chinese immigration, which was extremely controversial among many xenophobic white Americans, especially in the West. Garfield denounced the letter as a forgery—as did most of his contemporaries as well as later historians. Hancock's refusal to do likewise offended Goddard's strong moral sense and persuaded him to vote for Garfield instead of his beloved wartime corps commander.

Springfield Republican, September 15, 1908
"Politics in Maryland
Mr. Bryan's Recent Appearance
Correspondence of *The Republican*"

Baltimore

The arrival of 'the peerless one' in Maryland, where he has made a few speeches this week, has made but a mild ripple in the quietest political campaign I have ever known in my 26 years of residence in Maryland—and everybody knows that from the foundation of the republic (and even before) Marylanders take their politics 'hot.' But, honestly, there is far more excitement over baseball here, now that, after holding and losing a National League championship, we have a local nine that is apparently to win out as champions of the Eastern league, their only dangerous opponents being those Providence "Clamdiggers," and on Saturday there were actually 20,000 people out to see two closely contested games between these two leading nines. Although Mr. Bryan spoke at our big armory last night, from which all the seats had been removed, no one claims over 15,000 to have been present during the whole evening. It is pleaded that the place was hot, crowded and uncomfortable, but so was the baseball park, and as a rule those of us who stayed away from both places were congratulated by those who did not. Yet the general verdict was that the Baltimore nine never played better, and that Bryan[1] was never less interesting. How Maryland will vote is another question. Many prominent Democrats won't vote for Bryan, but a good many are going to "hold their noses" and swallow the ticket, and I have a suspicion that the negro vote is far less surely to be depended on by the Republicans than it has been of old. Never before have I found Maryland negroes reticent, but this year they seem to keep very quiet and avoid the subject. The local leaders of both parties are not the best men in them, by a long shot, and aside from interest in the presidential candidates in favor of Taft, one would not care too much who whipped whom.

1. William Jennings Bryan (1860–1925), known as the Great Commoner, was a leader of the Populist movement of the late nineteenth and early twentieth centuries and a rousing political orator. A three-time Democratic presidential nominee, he lost to Republican William McKinley in 1896 and 1900 and to Republican William Howard Taft in 1908. He served as President Woodrow Wilson's secretary of state from 1913 to 1915.

Springfield Republican, October 1, 1908

"Hughes' Great Speech"

Baltimore

To the Editor of *The Republican*

Since that eventful night in 1860 when I heard one Abraham Lincoln, of Illinois, discuss the issues of that hour in the little city of Norwich, Ct., I have never heard a campaign speech comparable to that of Gov. Chas. E. Hughes[1] here in Baltimore last evening. For cool, calm, dispassionate reasoning it was magnificent, and I only wish every Democrat in Maryland who is hesitating as to his duty in this campaign could have heard it. Not an offensive word or bitter epithet was applied to Mr. Bryan, but the analysis of his weakness as a presidential candidate was unanswerable.

The Abraham Lincoln whom I heard in 1860 became president of the United States. In God's good time I predict that if he lives Charles E. Hughes will hold the same office. Meantime, it behooves us all to help elect the man of his choice, William H. Taft.

1. Charles Evans Hughes (1862–1948), Republican governor of New York, 1907–10, was the GOP presidential nominee in 1916, losing to President Wilson. He served as secretary of state under presidents Harding and Coolidge from 1921 to 1925 and as chief justice of the United States from 1930 to 1941.

Baltimore Sun, December 27, 1911

"Self-Respecting Union Veteran, He Thinks, Should Oppose the Sherwood
  Pension Bill" [Letter to the *Baltimore Sun*]

Sir: At a gathering of Union veterans in Baltimore several years ago, Gen. 'Joe' Hawley, then United States Senator from Connecticut, a soldier with a magnificent record in the Civil War, was appealed to to further the passage of some bill for an increase in pensions. He refused, indignantly, saying: "For Heaven's sake, don't let people think that we're all beggars."

This utterance comes to my mind in connection with the Sherwood Pension bill, which has just passed the House of Representatives, and is shortly to come before the Senate as, I understand this bill, it provides a pension of $15 per month for a service of 90 days, and $30 per month for a service of one year or more, during the Civil War. The official estimate of the Secretary of the Interior is that this bill will cost the country $75,000,000 a year.

In a recent article in the December *World's Work*, by Gen. Charles Francis Adams, of Massachusetts, who served for over three years in the Civil War, he asserts that in 1866 the total pension list was about $15,000,000, which, 44 years later—1910—had increased to $160,000,000. Concerning this General Adams writes: "No precedent exists in the history of the human race for such indiscriminate and pernicious giving as that already provided for under the existing pension laws of the United States, or for anything approaching it."

Under all these circumstances, should not self-respecting Union veterans oppose this bill, and what reasonable excuse can members of Congress of either party offer the public for its support?

Springfield Republican, December 22, 1895
"Hear What War Veterans Say"

To the Editor of the *Republican*

Let me send you a word of congratulation on the editorial in your issue of the 18th, concerning the present war craze. It is sad to see this wave of passion sweep over the country to the extent that it does. You are right in saying that those who cry for war think only of its glamour and cannot realize the extent of the horrors and suffering that would be occasioned thereby in these days of large armies and destructive missiles.

For one, I never wish to see another war, unless it is absolutely necessary for the defense of our own country or against downright wrong to morality. I am glad to say that this view of the case is that of many of the most distinguished soldiers of both armies who served in the late war and are now dwelling together in harmony in Baltimore.

28

The Civil War Redux?

Baltimore News, January 12, 1904
"A Queer McClellan Story"

Baltimore

To the Editor of *The News*

In the *Baltimore Sun* of Jan. 11 is a communication from Benjamin J. Keiley, Bishop of Savannah, Ga., who states that he was informed by the late Confederate General Longstreet that immediately after the battle of Antietam, Md., in 1862, Gen. Robert E. Lee showed to Longstreet a letter which he had just received from Gen. George B. McClellan, commanding the Union Army, proposing an interview between Lee and himself for the purpose (as Lee and others who saw the letter inferred) of arranging to end the Civil War by uniting their forces to march upon Washington and compel peace.

The *Sun* comments editorially on this communication, and apparently thinks that McClellan's suggestion was a good one.

In the communication it is stated that General Lee told Longstreet that "President Davis, and not General Lee, is the one to whom such a message should be sent," and for that reason he declined to meet General McClellan. The writer adds that McClellan's letter evidently came into the hands of Col. Charles Marshall of Baltimore, by whom it was mislaid or lost.

The present writer has never been an ardent admirer of General McClellan, but it would require very strong evidence to convince him that McClellan was guilty of the act alleged by the Sun's correspondent, which would have borne too close a resemblance to the treasonable case of Benedict Arnold in opening correspondence with Sir Henry Clinton while the former was an officer of the Continental Army.

If this astounding story is true, it can reflect only dishonor on the memory of the Federal commander and honor General Lee, who was loyal to his commander in chief, while McClellan was disloyal to his; but for one I cannot believe that, whatever may have been his ingratitude to the great Lincoln, who was ever so forbearing toward him, Gen. George B. McClellan was disloyal to his Government, as he certainly was if this allegation of the Bishop of Savannah is true. In repeated talks with Colonel Marshall on the Civil War, he never once hinted to me that he had ever heard such a story or seen such a letter.

Baltimore News, January 14, 1904
"That McClellan Letter" by John R. King

To the Editor of *The News*:

Referring to the letter of Bishop Keiley in a morning paper, relative to the letter General McClellan is said to have written to General Lee after the battle of Antietam, I must say that I was as much surprised as Captain Goddard, and could scarcely credit it. The very day of its publication I called on Gen. Joseph Dickinson, now residing in Washington, and who was General Hooker's adjutant general, and, calling his attention to the publication of Bishop Keiley's letter, asked if he had ever heard of the McClellan letter. He very promptly replied that he had not seen the Bishop's letter, but was perfectly familiar with the McClellan letter incident, as he and General Longstreet became very warm friends and neighbors after the war, and that the old General had often spoken of it, and said his copy of the letter was destroyed, with his house, by fire some years ago. General Dickinson substantiated in every particular the statement of Bishop Keiley.

General Dickinson also made the startling statement that at Antietam some of the high-ranking officers were so incensed at McClellan's delay that they went to General Hooker, who was in an ambulance wounded, and demanded that he take command of the army and move.

Baltimore News, January 12, 1904
Gen. McClellan for Peace [author unknown]

The *Baltimore Sun* of Jan. 11 says that the following communication, addressed to a gentleman in Baltimore, makes a very interesting contribution to the political history of the civil war, to the effect that Gen. McClellan in 1862 sought an interview with Gen. Lee with the supposed purpose of making peace over the heads of the Governments at Washington and Richmond:

Bishop's House
222 East Harris Street
Savannah, Ga., Jan. 3, 1904

My Dear Friend: Your letter of the 1st inst. to hand. My recollection of the conversation to which you refer is clear.

Gen. Longstreet told me more than once that immediately after the battle at Sharpsburg, or Antietam, while he was in Gen. Lee's tent, the General handed him a letter which he had just received from Gen. McClellan, the commander of the Federal armies. Gen. Lee gave Gen. Longstreet a copy of the letter and asked him to give it his serious attention, and on the following morning advise him (Gen. Lee) what he ought to do in the matter. The letter from Gen. McClellan proposed an interview between himself and Gen. Lee. Gen. Longstreet said to me: "I told Gen. Lee that in my judgment there was no other construction to be placed on it save one, and that was that Gen. McClellan wanted to end the war then and there."

Gen. Lee said: "That idea occurs to me also, but President Davis, and not Gen. Lee, is the one to whom such a message must be sent."

Gen. Longstreet took the letter to his own quarters, where he found Gen. T. R. Cobb of this State. He gave it to Gen. Cobb, pledging him to observe secrecy with regard to it, but not saying a word as to the construction he placed on it.

After reading the letter attentively, Gen. Cobb said there was no doubt in his mind that Gen. McClellan wanted Lee to help in the restoration of the Union by marching to Washington with the combined forces. Gen. Longstreet told me of the circumstances more than once, and added that he thoroughly coincided in Gen. Cobb's views, but that Gen. Lee, for the reason stated, declined to meet Gen. McClellan.

The copy which Gen. Lee gave Gen. Longstreet was sent after the war to Col. Marshall. I tried to get it from Col. Marshall, who told me he had mislaid and could never find it. I do not know, of course, what became of the original letter.

I forgot to say that Gen. Longstreet strongly advised Gen. Lee to meet Gen. McClellan in order that he might know definitely what McClellan wanted.]

Baltimore Sun, March 10, 1905

"Talked of Lee and Grant: Major Denny and Capt. Goddard at Lutheran Social Union" [author unknown]

The fine Christian character and bravery of Gen. Robert E. Lee and the military ability and magnanimity of Gen. Ulysses S. Grant were exploited last evening by Major James W. Denny and Capt. Henry P. Goddard, who spoke before the Lutheran Social Union at its third quarterly meeting, in Grace Lutheran Church, Broadway and Gough Street.

Major Denny entertained his audience with personal recollections of the Confederate commander during the time between the battle of Gettysburg and the surrender at Appomattox.

He said: General Lee was a man of fine Christian character and was one of the bravest of soldiers. He was always courteous to the men of his command, and I recall one instance where he displayed his magnanimity toward a private soldier. The man came to General Lee to complain of the treatment accorded to him by his captain.

Instead of ordering the man to report to his captain and forward the complaint through the regular channels, he listened for 10 minutes to the story of that individual private soldier, and then said, "My man, you go to your captain and tell him that I say for him to treat you better."

When we were in the Wilderness, we were set upon by a large force of Yankees. They charged down while our men were forming, and their charge broke our columns. General Lee determined to restore his line, so he placed himself at the head of a regiment and ordered them to charge. But they grabbed his bridle and told him they wouldn't budge an inch till he went to the rear. He did this, and that regiment of Virginia infantry went forward and re-established the line.

I will never forget as long as I live Lee's last order. It was at Appomattox Courthouse, after his surrender, and I've found that it has never been recorded in history. After he had surrendered in an open field, he said, "General Longstreet, form the wagons on each side of the road and march the prisoners to the Union lines. Then send word to the front to cease firing." You see, the Confederates, some of them not knowing of the surrender, were still keeping up the battle.

Captain Goddard then spoke of General Grant. He said that he first saw Grant at the Willard Hotel, in Washington. He was entering the hotel, and was pushed forward up the stairs by a great crowd of people. Being forced in an alcove, he saw that General Grant was being introduced by another officer, and from where he stood he obtained a good view of the great soldier.

"As I looked at him," Captain Goddard said, "I asked myself if there was any striking feature about him that would attract attention if one passed him on the street. At first I failed to note any, but at last I admitted to myself that Grant had the most firmly set and strongest chin of any man I had ever seen."

Captain Goddard then recalled instances of Grant's boyhood and his career throughout the Civil War. He concluded by saying, "General Lee, no doubt, had a magnificent character, but I think that General Grant equaled it." Some time after the war I invited two United States Senators and Col. Charles Marshall, of Baltimore, to dine with me. Colonel Marshall was military secretary to Lee, and witnessed the surrender. He said that all admired the Union commander when he rode upon the field, dressed in a simple soldier's blouse and without a sword, and allowed the men of the Confederate Army to take their sidearms home with them.

"Colonel Marshall was present when the papers were drawn up after the surrender, and he told us that the conduct of Grant toward the defeated Confederates made them feel as if they were the conquerors and not the conquered."

Springfield Republican, **February 26, 1907**
"General Lee and Others"

Baltimore, Md.

To the Editor of *The Republican*

The writer has always been greatly interested in the Adams family of Massa-chusetts, and was one of those who ardently hoped that the senior Charles Francis Adams[1] would have been nominated for the presidency at that ill-starred liberal Republican convention of 1872, in which the *Springfield Republican* was so much interested. He has read with attention and general approbation the published speeches of the present Charles Francis Adams,[2] and, although bearing arms against the South in the civil war, has most profound respect for the character and memory of Gen. Robert E. Lee, whom he believes to have been not only a very great warrior but an honorable, straightforward gentleman, who followed his honest convictions of duty when he espoused the cause of the South. He has read Mr. Adam's recent oration at Lexington, Va., and indorses much of what he said, and yet, I go even farther than does Gov. D. H. Chamberlain[3] in his communications to you in the line of criticism. Unfortunately I have not a copy of Mr. Adam's speech at hand, but my most serious criticism is that it left on my mind and that of others the impression that the orator not only fully justified Gen. Lee in going with the South, but intimated, to say the least, that Gens. [Winfield] Scott and George H. Thomas [both Virginians] deserved no more praise, and hardly as much, for being loyal to the Union cause after being educated and honored by the federal government.

If this was Mr. Adams' intent, I can but part company with him on that issue, for, condone or disguise it as we may, back of all questions of loyalty to state or nation was the question of African slavery, the bedrock on which the southern confederacy was founded. Mr. Adams may plead very plausibly that Lee loved Virginia the more, not the Union the less, but he never can convince many Union soldiers that the great Virginia soldiers who loved the flag and the country that had educated them, and that was fighting the battle of human freedom, more even than they did their grand old state, were not entitled (to put it very mildly) to as much honor from the grandson of "The Old Man Eloquent,"[4] who for so many years fought for the cause of human freedom on the floor of the national House of Representatives.

Let us honor southern valor, chivalry and honesty as it deserves, but don't let northern men asperse those of our southern brethren who, like Scott and Thomas in the army, and Farragut [Adm. David G. Farragut, native of Louisiana] and that other grand old admiral (now living in Baltimore in his 85th year), George B. Balch [native of Tennessee], in the navy, were loyal to the Union.

1. Charles Francis Adams Sr. (1807–1886), son of President John Quincy Adams, was a member of the U.S. House and Senate from Massachusetts before the Civil War and served as U.S. ambassador to Great Britain during the war.

2. Charles Francis Adams Jr. (1835–1915) served in the 1st Massachusetts Cavalry, 1861–65, beginning as a lieutenant and ending as a brevet brigadier general. After the war he was a historical writer and president of the Union Pacific railroad.

3. D. H. Chamberlain, a Republican, was elected governor of South Carolina in 1874, with the support of many Democrats as well as the solid support of African American voters. In 1876, following the Hamburg and Ellenton massacres of blacks and other acts of intimidation by bands of white vigilantes, Chamberlain was defeated by the ex-Confederate general Wade Hampton.

4. President John Quincy Adams was elected to the U.S. House of Representatives from Massachusetts following his presidency.

Springfield Republican, **November 23, 1910**
"Affairs at Baltimore
Gettysburg
Correspondence of *The Republican*" [Excerpt]

One of the dearest of these (ex-Confederate officers) was the late Col. Charles Marshall of Gen. Robert E. Lee's staff. He used to tell me that before he read 'The Battles and Leaders of the Civil War,' in four ponderous volumes, written by gallant soldiers for each army, he thought he knew something of that war, but after perusing that book changed his mind. I have long felt the same way, but the other day was presented by my friend, Col. D. G. McIntosh of Towson, a distinguished confederate soldier, with his privately published 'Review of the Gettysburg Campaign,' in which he was a distinguished actor, and I cheerfully bear tribute to the care and fairness with which it is written. Of course it is from a confederate standpoint, but it weighs with care the evidence as to the conduct of Gen. Lee and Gens. Longstreet and Stuart before and during that great battle, and is to me convincing that Gen. Lee's plans were greatly upset by the conduct of both Stuart and Longstreet. Col. McIntosh makes the astonishing statement that Col. Marshall told him that he (Marshall) had reported to Gen. Lee that Stuart should have been court-martialed and shot for disobedience of orders. As to Gen. Longstreet, it is evident that he did not believe in Gen. Lee's plan of campaign, and delayed action as long as possible on this account. One may not be sure that Col. McIntosh is right in all his conclusions as to what would have happened had Stuart and Longstreet done exactly as Gen. Lee desired, but his work is thoughtfully and carefully done, and of deep interest to all students of the Gettysburg campaign.

New York Times Book Review, March 15, 1905
"The Custer Controversy"

Baltimore

With much reluctance I feel compelled to enter into the controversy as to Gen. [George Armstrong] Custer's course in the last campaign of his life, and I do it solely in justice to two gallant soldiers who, like the brave Custer, have no longer opportunity to speak for themselves. The one was Gen. Alfred H. Terry, who kept silent after Custer's death and for years suffered criticism, when if he had spoken he could have shown that, although he had done everything possible to help Custer when the latter was in ill repute at army headquarters, the latter in his last campaign acted in direct disobedience of Terry's orders in not keeping his column in direct touch with the column of Gen. [John] Gibbon. The whole story was clearly set forth by Col. (now Gen.) R. P. Hughes in the Journal of the United States Military Institute for January 1896, in which General Hughes properly holds that Terry dead is entitled to vindication even if Custer was also dead.

When Gen. Hughes's paper was published the writer discussed it with his old army friend, Gen. John Gibbon, than whom no braver ever lived, who said: "When we separated in two columns I said: 'Now don't be greedy, Custer. Wait for me.' But perhaps it was too much to expect of him, as he was always ready to fight."

Gen. Gibbon spoke tenderly of Custer, and felt, as did all old army men, that he was reckless to a fault, but that his gallant death made it unpleasant to criticize him, but it is unfair to the memory of Terry and Gibbon to justify his disobedience to the command of one and the request of the other.

Springfield Republican, July 11, 1876
"Our Hartford Letter
From Our Special Correspondent"

Hartford

. . . Poor Gen. Custer! I met him once, about 1864, at the Ebbitt House in Washington, just after one of his sharp cavalry fights. One of those old growlers, a retired regular army field officer boarding at the house, saw him enter, and grumbled out, "What excuse have you for being in Washington in war-time?" "This," said the young general, as he rolled up his pants and showed a bullet-hole in his leg. As in the old war days I gazed on him as he rode at the head of his command, with his golden hair floating from under his great sombrero, and his red neck-tie flaming in the wind, brilliant as the colors of the scarlet-tinged or Baltimore oriole, the "boy general, with his golden locks," seemed to me, as he flashed by, like the picture of one of Charles's cavaliers of the 17th century, rather than a real creation of the 19th.

In this connection the exploit of one of Custer's former aides, Gen. E. W. Whitaker (ex-postmaster of Hartford), comes to mind. It was near the close of the war, when one of the generals of the army of the Potomac (Wilson, if my memory serves me) made a movement of his command to far to the left of Grant's main army that he found himself finally entirely cut off therefrom. As Lee's whole army was between him and Grant, he dared not risk a general engagement by an attempt to cut his way through, and so summoned Whitaker, who selected 30 picked men, and with them rode seven miles through the camps of the confederate army ere he reached our lines. This he accomplished with the loss of about half his men, delivered Wilson's message, and secured the immediate sending of reinforcements that insured a safe road for the return of the lost army corps. For this feat Whitaker was breveted brigadier. Like the raid of Sergeant McDonald, one of "Marion's men"— the subject of a poem by Paul H. Hayne in the August *Harper*—the secret of this dash through the enemy was its utter unexpectedness and reckless daring. Whitaker told me afterward that in the first of the rebel camps they rode through not a shot was fired at them, as the soldiers did not dream that Yankee soldiers could thus be riding through their lines. Doubtless such examples and memories as that inspired poor Custer to his final and fatal charge of death. Well may his old comrades pray for his soul and for those of the ones who fell with him. And whatever the creed of the clergyman, whom they may seek for this office, it does not seem that any could refuse, while

> *"The knight's good bones are rust,*
> *And his good sword dust,*
> *His soul is with the saints, I trust."*

Springfield Republican, January 7, 1876
"Our Hartford Letter
From Our Special Correspondent"

A very cursory glance through Gen. [Abner] Doubleday's newly published "Recollections of Fort Sumter" inclined me to the belief that he does not fully do justice to Maj. [Robert] Anderson. While he recognizes the beauty of the Christian character of that officer, he asserts that he took but little, if any, interest in the cause of the Union. While it is doubtless true that Maj. Anderson hoped, even when it was hopeless, that war might be averted, and, while he undoubtedly shrunk back as long as possible from absolute hostilities against the section which contained so many near relatives and intimate friends, yet I have excellent authority for stating that he held the Union as sacred above all. Mr. S. H. Moseley, now of the New Haven house, was, at the time of the siege of Sumter, one of the firm of Moseley and Waite, proprietors of the Brevoort house in New York, whence Maj. Anderson went to Charleston, and whither he returned, after the surrender of the fort. His wife was a boarder at the house all through the winter of '60–61 and the spring of '61, and her letters from her husband, during this period, were seen and read by this gentleman who states that in them Maj. Anderson repeatedly assured his wife, who was a Georgia lady, that he would never disgrace the country which had educated him, nor the proud family whose name he bore, by disloyalty to the flag. Although her own relatives disowned her and insulted him for his loyalty, Mrs. Anderson was wont to reply to him that he was right, that she could not have endured that their son should ever bear the reproach that would attach to one whose father forswore his country. And so the loyal father and husband chose to do right at the expense of the loss of fortune, for the Georgian, who had bought his place in that state, never paid for it, on the ground that Anderson's course destroyed slavery and thus ruined the value of the place. With health shattered by the mental struggle and the privations of Sumter, the soldier came back to New York, seeking rest and recuperation, which he never found this side of the grave, though he did have the honor and happiness of hoisting over the ruins of Sumter, in 1865, the very flag that he had been compelled to haul down—through with a salute—in 1861. Surely Gen. Doubleday can claim honor enough as a member of the historic garrison, to be very tender of the memory of his old chief. It is to the credit of the proprietors of the Brevoort that no bills were ever sent to Mrs. Anderson, while her husband was shut up in Sumter, and to the credit of the whole-souled William H. Aspinwall that, on learning this, he insisted on assuming any indebtedness that she might incur.

29

Goddard's Friend and Dinner
Companion, Mark Twain

Springfield Republican, March 16, 1875
"Our Hartford Letter
From Our Special Correspondent"

Mark Twain's lecture in behalf of the poor of Hartford filled the opera house and netted over $1,200. His manner was inimitable, and the lecture, "Mountaineering in Nevada," far better than the one on the Sandwich Islands [Hawaii], delivered for the same object, two years ago, in that it was far more delicate in its humor and almost entirely free from that coarser wit that blemished the former. Mr. Clemens's progress is this direction is marked and most creditable.

Springfield Republican, July 14, 1876
"Our Hartford Letter
From Our Special Correspondent"

Hartford

They say Mark Twain is to lecture here again, next winter, for $200 per night. Wonder whether he will tell the true story of how he persisted in getting the measles, when he was a boy. It seems that they were prevalent in his neighborhood, but wouldn't strike Mark. As all other boys had them, he did not think this half fair, and so determined he would have 'em anyhow. To achieve this happy result, he trice essayed a visit to a sick lad in his neighborhood, who was very much broken out. Twice was Mark driven from the house; the third time he stole up the back stairs and into the child's room, and was in bed with him five minutes ere he was discovered and driven out with a broomstick. The result was as fine a case of measles as was ever known in that village. As Twain says in "*Tom Sawyer,*" the secret of making anything desirable is to make it difficult of attainment. This is as true of the measles as of whitewashing a fence or running for the presidency.

Harper's Weekly, **February 24, 1906**
"Anecdotes of Mark Twain"

Mark Twain spent a goodly number of years of his middle age in Hartford, Connecticut. In many respects this was the golden era of his life. In the decade between 1870 and 1880 it was my good fortune to meet him not infrequently, and from notes made at the time, and after a few meetings elsewhere in later years, to be able to furnish some reminiscences of the man who today is our best-loved writer.

About 1877 or '78 there was a reunion of the Society of the Army of the Potomac at Hartford. Many distinguished officers were present, including General W. T. Sherman, most of whom were present at the banquet of the society at Allyn Hall. On this occasion Mr. Clemens was to respond to one of the toasts. He had hardly got under full headway before a military band passed by the hall, playing "America." Instantly stopping his speech, the orator waved his handkerchief and led the entire audience in singing the hymn. At its close he resumed his speech, but when a little later the band passed in the other direction playing the "Star-spangled Banner," again he took up the tune and led the singing, after which he finished his speech in perfect coolness. "You will find my speech, but without the music, in tomorrow's Hartford *Courant.*"

WHAT HE WOULD HAVE DONE

In conversing with Mr. Clemens on this incident, I told him a story of Bret Harte's concerning an experience of his when lecturing at Syracuse, New York. He was seated on the platform, waiting to be introduced, when the chairman stepped up to the front and said, "Is Dr. Perkins in the house? If so, will be please step out to the entrance, as he is wanted. I have the honor to introduce to you the gifted novelist and poet of our Pacific coast, Mr. Bret Harte." The effect of this upon the sensitive nerves of Mr. Harte was such that, in his own words, "it spoiled my lecture, for through it all I occasionally saw people turn their heads and crane backward to see whether Dr. Perkins (who had at once risen and left the hall) was coming back."

When told this story, Mr. Clemens replied that "Harte made a big mistake in not satisfying the curiosity of his audience. At the first sign of their restlessness I should have stopped to advise my auditors as to who it was that wished to see Dr. Perkins, for what complaint, and when he would return. They should have had plenty of information, and then they would have been attentive to the rest of the lecture."

THE INCIDENT OF THE 9:30 TRAIN

That the speaker was not altogether in jest is evidenced by an incident that I witnessed some years later, when he was giving readings in Baltimore with George W. Cable.[1] The latter had finished, and Mark Twain had hardly begun his "stunt" when a party of young ladies with an elderly matron (presumably a boarding-school party) rose from the front row of seats and crossed the hall to a door on the right, which they found locked; whereupon they were compelled to retrace their steps and cross over to a door on the left, when they made a hasty and confused exit as the speaker, who had stopped short to gaze intently at them, said in his inimitable slow drawl: "Got to take the slow train, I suppose. Funny, whenever I read, people always want to take the 9:30 train."

On a later visit to Baltimore, Mr. Clemens performed a generous act that should no longer go unrecorded. He came to read with dear old Colonel Richard Malcolm Johnston, then the dean of our Southern literary men, supplying the place of Thomas Nelson Page,[2] who had been compelled by a domestic calamity to cancel his engagement at very brief notice. After the readings were over, Mr. Clemens went over the financial statement of expenses and results with care, and after a check had been handed him for his share (several hundred dollars), took a pen and quietly endorsed it over to the order of Colonel Johnston, who was far from well off financially. When the latter, with tears in his eyes, tried to refuse the gift, Mr. Clemens said, "Keep it, colonel, and some day when you find another author who needs help, pass the favor along." Curiously enough, within a year Colonel Johnston had opportunity to give his services at a reading in behalf of another Southern writer in distress and "passed the favor along."

In acknowledgment of this act of Mr. Clemens, several friends of Colonel Johnston arranged a little dinner at the University Club of Baltimore, to which both authors were invited. Mr. Clemens had for the same evening an invitation to a dinner-party at the house of a wealthy citizen, where he knew he would be lionized, but accepted our little club dinner in preference, writing me, "There I must be on my good behavior and try to be entertaining, but at your club I can smoke in peace and say to you men, 'Talk, hang you! I'll listen.'" However, in course of the evening, when toasted, he paid a loving tribute to Colonel Johnston, and said some very pleasant things about Baltimore, but, in conclusion, told us that many years before he had a striking illustration of genuine Maryland hospitality. In company with George Alfred Townsend,[3] he had arrived late one summer evening at Barnum's famous old hostelry here. After being shown to their room the two impecunious journalists, as they were then, sat with their door open into the hall, bemoaning the fact that they had no spare money with which to pay for a drink, when suddenly a gentleman entered the room, with three bottles of whiskey, one under each arm, and the other inside him, who said: "Gentlemen, I am from the eastern shore of Maryland. I have the next room, and happened to overhear your conversation. I have whiskey. Let us make a night of it."

MARK TWAIN'S MEMORY

At a little dinner given by the writer in Hartford about 1879, to Donald G. Mitchell,[4] Mr. Clemens and his lifelong friend, the lovable Charles Dudley Warner[5] were guests. The talk ran along the lines as to methods of public reading and speaking, and Mr. Mitchell was much interested to hear Mr. Clemens describe those he had followed. In the beginning he had used a manuscript, which he gradually reduced in size till it became simply a little card of hieroglyphic pictures to suggest the subjects to be treated. This he kept in his vest pocket to consult as needed, but later dispensed with it altogether, substituting for a while a few marks on the back of his finger nails, until at last he was able to trust entirely to memory.

Few men have ever been so ready and witty in introducing others to public audiences. Introducing General Joe Hawley, United States Senator from Connecticut, to a political gathering in a city in New York State, Mr. Clemens told the audience that they could bank on the Senator's honesty, for although his back yard at Hartford adjoined that of General Hawley, he had never lost a single chicken, and although he had closely watched the General as he passed the plate in the Asylum Hill Congregational Church, he had never seen him take one cent out of the plate. In closing, he said, "Now, my friends, I have paid high tribute to General Hawley, but I assure you not one word have I said of him that I would not say about myself."

1. George Washington Cable (1844–1925) was a novelist of his native Louisiana and its Creole culture and a social critic of political corruption and racism.

2. Thomas Nelson Page (1853–1922) was a writer, lawyer, and U.S. ambassador to Italy during World War I.

3. George Alfred Townsend (1841–1914) was a leading Civil War correspondent and postwar journalist and author.

4. Donald G. Mitchell (1822–1908) was the Washington correspondent for the *New York Morning Courier* and the author of satirical, historical, and agricultural books.

5. Charles Duley Warner (1829–1900) was an essayist, a novelist, a lecturer, a coeditor with Joseph R. Hawley of the *Hartford Courant*, a *Harper's Magazine* writer, and an advocate of prison and other social reforms.

Harpers Weekly, March 24, 1906
"Further Anecdotes of Mark Twain"

In his early Hartford days Mark Twain took an active interest in baseball in common with most of his fellow citizens. While attending an exciting match he lost a gold-headed umbrella, which he advertised in the local papers somewhat after this fashion:

"Lost—$10 Reward. A gold-headed umbrella was lost by the undersigned on the grand stand at the baseball ground on Saturday. It was probably stolen from him while he was engaging in cheering the Hartfords for their victory over the Providence nine—presumably stolen by a red-headed, freckle-faced boy about twelve years old. For the body of the boy and the umbrella delivered at my house on Farmington Avenue, $10 will be paid. For the body of the boy and the umbrella separately, $5 for either. For the boy alive, nothing under any circumstances." This advertisement was signed with his full name and address.

At a dinner given by some local mercantile or business organization Mr. Clemens responded to the toast of "Hartford." In his speech he glorified the city as the one place in the world which provided for every possible human need. He said that Hartford provided life-insurance policies to protect men's lives, accident policies to protect their persons, and fire-insurance policies to protect their future. It made guns and pistols with which to kill men, but printed books to tell them how to live and Bibles to tell them how to die. In short, it supplied all their needs, not only here but even hereafter.

The following characteristic letter was written in Montreal in February, 1885, in response to an invitation to Mr. Clemens and George W. Cable, who were reading together, to be guests of the writer and some friends when they should reach Baltimore.

> MY DEAR CAPTAIN,—We thank you ever so much, but we can't. The readers connected with this circus must attend strictly to business—no social life allowed them.
>
> Sincerely yours,
S. L. Clemens

Hartford Courant, 1910
"Reminiscences of Mark Twain
Letter to the *Hartford Courant*"

Hartford, Connecticut mourns for Mark Twain, who spent many of the happiest years of his life and made abiding friendships in that city. From notes made during the years between 1870 and 1882 and from pleasant memories I can give a few unpublished reminiscences of our acquaintance.

In the social life of that ever intellectual city, Mr. Clemens was always a prominent figure. I well recall seeing him in a handsome Revolutionary costume at a "Martha Washington Tea Party" for a local charity sometime in 1875. Standing near him on the stage, I noticed that he was sadly bored by his companion, a very enthusiastic young Miss, daughter of an ex-governor of the state. She was so effusive in her flattery of the author that he at last turned to me with a gesture of despair, and said, "I can't stand this rot; I'm going to clear out." And he quietly slipped down into the hall.

Devotedly fond of his pastor, the Rev. Joe H. Twitchell (who was one of the clergy at his funeral) Mr. Clemens was always joking with or at him. For instance, he once wrote an endorsement of some patent fly screen which he had found useful, suggesting that it would be well for the manufacturer "to furnish one for the

Asylum Hill Congregational Church, to be spread over the congregation, who could then equally enjoy the service, and the sight of the flies taking it out on poor Parson Twitchell."

On one occasion he planned to walk to Boston with the parson. They made a fine start, but, after walking ten miles, found it convenient to take a train for the rest of the journey. In an account of this trip written for the "*Courant*," Clemens began as follows: "Having long been in the habit of taking strolls with my pastor in order that he from my conversation might gather subjects for sermons, and I from his subjects for jokes, we planned to walk to Boston."

The Rev. Dr. L. R. Parker of Hartford was also a warm personal friend of Mr. Clemens. He tells a good story told by Mr. Clemens of his once attending an evening service at Dr. Parker's South Congregational church. These evening services were very popular in Hartford, were attended by many prominent folk of other denominations, and included a good deal of music and a good deal of ritual. As Clemens told it, he listened with great interest to the service, till the organ began to play a voluntary, and four gentlemen began to pass plates, when he felt in his pocket and found that he had left his pocketbook at home. Turning to his wife, he asked her for some change, to find that she too had not a cent. Just then the collector approached the pew in which he sat, when Clemens drew the man's head down and whispered in his ear, "Charge it."

On a New Years Day in the seventies, Mr. Clemens, in a fine Russian sleigh, and resplendent in an elegant fur coat, started out to make New Years calls, as was then the custom. At the very first house at which he called, he was somewhat startled when told by his hostess that he had forgotten to put on a necktie. He apologized, and left after a short call. About an hour later the lady received a note from him. Inside the envelope she found a necktie and a slip of paper with these words: "Here's the rest of me. S. L. Clemens."

At his famous seventieth birthday party in New York, the fair Amelie Rives (Princess Troubetzkey)[1] was sitting at table not far from the hero of the hour when, early in the dinner, she noticed that he was looking wretchedly. Divining the cause, she said to her nearest neighbor, "I believe Mark Twain wants a smoke; haven't you a cigar?" One was quickly produced, when she arose and took it to the author. He accepted it with his most gracious smile. "You don't happen to have a match too?" he suggested. She secured one and gave it to him, whereupon he seized her hand and said, "Madam, you have saved my life."

1. Amelie Rives (1863–1945) was a novelist, a playwright, and the wife of Prince Pierre Troubetzkoy of Russia, the second son of Prince Pierre and Princess Ada Troubetzkoy.

30

Preserving the Legacy,
Welcoming Former Foes

Baltimore Sun, February 14, 1910

"Capt. Goddard Pays Tribute to General Leary." [Letter to the *Baltimore Sun*]

Messrs. Editors:

The death of Gen. Peter Leary is one that is sadly mourned by all who know him well, but falls with especial severity upon the Maryland Commandery of the Military Order of the Loyal Legion.

This commandery was organized in 1904—over 39 years after the close of the Civil War—being composed of commissioned officers of the Union Army. Organized first in 1865, most of those who started our commandery had been for years members of the order. The Maryland organization was a direct outcome of a disagreement with the District of Columbia Commandery, to which most of its members belonged. Gen. Leary was the first to suggest a local organization and was very proud of the fact that, starting with but 26 members and with a limited field for recruits, the order now boasts over 60 members. He was unanimously chosen the first commander of the order, and himself insisted on rotation in office, so that every year a new commander is chosen, as he felt that "the boys are growing old and the honor should be passed around."

A brave soldier and loyal to the Union in the days that 'tried men's souls,' he was full of loving kindness to our old foes, and it is largely owing to him that we have had so many addresses by ex-Confederates of late years.

A gentleman by every instinct, he won our love and that of his old foes, and as he goes hence I know of no other old soldier of either army, who knew the man, who will not say with me, *Friend and true hero, hail and farewell!*

Baltimore American, **January 4, 1907**

"Loyal Legion Holds Meeting,

Gets 'Little Breeches' from Vermont Veterans." [author unknown]

The January meeting and dinner of the Maryland Commandery, Military Order of the Loyal Legion, was held last night at the Hotel Altamont, and proved one of the most interesting in the history of the commandery, which was formed in 1904. . . .

Being the latest branch of the order to be formed, the local commandery was entitled to a pair of little lace breeches which were started on the rounds by the Kansas Commandery in 1888. They were first passed on to the Iowa Commandery, then to the Washington Commandery, then to the Vermont Commandery and by it to the Maryland Commandery as the "baby" of the highly honorable Order of Civil War Veterans who saw active service in battle and plenty of it. . . .

The breeches will be acknowledged by the local commandery with a fine drawing, the work of Mr. Spencer B. Sisco, and a poem in ink by Mr. Calvin Hooker Goddard. [Goddard's son (1891–1955), who pioneered the science of forensic ballistics in the 1920s and 1930s]. All on a large card. There is a picture of a sturdy father handing a pair of breeches down to his little son. On the card is a reproduction of the coat-of-arms of Vermont and Maryland and the badge of the order. Here is the verse:

> *Oh, brothers, now receive our thanks*
> *For all your greetings kind.*
> *We're very pleased to join your ranks*
> *And happy ties to bind.*
> *We thanks you for the breeches too—*
> *Although they are too small—*
> *For now we're 'most as big as you*
> *and still are growing tall.*
> *So now, good friends, we'll say good-by.*
> *Come see us when you will,*
> *There'll be refreshments wet and dry*
> *And you may have your fill.*

. . . The local commandery holds five meetings and dinner each year in the months of January, March, May, October and November. Rear Admiral John D. Ford, the commander, was unable to be present last night because of a death in the family. Capt. H.P. Goddard, the senior vice commander, occupied the seat of the commanding officer.

The individual ices at the end of the dinner were in the form of battleships, with a real flag floating from the stern of each.

Baltimore Sun, October 8, 1912

"Tells of Civil War Poems: Captain Goddard Reads Paper before the Loyal Legion." [author unknown]

. . . A paper on the poetry of the Civil War was written and read by Capt. Henry P. Goddard. Capt. Goddard treated of the following poets, reading the poems referred to and giving a little sketch of each author: The Union poems were "All Quiet on the Potomac," by Mrs. Ethel L. Beers; "Marching Through Georgia," Henry C. Work; "Sheridan's Ride," Thomas B. Read; "Harvard Commemoration Ode," James Russell Lowell; "Bay Fight," Henry Howell Brownell; "The Advance Guard," John Hay; "Oh Captain, My Captain," Walt Whitman; "Battle Hymn of the Republic," Mrs. Julia Ward Howe, and "The Blue and the Gray," Francis Miles Finch.

Among the Confederate poems that were read were "Stonewall Jackson's Way," Dr. John Williamson Parker; "Maryland, My Maryland," James Ryder Randall; "The Good Old Rebel," Major Innes Randolph, and Rev. Abram Joseph Ryan's "The Conquered Banner."

31

Conclusion

Baltimore Sun, December 21, 1910

"The World Is Growing Better, and Most People Have Kind Hearts When Afflic-tion or Trouble Is Brought Home to Them." [Letter to the *Baltimore Sun*]

Messrs. Editors:

One who witnessed the gathering of the Empty Stocking Club and saw the 2,500 children of the poor made happier at Ford's Theatre Tuesday afternoon was impressed with the truth that comes to us more and more the older we grow, which is that the world is steadily growing better and that most people have kind hearts when affliction or trouble is really known to them.

As I watched those who took part in the exercises and heard the gleeful cries of the children I felt anew the truth of Longfellow's lovely verses:

> *And I remember still*
> *The words and from whom they came,*
> *Not he that nameth the name,*
> *But he that doeth the will.*

The ladies of the club, the proprietors of the theatre who gave it for the meet-ing, the actors who played Santa Claus and the children who acted, all are entitled to praise and thanks and deserve a very Merry Christmas.

Part 4

THE BROTHER WHO DID NOT RETURN

32

Alfred Mitchell Goddard

Alfred Mitchell Goddard was working as an engineer in the Sandwich Islands (Hawaii) when the war broke out. His inner conflict between finishing his work in the Pacific and heeding his country's call to duty was intensely felt. Finally returning home, he received a commission as a first lieutenant in the 8th Connecticut Infantry in July 1863 and was soon detached as a general staff officer. But wanting to fight alongside his regiment as the Army of the James prepared to move west toward Petersburg and Richmond, he left the relative safety of his staff position in March 1864. His first engagement, the battle of Walthall Junction on May 7, 1864, was to be his last. Mortally wounded, he died two days later at age twenty-seven.

~

Excerpts from *The Norwich Memorial: The Annals of Norwich, New London County, Connecticut, in the Great Rebellion of 1861–65,* **by Malcolm McG. Dana (J. H. Jewitt and Company, 1873)**

Alfred M. Goddard, First Lieutenant, Eighth Regiment, was born in Marietta, Ohio, June 19, 1836. His parents removed to Norwich when he was quite young, and here he grew up, developing a character of rare beauty and force. Leaving his home at an early age to commence life for himself, he for that reason was less generally known than otherwise he would have been. Yet in the home where a peerless devotion to those he most deeply loved distinguished him, and by friends who were aware of his noble nature, he was held in reverent and affectionate esteem. . . .

Immersed, when quite young, in the cares and duties of a responsible business, yet he displayed a culture ordinarily looked for only in the man of letters. . . . His journal while in the Pacific abounds in the most graphic portrayal of life on ship-board, and on the Islands. Susceptible to all that was grand and beautiful in Nature, his descriptions of scenery in the Tropics and of the changeful ocean, near and upon which so much of his life was spent, can hardly be surpassed.

Entering, when still under age, the employ of Williams & Haven, of New London, Connecticut, he was by them sent out to the Sandwich Islands [Hawaii], and in connection with a branch house, resided about five years at Honolulu. During that period he made several voyages to the Arctic Ocean, passing two years on McKean's Island, in the Southern Pacific. At the breaking out of the war, he was about leaving Honolulu for Mauritius. When the news reached him that hostilities had actually commenced, he was eager to leave at once for home, that he might enroll himself among those hurrying to the government's defense, but such were his business engagements, that fidelity to his employers required the prosecution of the voyage. So, with a disappointed heart, he endeavored to do the work to which he was committed, though his thoughts were with the brave men who were already marshaled for deadly conflict with our foes.

He writes in his journal as he started on this voyage, "I have been reading the *Atlantic Monthly*. It is all war. How is this? I am trying to do my duty, and yet a deadly sickness comes o'er me when I think what a feeling of joy it would have given me could I have gone home and given up all for my country." At a later date he adds, "All my hope now is, that having chosen this path, I may command myself and give myself to the present, trusting that through some great good luck I may yet find myself among the New England heroes." Who of us imagined that on the far Pacific main there was a heart beating with such lofty patriotism; reckoning as its chief trial that it could not share in our struggle for national existence. And yet, like thronging doves to their windows came the patriots of our land, traveling homeward from every quarter of the globe that they might swell the hosts who battled for truth and freedom.

He . . . remarks, "I begin to think the war is the best thing which could have happened to us. I know it must stir up our young men to action and fill their veins with new life. I honor the brave fellows and am proud of dear old Connecticut. The spirit of our Puritan Fathers is not yet dead."

While at Mauritius, hearing of his father's sudden death, young Goddard hastened back with the utmost expedition that he might visit his bereaved mother and mingle with the afflicted family. Taking the East India route through the Red Sea and Europe, he arrived at his home in the fall of 1862. He hoped then to enter the army and gratify thus the deepest longings of his heart. But his business engagements compelled him to go back once more to the Sandwich Islands, and with great reluctance he turned his face toward the Pacific. He seemed at this time keenly sensitive lest his absence from the country while in so critical a condition should not be understood. . . . "If my choice could be recalled," he writes in one place, "I would go through anything to get upon the battle field." He speaks also of the moral issues of the conflict, demonstrating his ardent love of liberty for all classes—"It seems strange the country should have been ruled so long by this small party. (Slaveholders.) But the time for a change has come, and I think the curse of slavery will now be removed from our beautiful land."

Dispatching with promptness his business at the Islands, and closing his connection with the firm he had served so long and well, he was enabled to return home in May 1863.

On the following July, he received a commission as First Lieutenant in Company B of the Eighth Connecticut Regiment, but was at once detached for duty on the Staff of General Harland [Edward, Brig. Gen. of Volunteers, from Norwich, Conn.], the former Colonel of the Eighth Regiment. In this capacity he rendered faithful service until March 1864, when, at the request of officers and men, he rejoined his regiment. "It is a hard thing to do," says his diary, "but I am sure it is right." His associates on the Staff parted with him, not without the greatest reluctance and the most genuine regret. To General Harland he was strongly attached, and by him in turn was esteemed as an able officer and a personal friend. The heart which had chafed so when business prevented his connection with the army, was still dissatisfied with the less arduous duties of staff officer, so he took his place in the ranks. . . .

March 13, 1864, the regiment, under command of Col. J. E. Ward, left its old camp at Portsmouth, Va., and marched to Deep Creek, where it performed outpost and picket duty until April 13. Thence it was ordered to Yorktown, and was assigned to the Second Brigade of the Eighteenth Corps. Forming part of General [Maj. Gen. Benjamin] Butler's command, it was engaged in a reconnaissance of the enemy's lines before Petersburg. On the morning of May 8, the regiment led the advance in an attempt to press back the enemy. Forming in battle line, it repeatedly charged the foe, driving him before them, and continued fighting till the ammunition was exhausted and the regiment was relieved by order, receiving, as it returned from the bloody field, the cheers of the whole brigade. It was in this action that the fatal bullet struck Lieutenant Goddard. While bravely fighting and cheering on his men in this his first battle, he fell, mortally wounded.

The day before, his entry in his diary, when it was apparent an engagement was imminent, was both touching and significant—"And the children of Israel prevailed, because they trusted in the Lord God of their Fathers." . . . Before sundown he was borne from the field, and ere another day had gone, the knightly youth of high hopes and unflinching courage passed away. . . .

Upon the examination of his wound, he asked the regimental surgeon whether it was likely to prove fatal, adding, at once, that he thought it must; in which opinion the surgeon was obliged to concur. Immediately he added: "Tell my mother that I die in the front, that I die happy." Removed to the Chesapeake Hospital at Fortress Monroe, he lingered for little more than a day, suffering intensely but patiently.

Writes one who knew him well: "He was one of the few men whom I have known in my life whose steadfast honesty was proof against all temptations, and his varied life exposed him to not a few." Another friend, intimately associated with him while in the army, wrote when the news of his death was received: "May God rest the soul of our martyr-hero. . . . How kind and unselfish he was. What a sturdy champion for everything just, noble, and right. How he loathed oppression and injustice. How he loved his country."

. . . While in the strength of his young manhood, God permitted him to die, and his death adds another to the list of heroes whose memory and example are the nation's heritage (29–34).

Oct. 27, 1861.

Dear Alf,

Your very entertaining and affectionate letter of the 2nd of September came to hand on Friday and was read with the liveliest satisfaction.

I have just returned to the office from a conversation with a Capt. Morse of New London, late of the ship Polynesian, a casual acquaintance. He says he knows you and shall be out your way pretty soon and sends his regards.

I am a little in the "marine" line myself just now as Ike [Bromley] is in Washington trying to get me a berth in the Marine Corps, and here at home I am flirting with Miss Lillie Welhams, daughter of Capt. Jerome Welhams.

You wrote that you supposed I wanted to change the pen for the <u>rifle</u>—I do want to change it for the <u>sword</u> as I want to earn money enough to do something for the people at home, which I could do if I could get a lieutenancy, but not as a private. Besides, I am satisfied, or nearly so, that I could not stand the life of a common soldier. If there are any vacancies in the Marine Corps, Bromley can get me a place as his influence with [Gideon] Welles, the Secretary of the Navy, is great. He has already got some eight or ten places for his friends from that department. If you were here he could easily get you a Sailing Master's place as there are more vacancies of that sort than any other.

I am just reading proof of dispatches from San Francisco Oct. 27th which appear in the Bulletin Oct. 28th. The completion of the electric link between the Atlantic and Pacific binds me nearer to my far distant brother than ever before.

Oh Alf. It does seem a shame to be staying around home at this time when such boys as Kemp, much younger than I and a 3 month's volunteer, is serving in a company for three years. Before this war is over, I will go—as a private even—if no other chance offers.

Yours, H. P. G.

Excerpts from the Diary of A. M. Goddard

[Composed on board a passenger schooner and after Goddard's arrival in Honolulu]

<u>September 26th, 1861. Thursday.</u> I do believe I have committed a sin in giving so little thought to my country. . . . I have been too much bound up in the world and in business and now comes the reaction when it is too late. O gold, gold, how many warm hearts hast thou turned to stone, how much misery hast thou caused. Tennyson is right when he says (in Maud), "Give us war"—'Tis better than the miserable endeavors to be rich, the grinding down the poor and quarreling over some mean political questions. . . .

<u>September 29th. Sunday.</u> . . . I have been reading a paper in the "Atlantic" on Theodore Winthrop, one of the hero's of 1861, who fell in just in his budding glory on the battle field of Great Bethel [fought June 10, 1861, a Confederate victory near Hampton, Virginia; novelist Winthrop was on the staff of Brig. Gen. Ebenezer Pierce]. What a noble fellow he was and what a noble death he died—such men as he will live forever, and although in his military life he had opportunity to do but little, in his death he did a great deal and thousands of young men will feel their pulses throb with noble emulation when they read the story of his life and death. Such names as his and Ellsworth's will be household names through our land—God reward them.

We know so little what is best for us that it is folly to think "what might have been." Yet I cannot help feeling that it is hard for me to be thrown so far away from home and from those brave fellows, friends near and dear, who are going forth in their grand young strength to maintain our flag and our country's honor and to avenge those who have already fallen in their tracks, doing their duty to God and Country. . . .

<u>November 8th. Friday Evening.</u> . . . I have been blue enough for a few days passed and the last three nights I have dreamed of home, which is unusual. I hope and trust they may all be well there. Sometimes my dreams are very pleasant but often the reverse. Once and only once have I dreamed of the war; it was a glorious dream. It seemed as if I was at home with my comrades and schoolmates, a member of Ned Harland's[1] company. I thought we were in the thickest of the fight. I was doing my duty valiantly. Would that the dream had been true. Yet after all, it is horrible this war between brothers. What strange victims of fate this great human family is made up of. Though after all it is not fate, but a just punishment this war, which our sins have brought upon us. Let us then humbly and devoutly go to Him the God of battles, praying for His guidance and entreating His forgiveness for the dear Christ's sake.

<u>November 22nd. Friday.</u> . . . Mother and Sister write very dismal news of the war, yet they are most hopeful of success and both ready to do all in their power for our dear country's cause. . . .

<u>November 24th. Sunday.</u> . . . The letter from Mother dated Sept. 4th was full of home news. Very proud am I of dear old Norwich when I hear such good accounts of her sons; many of my old school-fellows have already won great credit for their soldier-like conduct on that unfortunate field of "Bull Run."

<u>December 15th. Sunday Evening.</u> . . . Dear Jule, what a change has ten years made in our lives. Only ten years ago we were children, such happy children, no sorrow, no care, touching us then, now how different, now we are men and women with all the cares and trials of life hanging about us and thousands of miles of land and sea lying between us. Even our dear country has changed. A little while ago so glorious and united, the envy of all nations—now disunited and torn by discord, its dear air rent by the booming of cannons and the clash of arms, the din of death where for many years only the hum of industry had been heard. Now, the whirling of the mill wheels, the lowing of the cattle, the whetting of the scythe and all the cheering sounds of all the arts of peace are drowned and deadened in this great clang of arms, borne to us from the bloody battle field. . . .

<u>December 31, 1861.</u> Tuesday. And this is the last day of the year 1861, but a few hours more and this year, which had been so full of startling events, will have passed into history. Thus the years glide swiftly on, sweeping all things into the gulf of time. Despotic Russia has justly the admiration of the world by the liberation of her surfs; henceforth the Czar of all the Russias can be quoted as the friend of freedom. And our own dear free country is in the midst of a tremendous struggle to preserve the only purely republican government in the world, and to keep secure and sacred the rights and liberties which our forefathers fought and died to maintain. Yet the South, forgetful of her solemn oaths, ungrateful to the government which has petted her so long, forgetful of the precepts of the great and good who have gone to their rest, the rebellious South has raised her bloody hand of treason, insulted our flag and trampled under foot our laws, deluged our land in blood in the hope of establishing in her own great maelstrom of corruption an empire founded on slavery—an aristocratic slave empire on the ruins of our free institutions, our sacred self-government and civil liberty. God forbid it, and God defend and bless the right. Soon may all the din and discord of war cease and the cry of distress cease forever in our beautiful and free country. Again may the sounds of peace, the song of industry and wealth drown the tumult of battle. . . .

<u>May 10th.</u> War, by land or by sea, is very horrible, and yet I believe it is a necessary evil until the world is nearer perfection than today. Wars purify the earth and the battle is an ordeal which tries and schools our manhood and proves our faith. Would He without whose knowledge not even a sparrow falleth to the ground allow all the misery of war for naught? No. No—it is for a great purpose that wars

are waged and will be, until at last that happy day of brotherly love reigns over all the world, when the lion and the lamb shall lie down together and a little child shall lead them. Then Satan shall have no more power, the sword shall be beat into plowshares and the spear into a pruning hook.

1. Edward Harland, from Norwich, Connecticut, was a captain in the 3rd Connecticut Volunteer Infantry in May 1861; a colonel of the 8th Connecticut Volunteer Infantry, in which Goddard was to serve, in October 1861; and a brigadier general by November 1862.

Telegram from Alfred Mitchell Goddard to His Mother in Norwich, Connecticut

May 9, Fort Monroe.

Tell mother to come. Am badly wounded and at Chesapeake General Hospital.

A.M. Goddard

Letter from A. M. Goddard's Company Commander to Goddard's Mother, Mary Woodbridge Goddard

Camp of 8th Conn. Vols.
In the field, May 11th

My dear Madam,

Most sincerely do I mourn with you the death of dear Alfred. While most bravely fighting and cheering on our men, the fatal bullet struck him and he was taken from the field. As he was carried past me, he said he was wounded but that he had done his duty. Most truly can I echo those last words. He had done his whole duty and no man could have better conducted himself during the trying hours of that day.

Our company, with one other, was detailed in the morning to skirmish in front of our line, so Alfred was one of the first under fire. Later in the day we returned to the Regiment and advanced with them in the charge and severe fighting. It was during the last heavy fighting that Alfred was struck.

I have no words to express my appreciation of his behavior in this his first action. He was so thoughtful, considerate and courageous, and not rash or impetuous, but cool and collected, ready for every emergency, willing for every duty.

After the battle I saw Alfred a few moments at the field hospital. He could talk but with difficulty. Said that he did not expect to live, that he was ready to go, that he could trust in the Savior. He only desired that any property that he should leave should hereafter be his mother's. I attempted to cheer him but he said he knew his condition and that he could not live. When I told him that our expedition had been successful, that something had been gained though with heavy loss, he pressed my hand and said he was satisfied. He also wished me to thank our company, for him, that they had fought so well. As he seemed somewhat excited at this time, I left him, promising to see him the next morning, but during the night he was removed and I saw him no more.

Alfred is truly mourned throughout the entire regiment. For the short time that he had been with the regiment, he had in no common degree won the regard and esteem of all the officers, but on my self does his loss fall the most heavily. During the five months we have been together, I have most highly prized our constant companionship. Our many common interests brought us into the closest communion, and converse of the near ones at home strengthened and encouraged us in many trying hours.

I send by this mail the articles that were left with me, a photograph album, diary and letters. The sword I fear was lost. The men who carried him from the field say that it was taken off to relieve him and they think left in the woods.

I cannot say half of what I would in any letter, only when I can talk with you can I truly express my sympathy with you in this great affliction.

I am truly,

Charles Coit

INDEX

Abbott, Kemp, 51, 72–73, 81, 123, 142, 227, 334

Adams, Gen. Charles Francis, 308–9, 314

African Americans: abolition, feelings about, 123, 126, 130; banjo picking, 199; contrabands, 19, 95; conversation with a former slave, 14; food given to soldiers, 119; food purchased from, 20, 116, 119, 124; service as servants to Union officers, 19, 61, 77, 93, 138, 143, 193, 199; theft by, 197; view of, xv; voting rights, 269–71, 278; waiters refuse to serve agents of *The Clansman,* 274; welcome Union troops, 23. *See also* race relations

Aiken, Gen. William A., 294

Alcott, James P., 232

Alexander, Col. Mark, 275–76

Alexandria, Va., 186

Allan, Maj. Gen. Ethan, 160

Almy, A. H., 7

Almy, Col., 48

Alstadt, John, 63–64, 68

Ames, Capt., 191

Anderson, Brig. Gen. A. P., 25

Anderson, Gen. J. R., 29

Anderson, Maj. Robert, xvii, 317–18

Andrews, Brig. Gen. George, 100

Antietam, battle of, xi, xiii, 33, 55–61; casualties, 58; 1886 reunion at, 254–58; Lincoln's review of troops, xii

Appomattox, xi, 217, 285, 287

Aqueduct Bridge, 5, 49

Aquia, Va., 27

Aquia Creek, Va., 91, 128, 153

Arlington, Va.: Arlington House, 1–2; Camp Palmer, 8–13

Arlington House, 1–2

Arms, Adjt. Charley, 84, 180

Armstrong, Adjt., 6

Army of Northern Virginia. *See specific battles and officers*

Army of the Potomac. *See specific battles and officers*

Arnold, Capt., 191

Arnold, Samuel, 300

Arnold, Mrs. William A., 198, 206

Arthur, Chester A., 289

artillery brigade, xiv, 188–217

Ashby, Thomas A., 239

Aspinwall, William H., 318

Auburn, Va., 187

Auger, Brig. Gen. Christopher, 18, 20

Austin, Lt. Charles, 53

baggage: Falmouth, list of what quartermaster will carry, 139; guarding baggage train, 88; noncommissioned officers and amount allowed, 59; problems with, 63, 71, 81, 83–84, 89–90

Bailey's Cross Roads, 57; review of troops, 10

Balch, George B., 314

Baldwin, Lt. Charles O., 42, 71, 79–80, 90

Baldwin, Sgt. George W., 156

balls: Governor Bradford's Baltimore ball, 172; Kilpatrick's headquarters ball, 199; 2nd Corps grand ball, 207, 209–10, 216

Baltimore, Md.: "Fighting 14th" parades through, 47, 53; Goddard visits on return from sick leave, 154, 158; Goddard joins Maj. Gen. Tyler's staff in, xiii, 154, 158–59; Goddard moves to, xv, 228; Goddard seeks return to regiment in, 169–70; Goddard's death at, xviii; Governor Bradford's ball, 172; politics, postwar, 266–79; Pratt Street riot, 228–29, 286–87; Southern sympathizers, 259–65; veterans' reunions, 286–87

Baltimore American: Antietam reunion (1886), 254–58; Loyal Legion meeting, 326

Baltimore Evening Sun, plays about the war, 264

Baltimore Herald: letter about *The Clansman,* 273–74; obituaries of veterans, 237–38; story about purchase of paper, 265

Baltimore News: election results (1907), 276–78; Fredricksburg reunion, 288–90; McClellan letter to Lee, 310–12; obituary of General Leary, 325; President Theodore Roosevelt and race relations, 279

Baltimore Sun: Barbara Fritchie, 280–81; election results (1910), 272–73; Empty Stocking Club, 328; Hetty Cary, 260–64; Lee's and Grant's characters, 312–12; Loyal Legion meeting, 327; race relations, 275–76; Sherwood Pension Bill, 308–9

Baltimore Sunday Herald: obituary of Gen. John Kenly, 239–45

Baltimore Sunday Record: Judge Bond's memories of Maryland men, 227–31;

obituary of Henry Kyd Douglas (1903), 234–37

Banks, Maj. Gen. Nathaniel, 7, 51, 73, 240

Bank's Ford, 152

Barlow, Brig. Gen. Francis, 213

Barrett, Lawrence, 264, 275

Barton, Clara, 251–52

baseball, 307

Bates, Edward (attorney general), 7

battles. *See names of specific battles*

Beaumont, Nelson J., 107

Beauregard, Maj. Gen. P. G. T., 14, 261; Bull Run headquarters, 14; war flag made by Hetty Cary, 261

Beaver Dam Creek, battle of, 43

Beebe, Cpl. Fred, 61

Belair Heights, 81, 83

Berkeley, Annie, 74–75, 123

Bermuda Hundred campaign, xv

Bernard, Fort, 178

Berry, Fort, 178

Berry Hill, Va., 191–92

Bierne, Charlie, 93

billiards, 170–71

Birge, Gen. Henry, 295

Birney, Brig. Gen. William, 210, 213

Birth of a Nation (film), xvi

Bishop, William H., 275

Blenker, Fort, 178

Blenker, Brig. Gen. Ludwig, 88

Blinn, Capt. Jarvis E., 58, 85, 118

Bliss, Dr. William, 158, 169

Bliss Farm, Gettysburg, 155

Bloody Lane. *See* Sunken Road (Bloody Lane)

Bolivar Heights. *See* Harpers Ferry

Bonaparte, Charles Joseph, 294

Bond, Frank, 44

Bond, Hugh L., 227–31

Bond, William, 5

Boone, Kit, 118

Boonesboro, Md., 57–58, 63

Booth, Edwin, 273

Booth, John Wilkes, xvii, 280, 300

Bowman, F. C., 232

Bradford, Edward G. (governor of Maryland), 172

Bragg, Maj. Gen. Braxton, 174, 256

Brand, Lt. C. A. "Kit," 68, 73, 75, 78, 93, 134

Brandy Station, Va., 192–94, 196

Brige, Maj. H. W., 227

Brigham, Lt. George N., 157, 214; reunions, 232

Bristoe Station, Va., xiv, 13–15, 166–68, 185–86, 212

Broatch, Lt. John C., 78; conscript camp duty, 177; friendship with, 90–91, 125; Gettysburg, battle of, 157, 160–61; promotion, 90, 126; resignation disapproved, 127; returns to duty, 123, 144; sickness of, 91; visits Goddard in hospital, 183; wounded at Morton's Ford, 203

Broatch, Col. Johnny, 46, 54

Bromley, Ike, 42–43, 138, 226–27

Bronson, Capt. Isaac R., 97, 115, 127, 141; arrest, 129–30, 139; commands regiment, 122, 148; court-martial, 131, 135; death, 153; disagreements with, 118; Goddard's opinion of, 131; leave, 145; musters regiment, 117; wounded, 107, 151–52

Brown, George William (mayor), 228

Brown, John, 62, 64, 287–88

Browne, Dunn. See Fiske, Samuel

Brownson, Capt., 209

Brownson, Orestes A., 209

Bryan, William Jennings, 307

Bryan, William S., 269, 277

Buck, Cpl., 20

Buckingham, Maj. Philo B., 84

Buckingham, William A. (governor of Connecticut), 15, 24, 295; call for more troops, 34–35; Norton sent to investigate lack of clothing, 81; recommends Goddard to Fighting 14th, 37; reelection campaign, 133–34, 141–42; visits Camp Foote, 45

Buckley, Charley, 179

Buckner, Maj., 202

Bull Run: description of, 13; 1st battle of, 4; 2nd battle of, 47, 49, 51, 57

Burlingame, Anson, 223–24

Burnside, Gen. Ambrose, xiii, 13, 57, 62; Goddard's opinion of, 98, 107, 123, 126, 208; goes to Washington, 93; mud campaign, 123–24; orders troops into action, Jan. 1863, 121–22, 124; replaced by Hooker, 124; reunions, 245, 254; review of troops at Falmouth, 121; review of troops at Warrenton Junction, 87, 89; rumor of order dismissing Hooker, 146; takes command of Army of the Potomac, 87, 89; troops taunt, 123

Burpee, Thomas F., 45

Butler, Maj. Gen. Ben, 52, 201, 229, 246

Butterfield, Brig. Gen. Daniel, 88, 256

Cable, George W., 320

Cairnes, Jim, 60

Caldwell, Brig. Gen. John, 205, 213

camp life: allottment per officer under Halleck, 120; baggage allowed noncommissioned officers, 59; bathing, 18–19, 130; converse with rebels across river, 127, 147; daily routine, 11–12, 39, 45–46, 53, 77–78, 119–20, 130, 190–91; dances (see balls); dress parades, 43, 64, 67, 80, 90, 115, 127, 129, 141, 143, 176, 179; drills, 10–11, 40, 66, 68, 70, 78, 83, 138, 176; Falmouth quarters description, 21, 124; foraging, 15–16, 20, 60, 97; guard

camp life (*continued*)
duty, 96, 118; Harpers Ferry, 62–86; horse race, 208; lice, 81, 87, 94; liquor, lack of, 129; meals (*see* meals); morning reports, 61; picket duty, 16, 24–25, 63–64, 68, 70, 72–73, 76, 78–79, 116, 124, 140; practical jokes, 12, 126–27; roll call, 14; St. Patrick's Day, 132; Sibley tents, 70–71, 78, 89, 93–94, 120, 122, 126, 130; sickness, 43, 64–66, 68–71, 77, 80, 85, 126, 166; theft, problem of, 12–13, 19, 54, 107, 197; trading coffee and tobacco with rebels, 113; uniform straps, problems with, 69; washing clothes, 65, 77, 94; winter entertainments, 212; wood huts, winter quarters, 95

camps. *See names of specific camps*

Canfield, Lt. Daniel E., 106, 109, 116, 118

Cannon, William (governor of Delaware), 147

capitol, U.S.: dome, 179; tour of, 6–7

Carpenter, Capt. Samuel W., 60, 97, 177–78; transfer to invalid corps, 181; wounded, 106, 116, 129, 141, 189

carpetbaggers, Southern contempt for, 299–300

Carr, Brig. Gen. Joseph, 213

Carroll, Dr., 204

Carroll, Col. S. Sprigg, 213

Carruthers, "Billy," 294–95

Cary, Constance, 260–61, 264

Cary, Hetty, xvii, 259–65, 282

Cary, Jenny, 259–61, 264

Cary, William M., 263

Casey, Gen. Silas, 49

casualty lists, 168; Antietam, 58; Bristoe Station, 168; Chancellorsville, 151; Fredericksburg, 115; Gettysburg, 155

Catholics, Goddard's view of, 144–45

Catlett's Station, Va., 16, 191

Cemetery Ridge, 33, 154–55, 157

Chain Bridge, Va. *See* Ethan Allen, Fort

Chamberlain, D. H. (governor of South Carolina), 314

Chancellorsville, battle of, 149–53; "Fighting 14th" band, 33, 150–51; Goddard wounded at, xii–xiii, 149, 152

Charlestown, W. Va., 74–75

Chase, Miss Kitty, 6

Chatfield, Col. John L., 81

Cheeseboro, Col. William H., 158, 260

Chesapeake Hospital, Fortress Monroe, 333

Chester, Capt. Frank, 222

Chickamauga: death of General Lytle, 285; monument to Maryland dead, 258

"Christian Expediency," 290–91

City of Hartford (steamship), 35, 48

Clansman, The (Dixon), xv–xvi, 273–74

Clanton, Maj. Gen. James, 297

Clark, Maj. Cyrus C., 67, 80; Antietam, 58, 61; court-martial, service on, 70; floor for tent, 77; Fort Ethan Allen, 48; friendship with, 65, 91; Harpers Ferry, 64–65; home on furlough, 116; paralyzed arm, 118; paymaster to army, appointment, 131; resignation, 129; visit with Goddard, 178; wounded, 106, 118, 125

Clarksburg, Md., 51–52

Clay's Hotel, 49

Clemens, Samuel. *See* Twain, Mark

Clement, Sgt. Nathan C., 156

clothing: coat from home, 135; Deers coats, 118; improved supplies under Hooker, 113; need for, 79, 81, 84, 117, 141; purchase of coat, 170; requests for, 65, 80, 118

Cobalt, Conn., reception of troops, 35

Cobb, Gen. T. R., 312

Coit, Charley, 132, 337–38

Coit, Capt. James B.: burial of McVay, 52; commissioned major, 186; election as captain, 45; Gettysburg, battle of, 160, 168–69; Goddard's opinion of, 43–44, 96; senior captain, 182; treatment of troops, 53; visit from parents, 208; wounded at Antietam, 58–59, 69; wounded at Morton's Ford, 203

Colegrove, Gen. C. S., 257–58

Coleman, Mrs., 197

Comes, Sgt. William A., 67; burial, 115; death, 115, 118; wounded at Fredricksburg, 104, 107, 109

Comestock, Lt. James. E., 61

Compton, Lt Fred.: bath in Rappahannock River, 18–19; death of, 51, 57; foraging, 151; Goddard sleeps in tent of, 12; Goddard's friendship with, 4

Confederates: generals (*see specific generals*); obituary of Henry Kyd Douglas, 234–37. *See also* rebels

Connecticut Brigade, 9th Army Corps visits, 118

Connecticut Squadron. *See* 2nd New York Voluntary Cavalry

Connelly, John Robert, 280–81

Connor, Brig. Gen. Selden, 253

conscripts and substitutes, 166–68, 175–77, 180, 184–86; N.Y. draft riots, 181

contrabands, 19, 95

Cook, Capt., 195

Cook, Maj. Edward W., 195

Coon, Capt. Marcus: camp at Fredricksburg, 24–26; conversation about, 41; Goddard's dislike of, 20, 28–29; dismissed from service, 196; Goddard plays prank on, 12; shot by own men, 49

Corbett, Jerry, 63

Couch, Maj. Gen. Darius N., 61, 80, 85, 88, 135; Fredricksburg, battle of, 102;

St. Patrick's Day, 137; succeeds Sumner, 126

courts-martial: Bronson, Capt. Isaac R., 131, 135, 139; Davis, tried for drunkenness, 127, 131, 139; Ellis sits on, 208; Galpin, Lt. Charles W., 146; judge advocate, acts as, 146; Kilpatrick, Col. Hugh Judson, 132; recorder, acts as, 70; testifies at, 80, 146

Cowan, Sen. Edgar, 7

Crampton, Cornette M., 76

Crosby, Lt. George H. D., 58–59, 70, 80, 85–86, 90, 118

Cross Keys, battle of, 37, 69, 82, 84

Crothers, Austin L. (governor of Maryland), 272, 278

Culpeper, Va., 212–13

Curtin, Andrew G. (governor of Pennsylvania), 209, 244

Custer, Brig. Gen. George Armstrong, 182, 316–17

Custis-Lee Mansion. *See* Arlington House

Dahlgren, Col. Ulric, 210

dances. *See* balls

Davies, Gen. Henry E., 38, 196

Davies, Mrs. Henry E., 30

Davies, Col. J. Mansfield, 3, 129; advises Goddard to resign, 30; appoints Goddard acting battalion adjutant, 20; Beaver Dam Creek, battle of, 43; first meeting with, 5–6; Goddard calls on wife of, 30; Goddard's opinion of, 20; nightly recitations in tactics, 10; reconnoiters Fredricksburg, 22; sick, returns to D.C., 21; Sunday church address, 16; transferred to 12th N.Y. Cavalry, 132

Davis, Henry Winter, 277

Davis, Col. Jefferson, 244, 302

Davis, Capt. Samuel H., 60, 79–80, 91, 93, 97, 141; arrest, 127, 129, 139; Chancellorsville, battle of, 152; command of regiment after Fredricksburg, 104, 107–8, 148; command of regiment after Gettysburg, 170; conscript camp duty, 177; ten-day leave, 127

Davis, Varuna, 178, 183

death, view of, 211

Decker, Lt. J. Nelson, 9–10; killed at Stafford, 17–18; plays prank on, 12; reflections on death, 42, 47

Decoration Day: address at Winchester, Va. national cemetery, 1893, 284–85; observation of, 284–85

Defiance, Camp, 51

Delaware, Fort, 166, 168

Dellaplain, Va., 91–94

Deming, Lt. Henry C., 38

Dennis, Dr. George, 261

Dennis, Capt. John, 227

Dennis, Capt. Oscar, 227

Denny, Maj. James W., 312–14

deserters, 121, 138, 145, 167, 183, 199

Devens, Brig. Gen. Charles, 246

Dibble, Lt. Charles F., 38, 148

Dickinson, Col. Joseph, 256, 311

Digges bills, 271–72

Dix, Dorothy, 166, 180

Dix, Maj. Gen. John A., 45

Dixon, Sen. James, 42; description of, 7; dines with in D.C., 190, 193

Dixon, Mrs. James, 45, 193

Dixon, Thomas, xv–xvi, 273–74

Doten, Cpl. Frederick B., 126–27, 138, 144, 148; arrival in Washington on sick leave, 181; commissioned captain, 186; Gettysburg, battle of, 157, 160–64; return from leave, 142–43; taken prisoner at Morton's Ford, 203, 206; ten-day leave, 127

Doten, Mr., 58

Doubleday, Col. Abner: book about Fort Sumter, 317–18; commander of Fort Ethan Allen, 47, 49–50, 53

Douglas, Benjamin, 46

Douglas, Col. Henry Kyd, xvii, 257, 281; campaigns for, xv, 235; obituary, 234–37; removal of Confederate dead from Antietam, 255

Douglas, Lt., 88

Dranesville, battle of, 13

dress parades, 43, 67, 80, 90, 115, 117, 127, 129, 141, 176, 179; rebels, 143

Dudley, Frederick A., Surgeon, 63, 143, 168–69, 176, 187, 189, 194–95

Dudley, Brig. Gen. William, 256

Dudley Buck (transport ship), 35

Duffie, Maj. Alfred N.: approach to Antietam, 57; distinguishes himself in Fredricksburg skirmishes, 138; reconnoiters Fredricksburg, 22, 24, 28

Dunn, Capt., 191

Dupont [Du Pont], Adm. Samuel, 168

Duryée's Zouaves, 5th Regiment New York Infantry, 4

Dutton, Col. Arthur A., 118

Dwight, Lt. G. Lyman, 191, 193, 204, 210–11, 214

Dyer, Charles, 180

Early, Gen. Jubal, 167

Ebbit House, lodging in D.C., 5–8, 153, 177, 314

8th Connecticut Volunteer Infantry, xv, 166, 174, 207, 331, 333. *See also* Goddard, Alfred Mitchell

elections: Connecticut gubernatorial election (1863), xiii, 130–31, 133–34, 141–42; fraud in, 304; presidential (*see* presidential campaigns); trick ballots, 272–73; voting rights of

African Americans, 269–71. *See also*
Maryland politics, postwar
Elizabethport, N.J., 48
Elliot, Capt. Charles B., 198
Elliot, Capt. J. Thomas, 187, 191
Ellis , Adjt. Theodore G., 43–44, 53, 57,
142, 172–74; behavior under fire, 58,
61, 156–57, 161; casualty lists, 168;
Chancellorsville, battle of, 151–52;
commander of 14th, 129–31, 151;
comments on paperwork, 114; commissioned colonel, 186; considers
promotions, 186, 193–94, 208; court-
martial, sits on, 193, 208; description
of, 39–40; dines with Goddard in
D.C., 190, 193; disliked by troops, 50;
friendship with, 48, 187–88, 190, 197,
215; Gettysburg, battle of, 156–57,
161; Goddard's opinion of, 130, 147;
ladies, and, 172, 209–10, 216; medical
treatment in Baltimore, 168–69; promotion, 66, 129, 143, 186; return
from sick leave, 94, 124, 142; return
to regiment, 177; reunion of 14th,
233; 2nd Corps ball, 209–10, 216;
sends Goddard to hospital, 152; sick
furlough, 71; strictness of, 61, 145;
visits with Goddard, 169–70, 172–74;
West Point Academy, 200
Ells, Lt. Ed, 68
Ely, Col. William B., 73
Elzey, Maj. Gen. Arnold, 260
Emancipation Proclamation, xi–xii,
55, 62
Empty Stocking Club, 328
Ethan Allen, Fort, 47–50, 53, 214
Eutaw House, 48, 158–59, 169, 176
Ewell, Maj. Gen. Richard, 260

Fair Oaks (Seven Pines), battle of, 37
Falmouth, Va., 4; Harris Light Calvary,
Camp Auger, 17–27; hospitals, 101,
103–5; winter camp (1862–63) for
the 14th Conn., 95–148
Farnsworth, Charley, 227
Farnum, William, 264
Farragut, Adm. David G., 314
Farrell, Lt., 195
Fessenden, Sen. Charles, 7
"Fighting Fourteenth." *See* 14th
Connecticut Volunteer Infantry
Fillmore, Millard, 221
Fisher, Ellen, 227
Fisk, Lt. Wilbur D., 90, 165, 189
Fiske, Samuel, 189; as captain, 128–29;
delivers Goddard's coat, 135; detailed
as assistant inspector general, 140;
Goddard visits, 196; lieutenant, 92,
121; medical treatment in Baltimore,
168–69; seeks resignation, 177;
wounded, 151, 185
Fitch, Capt. W. G., 281
Fitch, Gen. William, 83
Fitzhugh, George R., 288
food. *See* meals
Foot, Sen. Solomon, 7
Foote, Camp, 34–35, 37–46, 48; visit of
Goddard's mother and sister to,
175–76
Foote, Commodore, 34
foraging, 15–16, 20, 60, 97
Forrest, Edwin, 192
forts. *See names of specific forts*
Foster, Sen. John, 7
14th Connecticut Volunteer Infantry: at
Antietam, battle of, 33, 55–61; arrival
in D.C., 49; Bristoe Station, battle of,
xiv, 13–15, 167–68, 185–86; camped
at Harpers Ferry, 62–86; captaincy in,
xi, xiv, 214; Chancellorsville, battle
of, 149–53; company books, keeping
of, 90, 95, 120; conscripts, 175–77,
184–86; demoralized troops, 81, 108,
112–148; departure from Hartford,

14th Connecticut Volunteer Infantry (*continued*)

    35, 46–48; deserters, 183; enlists as sergeant major, xii–xiii, 37–38; Falmouth, winter camp (1862–63), 95–148; first marching orders, 49; Fredricksburg, battle of, 98–111; furloughs, granting of, 128, 139; Gettysburg, battle of, 154–65, 168–69; Goddard mustered out, 217; Goddard promoted to lieutenant, xii–xiii, 62, 64, 66, 118, 125, 131; history of, 3–4, 34–38, 45–47, 53–56, 60–63, 86–87, 97–100, 108–9, 112–14, 148–51, 155–57, 165, 166–68, 189, 200–203, 206, 212–13, 216–17; honorable discharge, xiv; Lee pursed into Maryland, 47–54; Morton's Ford, battle of, xiv, 201–6, 212; obituaries of veterans, xvii, 237–38, 247–51; officers refuse to leave Harpers Ferry without baggage, 83–84; organization of, 33–36, 44–45; parades through Baltimore, 47, 53; pay, slowness of, 67, 91, 94, 114, 123, 126; practical jokes, 126–27; rebel prisoners' opinion of the 14th, 187; recommendations for promotion, 120; regimental band, 33, 46, 63, 84, 113, 139, 150–51, 176, 189, 195; resignation from, 216–17; return of Goddard from staff duty, 175–76; reunions, xviii, 232–33, 294–95, 297, 306; Stoney Mountain, winter camp (1863–64), 188–217; training at Camp Foote, 37–46; Turkey Run camp, Va., 186–89; visit of Goddard's mother and sister to camp in Hartford, 175–76; visits at Morton's Ford, Va., 194

Fourteenth Street Bridge. *See* Long Bridge

Francis Scott Key Bridge. *See* Aqueduct Bridge

Franklin, Brig. Gen. William, 15, 124, 126; reunions, 245, 253

fraud, election, 304

Frederick, Md.: Barbara Fritchie, 280–81; march through, 55, 57

Fredericksburg, battle of, 98–111; anticipation of, 92; balloon, rebels fire at, 108; canteen, rescues Goddard, xiii, 98, 102–4, 106–7, 109, 112, 250, 293; Goddard wounded, 101, 103, 106–7

Fredericksburg, Va., xi; advance skirmishes, 17–18; flag of truce, 28–29; parading through, engaging rebels, 22–26; reunions, 288–90

Fremont, Jessie Benton, 178, 183

Fremont, Maj. Gen. John C., 39, 178; presidential campaign of 1856, xii; rumors of replacing Hooker, 146; treatment of, 89–90

French, Lt., 144

French, Maj. Gen. William, 51–52, 61–62, 200; division inspection, 78; Fredricksburg, battle of, 102, 105, 107, 109; reviews troops at Harpers Ferry, 67; St. Patrick's Day, 137

Fritchie, Barbara, xvii, 280–81

funerals: Clemens, Samuel, 323; Crampton, Cornette M., 76; Gibbons and Comes, 115; Lander, Gen. Fred, 224; McVay, Michael, 52; Perkins, Lt. Col. Sanford, 109, 293

Gainsville, Va., 187

Gaither, George R., 277–78

Gallaudet, Thomas Hopkins, 5

Galpin, Lt. Charles W., 61, 92–93, 118; court-martial, 146

Garfield, James A., xvii, 306

George, Misses, 189

George C. Collins (propeller ship), 48

Georgetown officers' hospital, 166, 176, 178–86

Gerard, Col., 83

Gettysburg, battle of, xiv, 33, 154–65, 168–69, 212; remembrances of, 315

Gibbons, Capt. Elijah W., 60, 77–79, 91, 103–4; burial, 115; death, 114–16, 118; Goddard's opinion of, 100; wounded, 106, 109

Gibbons, Brig. Gen. John, 213

Gieske, Alfred W., 279

Gillette, Capt. Robert, 58, 71, 79

Gillette, William, 264

Gillmore, Maj. Harry, 159

Gilman, Daniel C., 294

Goddard, Alfred Mitchell, 331–38; Arctic, trips to, 332; Cheasapeake Hospital, Fortress Monroe, 333; death, 334, 337–38; departure from friend, Capt. Griswold, in Hawaii, 286; diary excerpts, 334–37; engineer in Sandwich Islands, xiv, 331–32; first lieutenant in 8th Conn. Vol., xv, 166, 174, 207, 331, 333; Goddard writes of desire to enlist, 334; Goddard describes actions of 1862–63 to, 135; leaves Harland's staff for line duty, 333; Mauritius, trip to, 332; mortally wounded, xv, 333; pleas from brother to stay out of fight, 62–63, 125, 128, 136, 142–43, 148; praised by brother, 215, 298; staff position with Gen. Harland, 333; telegram to mother after mortal wound, 337; visit home, 198, 333; visit with brother, 159, 173–74; wants place on Gen. Tyler's staff, 159

Goddard, Calvin Hooker, xviii, 326

Goddard, George, 171

Goddard, Henry Perkins: African Americans, view of (*see* African Americans); Antietam (*see* Antietam, battle of); Appomattox, xi; artillery officer, 1863, xiv, 188–217; Baltimore (*see* Baltimore, Md.); campaign for Maryland legislature, xv, 276–78; Chancellorsville, wounded at (*see* Chancellorsville, battle of); clothing (*see* clothing); commanders, frustration with (*see specific commanders*); death, xviii; discharged from hospital, 186; father's death, 27; father's gravestone, purchase of, 170; father's illness, 23, 26; food, requests for, 123; 14th Conn. Vol. Infantry (*see* 14th Connecticut Volunteer Infantry); Fredericksburg, battle of (*see* Fredericksburg, Va.); friendship with Mark Twain, xvii, 319–24; Georgetown officers' hospital, 166, 176, 178–86; gifts from home, xviii, 3, 93, 121, 139, 141, 146; Harpers Ferry (*see* Harpers Ferry); Hartford, move to, xv; honor, opinions on, xviii, 17, 94, 125, 132, 233; joins Maj. Gen. Tyler's staff as aide-de-camp, xiii, 154, 158–59, 164, 166–72; Lincoln, memories of, 221–25; marriages, xvii; military life, opinions on, 132, 164; military strategy, opinions on, 90, 131, 136–37, 183, 208; money, requests for, 72–75; *New York World*, works for (*see New York World*); Norwich, Conn., native of, xi; obituaries of fellow veterans, 234–45, 247–52; pay, problems getting, 67, 91, 94, 114, 123, 126; Sanford Perkins, relationship with (*see* Perkins, Maj. Sanford H.); poems, requests for, 123, 128; politics, early interest in, xii; postwar

Goddard, Henry Perkins (*continued*)
history, xv–xviii; practical joke played on, 126–27; recommendations for promotion, 120; Reconstruction, view of, xvi–xvii; reflects on status of war, 40; religious views, 52, 75–76, 144–45; reminscences of Norwich, 221–22; reporter for Norwich paper (see *Norwich Bulletin*); reputation of, 53; reunions (*see* reunions); Richmond, Va., visit to, 1905, 300–303; 2nd New York Voluntary Cavalry (*see* 2nd New York Voluntary Cavalry); sends money home, 141, 180; sickness of, 126, 166–74, 178–87; summary of war service, xii–xv, 135, 181; things proud of, 139; visit with brother, 159, 173–74; visit with Gov. Fitzhugh Lee, xvii, 302; Washington, D.C. (*see* Washington, D.C.); women, opinion of, 132, 158, 168, 198–99, 205, 299

Goddard, Lida Acheson, xviii

Goddard, Mary "May": attention from soldiers, 42; praised by brother, 123, 182

Goff, Thomas, 238

Goodale, Ransler, 232

Goodwin, Sgt. E. L., 232

Gorham, Sen. Arthur P., 267–68

Gorham, William, 232

Grant, Lt. Gen. Ulysses S.: at Appomattox, 287; character of, 312–12; Goddard's opinion of, 207, 217; pleases troops, 213; reorganizes army, 213

Greenmount cemetery, 280

Greenwich, Va., 187

Griffith, D. W., xvi

Griggs, Capt., 186

Grinton, Capt. Henry, 186, 195–96

Griswold, Capt. John D., 59, 286

Hale, Capt., 176, 188

Hale, Lt. Charley, 72, 80

Hale, Sen. John P., daughters of, 209

Hale, Lt. Morton, 42, 52, 60, 95; detached to Gen. French, 71, 96; friendship with, 44

Hale, Rev. Dr., 8

Halleck, Maj. Gen. Henry, 58, 62, 90, 120, 154, 212, 256

Hamlin, Hannibal, 7, 207, 209

Hammock, Capt. H. Polk, 79

Hampton, Wade, 305

Hampton Roads, Va., Merrimac raids, 8

Hancock, Camp, 194–216

Hancock, Maj. Gen. Winfield Scott, 75, 78, 211; campaign for president, xvii, 306; Gettysburg, battle of, 163–65, 169; Goddard's opinion of, xi, 187, 190, 199, 215; protection of Roulette farm, 257; recruiting service, 199; reunions, 245; St. Patrick's Day, 137

Hardee, Gen. William Joseph, 300

Harland, Col. Edward B., 118, 132, 145, 227, 295, 333

Harpers Ferry, xiii, 47–48, 51, 55, 62–86

Harper's Weekly: Gettysburg, description of, xiv, 154, 160–64, 185; Lincoln, memories of, 222–25; Mark Twain, 320–23

Harris, Capt., 80

Harris, Sen. Ira, 3, 7

Harris, Miss (of N.Y.), 141

Harris Light. *See* 2nd New York Voluntary Cavalry

Harrisburg, Pa., 48

Hart, Cpl., 103–4

Hart, Lt. Edward W., 64–66, 68, 70, 90, 194–95

Hart, Marion, 70

Hart, Mr., 119

Hart, Mrs. (of Madison), 118

Hart, Capt. William H., 60, 72, 79, 114, 130

Hartford, Conn.; Camp Foote, 34–35, 37–46, 46–48, 175–76; move to, xv; poor, plight of, 291–92; race relations, 290–91; veterans' reunion (1875), 233–34; veterans' reunion (1906), 292–84

Hartford Courant: Gen. Hancock, election of 1880, 306; Mark Twain, 323–24

Hartford Evening Post: reunion of 14th Connecticut Volunteers (1872), 232–33

Hasty, Capt., 24

Hasty, Lt., 22, 24–27

Hawaii. *See* Sandwich Islands

Hawley, Lt. Frederick B., 95; wounded, 107

Hawley, Maj. Gen. Joseph, 233, 245–47, 308, 322

Hayes, Rutherford B., xvii, 304–9

Hays, Brig. Gen. Alexander, 155–56, 162, 170, 177, 213, 217; Morton's Ford, 201–4

Hays, Mrs. Alexander, 197

Hays, Brig. Gen. William, 128, 130; captured, 152; St. Patrick's Day, 137

Hazard, Capt. John G., 191, 198

Heffelfinger, Lt. Chris, 83

Heintzelman, Maj. Gen. Samuel P., 121

Held by the Enemy (Gillette), 275

Herndon, Belle, xvii, 29, 80, 107, 199, 290

Herndon, William, xvii, 30, 80, 107, 289–90

Hewes, James, 263

Hicks, Thomas (governor of Maryland), 228–29

Hill, Gen. D. H., lost dispatch, 257–58

Hill, Maj. John T., 177

Hill Von Hull (ship), 48

Hincks, William B., xvii, 157, 165, 186–87, 202; Medal of Honor, 238; obituary, 238–39; reunions, 232

Hirst, Sgt. Benjamin, 113, 167, 294

Hitchcock, Col. Frederick L., 150, 160

hoe cakes, 20

honor, Goddard's opinion on, xviii, 17, 94, 125, 132, 233

Hooker, Maj. Gen. Joseph: Goddard sees in Baltimore, 158, 160; Goddard's opinion of, xi, 62, 126, 128, 130, 164, 207–8; praise of "Fighting 14th" band, 33; removal from command, 256; replaces Burnside, 124; reunions, 252–53; revamps army, 112; review of troops with Lincoln, xiii, 112–14, 131–32, 142; rumors of removal, 146; St. Patrick's Day, 137; serenaded by band, 113; and the spring 1863 campaign, 135; wounded at Chancellorsville, 149–53

Hooker, Rev. Thomas, xviii

hospitals: Chesapeake Hospital, Fortress Monroe, 333; Fredricksburg, battle of, 101, 103–5; Georgetown officers' hospital, 166, 176, 178–86; Julia Goddard Piatt visits, 147; Washington, D.C., 153

Howard, Maj. Gen. Oliver O., 107, 126; Chancellorsville, battle of, 149–50; St. Patrick's Day, 137

Howe, Capt. Church, 83

Hubbard Rhetorical Society Exhibition, 123

Hughes, Charles E., 308

Humphreys, Maj. Gen. Andrew, 209–10

Hunt, Brig. Gen. Henry, 196, 204

Hunter, Maj. Gen. David, 39

Hunter's Chapel, Va., 49

Huxman, Cpl. Samuel, 161, 165

Hyattstown, Md., 56–57

Ingersoll, Charles R. (governor of Connecticut), 247
Irish Brigade, 100, 102, 106, 122; St. Patrick's Day celebration, 137
Irving, Sir Henry, 273

Jackson, Gen. Thomas "Stonewall," xiii, 33, 37, 239–40; Chancellorsville, battle of, 149; Harpers Ferry, 47–48, 55
Jacobs, Lt. Harvey, 173
Jefferson, Joseph, 273
Jefferson's Rock, 75, 85
Jewett, Dr. Levi, 34–35, 94, 114, 116
Johns Hopkins University, 263
Johnson, Brig. Gen. Andrew, 7
Johnson, Brig. Gen. Bradley T., 237, 239–41, 259, 261
Johnson, Col. Robert C., 115
Johnston, Gen. Joseph E., 37, 300
Johnston, Col. Richard Malcolm, 321
judiciary, reform of, 267–69

Kane, Brig. Gen. Thomas L., 69, 82, 84, 160
Kearney, Maj. Gen. Philip, 50, 107
Keedysville, Md., 57–60
Keenan, Frank, 275
Keiley, Bishop, 310–12
Kelly's Ford, Va., 192
Kelsey, Alson A., 103
Kenly, Col. John R., obituary of, xvii, 239–45
Kenly, Maj. William L., 245
Kilpatrick, Col. Hugh Judson "Kill Cavalry": acquitted at court-martial, 132; Beaver Dam Creek, battle of, 43; Brandy Station, 193, 195; commander of Connecticut Squadron, xii, 3; dance at headquarters, 199; foraging, 15; Goddard dines with, 199; holds horse race, 208; introduction to, 6; letter of commendation, 30; praises

action at Stafford, 19; promoted to brigadier general, 132; reconnoiters rebel pickets in Fredricksburg, 28; ride to Richmond, 211, 214; 2nd Corps ball, 209–10; wife, Goddard calls on, 30, 38
Kimball, Brig. Gen. Nathan, 100
King, Sen. Preston, 7
King, Brig. Gen. Rufus: Goddard requests leave of absence of, 25; grants forty-eight-hour pass, 27; reconnoiters Fredricksburg, 22
Kingley, Col. Tom, 68
Kingsbury, Col. Henry W., 59
Kirby, Ella, 158, 172
Knowlton, Commissary Sgt. Julius W., 58, 232
Knoxville, Md., 74–75
Kraft, Charles, 232
Ku Klux Klan, xvi

Lacy, Maj. Horace J., 140
Lacy House, 4, 96, 101, 105, 113, 127, 140–41, 199
Landau, David, 264
Lanman, Charles, 182–83
Lanman, Adm. Joseph, 295
Leary, Gen. Peter, 325
Lee, Bishop Alfred, 164
Lee, Fitzhugh (governor of Virginia), Goddard visits with, xvii, 302
Lee, Capt. Henry, 148
Lee, Lt., 60
Lee, Gen. Robert E., 198, 244; at Appomattox, 287; assumes command Army of Northern Virginia, 37; Bristoe Station, battle of, 167; Chancellorsville, battle of, xiii, 149; character of, 312–13; crosses Rapidan, 211; Gettysburg, battle of, 154–65, 315; Goddard's opinion of, 207–8, 213, 302–3; lost dispatch, 197, 257; and

McClellan's proposal to end war, xvii–xviii, 310–12; pursued into Maryland, 47–54

Leffingwell, Ozias C., 117

Leggert, Lt. Col. Robert, 247–48, 251–52

Lester, Hattie, 227

Libby Prison, 175, 199, 213

lice infestations, 81, 87, 94

Lincoln, Abraham: Antietam, review of troops at, xii; and assassination conspiracy, 300; call for more troops, 35, 37, 45; Emancipation Proclamation, xi–xii, 55, 62; Goddard's memories of, 221–25; Judge Bond calls on, 228–29; presidential campaign of 1860, xii; reviews troops at Harpers Ferry, 62, 67; reviews troops with Gen. Hooker, xiii, 112–14, 142; slavery, views on, 225–26; speech in Norwich (1860 election), 296; stories of, xvii, 222–25, 229–31

Littlest Rebel, The (Peple), 264

Lloyd, Cpl. Harry, 60

Long, John D., 289

Long Bridge, 49, 179; horse refuses to cross, 8

Longstreet, Maj. Gen. James, 155, 197, 310, 315; reunions, 289

Loudon, Lt. Robert, 195

Loudoun Heights. *See* Harpers Ferry

Lovell (regimental adjutant), 6, 8

Loyal Legion, 263, 281, 325–27, 376

Lucas, Lt. Walter M., 57, 60–61, 72, 78; returns to duty, 144; sickness of, 64–65

Lulls, Captain, 71

Lusk, Will, 158, 170–71, 175–76, 213

Lyman, Lt. Charles, 144, 289

Lytle, Brig. Gen. William H., 182, 285–88

Mackubin, Florence, 272

Madison, Conn., xviii, 232

Magruder, Gen. John B., 302

Mallory, Capt. William H., 3–4, 23; Goddard visits in Baltimore, 169; Goddard plays prank on, 12; promoted to major, 84

Manassas Gap Railroad, 88–89, 186

Mansfield, Richard, 273

Markoe, Col. Frank, 242

Marlowe, Julia, 236

Marshall, Col. Charles, xvi, 80, 241, 285–88, 302, 310–13, 315

Marshall House, 186

Martin, Harry B., 263

Martin, Mrs. *See* Cary, Hetty

Marye's Heights, xiii, 98, 108, 250, 289

"Maryland, My Maryland," xvii, 259, 281–82

Maryland Heights. *See* Harpers Ferry

Maryland politics, postwar, 266–79, 307

McCabe, Col. Gordon, 303

McClellan, Maj. Gen. George: Goddard's opinion of, xi, 89, 93, 120, 126, 128, 130, 143; Peninsular campaign, 37; politicians' treatment of, 89–90; proposal to end war, xvii–xviii, 310–12; relieved of command, 55, 87, 89; replaces McDowell, 4; replaces Pope, 47, 51; reviews troops at Frederick, 57; reviews troops at Harpers Ferry, 62, 67; reviews troops at Warrenton Junction, 87, 89; treatment of, 89–90

McComas, Louis, 235

McCoy, John W., 280

McDowell, Maj. Gen. Irwin, 4; army's lack of confidence in, 47; asks Goddard's opinion of officers, 29; Bailey's Cross Roads, review of troops, 10; commander Army of the Potomac, 7; commander Dept. of Rappahannock, 13; reconnoiters Fredricksburg, 22; refuses Goddard's leave application, 27; reunions, 245–46; view of, 16, 62

McDowell, Va., 37

McGowan, Brig. Gen. Samuel, 156

McIntosh, Col. D. G., 315

McKinley, William, 236, 281, 289

McMahon, Gen. John E., 289

McVay, Michael, 52

Meade, Maj. Gen. George: attends 2nd
Corps ball, 209; Gettysburg, battle of,
154–65, 168; Goddard's opinion of,
207–9; Philadelphia, 197; popularity
of, 192; review of troops, 210; succeeds Hooker, 126, 154; tribute to,
246

Meager, Brig. Gen. Thomas F., 100, 137,
160

meals: apples and potatoes received, 119;
cost of, 11, 14, 140, 196, 215; descriptions of, 72, 89, 128, 130; dines at Mr.
Lamont's in Wilmington, 170–71;
dinner party in D.C., 190, 193; dinner
party with Capt. Tubbs, 78–79; Ebbitt
House, 153; food purchased from
blacks, 116, 119, 124; griddle cakes
and molasses, 120; with Harpers
Ferry planter, 63; Capt. Hazard, dinner with, 198; improved supplies
under Hooker, 113; Mr. Milligan's
dines at, 172; settlement of mess bill,
129; Thanksgiving celebration, 91–93,
97; trading with rebels, 113

Medal of Honor winners, 33

Meigs, Sgt. John, 232

Mencken, Henry L., 270

Mercer, Count (French ambassador), 193

Merrill, Dr., 191

Merrimac: destruction of, 25; Hampton
Roads, raids on, 8

Middletown, Conn., reception of troops,
35

Middletown, Md., 57

Military Order of the Loyal Legion of the
United States. See Loyal Legion

Mills, Sgt. Thomas, 58, 61

Milroy, Brig. Gen. Robert H., 158, 160

Mitchell, Donald G., 38, 294, 321

Mitchell, Maggie, 186

Mitchell, Maj. Gen. Ormsby, 81

Monroe, Fortress, 333

Monroe, Lt. Col. J. A., 188, 198; compliments Goddard, 198; headquarters,
193; Morton's Ford, 204–5; repri-
mands Goddard, 196; review of cavalry, 199; serenaded by band, 195;
wife, description of, 194, 206

Montgomery, Ala., xvi, 297

Moore, Capt. Samuel A., 131, 156, 161,
165, 170, 177–78, 208; command of
the 14th Conn., 208; commissioned
lieutenant colonel, 186–87; dines
with, 194; Morton's Ford, 202–3,
206

More, Capt. Augustus, 80

Morehouse, Lt. George A., 66

Morgan, Edwin D. (governor of New
York), appoints Goddard second lieutenant in 2nd N.Y. Cav., 6, 8, 28

Morgan, Capt. Frank, 216

Morrill, Sen. Lot, description of, 7

Morris, Col. Dwight, 34, 45, 48, 51,
128–30; Antietam, 58, 61; commander of "Fighting 14th," 53–54,
67, 250; discharged for disability,
177; first meeting with, 38; parade
through Baltimore, 53; poem about,
119; return to duty, 124; sickness of,
91, 102, 116, 175; speaks highly of
Goddard, 117; Thanksgiving celebration, 91

Morton, Dr., 202

Morton's Ford, 202–3, 206; battle of, xiv,
194, 201–6, 212

Moseley, S. H., 317

Mudd, Dr. Samuel, 300

Mullen, A. Y. (hospital steward), 92

Murdock, Capt. William, 109, 202, 293

Myers, William Starr, 266–67

National Republican: report on appointment of "outsiders" as officers, 11–12

Naylor, Maj. John E., 195

New Hampshire Journal, speech at 1874 reunion, 297–98

New Haven, Conn., 1874 reunion, 297–98

New York Sunday Times, obituary of Gen. Douglas, 237

New York Times Book Review, Custer controversy, 316

New York World, Goddard refuses job as correspondent for, xii, 25

Newcomb, J. W., 74

Newton, John, 289

Nichols, James R., 39, 96, 118, 134, 135, 138, 139, 142; captures rebels, 216–17; Goddard's friendship with, 144, 298; promoted to captain, 181, 186; Stoney Mountain, 195; wounded, 238

North and South compared, 292–94

Norton, Frank, 127

Norton, Henry B., 69, 80–82

Norton, Mrs. Henry B., 109

Norwich Bulletin: announcement of Goddard's appointment to Harris Light Cavalry, 4; Camp Hancock, report from, 212–13; Connecticut election of 1863, 133–34; Fredericksburg, advance on, 17–18; Fredericksburg, battle of, xiii, 105–7; Lincoln's views on slavery, 225–26; personal connection with paper, 226–27; reminiscences of old Norwich, 221–22; speech to Board of Trade dinner, 1908, 295–96; winter quarters at Falmouth, 96, 124–25

Norwich, Conn., xi; postwar visits, 294–96; reminiscences of, 221–22

Norwich Free Academy, 294

obituaries of veterans, xvii, 234–45, 247–52, 281–82, 325

officers, appointment of "outsiders," 11–12

Orange and Alexandria Railroad, 175, 186

Owen, Gen. Joshua T. "Paddy," 177, 204

Packard, Joseph, 264

Page, Thomas Nelson, 321

Palmer, Camp, Arlington, Va., 8–13

Palmer, Dr. John Williamson, 283

Palmer, Col. Oliver H., 91, 102, 114

Pargond, Gen. Frank, 233

Parian, Thomas, 272

Parker, Dr. L. R., 324

Patrick, Brig. Gen. Marsena: approach to Antietam, 57; flag of truce, treatment of German consul arriving under, 28–29; reconnoiters Fredericksburg, 22, 24

"Peace Democrats," 207; rebuke of, xi, xiii

Peale, Henry, 222

Pearre, George A., 281

Pegram, Brig. Gen. John, 263

Pelton, Sgt. Maj. John C., 64–66, 78, 121, 125, 187, 196, 209, 215–16

Peninsular campaign, 37, 43, 53

pensions, 308–9

Peple, Edward, 264

Perkins, Capt. Joe, 179

Perkins, Maj. Sanford H., xvii, 40, 66, 177; aide-de-camp to, 63, 188; Antietam, 58, 61; bravery under fire, 99–100; floor added to tent, 77; Fredericksburg, battle of, 101–3; friendship with, 91; home on furlough, 116; inspects

Perkins, Maj. Sanford H. (*continued*)
    regiment, 101; obituary, 247–48,
    250–51; points out errors in drilling
    troops, 68; praise of, 121, 145; resig-
    nation of, 146; returns to duty, 132;
    stealing, treatment of offenders, 54,
    60; thanks Goddard for saving life,
    110–11, 124; Thanksgiving celebra-
    tion, 93; visit with Goddard in Balti-
    more, 173; visits Goddard's sister
    Julia, 125; wounded, Goddard saves
    life, xiii, 98, 102–4, 106, 109, 112, 250,
    293
Phipps, Col. Frank H., 280
Piatt, Col. Donn, 158–59, 164, 169,
    171–73
Piatt, Mrs. Donn, 158–59, 172–73
Piatt, Capt. J. H., 108, 114, 116
Piatt, John J., 7, 28, 144, 153, 175, 179,
    227
Piatt, Julia Goddard, 144, 147, 153
Piatt, Sallie M. B., 179
picket duty, 16, 24–25, 63–64, 68, 70,
    72–73, 76, 78–79, 116, 124, 140
Pleasanton, Brig. Gen. Alfred, 209–10
Plum, Capt. Francis M., 195
Plumb, Lieutenant, 24–25
Plunkett, Joe, 73
poems of war, 327
politics: Goddard's early interest in, xii;
    in postwar Maryland, 266–79, 307.
    See also presidential campaigns
pontoon bridges, 22–23, 74, 98, 121,
    144–45
poor, plight of the, 291–92
Pope, Maj. Gen. John, 47, 49–50, 62;
    Goddard's opinion of, 67, 84, 93, 108
Port Royal, Va., 88
Porter, Maj. Gen. Fitz John, 83, 93, 108,
    255–56
Postles, Capt. James P., 156

Potomac River: Aqueduct Bridge, 5, 49;
    crossing to Harpers Ferry, 62–63, 86;
    Long Bridge, 8, 49
Powell, Sen. Lazarus, description of, 7
Pratt, George, 6
presidential campaigns: Fremont vs.
    Buchanan (1856), xii, 221; Garfield
    (1880), xvii, 306; Hayes (1876),
    xvi–xvii, 304–9; Lincoln (1860),
    xii, 222, 296; Taft (1908), xvii,
    307–8
Prior, "Pony," 54
prisoners: exchanges of, 229–30; oath
    of allegiance, prisoners anxious to
    take, 85; paroled prisoner returns,
    122; parolees, talks with, 64; reb pris-
    oners opinion of the 14th Conn., 187;
    rebels at Fort Delaware, 168; scout to
    General Sigel, 173; Stafford, Va., in
    charge of, 18
provost duty, 69, 82–85, 88, 189

race relations, xi–xii, 266–79; and
    "Christian Expediency," 290–91; in
    postwar South, 299–300. *See also*
    African Americans
Randall, James R., 259, 281–82
Randolph, Maj. Inness, 281
Rapidan River, Va., 192, 201–6
Rappahannock, Dept. of; formation of,
    13
Rappahannock River: bath in, 18–19;
    converse with rebels across, 127, 147;
    crossing of, 98, 138, 192, 212. *See also*
    Fredericksburg, battle of
Rayner, Isadore, 269–70
Ream's Station, battle of, 238
rebels: capture by Captain Nichols,
    216–17; converse with across Rappa-
    hannock, 127, 147; deserter tells of
    lack of food, 145; deserters, problem

of, 199; dress parade, 143; intercepted letter about Lee's movements, 197; opinions of, 197; playing ball and pitching quoits, 140; prisoners at Fort Delaware, 168; sharpshooters, 33, 55, 58, 101, 105, 155–56, 161, 163, 201, 203; trading coffee and tobacco with, 113; Union reunions, participation in, 233–34

Reconstruction, xi, xv–xvii, 304

Rectortown, Va., 88

Redfield, John D., 117

religion, view of, 52, 75–76, 144–45

Reno, Maj. Gen. Jesse, 51, 57

reunions: Antietam reunion (1886), 254–58; Baltimore, Md., 286–87; Camp Carroll reunion (1884), 244; 1873 reunion, 245–47; 1878 reunion, 252–54; 1880 reunion, 306; 14th Connecticut Volunteer Infantry, xviii, 232–33; Fredricksburg, Va. reunion, 288–90; Hartford reunion (1875), 233–34; Hartford reunion (1906), 292–94; Middletown reunion, 1907, 294–95; New Haven, Conn., reunion (1874), 297–98

Reynolds, Maj. Gen. John, 160

Reynolds, Lou, 42

Richards, Miss, 209

Richardson, Fort, 178

Richmond, Va.: Goddard's visit to (1905), 300–303; and Gov. Fitzhugh Lee, xvii, 302

Ricketts, Captain, 191

Rigney, Edward, 238

Ripley, Brig. Gen. James W., 121

Ripley, Martha, 227

Ripley, Will, 184

Robinson, Len, 44

Rockville, Md., 51

Rockwell, Gen. Alfred, 238

Rockwell, Joe, 118–19; exchanged, 213; Libby Prison, 175, 199, 213

Rockwell, Lt. Newell P., 177, 200

Rockwell, Dr. Philo G., 103, 143

Roosevelt, Theodore, 268, 279

Root, Elihu, 281, 289

Rosencrans, Maj. Gen. William, 174

Ross, Col. Samuel, 69, 82, 84

Roulette, William, 254, 256–57

Roulette Farm, 55–56, 61, 100, 254, 256–57

Russell, Sgt. Robert, 152; begs Goddard to return, 194; promotion, 214

Sailor's Creek, 3

St. John, Mrs. E. J., 289

St. Patrick's Day celebration, 137

Salem, Va., 895

Sandwich Islands, xiv, 331–32

Sandy Hook, Md., 74–75

Scarsdale, N.Y., 3

Schenck, Misses, 181

Schenck, Maj. Gen. Robert C., 77, 158, 160, 164, 171, 260

Schimmelfening, Brig. Gen. Alexander, 230

Schoepf, Brig. Gen. Albin, 168

Schoepf, Mrs., 168

Scott, Maj. Gen. Winfield, 229, 314

Scranton, Mr. S. H., 232

Scranton, Lt. Sam, 165, 232

scurvy, 166, 178, 185–86, 189, 194, 195

2nd New York Voluntary Cavalry: Bailey's Cross Roads, review of troops, 10; commissioned 2nd lieutenant, xii, 4, 8; Fredricksburg, Va., 18–27; Goddard visits at Brandy Station, 193, 195; Goddard's resignation from, 27–30; horse and equipment purchases for, 8–9; Kilpatrick, commander of Connecticut Squadron,

2nd New York Voluntary Cavalry (*continued*)

xii, 3; Manassas, orders received to leave for, 13; Stafford, Va. skirmish, 17–18

Sedgwick, Maj. Gen. John, 49, 52, 149, 197, 209

segregation. *See* race relations

Selden, Lt. Col. Joe, 68

Seward, Camp, 49

Seymour, Lt. Frederick J., 95, 108, 117, 168

Seymour, Tom, and campaign for governor of Connecticut, xiii, 130–31, 133–34, 141–42

Shalk, Lt. Frederick E., 203

Sharpsburg, Md. *See* Antietam, battle of

Shenandoah River: crossing of, 88; washing clothes in, 65

Shenandoah Valley, 69

Shenandoah Valley campaign, 37, 69

Shepherd, Dr. Henry E., 282–83

Sheridan, Maj. Gen. Philip, 245–47

Sherman, Lt. William J., 77–78, 82, 84, 95; commands at president's reception, 68; friendship with Goddard, 68–69, 91, 94; Goddard's opinion of, 90; Hartford reunion, 320; lack of confidence, 70, 90; lack of money, 72; picket duty, 78; promotion, 64, 66; resigns as captain, 130; sickness of, 64, 92, 108, 114, 118; visitors, 80; wounded, 58–59, 64, 66

Sherman, Maj. Gen. William Tecumseh, 245–47

Sherwood Pension Bill, 308–9

Shields, Brig. Gen. James, 243

Sibley tents, 70–71, 78, 89, 93–94, 120, 122, 126, 130

Sickles, Maj. Gen. Dan, 88, 128, 253, 289

Sigel, Maj. Gen. Franz, 50–51, 62, 160

Simpson, Lt. James F., 65, 90, 102, 180, 189; captured, 152; friendship with, 144; medical treatment in Baltimore, 168–69; Goddard's opinion of, 138; promotion, 186; wounded, 106

Sisco, Spenser B., 326

skedaddling. *See* deserters

Slater, John F., 295

slavery: as basis of Confederacy, 314; Lincoln's views on, 225–26

slaves, former. *See* African Americans

Smith, Charley, 94

Smith, Prof. Elbridge, 294

Smith, Ned, 54

Smith, Col. Orlando, 187

Smith, Robert H., 277

Smith, W. F., succeeds Franklin, 126

Smithsonian, Goddard's visit to, 179

Snagg, Capt. Henry, 186, 189, 203

Snicker's Gap, 88, 97

South: Goddard's impressions of changes, 297–303; North compared to, 292–94

South Mountain, battle of, 55–56, 60

Southern sympathizers, 259–65, 281

Spangler, Edman, 300

Spencer, Sgt. L. A., 232

Sperry, Nehemiah, 246

Spiedel, Col. John, 73, 81

Sprague, Sen. William, 209

Springfield Republican: John Wilkes Booth, 280; General Custer, 314; Decoration Day, observation of, 284–85; Doubleday book about Fort Sumter, 317–18; 1873 reunion, 245–47; 1878 reunion, 252–54; Gettysburg, remembrances of, 315; Hartford reunion, 1875, 233–34; Charles Evans Hughes speech (1908 election), 308; General Lee and others, 314; Maryland authors, 281–82; Maryland politics, postwar, 266–73, 275–76, 278–79,

307; Middletown reunion, 1907, 294–95; North and South compared, 292–94; poor, plight of, 291–92; race relations, 290–91; Richmond, Va., visit to, 1905, 300–303; Southern women and contempt for carpetbaggers, 299–300; Mark Twain, 319; veteran obituaries, 247–52, 281–82; veterans' feelings about war, 1895, 309; visit to grave of Hetty Cary, 262–63

Stafford, Rev. T. J., 281

Stafford, Va., 17–18

Stahal, Maj. Gen. Julius, 160

Stanley, Lt. Joseph, 73, 107

Stanley, Lt. Theodore A., 49; arrested for leaving camp without permission, 81; death, 109, 118

Stannard, J. E., 294–95

Stanton, Dr. David, 178–81, 184

Stanton, Edward (secretary of war): friendship with Judge Bond, 229–30; religious services proclamation, 16

stealing. See theft, problem of

Stedman, Edmund C.: becomes broker in N.Y., 181; Goddard visits in D.C., 28; Goddard visits in Norwich, 294; obituary, 282; reporter with Army of the Potomac, 7

Stedman, Col. G. A., 118

Stevens, Chaplain Henry S., 52, 59, 65, 92, 99; reunions, 232–33, 257

Stocking, Lt. George A., 203

Stone, Chaplain, 9, 16

Stone, Gen. Charles P., 83

Stoney Mountain, winter camp (1863–64), 188–217

Stoughton, Lt. Frank E., 168

Stowe, Harriet Beecher, 273; defense of, xv; Goddard reads The Pearl of Orr's Island, 171

Stuart, Maj. Gen. J. E. B., 154, 260, 302, 315

suffrage. See voting rights

Sully, Brig. Gen. Alfred, 115

Sumner, Sen. Charles: description of, 7; Goddard dines with in D.C., 190, 193

Sumner, Maj. Gen. Edwin, 51–52, 54, 62, 90; Goddard's opinion of, 107, 126; relieved of duty, 124–25; review of troops at Falmouth, 115; review of troops at Harpers Ferry, 67; sick furlough, 71

Sumter, Fort, 317–18

Sunken Road (Bloody Lane), xiii, 55–56

Swann, Thomas (governor of Md.), 266

Sykes, Maj. Gen. George, 167

Taft, William H., xvii, 307–8

Taliaferro, Miss, 199

Tarr, Lt. Col. Fred C., 243

Taylor, Fred, 54

Taylor, Zachary, 221

"Telegraph" road (Fredricksburg camp), 23–26

Thanksgiving celebration, 91–93, 97

theft, problem of, 12–13, 19, 54, 107, 197

Thom, Col. John Watson Triplett, 192

Thomas, Brig. Gen. Edward, 156

Thomas, Gen. George H., 314

Thomas, Col. John L., 243

Thompson, Capt., 191, 209–10

Tibbetts, Lt. John, 163, 165, 168, 170

Tidball, Col. John C., 214–15

Tiffany, Charley, 57

Tilden, Samuel J. (governor of New York), xvii, 304

Times, and 1876 election, 304–6

Tomlinson, Charles (asst. surgeon), 177

Townsend, George Alfred, 321

Townsend, Capt. James L., 108, 141, 145, 161–62, 175, 178, 185, 187, 189; dismissal of, 193–94, 214; sick with scurvy, 195

Trott, Stanley, 119
truce, flag of, 28–29
Trumbull, John F., 223–24
Tubbs, Charley, 141
Tubbs, Capt. William H., 39, 61, 70, 88;
    dinner party with, 78–79; on march,
    88, 107; missed by regiment, 125;
    Goddard's opinion of, 135; resigna-
    tion, 127; sickness of, 96; visits God-
    dard in camp, 176; visits Goddard in
    D.C., 176; in Washington, 128;
    wounded, on leave, 105–6, 108–9,
    119, 123
Turkey Run camp, Va., 186–89
Twain, Mark, xvii, 319–24
Twitchell, Rev. Joe H., 323–24
Tyler, Maj. Gen. Dan, 132, 160, 249, 273;
    Camp Foote, 44–45; comments on
    staff, 173; friendship with, 228, 295;
    grave of, 287; joins staff as aide-de-
    camp, xiii, 154, 158–59, 164, 166–72;
    memories of, 227–28; Goddard's
    opinion of, 169; patriotism, quote
    about, 123; visit to Fort Delaware,
    168; visit to New York, 171
Tyler, Brig. Gen. E. B., 158, 160
Tyler, Sgt. E. B., 167
Tyler, Frederick, 249
Tyler, James Hoge (governor of
    Virginia), 289
Tyler, Ned, 158, 164, 170–71
Tyler, Gen. R. O., 175, 191
Tyler, Col. Robert G., 40, 93; obituary,
    247–50

Uncle Tom's Cabin (Stowe), xv, 273
Union Relief Rooms, 48
Union scout, conversation with, 73
United States Ford, 137, 152–53
United States Sanitary Commission
    nurses, 153

Upperville, Va., 88
Urbana, Md., 57
Usher, John (secretary of interior), 209

Van Dorn, Gen. Earl, 261
Van Zandt, Charles (governor of Rhode
    Island), 253
Vaughan, Dr. J. Frank, 170
veterans: feelings about war (1895), 309;
    Loyal Legion (see Loyal Legion); obit-
    uaries (see obituaries of veterans);
    reunions (see reunions); Sherwood
    Pension Bill, 308–9
Vicksburg, Miss., reports of battle,
    168
volunteers, appeals for, 34–35, 37
voting rights of African Americans,
    269–71, 278

Wachter, Frank, 277
Wadhams, Lt. Henry W., 200
Wadhams, Jessie, 200
Wait, Lt. Marion, 64, 70
Walker, Charlotte, 275
Walker, Col. Francis A., 197, 211
Wallis, Col., 78
Wallis, S. Teackle, 277
Walter, Lt. Col., 84
Walters, Capt., 24–25
Walthall Junction, battle of, xv
Ward, Fort, 178–79
Ward, Capt. Frank X., 243
Ward, Capt. Frederick S., 80, 90, 103,
    107–8, 116–17, 194
Ward, Maj. Henry, 116–17
Ward, Col. J. E., 334
Ward, Maj. John, 95
Warfield, Edwin S. (governor of Mary-
    land), 268–69
Warl, William, 14
Warner, Charles Dudley, 321–22

Warren, Maj. Gen. Gouverneur, 187–88, 215, 217; attends 2nd Corps ball, 210; Goddard's opinion of, 190, 200, 215; at Morton's Ford, 201, 205

Warren, Gen. Joseph, 235–36

Warrens of Virginia, The (De Mille), 275

Warrenton Junction, Va., 89–91, 166, 175, 191

Washington, Booker T., 279

Washington, D.C.: forty-eight-hour pass for travelers, 27–28; Georgetown officers' hospital, 166, 176, 178–86; Goddard first arrives at, 5–8; Goddard recuperates in, 153; Goddard returns to after resignation from artillery, 211, 216; Goddard returns to after resignation from cavalry, 29–30; Goddard visits Virginia forts from, 178

Watson, Col. William, 241

Webb, Brig. Gen. Alexander, 205

Webb, Charles H., 28

Webster, Sgt. Samuel, 97

Weir, Lieutenant, 191

Weld, Lt. Charley, 39

Weld, Maj., 44

Whitaker, Lt. Daniel, 129

Whitaker, Edward W., 177–78, 196; cuts way through enemy lines, 317; Goddard's friendship with, 84; Goddard's opinion of, 41; made second lieutenant, 57, 129; offered position of sergeant major, 25, 28; ride to Richmond, 204

White, Capt. Alexander, 243

Whiting, Frank, 175

Whyte, Sen. Pinckney, 267

Whyte, William P., 282

Wide Awakes, xii, 222

Wilcox, Sgt. Edwin, 39

Willard, Capt. Samuel F., 58–59, 64, 85, 90, 118, 232

Willard Hotel, 28, 313

Williams, Maj. Gen. Alpheus, 62; reviews troops at Harpers Ferry, 67

Williams, Winslow, 272

Wilmington, Del., xiv, 164, 166–72

Wilson, Henry, 246–47

Wilson, Gen. William, 288

winter camps: Falmouth (1862–63), 95–148; Stoney Mountain (1863–64), 188–217

Winthrop, Theodore, 335

women, Goddard's opinion of, 132, 158, 168, 198–99, 205, 299

Women's Christian Association and race relations, 290

Wool, Maj. Gen. John E., 13, 48, 230–31; parades through Baltimore, 53

Woolsey family, 141, 153

Wooster, Miss Boots, 264

Wooster, Lt. Col. William B., 69, 82

Wright, Lt. Col. Dexter R., 42

Wright, Lt. Miles S., 138

Zinn, Col. George W., 115

Zinn, Col. Henry I., 65

Zon, Mary Goddard, xviii

ABOUT THE EDITOR

CALVIN GODDARD ZON, great-grandson of Henry P. Goddard, is a journalist and historian living in Washington, D.C. A former staff writer for the *Washington Star* daily newspaper, Zon has a B.A. in American history from Davidson College and an M.A. from the American University. His articles have appeared in such varied publications as the *Civil War News,* the *Progressive,* the *National Catholic Reporter,* and *People.*